THOMMO

Stand Up Pinocchio

From the Kop to the top.
My life inside Anfield

With Ken Rogers

Sport Media
A Trinity Mirror Business

This book is dedicated to my wife Marg, my four
wonderful boys, my mum, dad, brothers and sisters and
fans everywhere who inspired me on this memorable
journey. It would never have happened without the vision
and passion of Bill Shankly, who trusted this skinny
Kirkby kid to live his dream.

Sport Media
A Trinity Mirror Business

Published in Great Britain in 2005 by:
Trinity Mirror Sport Media,
PO Box 48, Old Hall Street,
Liverpool L69 3EB

Executive Editor: KEN ROGERS Editor: STEVE HANRAHAN
Art Editor: RICK COOKE Production Editor: PAUL DOVE
Editorial Assistant: JAMES CLEARY
Sales and Marketing Manager: ELIZABETH MORGAN

ISBN 1905266057

Printed and finished by Scotprint, Haddington, Scotland

PHIL THOMPSON

BORN: 21 January, 1954, Kensington, Liverpool.
KOPITE: 1964-1970 (age 10-16).
LIVERPUDLIAN: Lifetime.

Schoolboy Honours:
With Kirkby Boys, Dimmer Cup Winners (1969), Joint Winners Welsh Shield (1969).
Signed as apprentice for Liverpool: 29 August, 1969 (from Kirkby Schools).
Signed as professional for Liverpool: 22 January, 1971.
Positions played: Central midfield, Central defender.

Liverpool Career:
1970/71–1984/1985 (player); 1986/87–1991/92 (Reserve-Team Manager);
November 1998– June 2004 (Assistant Manager);
October 2001–March 2002 (Caretaker Manager).
Liverpool debut: 3 April, 1972 v Manchester United (Old Trafford, League, as substitute).
Full debut: 28 October 1972 v Norwich City (Carrow Road, League).
Appearances: League - 340, goals 7; FA Cup: 36, goals 0; League Cup 43, goals 1; Europe
50, goals 5; Other games 8, goals 0.
Total: 477, goals 13.
Liverpool captain: April 1979–January 1982.

Liverpool Honours as a player:
Three European Cups: 1976/77 (did not play in Final), 1977/78, 1980/81 (as captain).
Two UEFA Cups: 1972/73, 1975/76.
One Super Cup: 1977. Finalist 1978.
World Club Championship: Finalist 1981 (v Flamengo).
Seven League Championships: 1972/73, 1975/76, 1976/77, 1978/79 (as captain),
1979/80 (as captain), 1981/82, 1982/83.
One FA Cup: 1973/74. Finalist 1976/77.
Two League Cups: 1980/81 (as captain), 1981/82.
Six Charity Shields: 1974, 1976, 1977, 1979, 1980 (as captain), 1982.
FA Youth Cup Finalist: 1972 (v Aston Villa).

Liverpool Honours as Assistant Manager:
2000/2001: UEFA Cup Winner, FA Cup Winner, League Cup Winner.
2001/2002: Super Cup Winner, Charity Shield Winner.
Premier League Runners-Up.
2002/2003: League Cup Winner, Charity Shield (Finalist).

England Honours:
Mini World Cup Winner (v West Germany in Spain) 1972.
England Youth International.
England Under 23 caps: 2.
England 'B' caps: 1.
Full caps: 42 (six times captain), goals 1.

For the record:
Manager, Falcon FC, Kirkby Newtown League, treble winners.

Contents

The Liver Bird Upon My Chest and ready to do anything for my team

Football is a remarkable business. It can send you soaring to the heights or it can leave you in total despair. The longer you are in this great game – and I have had a lifetime of involvement first as a player and then as coach, assistant manager and caretaker manager at the highest level – the more chance there is that you will take this emotional roller coaster ride of highs and lows.

They say that when you are drowning or facing a disaster your whole life suddenly flashes before you. I've learned that this can also apply when your situation is suddenly transformed in an incredibly positive way and your football dreams come alive again.

I was the passionate Kopite who had the honour of signing for the immortal Bill Shankly, my all-time hero. I fulfilled a boyhood dream by going on to skipper the club I adored. I captained England and played in a World Cup. I won a Championship medal and a UEFA Cup medal at the age of 19 and fulfilled every young man's dream by lapping the famous Wembley Stadium clutching the FA Cup. I climbed to the pinnacle of club football and played my own game of 'Fantasy Football' by striding up to collect the European Cup on a never-to-be-forgotten night in Paris, having helped the Reds vanquish the mighty Real Madrid.

For a skinny kid from Kirkby who looked more like a long distance runner than a footballer, my soccer existence was like winning the Lottery every day. Even when my playing career had ended I was able to power on after being invited to join Liverpool's famous Boot Room. I was looking after the reserves and determined to put in as much as a coach as I had taken out as a player.

The trouble is, all good things must come to an end. I'd witnessed one of Liverpool FC's greatest-ever legends, Kenny Dalglish, forced into early retirement by the sheer pressure of trying to keep the Anfield dream alive.

Kenny was a god in a football sense, but he woke up one day and found himself drowning.

I don't know if his previous football life flashed before him when it happened on an amazing day in February, 1991, but I can assure you that mine did when my own world came crashing down just over a year later after Kenny's successor, Graeme Souness, controversially sacked me from the Anfield Boot Room team.

I would lie awake at night and see myself with the Championship trophy, the FA Cup and the European Cup. I would constantly be preoccupied with thoughts about the young players I had been coaching just days earlier. They all harboured the same dreams that had inspired me at their age. I had desperately wanted to help each and every one of them progress in the game and experience some of the highs that had been part of my life while playing alongside some of the greatest players this country has ever seen.

I will give you my side of the Souness affair later. This book is my eventful journey through the Fields of Anfield Road. It is written by a Red for the Red Army that remains central to my life. I don't look on myself as an ex-footballer. I don't look on myself as an ex-coach. First and foremost I'm a LIVERPUDLIAN and I'm proud of it.

I was a fan while I was a player and I was the same fan when I sat in the Boot Room. If you are reading these words you will know exactly how I feel because there is every chance you will be a Red as well.

You will feel inspired just by looking at a picture of the great Bill Shankly or hearing his name mentioned. You will know exactly what it means when a Kopite holds five fingers up to his Manchester United, Arsenal and Chelsea counterparts. You will have the Liver Bird upon your chest. You will feel ten feet tall just walking through the Shankly Gates. And when you stand inside the fortress that is Anfield there will never be a single moment when you will have to Walk Alone.

We are all part of a remarkable club and that is why my life was turned upside down when Souness showed me the door for reasons that still bemuse me. Thanks to my wonderful family and some true friends, who I will introduce you to later, I somehow managed to rebuild my life and get back on track. Business was good, my lifestyle was great and I was able to spend a lot of time with my wife Marg and sons Philip, Daniel, Max and Josh. As we focused our thoughts on our young family, I was also able to keep in touch with the game I loved through various newspaper and magazine columns as well as my increasing work as a pundit with SKY television. I didn't have any pressure and I could have maintained my comfortable and relaxed regime into the foreseeable future.

So why did I climb back on the roller coaster? Why did I put myself in a position in which my whole world would be turned upside down alongside a highly intelligent and likeable workaholic from France who had his own football dream?

Hold those five fingers up, understand the importance of one of the greatest clubs in the world competing again for football's greatest honours and feel that red heart pounding inside your chest and you will know that nothing can stop you answering the call from Liverpool Football Club.

When I was on the outside looking in and Roy Evans eventually took over from Souness, I always hoped that I might be asked to return. Then Roy appointed his own man and I simply had to get on with my life.

When it came to football, I was just a fan again and that's the way I thought it would remain. I will reveal how a phone call from Peter Robinson dropped a bomb into my comfortable existence.

However, when I realised it was an offer to work as Gerard Houllier's assistant I happily picked up that ticking device, tucked it in my bag and said: "When do I start?" We were determined that the explosion would be all about a rebirth of Liverpool FC and we came so desperately close to making it happen. I'm proud of what we achieved, yet frustrated that the Premiership prize – the most important goal of all – eluded us.

This book will cover all the angles – fan, apprentice, player, coach and those eventful months when Gerard was fighting for his life and I was working hard as caretaker boss to keep us on track. It will be a story told from the heart, with nothing held back and nothing hidden. I hope it will reflect my character and it will certainly demonstrate my pride in my Scouse roots, my loyalty to LFC and my love of the people, both in Liverpool and my spiritual home of Kirkby.

I talked earlier about that flashback feeling when you are drowning and suggested you can actually have the same experience when things turn for you in a positive way. I know this is fact because on the day I returned to Melwood as Gerard's right-hand man I can remember being on my own and leaning back against the slats of the grey stone wall that surrounds the training ground. It was in the corner facing what we always called the 'Mini Wembley', a pitch to the right of what was the old changing pavilion where the ghosts of Hunt, St John, Yeats, Smith, Callaghan and the rest still play their never-ending games of five-a-side under the watchful eye of Shanks, Bob Paisley, Reuben Bennett and Joe Fagan.

It was a beautiful day. The sun was shining. I was back and I was proud. I shut my eyes and I heard Shanks: "How are ye son? Are you eating well, are you sleeping well?"

I saw Reuben striding past with his bag of balls and growling about the Scots being a superior race to the English. I saw Bob, always thoughtful, always talking sound sense and diagnosing an injury even before you felt the twinge. Joe was in the distance, giving me that look that said more than a thousand words. "Come on lad, you know what's needed. Get on with it."

And as a young, skinny kid from Kirkby ran past in my mind's eye, leading from the front in the training runs, determined to prove to all and sundry that he was ready, willing and able to do anything in the cause of the Reds, I heard Tommy Smith's distinctive voice barking out some words of advice from the older pros. "Slow down kid and get back in line or I'll break yer fucking legs." Thanks Tommy.

In the twinkling of an eye I shook myself back into the world of the modern Liverpool. It was Gerard, in that unmistakeable French accent, calling me to arms to begin another chapter in my eventful Anfield career.

This is where I start my story, in an amazing week in 1998 when a mobile phone call pointed me back towards the Shankly Gates.

THOMMO

Chapter 1

Call to arms, player power and how my Kop roots inspired me to succeed

I had been out of the game for six years when I took the remarkable call that would turn my life upside down. I had literally given up any hope of ever returning to Liverpool FC.

I felt that if I had a chance, it was going to be in those first couple of years after leaving. Of course, it was never going to happen while Graeme Souness was still in charge. When he finally departed and Roy Evans claimed the Anfield hotseat I always wondered if he might give me a lifeline back into the club I still loved with all my heart.

However, that door also remained firmly shut. Instead, Doug Livermore was brought onto the coaching staff and I thought that was the end of it.

I had to get on with my life without football and slotted back into a business routine with my Phil Thompson Pine DIY shops. I tried to keep in touch with football and had a column in both the Liverpool Echo and the Kop Magazine that helped to keep my name in the public eye. I also started to speak on the After Dinner circuit after many conversations with my mate Tommy Smith who had gone down this route himself with a lot of success.

The media work, including SKY TV, kept me in touch with the game. After the upheaval of losing my coaching job at Anfield, my life was planned out again – or so I thought.

Wednesday, November 11, 1998, was intended to be an enjoyable reunion with some of my former teammates and Liverpool colleagues. SKY had been organising a very successful six-a-side football event for former stars called 'The Masters' in which Liverpool had done particularly well.

We had planned a training session for some of our lads at the Pitz Soccer centre in Everton Valley, which has a number of artificial pitches. You hear people talking about being caught with their trousers down. I had just dropped a not so trendy pair of stone coloured tracksuit bottoms when the mobile phone went in my bag.

I picked it up and hit the button to take the call. It was Liverpool Chief Executive Peter Robinson and I thought it prudent not to tell him that I had my trousers round my ankles. I tried to be as formal as I could, but my mind was already beginning to run away with me.

My first thought was linked with the Radio City match commentary I had been involved in the night before. The Reds had lost 3-1 to Tottenham in the League Cup and it wasn't the best of performances, to say the least. I wondered if I'd said anything that might have upset anyone. Possibly Peter was going to say: "Lay off, Phil."

I had certainly spoken from the heart on the radio that night, but as soon as the thought crossed my mind, I immediately thought about a letter that had been pushed through the door that morning at our Kirkby business premises in which a fan revealed that he had also listened to that broadcast. The letter, addressed personally to me, said: "The time has come for you to go back to Anfield. Bill Shankly would have been proud of your words last night."

The brain can be a wonderful thing. Peter Robinson had only said: "Good morning, Phil" and in the split second before I replied: "Fine, Peter" all of these possibilities, images and thoughts had flashed through my mind. I tried to compose myself, as much as you can with your trousers round your ankles, and repeated: "Yeah, I'm fine."

He immediately replied: "Can you come and see me?" It still could have been about a negative, but his voice sounded earnest and positive. I said: "Yes, no problem. Do you want me to come to Anfield?" Peter replied: "No, there will be too many Pressmen and TV cameras around."

At the mention of cameras, I finally thought it was time to pull up my trousers. Peter quickly added: "Roy has called it a day. Can you come to the chairman's house near Southport?"

Trying to keep calm and composed inside, I simply said: "Yes." Suddenly the phone went silent and he had gone. Most other people might have thought that Peter was being abrupt and disrespectful, but after working with him for years and knowing the man, this was just the way he was in every day life. I just stood there for a moment, wondering about the possibilities. It could have been anything.

I turned round and apologised to the lads who had no idea who I had been talking to and no information about the sensational events that were unfolding just half a mile away at Anfield. SKY presenter Rob Palmer, who fancies himself as a goalkeeper, was at the Pitz doing some filming for the show.

The camera was zooming in and out in our dressing room. Rob didn't realise that a major scoop was unfolding linked with the impending departure of the Liverpool manager, nor could I tell him. I remember that Alan Kennedy was also there. He had pulled on a pair of socks full of holes. We looked like Rag Arse Rovers, rather than Legends of LFC.

I apologised and mumbled something about being called away. As I got into the car park, David Johnson drove in and pulled up alongside my car. "Where are you going?" asked The Doc. "I thought we were training for the Masters."

I said that I had to do something for SKY. Later Johnno told me that he was completely bemused by that, not least because a SKY camera was in the dressing room I had just left! I quickly drove off.

Peter had asked me to go up to the chairman's house straight away. My mind was still spinning and I felt I had to ring my wife Marg. She helped out at St Edward's College, which our children attended. It was her way of giving something back and helping the younger ones with their reading.

She always told me never to ring her during those sessions and normally she would never have her mobile on.

Incredibly it rang and I said: "Marg, it's Phil." She immediately whispered: "I'm in with the children, I told you not to call me here."

I just said: "I've had a call from Liverpool. They want me to go for a meeting with David Moores."

She asked the most obvious questions: "Is it the manager's job? Is it a coach's job? Is it any job?"

I just had to say: "I don't know." I guessed they were going to offer me something. In these situations you usually speak to an agent or even a lawyer. I asked someone much more important. I said: "Marg, what do I do?"

She immediately said: "It doesn't matter what the job is. It's something you have always wanted. Don't turn it down."

I pointed out that a return to football would completely change our lifestyles. Our boys were still quite young at that time. It would mean total commitment to the club. She said: "We'll get round it."

I now phoned my brother Owen who works as warehouse manager in our business. I trusted Owen completely and knew he would give me some instinctive advice. He was the one who helped me gain all of my early Anfield experiences as a fan. His first words were: "I knew an offer would come. Whatever the job is, take it." I said that I was frightened of what it was going to be, but Owen remained positive.

The only other person I spoke to was a friend of mine called Len

McCormick, a lifelong Liverpool fan. Len is MD of a company called Batley's Cash and Carry on the M57. He was suddenly one of the few people in the city who knew Roy Evans was on his way out. I knew he would keep the information to himself.

Len was also extremely positive. My wife, my brother and a great friend had all told me what I already knew. If Liverpool wanted me back, in whatever role, I would be up for it.

Before I knew it, I was outside the chairman's house. My head was in the stratosphere. I tried to keep composed as I was shown in to meet David in his lounge. He actually looked quite distraught.

I had not been sure what to expect, but it was a bit like a funeral parlour. I glanced round and saw Peter, Tom Saunders, Rick Parry and financial director Keith Clayton. Everyone was quiet. I knew the chairman had been extremely close to Roy. They had been friends for many years. He shook his head and Peter immediately took charge.

He said: "Roy has decided he wants to go. He believes it will be better for the club if he leaves and Gerard takes sole charge."

My mind was racing. How did I fit into this? What about the other members of the backroom staff? Peter read my mind and added: "Doug Livermore is also going."

Peter added: "We have had a long chat about who to bring in as assistant manager to help Gerard with the discipline." He indicated that they wanted someone with a pedigree who could stand up to the players, someone who understood the club from top to bottom and who had seen it all before. Clearly, the wise and respected Tom Saunders had played an important part in the decision-making process. It appears that Tom had said there was only one person filling the criteria and that was me. Peter said this was why they were asking me to return to the club. I will always be beholden to Tom for thinking about me.

I immediately asked how Gerard felt about all of this. I had only met him previously for 15 minutes and here I was, being asked to become his assistant. Peter revealed that Gerard had been told about my qualities and that he wanted to give it a try. I was thrilled that the board had this belief in me, not least because Graeme Souness had let it be known that I was disloyal which was never the case.

I gave my answer immediately.

"Great, fine!" Then I tried to get my sensible head on as Peter said: "You will want to know about the financial package."

I replied that I had built a nice life for myself after being forced out of the club by Souness. I told them some of the things I was involved in, like being chairman of the Vernons Spot The Ball competition with David Johnson and Alan Kennedy. I had my own business, my media work and a relaxed social life, able to watch my family growing up without any pressure.

I said: "I will be taking a chance turning my back on all of this. I have a good reputation in the city. I could be putting it all at risk." I was trying to emphasise that I was not a pushover, although I would have walked halfway round the world to be involved with the Reds again.

Peter came up with a figure. I said: "Let's not be foolish. That doesn't come close to what I am already earning."

They asked what I wanted and I doubled it, not knowing if it was right or wrong. If they had laughed and stuck to their guns, I would have still taken the job, no doubt about that. They asked for a moment to discuss it and I stepped outside of the lounge. I was only out there two minutes when they called me back into the room and the chairman said: "We are ready to make you assistant manager."

That was it. It was as if all my Christmases and birthdays had come at once.

I took a deep breath. Houllier and Thompson. In many respects, we would be the odd couple. Gerard was sophisticated, calm, reassuring and steeped in knowledge about world football. I thought: "What will he make of me?"

We all shook hands and I said: "Where do we go from here?" They asked me to meet Gerard that same evening at his house near Calderstones Park. I came out and rung my wife, my mum and dad, and my brothers Owen and Ian.

Marg said: "You have done it now. This will change our life."

She was thrilled for me because she knew how much the sacking I had been forced to deal with had hurt me. It was as if a whole new future was opening up and I rang my pal Len McCormick who I had trusted with the news earlier to say he could go public. I also rang another friend, gynaecologist Peter Bousefield who had delivered all of our children.

I wanted to tell the world: "THOMMO IS BACK!"

My first meeting with Gerard would turn into a marathon all-night affair. It highlighted the work ethic of the Liverpool manager who was completely focused on the challenge of getting the club back to the top. Having finally disposed of my grey flannel tracky bottoms and sweat top, I got changed and arranged to meet Norman Gard, a close friend of Gerard's and the players' liaison officer, in the car park of the Fiveways pub in the Childwall district of the city. It's a well-known crossroads in Liverpool and that seemed quite symbolic in the circumstances. Norman asked me to be there about 5.30. I got there at 3 o'clock to make sure he did not pass me by. Seriously, after six years in the wilderness I was really looking forward to the exciting challenge that was looming.

When we finally arrived at Gerard's apartment, all of the people I had met earlier were there. Food had been organised and we began to talk about football in general. Finally Gerard and I were left alone to get to know each other. It was a strange situation, but we felt comfortable in each other's company. He immediately began to ask me about players and systems. I wondered what would have happened if we hadn't clicked as a partnership. I said: "Look Gerard, I will be something completely different. I am very disciplined and I will help you on this side."

We went through the rigmarole of what had allegedly gone on between Graeme Souness and myself. He said: "I have no concerns about that. It's the future I am interested in. It's now about you and me."

We sat and talked and it was fascinating. Here was this guru of football who was Gerard Houllier. I always thought I knew my football. We chatted for five, six, seven hours. It was an eye opener for me. He had this briefcase that was bulging with information. Then there was me with my homework on the back of an envelope. It was great. This was our first serious meeting together, apart from 15 minutes in Valencia when I was covering the second leg of Liverpool's UEFA Cup clash for Radio City. I was in the hotel bar having a drink and Ronnie Moran and Tom Saunders were on the trip. Ronnie had been my mentor while I had tremendous respect for Tom. Gerard walked through and stopped to introduce himself. He said: "I stood on the Kop and watched you many times as a player." Little did I know that three or four weeks later we would be forging this partnership.

I remember Tom questioning me that night about why I had not returned to the game. He said: "Phil, you have so much to offer." Later, as I reflected on our chat, I began to piece together why Liverpool had asked me to come back. I told Tom that many people in the game pigeon-holed me with Liverpool because I had been a fan, a player and a coach with a seemingly one-track mind about the Reds. I explained that it would be harder for me to commit myself to another club. Anyway, I always harboured these thoughts that I might get a call from Liverpool, a dream that retreated with every passing year.

Tom had taken a real interest in my comments. I wondered later if my words had stuck in his mind when the Reds began to consider the way forward with

Gerard in sole charge. As I sat in Gerard's apartment, all of these thoughts were in my mind. We had so much to discuss and could have stayed up all night. In the early hours we finally called a break and I set off home, mentally shattered but thrilled at the possibilities.

Back home in Knowsley Village, I could not sleep as I prepared myself for that first meeting with the players at 10.30am the following day. A press conference had been arranged for 11.30am. As far as I was concerned, the media were still blissfully unaware as to what was happening.

I got up early and chose a shirt and suit rather than the casual trackie I had donned just 24 hours earlier when the only thing on the agenda was that Masters training session with some of my former teammates. I was conscious that the whole of the city was still oblivious to the drama that was unfolding behind the scenes at Anfield. I was also conscious of the fact that my two young boys still did not fully know what was going on.

Locked in my mind was a memory that had haunted me since the day when Graeme Souness sacked me as Liverpool reserve coach. I was forced to break the news at that time to Philip and Daniel. I did not want them finding out by chance in school. When I explained that I was finished at Liverpool FC, they both sobbed and sobbed. It was heart-breaking.

Now I could make amends. The wheel had turned full circle. They looked smart in their St Edwards College uniforms and I was proud of them as they prepared for another busy day. Marg called them into the living room and I said: "Remember when I got the sack and we cried together?" They nodded.

I said: "Well, your dad is now the new Assistant Manager of Liverpool. We held each other, reminiscent of one of those famous Anfield player huddles before kick-off. We were jumping up and down as if we had won the Lottery. Tears were rolling down our faces and I said to them: "Your dad is back, but be careful. Don't tell your classmates until this afternoon."

What a secret to ask them to keep. When they went off to school I broke the news to my two smaller children Max and Josh. Although they were very happy they did not understand the consequences of what was happening as much as Philip and Dan.

I had two guys in decorating the house. They had just heard the 9.30am news bulletin on Radio City. One of them, Carlo, said to me: "Something is going down at Anfield today Thommo. I think the manager must be getting sacked or something."

They didn't realise I knew exactly what was going on and was part of it. Straight away, as I was just about to set off for Melwood, the phone rang at home. It was Ken Rogers, sports editor of the Liverpool Echo, who said: "Congratulations Phil."

I said: "What for?" He said: "For being named the new assistant manager of Liverpool FC." I knew Ken really well. He had given me a column in the Football Echo and the Kop Magazine after the Souness business. He had always had strong contacts within Anfield and I wanted to respond, but I tried to play it straight. I said: "Leave it there. I'm not denying or confirming anything." Of course, Ken knew what was going on and had the story prepared for that night's Echo hours before the formal press conference unfolded. I said goodbye to Marg. As she had predicted, our life was about to be turned on its head as I prepared for a new phase in my football career with Gerard Houllier. It would be an eventful, enjoyable and a highly emotional roller coaster ride and include a historic treble success. But this was day one and I couldn't wait to meet the players and get started.

I will never forget that first morning back at Melwood, newly appointed and ready for another challenging chapter in my career. Of course, the players were still unaware of what was going on. I arrived at around 10am and was wandering round. A few of the lads saw me, people like Jamie Redknapp, Robbie Fowler, Steve McManaman and particularly Steve Harkness. It may sound strange to single him out, but I brought him through when I was running the reserves. We became quite close.

Later, when I was out of the club and needed a ball or shirt signing for an event or something, Stevie would always help. He would even give me his complimentary tickets or 'comps' as we called them for the lesser games. I remembered that and really felt for him when I returned and he eventually left. Later he would reflect on that morning at Melwood when I returned like the Prodigal Son. He thought to himself: "What's Phil Thompson doing here?"

They would soon find out. We called a short players' meeting at Melwood to make sure the lads found out the breaking news before the Press. Gerard told the lads that Roy was going and that I would be returning as the assistant manager. Clearly, we needed to work out some new rules to ensure that everyone knew the boundary lines. I remember Steve Harkness coming to me and saying: "Does that mean we are going to get our arses kicked now?" It must have been in his mind that I had been brought back to the club to help Gerard with the discipline. Let's just say things had gone a little bit amiss.

Of course, we still had to get ready for the press conference because it was important to get the right message across from the word go. I think everybody knew that the joint manager thing with Roy and Gerard was never seriously going to work, but they had both been prepared to give it a go. The time had come to set a new structure. I suppose I should have expected it, but one of the first questions from the Press related to discipline.

I said: "If backsides have to be kicked, I don't mind doing that." It was a statement that proved unpopular with certain players and the early years were always going to be a challenge.

With Gerard and myself, it was the good cop, bad cop thing. I didn't mind if it made me unpopular with some people. It was needed and those who responded in a positive manner were the people we wanted to work with.

The press conference to announce Roy's departure and my appointment as Gerard's assistant was a surreal affair in many ways. For a start, departing boss Roy Evans and coach Doug Livermore were paraded in front of the media before we took centre stage. It was strange, but it highlighted the relationship Roy enjoyed with the club and the respect in which he was held, not least by chairman David Moores who he had known for years. It's gestures like this that make LFC different from the rest. The club is not a public limited company, unlike some of the other big guns.

It inspires the family atmosphere that makes Liverpool so special. Normally when a manager goes, he is out of the door in the twinkling of any eye with no looking back. It can be a cruel business in that respect. Liverpool operate under a different, more personal code and so it was that Roy and Doug were able to stand up at Anfield and speak to the Press on their final day. It was all very positive as you might expect.

When they finished, they made their way out into the corridor where I was standing. Press officer Ian Cotton had gone off with Gerard and so I was on my own. Both put their arms round me and Roy said: "Best of luck, Phil. The best thing that can happen to Liverpool FC is for you to come back."

Doug quickly added: "They could not have picked a better person to be Gerard's assistant. I'm thrilled for you."

They were instinctive thoughts on their part and I was grateful that, at such a difficult moment, two people chose not to think about themselves but about me and the part I could now play to help the club move forward.

However, I also had another thought. What went through my mind as I looked at Roy was: "Why did you not give me a chance to return on the staff if you think this is the perfect role for me?"

The thought came and went in a flash. I had finally been given the call, not by Roy but by Gerard Houllier. I knew that some big decisions would have to be made and I pledged to myself that I would not let the people down who had finally made my dream come true and opened the door once again to my beloved Anfield.

The final phase of Roy's reign had begun to be dogged by a little bit of player power. Gerard came into that situation when he linked up with Roy.

It's difficult when you are on the outside looking in, but I had heard all of the stories about what had been going on at the training ground. Commentators had begun to interpret it in different ways. I remember reading Tommy Smith's column in the Liverpool Echo. He had declared that you can't have the inmates running the prison or the crew telling the captain how to run the ship. Smithy pointed out that when that begins to happen it's a recipe for disaster.

Clearly, things had to change at Melwood. When I met Gerard to discuss my appointment he said that the only place he wanted Liverpool was on the back pages, not the front pages.

I have to say that as a player myself we had enjoyed ourselves and probably drank as much, if not more, than any other team. The difference is, we were successful and knew where the line stopped. You have to earn the right to celebrate and you have to put the club before everything else.

There were some big stars at Anfield when I returned to work with Gerard. I was not going to shirk the challenge. I was not there to win friends. I was brought back to act as the buffer between the manager and the players.

Gerard was a very positive person. He had this plan and the end game was all about Liverpool winning the Premier League and then the Champions League. I wanted to play a part in this success story. In my mind the Premier title was the most important thing because it had been so long since we had won it. Roy picked up the Coca-Cola Cup in 1995, while Graeme Souness won the FA Cup in 1992, but there had been a real shortage of top honours.

We knew we faced a tall order, sitting 11th in the table at the time. Let's be clear. This was a club that could have gone further down. As it was we improved to finish seventh and looked forward to Gerard's first full season in sole charge.

I wanted to give the younger fans who had not experienced a major triumph something to be really proud of. A club like Liverpool needs to be winning the Premiership. I knew it wasn't going to happen overnight. Gerard had his thoughts. I had my own ideas of players who might help us. I had studied it from the outside for a long time.

We felt in particular that we needed a centre-back. That was our priority. Gerard agreed and said that we needed to get one from somewhere. I thought and said: "No, we need two whether they both play from the start or not. That will show we mean business."

This became our immediate aim, linked with a determination to change attitudes on the training ground. Some players would feel uncomfortable with this. Others, the ones who mattered, realised we had to get our act together on and off the pitch. Along the way we would manage to win five trophies in one remarkable year, including an historic treble of League Cup, FA Cup and UEFA Cup. We would repeat our League Cup success and make significant progress on the Premier front. From seventh in 1999, we claimed fourth, third and second. In order to maintain this impetus we could only go one way on the domestic front and that was the biggest step of all into pole position.

It's something you can't guarantee. The competition is white hot and we would have two massive clubs challenging us for the top spot in Manchester United and Arsenal. I will reveal the inside story of our chase for glory and how it ultimately ended in total frustration for Gerard and myself, so near and yet so far from achieving our sky high ambitions. But my story is about a life-long love affair with Liverpool FC that started in earnest in 1965 when, as a young fan, I witnessed my first major game at Anfield. It was a night that would become part of Kop folklore.

May 4, 1965, is a date that Liverpudlians young and old remember as being one of the greatest occasions in the history of our famous club. Bill Shankly's first great team had fought their way to the semi-final of the European Cup in which Italy's mighty champions Inter Milan stood in their path. Liverpool FC was already my life. As a fan, every inch of my bedroom wall was covered with pictures of heroes like Ian Callaghan, Tommy Smith, Peter Thompson, Ian St John, Ron Yeats, Roger Hunt and Tommy Lawrence.

I had a wooden bed-head and used an ink marker to write on it the names of Sir Roger and the Saint. My mum, a big Liverpool fan herself, said that she wanted to wallpaper the room. I pleaded with her to leave it as it was. How could I take down my wall-to-wall LFC posters? She realised what they meant to me and the room was never decorated.

My passion for all things Liverpool was funny because the early games I was taken to actually featured Everton!

Kevin Marsh played for Kirkby Schoolboys and eventually signed for Liverpool as a pro. He lived just round the corner from me. I remember that Kevin was the idol of Kirkby at that time. He was the best player the town had produced in those early days along with John McLaughlin who had managed to play 39 league games for Bill Shankly between 1969/70 and 1971/72. We all thought Kevin was going to be the next big local star. The thing was, he was a big Evertonian.

Now and again, he would go to Goodison and take me along. I probably went on three or four occasions and can remember standing in what was the paddock on the Bullens Road side of the ground. It was not Everton that was the attraction. It was the bright lights and the green of the grass that was magical, but there was no way that I was going to become a Blue.

I was simply attracted by the opportunity to watch the professional game and it stirred my imagination about what it would be like to become a pro footballer myself.

I watched my first Liverpool game when I was eleven. I was incredibly lucky because it was a legendary occasion, the European Cup semi-final clash against Inter Milan in 1965. I can remember sitting right on the front row in the old Kemlyn Road stand. What a view! I was too small to get 'Kemlyn Roader's Knee' then. This was a famous ailment caused because the rows were jammed so close together. Every adult had his knees under his chin!

I can vividly remember Gerry Byrne and Gordon Milne parading the FA Cup around the pitch before kick-off. The roar from the Kop was deafening and I could almost reach out and touch the lads. I remember banging my knee on the front perimeter wall. Gerry, of course, had been the hero of Wembley after playing on with a fractured collarbone. Gordon missed the game because of injury. I have this image of Roger Hunt scoring against the Italians. He did a twirl in the air as he celebrated and that was one of the first specialist goal celebrations I had seen. He thrust a clenched fist in the air and spun round. Of course, I was repeating the celebration in the school playground the next day.

I have to thank my mum June for introducing me to Anfield. She somehow secured three tickets. My elder brother Owen joined us at Anfield that night. Mum and her twin sister May were great fans. They used to stand right next to the dugout in the paddock in the early Fifties. I have seen pictures of them by the tunnel prior to the players coming out. They were passionate about their football and idolised the likes of Billy Liddell and Cyril Done early on. There is no way they were going to lose me to Everton, a club my dad supported.

I should introduce you to the family. As I said, dad Owen was an Evertonian and a merchant seaman. He was often away and my mum June therefore had a great influence on my early life. The eldest child was Linda, then Owen and me, followed by Ian and Denise. Then there were the twins, May and June, named after mum and her twin. That's seven kids. Perhaps it's lucky dad was away a lot or we might have had to take on two Kirkby houses!

Mum's enthusiasm for the game ensured we became steeped in football. Aunty May had been a spectator at the FA Cup Final in 1950 when Liverpool lost to Arsenal at Wembley. Mum missed out because she was pregnant with our Linda, but she had the ticket stub and it was autographed. All seven of us were Reds. My dad didn't stand a chance.

When he used to come home from sea he would say to me: "If you agree to support Everton, I will give you your present." I'd shake my head and he would still give it to me.

We had a great time growing up. We originally lived in Kensington in Liverpool at 69 Ling Street. When the council started to move people out of the city, we set off for our adventure by the seaside, or the River Alt as we call it in Kirkby. It's no more than three or four feet at its widest, but still a river! It was 1957 when we arrived in Stone Hey Road in the Kirkby district of Southdene. My dad is still there.

Our house backed onto St Joseph's School field and that was a real dream. It gave me the ideal opportunity to play football on grass. Of course, we could also play in the street. There was hardly a car to be seen in those days. We would play lamp post to lamp post, every available minute of every day.

I also played about 500,000 games of 'Spot' against the front wall of the house. You had to hit a particular spot and if you missed you got a letter and started to spell out the word 'Spot.' You were out when you finally got the 'T'. In those days, even a cheap 50p football was hard to come by, but mum always managed to get us a ball. I remember when the Frido Orange plastic ball came out. If it became punctured on some glass you could mend it which was revolutionary then. Some people would use a hot poker to melt the plastic around the hole and smooth it over. These were the days of coal fires!

We had a different solution. We would take one of the sharp knives out of the cutlery draw and smooth it over the small hole. I could have become a plastic surgeon by the time I was 14, I was so good at moulding the Frido balls with that knife. The one drawback was that it left the skin of the ball wafer thin and it would soon burst again or get a large egg in it which meant the ball wouldn't run true. This became a way of life for us. I would have a ball until someone else got one for his birthday and then we would play with that for months until it succumbed to the knife treatment. Football was my life. There were no other distractions.

If I was on my own I would just practice control in front of the house. If there were two of us it would be Spot. Any more than that and we had a match going on St Joseph's field.

Looking back, if I had to describe the young Thommo I suppose I would be classed as a Scally. I would get very angry if we lost a match of any sort. I would be angry if I mis-controlled, angry if I missed a goal. I wanted to be perfect. My biggest problem was that I always wanted to fight bigger kids. I'd be swinging at older lads. My mum later said: "You didn't know when to back down." Possibly it helped me to get on in later life. I was so skinny that I needed that fighting spirit to survive.

My first school was Rushey Hey Juniors. We used to have to keep a diary. All I did was play football, but I used to lie in the diary that I was doing other things in case my teacher didn't believe that I only had one focus in life. In the summer we might play cricket, using old railings as stumps. If we didn't have a bat, we would use the widest thing we could find. The parents of the kids would field and these were happy times. There was no golf or tennis in Kirkby. Of course, the sooner the football season started again the better.

While Inter Milan was my first game at Anfield as a serious spectator, I had been following the Reds since the days when they were in the Second Division. I would get together with my mates and we would quiz each other about who was in the team and who our favourite players were. We used to have a little out-building at home which we kept the coal in. That was our den. We used to write the players' names on the floor and the walls using the coal. I hated it when the coalhole was used for its real purpose and I was sent out to get some fuel for the fire. Of course, many people still had open fires in those days.

It was coming into the early Sixties and all Liverpudlians were beginning to get excited about the arrival of a football messiah called Bill Shankly. These were whirlwind times if you were a Red. What a time it was to be on Merseyside with the music and the football combining to make Liverpool the centre of the universe. I was only a kid, but I sensed these were special days.

If I could have looked into a crystal ball at that time and saw what the future had in store, I would not have believed it. Every game I watched at Anfield was a stepping-stone towards the club becoming my whole life. I can remember queuing for tickets for the big games. The police used to leave gaps as they let a certain amount of people move forward at one time. Then there was an almighty charge as they allowed you to close up. Often they would sell out just before you got to the turnstiles. That was always in your mind until you got your hands on your tickets. It happened to me prior to the famous European Cup Winners' Cup game against Celtic in the mid-Sixties. I was totally demoralised.

When you started out as a young fan, your first stop was the Boys' Pen. It was in the top right-hand corner of the Kop as you looked at it from the pitch. I used to go with a lad called Tom Heaton who was a mad Liverpool fan. There was a drainpipe in the corner of the Pen, going right up to the roof. Lads would be climbing up it and jumping into the Kop. It was a tricky one. The stewards were always waiting for you. Achieving success was like some sort of initiation ceremony. Other kids would dare you to try.

We had this routine. One of us would climb over and be chased by a steward. This would give vital seconds for the next lad to take his turn. It became a way of life. The Boys' Pen could be a frightening place. It was the opposite of the closeted environment that is the modern Family Enclosure. Eventually you would progress to the next phase in your fan development and stand in the Paddock in front of the Main Stand. From there you moved up to the Anfield Road which was your apprenticeship for the final step on the journey and your formal introduction to the Kop itself.

My brother Owen started work at 15. He was earning £3.50 a week and he used to give me the 50p for pocket money as well as giving my mum money for his keep. I would use the money to go in the Kop. I'd get in at around 12.30 for a 3pm kick-off and make my way right into the middle where I would stand in front of a crush barrier. This was to avoid being swept forward by the army of fans who would eventually be lined up behind. I used to try and keep just enough space for my brother who worked in a garage in Mount Vernon Street. He would get in at about 12.45 and I would be hoping and praying that some big docker did not push into the space I was protecting. That was our spot and Owen knew exactly where to find me. We stood there for the next few years, watching those great Shankly stars sweeping all before them.

The crush in the Kop was something that you had to learn to deal with. It usually happened 15 minutes before kick-off by which time it was jam-packed. Supporters would seem to sweep forward in groups of 100. It was like a red tidal wave. You would suddenly be back in the position you started in. People would sympathise with me because I was so young.

Being in front of the barrier, you would be protected from the pushing from behind, but it would be happening sideways and backwards all around you and there were times when you would be on the point of blacking out. When someone had a problem, he would be lifted high above the heads of the fans and passed all the way down to the front where the St John's Ambulance men administered first aid.

There would be spells when nothing was happening, but then we would get a corner and one of the Kop's famous sways would lift you off your feet. It was quite dangerous for the younger lads, but you would be in school on the Monday, proudly telling your mates that you had been in the Kop and that you had done this and that. It was fantastic being a Kopite. No matter how far you were away from the pitch, you were just happy to get a glimpse of the action and feel the excitement. To stand in the middle of 28,000 singing, roaring Kopites was simply inspirational. It's sad that the standing Kop has gone but times had to change after Hillsborough.

I will still always remember my time in there and that square yard of terrace that was Owen's and mine. It was our spot, hallowed ground that was part of our life and all for 50p. I actually continued my Kop love affair until I was 17. Those two years of being an apprentice at Liverpool didn't stop my journeys onto the Kop with my red and white scarf still draped around my neck. It was a strange thing to be paying to go in, singing and shouting the players' names and then going in to train with them the next morning.

The only reason that I stopped going on the Kop and meeting Owen on our sacred spot was that all of a sudden people were stopping, staring and pointing and saying: "Isn't that the young Phil Thompson who plays in our reserves?" I started to feel uncomfortable with that and thought that it was maybe time to sit in the stands and use the one complimentary ticket I got from the club. When I eventually fulfilled my boyhood dream and found myself out on that famous Anfield pitch, I could stand on the 18-yard box and pick out our Owen in the middle of the Kop. That was what years of training as a fan was all about. Fortunately my younger brother Ian had stepped up to take my place alongside Owen and it was easy to recognise them and wave.

As I began to develop my ability as a young player it was Everton who offered me the chance to train with them every Tuesday and Thursday night. My heart was still set on playing for the Reds, but I was just happy to be part of some organised sessions. I was around 14 and playing for the Kirkby Boys team. These days people ask me if youngsters are over-played. All I can say is that my football agenda was non-stop as a kid. At 14 and 15 I seemed to be turning out every day of the week. I played five-a-side for a team called Digmoor. I was playing for the Brookfield School team and Kirkby Boys. I was also playing for a Sunday League team called St Joseph's on the field behind my house. I could just jump over the fence and be ready for action.

It was there as an Under 15 that my potential was first spotted. I owe a great deal to a man called Billy Gamble who was a steward at Anfield and also manager of my Sunday team. He got a scout to watch me play along with another kid called John Roberts. Thanks to Billy's intervention I was invited to go Tuesday and Thursdays to Liverpool.

Of course, I had been having a few sessions with Everton along with three or four lads from the Kirkby Boys. It was good that Everton were interested in me, but I looked on it as a bit of a betrayal and my heart was never in it. I was 14 and really taking my support of Liverpool seriously. When I got offered the chance to train at Melwood there wasn't really a decision to make although there was a minor dilemma right at the start. The first game was against a Kirkby Sunday League team called Medbourne. I knew most of their lads and they wanted me to play for them in the match. Liverpool often arranged games like this to see how their younger lads would fare. The Sunday teams often had a few older, experienced players.

I was on trial with the Reds and there was no choice but to play for them against my mates. I wanted to show Liverpool what I could do. We won 4-2 and I scored twice. It was a great starting point and I did myself a lot of good.

I continued to train on Tuesdays and Thursdays. It was coming towards the end of the season and I asked Liverpool's Tom Bush what was happening. They had already made a decision about their apprentice intake and I was not included. They used to have 15, but times were tight and the numbers were dwindling. Liverpool asked me to come on trial again pre-season. I felt a bit embarrassed because they had not signed me.

Instead they took on four lads who all had promise. Paul Johnston had played for Liverpool, Lancashire and England Schoolboys. John Caslon had done the same. Ken Pritchard was an incredible goalscorer for the Liverpool Boys and Lancashire sides. Then there was John Gidman who had already put pen to paper after leaving school early. All four had very good pedigrees. As it turned out, none of them went on to play for Liverpool although Gidman would play for Manchester United and Everton. Against this, I was this lad from Kirkby who was about eight stone soaking wet. Despite this I had a burning desire to do well whether I was cleaning boots or taking part in a game. I decided to give it everything in the trial period. After five weeks and with the season looming, nothing had been said to me. I was feeling a bit miffed. I didn't want to be hanging around. Here I was playing, putting out the kit for the seniors, cleaning the baths and mopping the floors and no one was giving me a hint if it would have an end product.

My dad was at sea and I had to look to my mum for support and guidance. I asked her to have a word with Tom Bush to see if she could find anything out. There was a midweek game against Bury 'B' at Melwood. We won 2-0 and I felt I played well. Afterwards my mum spoke to Tom. We were due to go into town to meet her sister, but I pestered her for news. She said Mr Bush didn't say one way or the other. I desperately wanted an answer, but we walked away from the training ground towards what is now the Bill Shankly Playing Fields. She was quiet and that made me worry, but suddenly she spoke up. "Listen Phil," she said. "I will tell you now but you must not say anything to Mr Bush. He's told me you will be signing apprentice forms tomorrow."

I jumped up and down. Despite the frustration, those five weeks had been the happiest time of my life. I had progressed from the Tuesdays and Thursdays under the guidance of George Patterson and Reuben Bennett to a situation in which I would find myself in the same room as the great Bill Shankly, Roger Hunt, Tommy Smith, Chris Lawler and all of my other heroes. From starting on the Kop to being part of the club itself was an amazing thing for me. We used to travel on the bus to training and I would be looking out of the windows, imagining all the fans were looking at me when they were really looking out for the giants of the first team at that time. No one could take that away from me. I signed as my mum had predicted for the princely sum of £7 a week. I was actually the last player Tom Bush signed as an apprentice because he died soon after that. He was a big imposing guy who always wore a trilby.

I made good progress to reach the reserves when I was 16. My debut was at Sheffield Wednesday and Ian St John was in the team. Over 30 years later I would have a bit of a rift with him as Gerard Houllier's assistant and with the Saint working for Radio City, but more of that later. At this stage the Saint was my idol and he played in that game at Sheffield. Ian was booked and the referee asked for his name. I was gobsmacked. I thought: "Cheeky bastard. Do you know who you are talking to? It's the Saint."

Ian had that competitive edge, even when he was playing for the reserves. It bordered on anger and determination. What sticks in my mind even more than Ian's confrontation with the ref was coach Joe Fagan's reaction to my performance in the dressing room. He actually gave me a bollocking. He said: "I know it was your first game son, but can't you play the ball forwards? Every ball was sideways or backwards. Use this as an experience and have the confidence to play the ball forwards."

Being my debut, Joe knew that I would remember his words. Of course, it was sound advice, even if it did shake a 16-year-old who thought he had done fairly well in a goalless draw. Joe was quite a relaxed guy and he never usually got angry. When he did react, you listened.

King Konk bloodbath, sparrow legs and a Red through and through

L iverpool's decision to sign me on and the good early progress I was making augured well for the future, but I often thought about what might have been. At the age of 13 a new teacher came to Brookfield School in Kirkby called John Crompton. He was big on athletics and cross-country running, things that had never really been part of the scene before then.

I had a prowess for cross-country although I don't know where it came from. I could run and run and not get out of breath. John had high hopes that I might become a successful athletics distance runner. At the age of 13 I was North of England cross-country champion. I remember taking part with 800 other schoolboys at Lymme Park. It was an unbelievable feeling. After a mile I was 60th, but I started to ghost ahead of people. My teacher was part way round the course and encouraging me. The feeling of hitting the front and then coming first was magnificent. I won a lot of races at that time.

My mum, to help out with the family funds, was a cleaner at Brookfield. Mr Crompton was always encouraging her to push me down the athletics front. He had a real belief in me. I was skinny, tall and had these long legs. Mum always told him that he would never persuade me to give up the real love of my life, football. John left not long after that and went to America.

A new teacher, Bob Downing, arrived who was absolutely passionate about his football. It was the love of his life. I immediately struck a chord with him. There was only one problem. He was an Evertonian!

Still, Bob allowed us to stay on in school until 7pm almost every night to have a kick-about in the gym. He would later become a great friend. He got me back on track on the football side and any thoughts of concentrating on athletics disappeared.

Bob was naturally delighted when I ultimately joined Liverpool, even if he would have preferred me in a blue shirt. My learning curve continued at Melwood. In these early days a guy called Tony Waiters was appointed as the club's first youth development officer. Tony had been a top-class goalkeeper with Blackpool. He had some quite futuristic thoughts about coaching and how youngsters should be developed and Bill Shankly was keen for these ideas to come through.

Tony was great. He used to have these big charts with a clear structure to the working day. He was keen on the use of weights to build up strength. He actually introduced a new fitness regime for the older players. They saw it as strange rather than visionary and a few eyebrows were immediately raised.

I remember watching one of Tony's sessions and recognising that some of the established stars like Tommy Smith, Ian St John and Geoff Strong were clearly not happy. Training had been all about working around the five-a-sides which were legendary. They were actually 7 or 8-a-side. You could hear the moans and groans in the dressing room about Tony's methods. People would be saying: "What a load of crap."

No one likes change, especially when the previous system has proved successful. Suddenly Bill Shankly had encompassed this way of moving things forward and updating things. The players were not up for it and went in to have a word with the boss. After a couple of weeks, Tony stopped working with the senior pros. His brief was now to concentrate on the youth side. Their loss was our gain. We were more open to the new ideas although it wasn't all plain sailing. Ronnie Moran was youth coach and, like the older players, he had been brought up on a different routine. There was a lot of friction early on between Tony and Ronnie. They argued, but Ronnie would later admit that the new man actually had some interesting thoughts.

Sadly, Tony only stayed for about a year. He decided to return to football as a player and joined Burnley, later going to Canada with Vancouver Whitecaps to expand his coaching thoughts.

He pulled me to one side just before he left and gave me a fascinating insight into how my career should progress. He said: "By 18 you should be making your first-team debut. By 19 you should have been clocking up at least 15/20 senior games a season. At 20 you should be established in the side. These are the challenges you should set yourself." I always remember Tony's comments. It is amazing, but my career actually took that line. He had set me clear targets and that is crucial for a young player. I learned a lot from that and throughout my life I continued to set myself targets.

The most important thing was that I desperately wanted to be successful as a footballer. I was this skinny kid who needed all the drive and aggression I could muster to achieve my aims. I was out of the norm for a footballer. I needed something different. From the 'B' team Ronnie Moran became my mentor and he remained influential throughout my football and coaching career. He was always there to give advice and help. He was also prepared to give you a kick up the backside if that was needed.

I remember getting in an argument in the dressing room at Melwood with a lad called Keith Milton. I didn't take kindly to him calling me King Konk. Keith had a big physique, but I thought I would give him a hiding.

There was blood all over the walls in the shower area. I looked at him and thought: "It's not his!"

I put my hand to my nose and it was covered in blood. I looked in the mirror and it was all bent. My nose was to be the big thing in my life. Who said: "Sit down Pinocchio?"

I had to see Ronnie and when he saw my nose, I said: "I caught myself on the door in the shower room." He could see right through that excuse and took me to Broadgreen Hospital. The doctor said: "We need to put your nose back into shape now." Ronnie was laughing and saying: "We'll call in Wimpeys for the scaffolding."

The doctor explained that if it wasn't dealt with immediately, it would be harder later. He put his two thumbs together and pushed things back into place. I nearly hit the ceiling, but the job was done. It wouldn't be the last time my nose got me into trouble.

I got back into the routine at Melwood. It was November, 1970 and I had a thigh strain. When you were injured you were left to your own devices. The age of 17 is a critical time for a young player. You either get an offer to stay on at the club, or you get the arm around your shoulder that suggests it's bad news. Everyone was so nervous on their 17th birthday. Our core of five apprentices were all worried about it. My birthday was still a couple of months off, in the January. I was walking round the 'B' team pitch as part of my recovery process. The great man, Bill Shankly, stopped me and chatted about the injury. That was unusual because normally you didn't get a peep out of him if you were in the treatment room. I distinctly remember we were standing in the area between the old 'A' and 'B' team pitches.

The boss said: "Are you sleeping well, Phil? Are you eating well?" I nodded, fearing the worst. He said: "Your 17th birthday is coming up soon." My heart skipped a beat, not knowing what was coming next. Shanks said: "We have discussed things and we like what you have done, on and off the pitch. Everyone is extremely pleased with you." He added: "I know this is a difficult time when you are a young apprentice. I wanted to put your mind at ease. We are going to sign you on your 17th birthday."

This came right out of the blue. It's hard to understand. He was a god-like figure to me and to all the fans. I used to go home and tell my mum with pride that I had spoken to him. He once said to me: "You must have told some lies when you were younger, Phil." It was the first reference to Pinocchio, but it would not be the last. I was always thrilled when he spoke to me, regardless of what he said.

The boss had a tremendous sense of humour and I was proud to be the butt of one famous quote. It was around 1971/72 when I was just staking a claim for a place in the first team. People were beginning to take notice of the young Phil Thompson. Shanks always had a story or a line for every player. I was his young prodigy and he produced one of his great quotes in my name when he said: "Aye, Phil Thompson. The boy tossed up with a sparrow for his legs and lost."

It was one of those asides people always remember, like: "Hey, Ronnie Yeats. He must be seven feet tall. What's that? Six feet three inches? No, seven feet is near enough for me."

I loved the little joke he made at my expense, even though he was taking the piss out of me. It meant I was accepted, but I'm jumping ahead of myself.

Now I had a wonderful secret about being signed on my birthday that I would have to keep from the other lads for a couple of months, but I couldn't wait to get home to tell my mum and dad. I just hoped he would not forget the conversation.

I had this warm feeling inside knowing that I could continue with my Liverpool dream. The other four lads, who had been signed as apprentices before me, were all released.

I signed pro forms in 1971. It was the year that the club went to Wembley to play Arsenal who were chasing an historic league and cup Double. I was included in the travelling party and can remember the pride in wearing my official blazer and badge. The game went into extra time and I could not watch.

I would go out onto the Wembley balcony and then race back in when I heard a roar. Naturally I was thrilled when Stevie Heighway put us in front, but I went straight back outside. The tension was really getting to me. I heard another roar. George Graham and Eddie Kelly had combined to score that calamitous equaliser. I stood outside again and another roar went up, clearly not from our end. Charlie George had fired in what proved to be their winner.

I just cried. It was so emotional. Later I attended my first official dinner. My career was up and running, but I wanted to be in the first team playing my part. 1971/72 was to prove a momentous year for me. I won England Youth caps and was playing for the successful Liverpool Youth team. We got to the final of the FA Youth Cup and beat rivals Everton on the way through. Our side had been thrown together. They had a lot of schoolboy internationals, all apprentices or young pros. The spirit and drive in our dressing room was what set us apart. We knew it was going to be a real game. People had classed it as a personal battle between Everton's Mick Buckley and myself. We were both midfield players and I was up for the challenge. We won 3-2 and I got a lot of plaudits after the game. The reports said I had been dominating. It was my first taste of stardom.

In the final, one of the apprentices who had been discarded by Liverpool turned up in the opposition – John Gidman. He had joined Aston Villa. We lost 1-0 in front of 17,000 people in the first leg. We then played at Anfield and finally lost 4-2 after extra time. Brian Little was also in the Villa team.

I scored in the last minute of normal time to keep us in the game. For my pains I was kicked in the chest by Bobby McDonald, the Villa defender. I was lying on the ground, doubled up in agony and clutching my ribs. I looked up hoping to see Ronnie Moran administering treatment. Instead, it was my brother Owen who had come running down from his place on the Kop onto the pitch, asking me: "Which one of those bastards did it?"

He wanted to beat them up. I answered: "Get off the pitch you soft get!" That was typical of Owen, showing the big brother attitude without taking into account it could have had him thrown out of the ground.

Because of what Bobby McDonald had done to me, Tommy Gore – our small right winger – squared up to the Villa man, only to take a right hook that knocked one of his teeth out. This led to McDonald being sent off. Even though they were down to ten men, Villa still went on to win the game 4-2 and secure a 5-2 aggregate victory.

Season 1971/72 was a great one for me. I had my first European trip, to Servette Geneva in the Cup Winners' Cup. I was not due to be involved. John McLaughlin, ironically another Kirkby lad, was taken ill and I was sent home to get some clothes before heading for the airport. I was not even sure where my passport was, but I got myself together. It was a whirlwind time, but I was young and a bit sheepish.

Shanks had said in the papers that he would have no fears if he had to play me. He said: "This is a young kid we have high hopes for." I had still not made my first-team debut. We arrived in Geneva and I was rooming with Alun Evans who was the game's first £100,000 teenager. The hotel was incredible, so grand and overlooking Lake Geneva. It was the most incredible place I had ever seen.

Alun was really good to me. He really took care of me on the trip and we would both look out of these huge windows in our room towards the Lake, which is beautiful. There was a big spiral staircase in our room with a red rope handle that led up to the bedroom. It had upstairs and downstairs toilets. The boy from Kirkby was astonished. It even had a phone in the toilet. This WAS luxury. Now you realise that it was a top of the range suite and all the players had one. At the time, we thought we'd been given the wrong room.

In the game we went 2-0 down before Chris Lawler ghosted in as usual to give the game credibility and offer us a real chance in the return match, which we won 2-0.

I was then selected for the 1972 Mini World Cup in Spain. We had gone through all the rituals and Lilleshall trials. I was named in the squad and won my first cap against the host country, which was special.

Liverpool's former cultured midfield player Gordon Milne, one of my schoolboy heroes, was the manager of the England Youth team. Ten years later I would play in the proper World Cup, but for now I was just thrilled to be on the way up. Ironically, Everton's Mick Buckley was my roommate. We also had a bit of a starlet in the squad called Trevor Francis. At 16, he was already rattling in the goals for Birmingham City. He was so highly rated, he never even turned up for the trials.

In an earlier friendly against Spain, I partnered Mick in midfield. After the game I got exceedingly drunk. I was sick in our room, but made sure I had cleared it up with towels and tissues before he woke up. I swore that it would never happen again. That Mini World Cup tournament was brilliant. We played at Valencia's ground. The final was against Germany at the Nou Camp.

I was this centre midfield player with defensive qualities, keener on the short ball rather than the long ball. Suddenly I rifled a shot from 30 yards out into the top corner. To cap it all, Mick scored in the second half and we lifted the trophy.

We had this player called Kevin Beattie. He was a man mountain, despite his age. Kevin was strong in the air, had a shot like a cannonball when he came forward and had all the qualities of a Bryan Robson type. His career with Ipswich was cut short by injury, but he could have been one of the greatest players in English football.

After the final I tried to get all the lads to sing 'You'll Never Walk Alone'. I wanted it to be the England song. Instead, however, Trevor had us singing Birmingham's 'Keep Right On To The End Of The Road.' He was a strange lad even then, but what a footballer. Of course, we have ended up working together again on the SKY team.

Although the '71/72 season was great for me at youth level, stepping up with the big boys was every young player's ambition. Speaking to Trevor Francis about his exploits in the First Division, I was hoping and wishing that my time would come.

Back at Anfield, I had much to learn alongside some real football legends. I've explained that I was quite a runner. I just got on with the job. I can always remember Tommy Smith saying to me: "I'm warning you, lad. Slow up or I'm going to break your legs." Smithy added: "I don't care how fast you can run. You will never be a player." During the runs he would shout: "Will somebody put a harness on that skinny bastard. Get back in line."

I would run alongside them. Towards the end I would sprint in. I never had blistering pace, but I was quick when it came to the 200 yard or 440 yard runs. I was even striding on in the 880s.

These were the days when apprentices had the boots to clean. My senior pros were Emlyn Hughes and Ian Callaghan. Cally was and is one of the nicest people you could ever meet. He seldom missed with his payment of 12/6d a week (62p). Emlyn occasionally missed, but he would eventually pay up. At Christmas they would give me a couple of quid as a bonus.

The great thing about Emlyn was that he was the same shoe size as me. He wore Adidas 2000, the Predator of their day. He would ask me to break them in for him which was a painful pleasure. When he discarded them he would pass them on to me. I would get them patched up. I'd be the only one in the 'B' team playing in Adidas 2000 and that made me feel really special.

Cally was my idol as a person. Roger Hunt was my idol as a player, probably because he was a striker and a lethal matchwinner. When my mates and I played 'Spot' against the wall, I was always Roger. It's incredible how things happen in your life. A few years ago I was at York races with my friend Len McCormick. I had heard that Roger Hunt was there on the day and like a star-struck schoolboy I asked Len if he could invite him up to our facility. I am never usually in awe of people, but this was different. We are talking about 'Sir' Roger Hunt. I was Assistant Manager of Liverpool at the time and he was coming up as though I was the star. The truth is, Len and myself were the groupies. He was and is an absolute Liverpool legend and that was one of the proudest days of my life to be able to spend some time with him.

The same thing happened with Gerard Houllier and Ian Callaghan. As Gerard's assistant, I had my staff room at Anfield on matchdays into which friends could come. We had a Boot Room for other members of staff. I would often bring in ex-players and Cally was one who would sometimes pop in with a friend. This day Gerard was coming down the corridor. He said: "Who is in the staff room today?" I just said: "Ian Callaghan." He said: "You are joking. I used to stand on the Kop and watch him when I first came to Liverpool as a teacher. He was my idol."

Gerard asked if he could come in and he was like a fan again, all starry-eyed when he met Cally who was standing there, bottle of Carlsberg in his hand and as down to earth as they come. I introduced them and Cally went as red as the Liverpool shirt he once wore with such pride and quality.

Gerard was genuinely pleased to meet a former player he had admired so much. When I later told this to Cally, he couldn't believe it. He thought I was winding him up. In fact, here were two men in a 'Mutual Admiration Society.' It really was a humble meeting and lovely to watch.

Of course, Cally was very much involved as a player as I started to make my way with the club. What a dressing room it was with other people like Ronnie Yeats and Smithy in there as well.

It started to break up in 1969 as Shanks started to build his second great team although Cally and Smithy would remain part of the scene until after the legendary 1977 European Cup Final when they both helped Liverpool win the European Cup for the first time.

As the Seventies dawned, men like Ray Clemence, Brian Hall and Steve Heighway started to come through and now I was also on the brink of taking the giant step that I had always dreamed about with my league debut within touching distance.

One special date will forever be etched in my memory. It was April 3, 1972 and I would finally make my debut on a truly unforgettable day. Not only was it at Old Trafford, but we thrashed Manchester United 3-0. I would get off the bench after being an unused substitute the week before at home to Stoke City.

Okay, maybe it would have been more memorable to step into the top flight at Anfield, but this was the next best thing. Let's record the goalscorers first. Chris Lawler (60), John Toshack (62), Emlyn Hughes (84). At 2-0, and with Liverpool crushing their rivals, my time had finally come.

Tosh came off feeling a bit groggy and the boss signalled for me to get stripped and ready. The words of Bill Shankly are still ringing loud and clear in my ears: "Son, just play behind Kevin Keegan. Leave him up front on his own. Slot in behind."

These days we would call it playing in the hole. Even though we were 2-0 up Shanks knew that it was important to strengthen the midfield and he was aware that my defensive qualities would be ideal for that position.

I clearly remember my very first touch in top flight pro football because it brought me face to face with the legend that was George Best. He tried to nutmeg me on the halfway line. I was older than my years and closed my legs as he tried to do it. The ball just rebounded off my skinny shins to set up a Liverpool attack. I would always recall this as a fantastic moment. Phil Thompson, new to the big time, had broken the George Best spell.

Soon after, I remember going down the inside-right channel to pick up a ball over the top before turning onto my weaker left foot. In the process, I glided, with a swagger, past the famous Martin Buchan and hit a left-foot drive from the edge of the box. Alex Stepney was forced to turn it behind for a corner with a full-length save.

To hear all the Liverpool supporters singing my name was an unbelievable feeling. That was the first time I had ever had the pleasure of the travelling Kop recognising my efforts. Things were to get better because Emlyn was to drive the dagger into the hearts of the United fans with the third goal. It capped a resounding victory and a fantastic 15 minutes of pure heaven for a young Phil Thompson. I can remember Bill Shankly being interviewed after the game and people asking who I was and what he felt would become my best position. They were probably flummoxed by where I played in the game. Shanks said I was a midfield player who could play in defence, but who could even make an attacker because of my shot, which could have made a fantastic debut even better.

I was not to play any part in the remaining games that season although I was an unused sub in the last match at Arsenal. There was still a chance that we could have won the title that day, but it wasn't to be. In the dressing room I sat in awe of the more experienced pros who were gutted that the Championship had passed us by.

This would be the beginning of a new era, not only for me but also for a young side that was being rebuilt by Shankly to take on the next challenge. Men like Stevie Heighway, Peter Cormack and even Alec Lindsay were helping to shape a new Shankly team.

This side, in the 1972/73 season, would now bring the League title back to

Anfield for the first time since 1966. I always remember when Emlyn Hughes was signed in '66. He always said he felt he was a jinx because the club failed to win honours from then until '73. Having made my first appearance from the bench, I would now make my full debut and begin to play the amount of games Tony Waiters had once planned for my career all those years before.

The 1972/73 season began with a home game against Manchester City, but I was not involved. I had been given the taste the season before and the boss knew I was straining at the leash for another chance to prove myself.

Manchester United then came to Anfield and I was desperate for a second crack at them, having made my debut in such a satisfying way at Old Trafford just months before. Again, I was not involved as Steve Heighway and John Toshack inspired a 2-0 win. I would have to wait until mid-September for a place in the squad at Arsenal, but didn't get on.

Another sub appearance without any action came at Leeds and then I was overlooked for three more games, including the derby at Everton. I had been really hoping for a call for that one, but this is all part of the learning curve as a young pro. You just have to make sure that when the call does come you are ready in every way.

My full debut was only a matter of time and the big day finally came at Norwich City on October 28, 1972. The previous week Emlyn Hughes had scored in a 2-1 home win over Stoke City, only to aggravate a thigh injury he had been carrying for weeks.

I knew he had a problem, but 'Crazy Horse' had been intent on playing through the pain barrier with the team playing really well at the start of that season. Stoke City was one game too far and my chance had finally come. I thought: "Great, I am going all the way to Norwich with Emlyn left behind for treatment. I must have a chance."

Shanks did not name the team until half-an-hour before kick-off. There were no mobile phones then to relay the messages back home to the family. The boss pulled me to one side for yet another surprise. He didn't tell me I was playing. He actually asked me if I wanted to play! I just said: "YES, YES, YES!"

I was going to make my full debut that afternoon alongside Peter Cormack. I must say that Peter was a fantastic help to me. He had something that Terry McDermott would later adopt as his own trademark, an ability to make perfectly timed runs into the box to get goals from midfield. Peter was a better header than Terry, but Terry knew more jokes.

Peter guided me through the game. I was happy to sit and play the anchor role. It was Peter Cormack who got us the goal in a 1-1 draw.

It was interesting to note who was substitute that day, none other than Kirkby's John McLaughlin. Shanks had chosen me ahead of him and that just emphasised my progress because John had been ahead of me with many games under his belt.

It would have been great if we could have held on to Peter's first-half goal at Carrow Road. A winning full debut would have been nice, but Norwich hit back. Still, nothing could take away the wonderful feeling of starting a senior game for the very first time.

What was to make it even better was the following day's papers and the great headlines. I had glowing reports from the Sundays and then the Mondays, all saying that I had made a very experienced debut. I knew Emlyn would be back. It was not a problem making way for the great Emlyn Hughes. I was only 18 and I knew more opportunities would come my way. I would have to wait until mid-December to get a run of six games and by now I was feeling more comfortable with the guys who I still looked on as heroes. I was then taken out again through March and early April, but actually played in the last four games as the title was won.

Bill Shankly knew what I was capable of and I remember a game in the February when he started me at Manchester City. He pulled me to one side and said: "Phil, play right in front of the centre-backs."

I was in for Peter Cormack and the boss was aware that City played direct football, missing out the midfield and chipping balls in for Franny Lee and Rodney Marsh who were both skilful forwards. He said to me: "Whether the play goes right or left, make sure you are in front of the ball. I played the whole game as a front sweeper. I can remember the City bench demanding that Marsh find more space.

He said: "This skinny prick is stopping me from getting any. What more do you want me to do?" That was music to my ears. When a rival player is upset you know you are doing a good job. This was one of the first times I had experienced it and how you could nullify your opponent's strengths. We drew the game and secured an important point. Manchester City were one of the best teams around at that time.

It was a pleasure to be involved with a side that was charging towards the title. The last two matches of the campaign were extra special, both home games against the great Leeds United and then Leicester City. To keep on course for the title we needed three points out of the four remaining, bearing in mind it was only two points for a win in those days.

I can remember our team coach approaching Anfield. I was sitting there and looking out at all the fans on Priory Road. I started singing 'You'll Never Walk Alone' to myself. Coming along Anfield Road I was still singing it, trying to psych myself up. As the words ran through my mind I was getting really pumped up for the action and, as it turned out, I played my best game for Liverpool up to that point.

We were 1-0 up through Peter Cormack just after half-time. I remember powering through a challenge with their experienced striker Allan Clarke. It was a 50-50 ball and I was so hyped up, I brushed him to one side and passed the ball on to a teammate, all in one aggressive movement. The Kop started singing my name. The buzz that it gave me was astonishing.

I thought: "You've arrived." Everything had gone right and I received the man-of-the-match award. I knew my position was always delicate at this time. I was still young and learning. I knew I had to fight for my place. Kevin Keegan scored a late goal to confirm a famous victory and the Championship was now in our grasp with one game left to play.

I can remember everyone being fit for that final match. Obviously all the players wanted to be part of an historic day, our first Championship for seven years. I was worried that I would be left out, regardless of how I played against Leeds. Shanks didn't name the team until we were all in the dressing room. He read out my name and the one to miss out was Brian Hall. I can remember stopping Brian in the corridor a few minutes later and apologising that he was the one left out. Brian said: "Don't worry son. I don't blame you. I blame that Scottish bastard for ruining my day."

Brian was 12th man and I was pleased that he got on. Alec Lindsay had returned for that final game, forcing the shuffle. It was a massive decision for Bill Shankly to make. I must have impressed him against Leeds.

The Leicester game was not a classic. The only scare for us was when Stringfellow headed past Ray Clemence, only to be ruled offside. My heart sank, but I was joyous seconds later when the linesman raised his flag. From the heady heights of a fantastic game against Leeds, we would win the title with a dour display, but no one was complaining, certainly not the Kop. There are some wonderful pictures of the post-match celebrations and lap of honour. There is one of me, standing behind the great man with his hands clasped as if in prayer in front of his adoring Kop. It always fills me with emotion when I see it.

It was during that fantastic Championship campaign, with my full debut finally under my belt, that I truly began to understand the workings of the mind of Bill Shankly. He had an honorary degree in psychology, earned over countless years studying at the University of Football. The boss knew exactly what made his team tick and he had this special knack of handling his players in tricky situations. Let me explain.

It was February 10, 1973 and the boss was plotting his first title success in seven years. Two weeks earlier the team had lost 2-1 in disappointing fashion at Wolves on a day when I was an unused sub. I'd also failed to get on at home to Derby County in the previous game and was desperate to make more progress in the first team, having made my league debut that season at Norwich as well as enjoying my first run in the side with six successive games between December 9 and January 6.

A home game was looming against Arsenal and Ronnie Moran thought I had a real chance of playing. I remember that the day itself was wet and the pitch was heavy. That might have swayed Shankly's mind when selecting his team, but the rumours persisted that I would be getting another chance to show what I could do.

Lo and behold, I was named 12th man and I didn't get on in a 2-0 defeat at Anfield that meant the Reds had failed to win in three outings. I remember Alan Ball and John Radford scoring for the Gunners. After the game Ronnie Moran, my mentor since I was a kid, said: "Listen, you should have played today, despite the conditions. It's important you see the boss and ask him why he left you out. You must see him. He will think more of you if you go in, even though you are only young."

All over the weekend I was talking to my mum, my other mentor, and asking what I should do. She pointed out that Ronnie had been good to me. Her verdict was simple. "If he feels you should speak to Bill Shankly then you should do it."

On the Monday I was walking along the corridor at Anfield getting the words straight in my mind. Suddenly, Shanks was coming out of his room. I asked for a word and we went back into his office. I just wanted to keep it simple and blurted out: "Why didn't I play on Saturday, boss?"

Bill looked at me and rapped back: "Play? Why didn't you play? Jesus Christ son, you are asking me why you didn't play with that load of rubbish."

He started to run through the names of the team and said: "These are all has-beens. You should be in here thanking me that I didn't play you with that load of crap. You are going to play for this club for years. You will captain this club one day. You will go on and play for England."

I felt fantastic. I had gone in to complain and come out buzzing. My head was so big it caught the door frame on the way out.

This was Shankly, the man who could turn any situation to his advantage. Whatever they say, he was the best in the country. I told everyone what he had said and waited with confidence for the next team selection the following Saturday, at Manchester City. He read out the names and I wasn't amongst them. He just said: "Phil Thompson, 12th man."

He showed his faith in the lads he had been hammering just a week before. That was Shanks. I'm sure he was delighted that I had gone to his office to question his selection. I was only 18 and he wanted me to confront him about my career. It showed I really cared. He would have seen that as the boy becoming a man. He built me up, but then he ensured my feet were firmly back on the ground with his next selection. Of course, Ronnie Moran knew exactly how their minds worked in the famous Boot Room. He had gone through it as an elder statesman. Possibly Ronnie had primed Shanks that I was going to see him, after telling me to stand up for myself.

It was their way of seeing what you were made of. I've spoken about my progress in that 1972-73 Championship season in which I managed 12 full appearances, plus two as substitute. That was enough for me to win my first medal although it was just magnificent to be around people who had been my heroes. It was still all new to me.

As an apprentice I can distinctly remember seeing Phil Boersma in the corridor counting his wages. He was moaning because he was only on £100 a week. The younger lads were gobsmacked. Now I was on the brink of the big time and I couldn't wait for my career to develop further, not so much for the money but for the glory of wearing the red shirt that had always meant so much to me.

I had figured in a Championship side and managed my first games in Europe as the lads made it a double trophy success by claiming their first Euro crown – the UEFA Cup. I had come on as a sub against AEK Athens, started against Dynamo Berlin and played in the semi-final, second leg against Tottenham.

I was to sit out the final, played home and away, but it enabled me to watch Bill Shankly at his tactical best. The teams actually met three times. On the first night a torrential downpour forced the referee to abandon things at Anfield after just 27 minutes. In that time Shanks took note of the aerial weakness of German opponents Borussia Moenchengladbach, a club we would meet years later in another famous final in Rome.

The boss seized the opportunity to change things the following night when the teams started all over again. You wonder if he was blessed. He left out the diminutive Brian Hall and brought in the giant John Toshack. It was to prove a masterstroke. The lads went on to blitz the Germans whose star turn was the great Gunter Netzer. We secured a three-goal first leg advantage which was to prove crucial because they proved worthy opponents on home soil.

We were two goals down by half-time in the second leg and this time they were murdering us. I was sitting on our bench, close to Shanks. He was strutting up and down the touchline for minutes on end, sometimes not looking at the game, but pointing to the Liverpool fans with his index finger as if to say: "Don't worry." I was panicking as they continued to take us apart and threaten an equaliser. During the interval the boss gave his rallying call. He told the lads to stick together. He said they had given it their best shot and that it would come right.

The longer the game went without them adding to their tally, the more skipper Tommy Smith and the lads were able to take a stranglehold of the game. There was a lot more confidence on the bench, but it was still an agonising wait as the seconds ticked away with Shanks still pointing his finger at the crowd. When the final whistle went, I looked for a UEFA flag amongst the fans that was being carried by my brother Owen. I had brought it back from the 1972 Mini World Cup in Spain as a memento and it seemed appropriate to take to a Euro final.

The fans were all over the pitch and we couldn't do a lap of honour. We were so shattered, Smithy could hardly lift the giant UEFA Cup. It was so sweet, a European first and the end of a remarkable season.

I had a League Championship medal and a UEFA Cup medal. In fact, I claimed a unique treble, also qualifying for a Central League medal with the reserves. The trophy count had started, although I have to admit to being slightly disappointed that we didn't get a proper medal for the Championship, but a plaque with a wooden back and a gold front. It reminded me of the hundreds of Sunday League trophies I had given out on amateur football presentation nights.

Nothing wrong with that, but there is something special about a medal. Later on we would get beautiful gold medals and I would receive four. They remain my pride and joy, along with the plaque which is a reminder of a fantastic year and the beginning of a wonderful era for me.

Having played a part in the double-winning Championship and UEFA Cup season of 1972/73, I now approached the new campaign determined to get even more games under my belt. I had been given a taste of the big time and now I wanted more of it. I was delighted when Bill Shankly, in the opening three games, handed me the number four jersey that I would later make my own although at that time it actually belonged to a Kop legend – Tommy Smith.

Smithy, of all people, wasn't going to part with it without a fight and it shortly came to that, although the battle was between Bill Shankly and the 'Anfield Iron'. When Tommy shook off an injury to return for the home game with Derby County four matches in, I was convinced I was the one who would make way. As it turned out, Alec Lindsay took ill and I claimed his number three shirt. It would be a memorable day for me because I scored my first league goal in a 2-0 win.

Derby were one of the top teams at that time, having won the Championship for the first time in 1971/72 under the enigmatic and often controversial Brian Clough. Ironically their title-clinching victory that season had been achieved at the Baseball Ground against Liverpool, who had been major contenders themselves, finishing third in the final reckoning.

The following year, as we grabbed their title crown, they dropped to seventh and trouble was brewing at the Baseball Ground. We were not fully aware of what was going on when they arrived at Anfield on September 4, 1973, but Clough and his assistant Peter Taylor were on a collision course with chairman Sam Longson over the manager's increasing TV work. Within a fortnight, both would be sacked, libel writs would fly and the Derby players would back Clough and Taylor in an unprecedented show of player power. They even laid siege to the Baseball Ground offices where the board was meeting, ready to announce the appointment of Dave Mackay as the new manager.

Of course, no one could have predicted this when the Rams arrived at Anfield with Cloughie still very much in charge and determined to try and put one over on his old adversary Bill Shankly. After 35 minutes I took up a covering position as we won a corner in case the ball was cleared and they tried to counter attack. As it happened, the cross was headed out and it fell to me about 30 yards out. I'm not a good golfer, but I know that feeling when you sometimes catch a ball perfectly, regardless of the sport. It flew from my boot and went right into the top left-hand corner as you look towards the Anfield Road End. Goalkeeper Colin Boulton was left completely stranded.

I had been used to being in the crowd and seeing a goal hero mobbed by his teammates with the crowd roaring his name. Suddenly I was in the middle of such a celebration and it was a wonderful feeling. I remember Kevin Keegan rushing up to me saying: "How did you kick it that far?" I just wish the BBC or SKY TV cameras had been there to capture the moment. These days every goal is recorded for posterity, but then it was different. I would score in the Kop End as my career progressed, but nothing could match this feeling because it was my first league goal. I'm sure every Liverpool-born player, people like Smithy, Chris Lawler and Ian Callaghan all felt the same about their first Anfield goal.

Kevin would grab a penalty to complete a 2-0 victory. When Clough and Taylor shook hands with Shanks on the final whistle, no one knew that they would be gone within a fortnight.

I would play four more games as the season began to take off and then be rested by the boss with Alec Lindsay now recalled and Smithy defiantly holding on to his number four shirt. Incredibly, on the crunch day when Shanks finally decided to leave him out, I was handed the shirt and received it with mixed emotions. Firstly I was thrilled to be recalled on November 3 at Arsenal, a fixture that was always one of the highlights of the season. However, I was nervous because Smithy was fuming when the boss finally named the team in the Highbury dressing room, just minutes before the kick-off.

This was the first time I had been selected ahead of Tommy on merit at number four with Emlyn reverting to Tommy's position at centre-back and me in midfield. He had been one of my heroes, a player I had idolised when I stood on the Kop. I think Tommy had an inkling that he was going to be left out, but he was furious that he had been forced to travel all the way to London with no formal confirmation from Shanks that the change was to be made.

I can remember that Smithy put his bag across the dressing room door. Every time someone came in or went out, they had to climb over it, even the boss. No one dared to move it. Tommy frightened the opposition and he could also be a fearsome character in our set-up. To be honest, I was frightened to death, not about the prospect of playing in front of 40,000 people, but about taking Tommy's treasured number four shirt. What would he make of this young lad claiming his place? He certainly didn't take it lying down.

He finally picked up his bag, walked out of the dressing room and right out of Highbury. Later we would learn that he met a few fans in the street who accompanied him to the tube station and then all the way home on the train from Euston to Lime Street. I knew he had stormed out, but I didn't realise he had gone home until after the match. Thankfully, we won the game 2-0 with goals from Emlyn and John Toshack. I felt I had justified my selection, but no one was looking forward to meeting Smithy at the training ground on the Monday morning.

As it happened, Shanks defused the matter in his own inimitable way. He called Tommy in and before the Anfield Iron could let fly with his own broadside, the boss declared that he would have walked out himself in similar circumstances. This calmed a simmering situation. The boss was brilliant at that. Smithy would fight his way back in, ironically claiming the number two shirt from his great mate and former roommate Chris Lawler who had suffered a knee injury.

Personally, I was now delighted to go on my longest run to date in the side. I only missed one game between the Arsenal fixture and the end of a season that would culminate with a famous FA Cup Final victory over Newcastle United.

It was the start of a fantastic spell for me although one well-known defender was less than happy and it wasn't Smithy who was now operating with all of his old power and determination at right-back. I will reveal the player's name shortly.

Cup Final heaven, Shanks' bombshell and 'tapping up' Terry by love letter!

A highlight for me had to be the derby game at Everton on December 8, 1973, when Alan Waddle scored a famous lone goal winner in front of 56,000 people. Big Willy as we called him (work it out yourself) had only played a handful of games, but he was the Red hero that day. Alan was 6ft 5ins with legs as long as they come. He swept home a goal at the Gwladys Street End to silence the Blue army and this brings me to one of my biggest apologies in this book. I didn't run to Alan to congratulate him. The young 19-year-old Phil Thompson, with his head momentarily back on the Kop, ran towards Everton's most partisan fans and gave them ridiculous 'V' signs with both hands. There is passion and commitment and then there is something that is unprofessional and steps over the mark. This fell into that category. It was one of the biggest regrets in my career. Down the years, more than a few Evertonians remembered those gestures although they didn't hold it against me, hopefully understanding that I was just a local teenager caught up in the emotion on the day.

Incredibly, only one newspaper picked up on my disgusting and degrading action and mentioned it. These days it would be all over the front and back pages, backed up by a huge FA fine. Even though it was over 30 years ago, I would like to apologise for my actions. This apart, it was a great day and a great result for a lad who was a fanatical Red, on and off the pitch.

Things moved on and I scored the winning goal in the January at home to Birmingham City in a 3-2 victory. I can remember knocking the ball past Kenny Burns who was looking for an offside. Instead, I ran on beyond him and found myself one on one with Gary Sprake at the Anfield Road End. My great memory about Gary as a fan related to that famous occasion when he was playing for Leeds and threw the ball into his own net in the Sixties, right in front of the Kop. That was the day they conjured up that now legendary

'Careless Hands' song from the Des O'Connor hit. I can remember the occasion perfectly. There was snow on the ground and the teams used an orange ball.

Gary was now with Birmingham and I must have run a full 20 yards before he confronted me on the edge of the box. I had plenty of time to think about what I was going to do. Gary stood up, making himself as big as possible which is the natural stance of an experienced keeper. The only gap I could see was between his legs and so I nutmegged him. When the ball hit the back of the net, it was one of the highlights of my career. The Kop didn't sing 'Careless Legs' but it would have been a thought!

Weeks later a decision was taken that would change my whole career. It was February 5, 1974 and Coventry City were due at Anfield. Larry Lloyd clearly had a problem. He had been struggling with a thigh injury, but had played through the pain barrier as we did in those days. This time he couldn't shake it off. Trevor Storton had been tried at centre-back. He had done okay, but it hadn't really worked. Larry had tried one comeback too many and split his thigh muscle. It was obviously going to keep him out for a good while.

I had played centre-back for the reserves when they were short of a few players. As I have previously mentioned, while I was a midfield player I was always defence-minded. When you can get the ball and keep hold of the ball, it ensures that your opponents can't play.

Ronnie Moran brought me up understanding this in the youth team. However, when the decision was taken to play me at centre-back in the first team, I was as shocked as anybody.

However, the coming together of Emlyn and myself in that partnership was the start of the Total Football, played skilfully from the back, that would be made famous by the Dutch that same year – 1974.

It was a clever decision by the boss and the staff. They were ahead of their time. No longer would they rely on a big, traditional centre-back like Ron Yeats or Larry Lloyd, as effective as they had been down the years. All of a sudden we were looking to build play from the back. If it took 50 passes to score we didn't care. We beat Coventry 2-1 that day and I was gutted. Yes, we had won, but I had wanted to keep a clean sheet. The Sky Blues grabbed one late on. However, we went on a great league and cup run and that was the only goal we conceded in about nine games.

I staked a permanent claim at centre-back. People would ask where I would rather play. I must admit I was now really enjoying it alongside Emlyn. We complemented each other. Whenever we were up against a big centre-forward,

I would take him. I wasn't dominant in the air like a big Yeatsy. I had good spring and if I couldn't win the ball, I would ensure my opponent didn't get in a clear header, ensuring the ball would run through to Emlyn. That is how we planned it. This was to shape Liverpool over the next few years. We would finish second, but there would be one final twist and a highly amusing one at that as we ended the season with two games in London.

The first was at West Ham. We were getting beat 2-1 and laying siege to the Hammers' goal in the closing minutes. Bill Shankly clearly thought we were not going to score and headed from the stand down towards the dressing room, anticipating the final whistle. Then Kevin Keegan scored, literally with the last kick of the match.

The boss heard the roar, but assumed it was the referee calling a halt to proceedings. We all trooped into the dressing room, delighted to have secured a last-gasp point. Shanks was already in there and looking exceedingly annoyed. He looked at the bubbly mood of the lads and started to have a go. He must have thought: "Bastards! They've lost and they're all smiling."

He started to say: "You should never lose to a team like this." Bob started to interrupt him and he looked even angrier. Then he heard Bob say: "Bill, we equalised in the last second. It was a draw." Shanks' face went the colour of the red tie he was wearing. He immediately said: "Great result lads. Fantastic. You deserved it."

We all started laughing but he couldn't see the funny side. He had wanted us to show our mettle as the season drew to a close and had clearly been frustrated by what he thought was our flippant approach to a defeat, when in fact we had secured a point. It was one of the great Shankly stories that everyone remembered for years to come.

Whenever people think about the 1973/74 season, they immediately focus on our outstanding FA Cup Final triumph over Newcastle United. Of course, it was a magnificent occasion, but it's worth reflecting that our FA Cup journey could have ended almost on the starting line against much less glamorous opposition. Liverpudlians will recall that our campaign began with what should have been a straightforward third-round clash with Doncaster Rovers. They held us 2-2 at Anfield and in the last minute they could have clinched a shock victory when one of their players went through one on one with Ray Clemence. He put it over Ray's head and it bounced into the Kop off the top of the crossbar. What a let-off. We lived to fight another day and claimed a safe passage with a comfortable 2-0 away win.

We then faced Carlisle United, one of Bill Shankly's old clubs. They put up a real fight in a goalless draw at Anfield and clearly felt a giant killing feat could be achieved at Brunton Park. They had a big, strong centre-forward called Frank Clarke who did the worst thing possible.

He criticised us in the Press and was particularly cutting about our giant defender Larry Lloyd. Clarke riled our entire team and we cruised to a 2-0 victory in the replay. Nevertheless, it had been something of a ropey start to our cup campaign. We had to get our act together and beating Bobby Robson's Ipswich at Anfield at the next hurdle was a decent performance.

In the sixth round Bristol City stood in our path. We knew we had to be on our game because they were a good team at that time. I remember Jimmy Hill saying on 'Match of the Day' that my form would be an important factor.

One of my main strengths was reading the game. I would get into a covering position and intercept danger without having to make a tackle. I didn't head the ball 30 yards away from goal. I would glance it to Smithy, or whoever, to ensure we kept possession. Hill, the game's leading pundit at that time, highlighted this ability and talked about my England potential.

One goal was enough to see off Bristol and set up a semi-final clash with Leicester City, a side who had a reputation for putting up a great battle against Liverpool. Old Trafford was the venue and they produced another fighting display in a goalless draw that took us to a replay at Villa Park. This was the ground where the Reds had beaten Chelsea to claim a Wembley place back in 1965 – the year of our first-ever FA Cup triumph.

We hoped it would be a good omen although the attention before kick-off surrounded their England star Peter Shilton who made a real fashion statement for a goalkeeper when he turned out for the first time in a white jersey and shorts.

In the end, it actually played into our hands. On a misty, drizzly evening, with the score standing at 2-1 in our favour, Kevin Keegan clearly spotted Leicester's white ghost off his line and hit a great shot right over him. It was all over and we all celebrated the prospect of a final confrontation against Newcastle.

They had a very good team, but we felt we had nothing to fear. In the league we had beaten them 2-1 at home and held them to a goalless draw away. However, I had cause to remember their powerful striker Malcolm Macdonald who could smash the ball when he had the chance. I got in the way of one of his piledrivers at St James Park and the ball flew into my wrist on the edge of the box. It was excruciating. I had never felt such pain before and despite treatment from Bob Paisley it continued to ache. The wrist was strapped but the pain was astonishing. I don't know whether it was the angle it caught me or the sheer power of the shot, but it caused me sleepless nights over the weekend.

In those days things were left until the Monday, hoping they would settle. It turned out that I had broken a small bone in the wrist and the medical people said they would have to put it in plaster up to my elbow. It never crossed my mind that this might prevent me from playing, first and foremost because of the danger to other players. Of course, I could still bend my arm and I didn't want to miss any games. I actually played from that point until it healed. A 'Tubigrip' bandage would be pulled over it to make the plaster less obvious. When the linesman came in to check the boots, I would shove this plaster down my shorts.

I recall that more than one striker was actually caught by my arm and yelled out: "What the hell was that?" They looked and just saw what they thought was a strapping. I got away with that for quite a while because after six weeks the specialist still felt the arm wasn't strong enough for the protection to be removed. Joe Fagan knew this specialist place in town and he arranged for them to make me a lighter plastic alternative. I could put my arm in and it had a slot for me to put my thumb through. I was able to use this every day in training and for matches. It became a bit of a ritual for our reserve goalkeeper, Frankie Lane, to strap it up for me.

Of course, I remembered the culprit who caused the problem, Malcolm Macdonald and I wasn't the only one in our ranks who would be looking for revenge against the self-proclaimed Supermac under the Twin Towers. He said in the Press that he was going to destroy Emlyn Hughes and the young Phil Thompson at Wembley. Macdonald had a decent partner in John Tudor who was good in the air. They said they would be too strong for us. Malcolm's words only served to stir us up. I had no nerves at all on the day. I had only just turned 20 the previous January. I just loved the build-up to the big day because it was all new and exciting.

We actually went to the cinema the night before the final. That was Shanks' way of getting us to relax. I can't remember what we saw. Some taxis picked us up to take us back to the hotel where I was rooming with Alan Waddle. It was only when we walked to the door of our room that I realised it was number 13. I thought: "This is getting off to a bad start!"

I can remember the room. Big Al's feet stuck out of the end of his bed, but because we were so young we just got on with it. I remember Brian Hall being very nervous before that final. He asked me how I was feeling and I said I was really looking forward to it. On the day of the game I can remember getting up and telling Brian at breakfast that I was going back to my room to watch TV. He couldn't believe I was so calm. It was just another final day for me. I had loved them ever since I had been a young boy. I always watched every minute of the build-up. I loved to see the players preparing to leave their hotel for Wembley and remember the pictures of the helicopters hovering over the stadium, filming those aerial shots of each team bus heading up Wembley Way. I also loved all of the old footage of previous finals and was determined to watch as much as possible before we set off.

When the time came to get on the bus, I was like a fan again, watching all the supporters with their flags en route to the stadium.

What was truly remarkable was that I had been helping to make two such flags just a few days before with my mum who was as big a Red as they come. She had these white sheets and rolls of red tape. I helped her as we spelled out 'SHANKS RED ARMY'. Suddenly the sheet was a fully-fledged banner, ready for Wembley. We made another one declaring: 'LFC – SUPER REDS'. It wasn't as if we put my name on one of them, even though I was playing. They were really good and it brought out the simple fact that I was just a supporter at heart who was lucky enough to be pulling on that famous red shirt and playing at one of the world's greatest stadiums.

I had revelled in every aspect of the build-up. Of course, we had to get our FA Cup Final suits. I remember they were a very smart grey pinstripe. There would be no all-white versions for this side. Emlyn was our captain then and must have played a part in the selection, but he didn't wear his club outfit at Wembley. He wore a brown suit and claimed he was superstitious because he had worn it right up to that stage. Probably one or two of the more senior players were looking at Emlyn with a bit of suspicion as to why he had really made that decision. The rest of us were in our pinstripes.

In the dressing room I can remember putting on my Stylo Matchmaker boots. They were clearly not the greatest, but Stevie Heighway had done a bit of a sponsorship deal. I think that was one of the first times any team had put together a 'Players' Pool' to make a bit of extra money. It was just before commercialism really took off.

It was to be one of the greatest days I have ever had in football. Possibly Newcastle were the in-form team going into the final, but Macdonald's prediction that they would destroy us had every single Liverpool player switched on like a prizefighter. I had the added incentive of that wrist injury and was determined to pay him back.

I remember going through the ritual in the dressing room with Frankie Lane who helped me on with the plastic cast that had become my own lucky omen. We then had that long walk out to the centre of the pitch with Shanks out in front looking so proud. I was looking round for my brother Owen. I knew which section he was in. He was wearing a bright yellow shirt that he had worn at all the games, even though it was coming away at the seams. I spotted him in this sea of red and white. We all had our little superstitions, so perhaps Emlyn was right.

I also looked for my parents. My mum had given the flags we had made to some of my Kirkby mates. It was great for me being in the privileged position of actually being part of the action on the pitch.

Although I was a young pro when we reached Wembley in 1971, I couldn't get tickets for my mates. This time I was able to help. We actually took a picture at my mum's house of all the lads with their Wembley tickets. Securing tickets was to become a big part of my life.

I'd be chasing around getting them for the lads for every game, even the pre-season matches. The fans even took their holidays to follow us around. I would ask Bob and Joe if there were any spare. They'd say: "Not again. How many mates have you got Thommo?"

Before matches I would dash down to the entrance with ten to fifteen comps. I did that for years to come. People remembered that later in my career. It was all down to my mum. She would say: "Always be nice to people when you are on the way up. You will meet the same people on the way down." That struck a chord with me and that is what happened in my career. I hope I was never carried away by stardom, not even as I prepared for an FA Cup Final.

Our first challenge against Newcastle was to keep a clean sheet in the first 15 minutes. As the game wore on I felt this steamroller effect building up as we began to increase the pace. As a player you could sense when your team was getting stronger and more confident. That day we knew a goal was coming and that we would take charge of the game.

We reached half-time and dear old Malcolm had not had a single shot. Into the second half we thought we had finally opened the scoring when Alec Lindsay fired a dipping volley past Ian McFaul. I can remember Alec with a wry grin, holding his arms in the air as he wheeled away. Then he turned round and realised he had been given offside. We were convinced it was a perfectly good goal.

That was the turning point. Newcastle lost their nerve and we were well on top. To go on and win 3-0 was absolutely brilliant. Kevin Keegan opened the scoring after 57 minutes and Steve Heighway rocked them back on their heels after 75 minutes. Of course, everyone remembers our final goal, conjured up with a magnificent move down the right. I think we put together about 16 passes before Smithy played a one-two and fired in hard and low for Kevin to turn the ball home. What a moment that was.

It was fantastic for Kevin. He was a real working class hero, having come from a humble background like many of us. I remember when he first joined us. He had this long hair and I thought: "Reuben (Bennett) is not going to like it." I could envisage our tough Scottish coach shouting: "You long-haired Jessie. Get yer hair cut!"

But Kevin had his own mind. I was playing in an infamous pre-season game with him at Southport soon after he arrived. After 45 minutes we had failed to score and a hard-faced Kevin Keegan said to Ronnie Moran: "We've not got anyone up front. We are never going to score a goal."

Ronnie shouted back: "If you can do any better, you play up there." Kev scored twice and his workrate and effort was sensational. Poor Southport didn't know what hit them.

Then we had the traditional first team versus the reserves game right before the start of the season. Kevin started in the first team because of his display at Southport. The reserves were often hyped up for these matches, but on this occasion they were beaten 7-3 and Kevin bagged three or four goals.

On August 14, 1971, Kevin made his debut against Nottingham Forest and scored his first senior goal in a 3-1 win. Every fan at Anfield that day knew we had something special. He was never blessed with silky skills, but he had this determination and quickness off the mark. He could leap to head the ball, despite his small stature, and I always admired him for his attitude to the game.

He would stop and sign an autograph for anybody, young or old. He would always give the fans his time and did that throughout his career. He achieved a tremendous amount with Liverpool and when he was honest enough to say he would be leaving to play abroad, people criticised him. I only had good things to say about Kevin. I remember him arriving from Scunthorpe with a brown Ford Cortina. I thought it was souped up because the engine used to always roar when he started it. He said: "No, it's just got a massive hole in the exhaust!"

Although Kevin was given local hero status after that FA Cup Final, the truth is that it was now superstardom and he deserved it. I can remember listening to the final whistle at Wembley and knowing we had won. At 3-0 we had been playing keep-ball and it was embarrassing for Newcastle as they chased around trying to regain possession.

This was the Total Football we were capable of. I felt we started it before Holland who claimed the phrase and the style as their own in the World Cup. It was about all of the good things Bill Shankly drilled into us about simplicity. It was there for all to see in that second half. I sought out Newcastle's Terry McDermott, another Kirkby kid, on the final whistle. We swapped shirts and he was clearly distraught, despite being their best player. I think we were the only players to swap jerseys. Tosh might have done so after the presentation of the trophy, but not before I was caught up in a remarkable incident.

As I started to make my way up those famous steps to the Royal Box to get my medal, two stewards grabbed me. They thought I was a Newcastle player going out of turn. I also had on this black and white bowler hat that someone had given me. Here I was, this fanatical Liverpudlian on the proudest day of my life dressed like a Geordie supporter on my way up to meet Princess Anne. I had to tell the stewards I was a member of the winning team. Someone came over to sort it out, but I still had that black and white striped top on as I got my medal.

The celebrations that followed our victory were incredible. The following morning I can remember Kevin Keegan asking me to go to the ITV studios with him. I said: "What do they want me for?" He said: "All the players made you man-of-the-match." That made me so proud. I can remember reading the London Evening News on the Saturday night and they made me their star man.

I went with Kevin and that was my first taste of being on the other side of the camera, something I'm used to now with SKY. I remember presenter Brian Moore saying: "I bet you have got your medal in your pocket Phil." I put my hand in and pulled it out. Brian said: "I knew you would never let it go."

I had a more embarrassing media engagement at the BBC radio studios. I was still on Cloud Nine and we had drunk a lot of champagne which I was not used to. Frank McLintock said: "Phil, how did the game go?" I said: "What about that fuckin' Supermac now?" All of these executives standing around spat their champagne back into their glasses. Frank roared with laughter.

I was so pleased we were able to ram Malcolm's words back down his throat. He got away from me a couple of times in the game. One shot went ten yards wide and the other ten yards over. That was it. The lesson is that you should never try to antagonise anybody in this game. It had become a ritual to pin up any Press cuttings in the dressing room if someone had slagged us off.

I carried this through into my coaching career. I even got them laminated, but we weren't quite so posh in those early days.

I was later to find out that Tommy Smith had already put the fear of God into Macdonald in the Wembley players' tunnel as we came out. Tommy had given him a finger-wagging. Smithy had this aura about him. If he could frighten his own teammates, he could certainly frighten the opposition and Malcolm had clearly got the message.

What we didn't know as we celebrated that 1974 Wembley triumph was that the great man, my hero Bill Shankly, was about to resign. We spent the early part of the summer looking forward to the new season, not least because the Charity Shield was to be played at Wembley for the first time. Our opponents would be champions Leeds United and while it would be billed as a prestige friendly, there was no such thing when these two sides met. It was the equivalent of the Liverpool and Manchester United affairs these days.

I couldn't believe it when the story broke on July 12 that the boss was resigning. My family couldn't believe it. It was as if there had been a death in the family. As a young player you never sniffed out stories like that. The elder statesmen in the dressing room might have heard a whisper and we heard later that he had offered to resign on many occasions. It makes you wonder. Shanks had just built another great team and he was still the messiah to the fans who idolized him. He was taking us to the Promised Land with the prospect of more cups and more glory. We felt invincible with Shankly in charge.

We all knew Bob Paisley was not the same person and that is no disrespect to Bob. Shanks had this aura that made you believe. Bob was always going to be different. He couldn't communicate the same. He couldn't motivate the same. But he knew the game inside out, even more than Shankly. I can understand why Bob was nervous about dealing with the Press and taking on this massive challenge.

The pre-season got underway and we got changed at Anfield and made our normal journey to Melwood by coach for the first day of training.

Shanks was already there, leaning over the veranda. We all said: "Morning boss." Training started and Bob would want to do something.

We thought: "Is it Bob or is it boss?"

The next day Shanks was there again, leaning over the veranda. "Morning boys," he'd repeat. We'd say: "Morning boss."

I was only young, but I could see it wasn't working. This is not how it should be. We all loved Bill, but we thought: "He's supposed to have gone."

Life became difficult for Bob. His working relationship with the players was difficult because Shanks was there, available to give advice. If we could have got round it we would have had the best of both worlds. I adored the guy and I had been his young prodigy, the last player he brought through.

I can't remember how long it went on for, but one day Shanks wasn't there and he didn't come back. He was asked to lead out the lads for the Charity Shield. It was meant to be his final goodbye to the fans. However, the occasion would be remembered for something else because we witnessed the first-ever sendings off at Wembley with Kevin Keegan and Billy Bremner involved.

Johnny Giles was actually the one who started it. He ran into Kevin's back. Leeds were good at that. They knew how to wind players up and Kev thought it was Billy Bremner who was a fiery little character in his own right. It was more handbags than anything else, but the referee didn't see it that way and they were dismissed. As Kevin was walking off he took off his shirt and threw it down in disgust. He was subsequently banned for ten games. This was an incredibly heavy punishment for a misdemeanour that didn't really deserve it. The game went on and finished 1-1 after normal time. We went straight into a penalty shoot-out.

While it was great to be back at Wembley after just a few months, I suddenly had a panic attack. The spot-kick score was 5-5 and the staff were beginning to select the next penalty takers. Ian Callaghan was number six, then someone else and then me. Cally scored our sixth and my hands started to shake. Then their keeper David Harvey strode forward and put the ball on the spot. Did I love him that day? He missed to relieve my stress and get me out of jail. I was never one to take penalties.

We would now move on, sadly without Shanks, but with an understanding that Bob and the rest of the staff had vast experience. The pre-season work always climaxed with a first team v reserves game that gave a clear indication of selection for the opening day of the season.

It was an important marker and having made that centre-back position my own and doing well in the FA Cup Final, Bob Paisley had made a big statement that I was now established in the first team. I was marking John Toshack who was in the reserves that day while our new signing Ray Kennedy was up front in our side. I remember this high cross coming over. I challenged Tosh and the ball sailed over the bar.

Larry Lloyd, who had lost his place through injury, shouted out: "If that had been a real centre-half he would have got the header." It was aimed at me for the ear of Bob Paisley. Our nickname for Larry was Albert Tatlock, the

Coronation Street character who was an old moaning get.

Smithy came over and said: "Just tell him to get his FA Cup winners medals on the table, Thommo." I appreciated his support.

Larry was clearly not going to play second fiddle and he soon moved on. I just took Bob's words as a clear message that I was doing the business and he was happy.

The season got underway, but it wasn't long before I suffered my first big injury setback. We were playing at Anfield against Stoke City and it was September 21, 1974. I can remember twisting and just felt something go in my knee. A sickly feeling came over me. I thought: "What was that?"

I tried to carry on, but as I turned quickly I just felt my knee go from beneath me. It was bent and I could not straighten it. I just felt very uncomfortable and knew something major had happened. I'd suffered thigh strains and a couple of broken noses. I'd also broken a bone in my wrist, but this was clearly more serious. I came off on a wheely stretcher, sitting up with a blanket over my legs. There are photographs of Bob looking very worried.

He was a wily old character and knew as soon as I went down what was wrong. He realised I would be out for while. In the treatment room Ronnie and Joe took hold of my ankle. They started to move it gently while trying to straighten my knee. All of a sudden the knee unlocked. The relief was fantastic. I asked what it was, but Joe just said: "It's early days. Don't worry."

They strapped it up and it wasn't until the Monday that I saw the specialist. He confirmed straight away that it was a cartilage problem. It was a common injury and my first serious setback. You are normally out for six weeks if all goes well.

I spent the first 13 days in Park House Hospital in Crosby. I was feeling groggy and was worried because my knee seemed to be twice its normal size. The nurse said: "Are you ready to do your exercises? Come on. Raise the leg. Tighten the muscle. I want you to do it six times every five minutes."

I couldn't even do one. I thought she must be an Evertonian and thought: "I'm going to give myself a few more days to get over the pain."

I remember when I first got home from the hospital. Bob Paisley called and said: "How are you Phil?" I said: "I'm still in some pain."

Bob just ignored me and said: "When are you coming in?"

My response that I wasn't up to driving didn't wash. He said: "When I did my cartilage and was at your stage, I was on my knees and ripping out my old fireplace."

I got the message and was back in training the next day. I had a little Ford

Escort at the time. Using a straight leg, I tried to work the clutch. I was sweating cobs just driving round the block in Kirkby.

There was no great magic cure. I was left to my own devices. I just placed an old cloth bag full of sand on my foot and raised it, tensing the quads.

Liverpool didn't allow you to wallow in any self pity. If you were playing well and had an ankle injury that was up like a balloon they would look you in the eye and say: "Are you fit?"

You would say "Yeah" even though your ankle was throbbing. When you were not playing well, they didn't even come near you. Everybody wanted to play and so you ignored the pain barrier. Of course, many paid for it later on.

I spent six weeks doing my own rehabilitation while receiving treatment from Joe and Ronnie. It was a frustrating time because just prior to my injury Don Revie had picked me for an England get-together.

He selected the 50 players from whom he would be picking his next squads. It suggested you had international potential and, at 20, I had been thrilled at the prospect of making progress with England.

While I was in hospital a basket of fruit and a message arrived from the FA and Don Revie subsequently phoned me to say my time would come. I really appreciated it and it gave me an extra incentive to get fit again.

That is where the Kop came in handy. In the afternoons I would run up and down the Kop stairs while people were brushing the terraces. Six weeks into my rehab I was feeling great. It was funny. I only played one 'A' team comeback game at Melwood on the 'Mini Wembley' and I can remember the opposing coach shouting at their striker to take me on because I was injured.

He was saying: "Get past him." It made me so determined to prove my worth. Maybe that helped me in the game. I was fine and was recalled to first-team duty on November 30 at Coventry, wearing the number five. A certain Terry McDermott had my four, having been signed from the team we vanquished in the FA Cup Final, Newcastle.

The story behind his transfer makes fascinating reading. Some might call it tapping up. I preferred to call it an exchange of correspondence with a Kirkby mate.

It was great to play alongside Terry Mac in that comeback game. He had been signed by Bob and I remember we had a laugh because he wore my number four shirt in my comeback game. The Press took a lighthearted picture showing us in a tug-of-war for the shirt.

I remember my first block tackle at Highfield Road. It was in the first five minutes and I went in without a second thought. I knew it was fine. I had no worries and never looked back.

We always laughed when Terry and I reflected on how Liverpool signed him. I was in my hospital bed when Bob Paisley rang me. He said: "The boy McDermott. I'm reading in the Press that he is not happy at Newcastle. Do you know him?"

I said: "Not really. He's a Kirkby lad, but he's a bit older than me. I only got to meet him in the Cup final where we swapped shirts."

Bob said: "I fancy him as a Liverpool player. Can you get in touch with him?" I said: "There is no phone for Macca, but I can write."

It seems ridiculous now with all the technology and all the controversy about players being tapped up in a high profile way. I sent Terry a letter from my hospital bed and said I understood he was not happy and that Bob Paisley had been talking about him. I explained that Bob felt he had all the attributes to be a Liverpool player, adding: "If you know what I mean."

I tried to word it as carefully as I could and soon got a letter back saying: "If you are trying to say would I be interested in Liverpool, it would be my dream."

I spoke to Bob who said: "Write and tell him not to do anything daft" (which was hard for Terry Mac!). Another letter went off and while Terry might have had to decipher it, the message was clear. Even at my young age I knew this was a sensitive issue.

A little bit of time passed and I got another letter from Terry, which said: "What's happening?" It was like James Bond with all of these cryptic messages changing hands. I told Bob and soon after it was in the papers that Liverpool were interested in Terry McDermott. After a little while longer and a few more 'love letters' to each other, he was to come to Anfield where we became firm friends and roommates for many years.

He moved back to his parents' house in Northwood, Kirkby. I was living close by in Southdene.

Terry was an unbelievable character. The lads nicknamed him 'Lege' which was short for Legend. He was such a bubbly and funny character and helped to make the dressing room light-hearted and relaxed. He was like that from the day he came. I should say that he had a strange sense of humour.

We went everywhere together and were to become well-known in the city centre nightclubs and bars. Whether that was a good thing or a bad thing, it was the norm. The LFC players were famous for enjoying a drink and a late night. People would say: "How can they do it and still win trophies?"

It was because we knew when to do it. We also worked tremendously hard.

Terry could drink and get home at two in the morning, but he could still get through any fitness regime you could throw at him the next day. That was never a problem for him. He could go in a sauna for 20 minutes without breaking sweat! He actually hated the sauna. I remember he had a chain that he wore round his neck. I can remember him being in the sauna and the chain must have been getting hotter and hotter. He suddenly screamed in pain. It was really funny.

Of course, our antics could lead to problems. There is the legendary story of Terry, out of his mind after a famous city centre European Cup trophy parade in 1977, peeing over the balcony onto some unsuspecting first aid girls below. Of course, he didn't know anyone was down there. I was standing next to him, but couldn't do anything about it.

The next day he said: "Tell me I was not having a pee over that balcony." When he realised it had happened he said: "You are joking." He couldn't remember.

In those days you could actually try and stop pictures being printed in the newspapers, unlike now. We actually got copies of the incident and stuck them up on the dressing room wall.

Maybe Emlyn Hughes inadvertently got Terry out of jail. He sang those unfortunate "Liverpool Are Magic, Everton Are Tragic" words from the same balcony and dominated all the headlines that day for insulting Blues fans, many who had joined their Red mates to welcome us home. That was an unfortunate error by Emlyn and I know Bob Paisley was furious with him.

But the antics apart, Terry McDermott was a fantastic player who was good enough to be named Footballer of the Year. I can still see his long runs from midfield into space and Ray Kennedy picking him out with that cultured left foot as Terry closed in to score. He netted some brilliant goals like the one at Tottenham – a sensational dipping volley from out on the wing. I said he missed his first touch. He said he flicked it up and volleyed into the far corner.

There was another at Aberdeen in a game that was billed as the 'Battle of Britain'. Terry was two yards in from the touchline, level with the six-yard box. With his weaker left foot he somehow chipped Jim Leighton in the Aberdeen goal. How he did it was astonishing. He always seemed to get 'Goal of the Season' like the famous derby goal he scored. He dragged the ball back and with Everton goalkeeper David Lawson trying to narrow the angle, he chipped him with an effort that was like a classic golf shot.

I know some of the high jinx was not right, but we were young and full of fun. I remember coming out of the city late one night. We stopped at a Chinese chip shop at the bottom of Duke Street and then drove home in my TR7 of which I was very proud. A policeman stopped us and when he saw me he said: "I suppose you've got McDermott in the car." We had been driving with our fish and chips on our lap. He gave us a right rollicking and thankfully just told us to drive on safely and get home.

Talking about fish and chips takes me back. These days most players have to live on a healthy pasta diet before and after games. When we played it was a nice fillet steak for pre-match, but our after-match diet would shock most nutritionists. Ronnie Moran would come round as we were travelling from the hotel to the stadium and the only choice we had to make was fish, pie or chicken with our chips. The chicken only came in during the later years because we were being extra successful.

Ronnie would hand this list to the coach driver who would give the order to the nearest chippy to the ground. We would stop immediately after the game to pick up our a la carte meal, with salt and vinegar as a bonus. You can't believe how much we enjoyed driving back to Liverpool, washing our local delicacy down with a few cans of lager.

Of course, this was manna from heaven for Terry. Sadly, I was to fall out with him later in life. He had moved on and I was at Liverpool as reserve-team coach. Terry would ring me for balls, shirts and tickets. I would always try and help. He was no longer in the game, but we kept in touch.

Our families were good friends. I took a call from him and he said: "Would you ask Graeme Souness if I could train at Melwood?"

Graeme had always found Terry funny and liked him. As a player, Graeme had roomed with Kenny Dalglish, but they used to like getting together with Terry and myself and we would talk and laugh into the night.

Of course, Graeme was pleased to have Terry back around the training ground and felt it would give him a focus. He was doing his own running and then we would all revel in a bit of 'craic'.

Then Terry got a call from Kevin Keegan, who had got the Newcastle job. Kevin asked him to be assistant manager and I was really pleased because it gave some new direction to his life.

Ironically, I was sacked by Graeme Souness and was making my own way, working in the media with SKY and Radio City. Terry met my sister Linda in Cyprus. He started to tell her that I should watch myself and that I was upsetting a lot of people at Liverpool with my comments.

He said: "Tell him to be careful and watch what he is saying on TV."

She couldn't believe his stance and said: "He was having a go at you and putting you in your place. He'd had a couple of drinks but he was not drunk."

I was really angry. Terry had phoned me because we shared the same accountant. He asked me for some info and started to chat. I steamed into him. He had done this big article in the newspapers saying how well Graeme Souness was doing. How every decision he made at Liverpool was a good one and how he would turn things round.

Did this include my sacking? I gave him a right rollicking on the phone and said: "You are supporting Souness in the papers."

He said: "What did you want me to say?"

My response was: "You should have said nothing. By backing him at this time you are insulting me."

My point was that I had helped Terry with many things over several years when he was out of the game. We had been good friends since 1974 when he first came to Anfield. He had not been involved with Souness for a long time when he made that phone call urging me to ask Graeme if he could train at Melwood. I'd been the one who kept in touch and tried to help. Now he was backing Souey.

Terry pointed out that he was not paid for the article, but that probably made it worse. He had indirectly had a go at me. I pointed out his conversation with my sister. He denied some of the things she told me and said: "She must have had a drink."

I told him my sister did not drink and he simply replied: "I've come on for a chat and you are giving me a bollocking."

We put the phone down and never spoke for years which is sad when you think how close we had been. No 'love letters' in the end. Just harsh words, but I felt justified.

Emlyn caught out, Bob's masterstrokes and the incredible legend of Molineux

That 1974/75 season still had its highlights for me, despite the cartilage operation and the fact that we had to settle for the runners-up slot for the second year running. On January 21, 1975, fittingly my birthday, I would win my first England Under 23 cap as Don Revie lived by his word and kept me very much in his thoughts.

It indicated that I was up and running again. I was part of an international squad that included Everton's Mick Lyons, Tottenham's Steve Perryman and Manchester United's Brian Greenhoff who I would later partner at centre-back in the full England side.

The Under 23 team included one or two over-age players. This was allowed at that time to help the younger ones develop. One of these was Colin Todd who I roomed with and then partnered in the heart of the defence against Wales. Colin knew it was my birthday, but he still didn't buy me a card or a cake! I had to settle for his experience on the pitch at Wrexham's Racecourse Ground where we won 2-0. Little did I know at that time, but that little stadium would play a big part in my international life. I later made my full debut there although unfortunately I scored an own goal in a 4-1 defeat. What made it worse was I was captain.

After recovering from my cartilage operation I was an ever-present for the remainder of the season. These were fascinating days with Bob Paisley still settling in as the new manager. Even though we finished second, the critics were out. People were still questioning whether he was the right man to replace Bill Shankly.

If they had only known what was to come, those doubters would have been completely silenced. Finishing second was no disgrace, but our 1973 Championship and UEFA Cup double, followed by our 1974 FA Cup success meant that the standards were higher than ever.

But this was actually the season in which we scored our highest-ever European win when we beat Stromsgodset 11-0 at Anfield in the Cup Winners' Cup. Believe it or not, it was only 1-0 away. Maybe that was because the lads were missing their new prolific goalscorer when the away leg dawned – ME!

I had grabbed the only double of my career at home, but then every other outfield player managed to score – except Brian Hall!

He felt a bit embarrassed, so I promised not to mention it in this book - I said I would concentrate on our third goal! I went on a run from really deep, aware that the cultured Alec Lindsay had the ball on his left foot which they used to call the can opener because it had a real cutting edge. He pinpointed a superb ball and I had to stretch and control it as the keeper came out. I managed to flick it over his head at the Kop end. It's funny how I can remember every detail of every goal I've scored, probably because they were so few and far between, just 13 in over 470 total appearances.

I can reel off all of mine while Ian Rush's massive catalogue of super strikes must all merge together and so I can tell you that my second against Stromsgodset was an easy close-range header at the Anfield Road end. This victory came just before my cartilage injury.

We moved through to meet Ferencvaros at the next stage at which point I was still on the recovery trail. They were a very good Hungarian side and the single away goal they scored at Anfield was good enough to see them through although both legs were very tight. I was pleased when Bob Paisley went in the Press to say he missed me at the back. It really encouraged me to power on with my rehabilitation.

We all understood the tremendously high standards that had been set by Shanks and it's fair to say that we all wanted the impending 1975/76 campaign to be a real success for Bob Paisley who had picked up something of a poison chalice in trying to replace his legendary predecessor, but who had all the knowledge that was needed to make us even greater.

We had finished the previous season on a high with a 3-1 home victory over an emerging Queens Park Rangers side. Ironically, they were our opponents again when the new season started at Loftus Road. They had a fine young captain in Gerry Francis. For our part, we had signed the leanest thing in football apart from me – a young and vibrant Joey Jones, who joined us from Wrexham. He was not born locally, but he might as well have been.

We always said Joey must have been born on the Kop because of his passion for the club and the supporters. He would become a legendary figure with his clenched fist salute and total passion for the Reds.

We felt full of confidence with Joey at left-back, Phil Neal on the right and Emlyn and myself in the middle. It looked a good defence with Tommy Smith also ready to give everything for the club after being so influential in the years before. The strange thing is, we got off to a mixed start – losing to QPR and managing just three wins from our opening seven games.

I had looked up to Emlyn and he had helped me at centre-back. I had never understood some of the nastiness aimed at him by some of the older players, but I soon got an understanding of what it was all about. He had been missing for a couple of weeks and had missed the final warm-up games because of a thigh injury. It was funny because he pronounced himself fit when most of us knew he was not 100 per cent.

Emlyn was such a strong character and obviously wanted to play, but we were 1-0 down at QPR and determined to close down the game and get a result. In the last 15 minutes he was charging all over the pitch, often leaving me at the back on my own. He was chasing balls that were going out for throw-ins. He was closing down on the opposing keeper when he was never going to get the ball. He was running into areas when there was no need.

We might still have been able to create a chance, but his cavalier play began to leave us open at the back and Gerry Francis played a one-two around me and raced on to score a memorable goal that settled things at 2-0. We were all gutted when we got down to the dressing room. This was not the start Bob had wanted and he stormed in and didn't hold back.

He focused on Emlyn and asked why he had been charging all over the field when we still had a chance to play some controlled football and get back in the game. Emlyn replied that he had not done much training of late and that he wanted to run round to build up his fitness.

Bob had steam coming out of his ears. He said: "There was no need for that. I got you the two fast full-backs you asked for."

Alec Lindsay had been the man to make way for Joey and he was sitting in the dressing room, fully clothed and listening to this. His head hit his chest and I thought it was going to hit the floor. You could have heard a pin drop in the dressing room. Bob realised he had let something slip, but the damage had been done.

Tommy Smith, also out of the side for this opener, was clearly not too happy to hear Bob's comment. Alec, ousted by Joey, certainly picked up on the significance of Bob's words. Emlyn must have been pointing the finger at one or two of the lads to the boss and asking him to make changes. You just don't do that as a player. You have your showdowns in the dressing room, but you don't go in the back door to the manager.

It was the first time I understood where some of the lads were coming from with Emlyn and I really felt for Alec Lindsay who was his big mate. That made it even worse. You don't mind coaches and managers making decisions, but you hate it if they are influenced by other people. As I said, Alec was Emlyn's best friend. When we drew our next game, at home to West Ham, the critics were turning the heat up on Bob. Incredibly, we would go on to have one of the greatest seasons in the history of the club. The team would get stronger and better and some famous moments were on the horizon.

Tosh and Kevin Keegan were now in overdrive. People had said they were telepathic and Granada TV chose to test it out. They sat facing each other in the TV studio, each holding a card up so the other could not see the symbol it carried. Everyone was completely astonished when they each guessed exactly right, calling out "square" or "triangle" or whatever it was. The truth was, they could each see each other's cards in reflected glass, but it was a great laugh and enhanced their telepathic reputation.

The way they played at times was astonishing, but it was not all happy partners. I can remember a game when Kev got exceedingly angry. Tosh could be a bit greedy and I remember his partner getting quite vocal in the dressing room after one game because John had not squared a ball for what would have been an easy strike for Kevin.

Kev wouldn't let it drop. He had let Tosh know his feelings on the pitch and he kept it going in the dressing room. The point is, you can't always be nice to one another. It's important to retain that edge.

When it came to growling, the king was Smithy. He taught me that you get nothing for being second best. Tommy would have a go at people, even if it temporarily hurt them. I would think: "You're a moaning bastard." Note I said I would think it!

Even when Smithy was having a nightmare himself, it didn't matter. He would still be driving the team on and giving you the biggest rollicking you have ever had. That's the sign of a good captain and we had several like that.

After missing out on joining that England get-together in 1974 because of my cartilage injury, I would finally make my full England debut on March 24, 1976 with Liverpool on track for another title success. I had made that belated U23 debut at the Racecourse Ground on my 21st birthday and would now return to this lucky venue for my first introduction to the senior scene. It was a strange day with several getting full caps for the first time. Don Revie put me alongside Manchester City's Mike Doyle who was a really tough customer. He helped me along and we forged a good understanding in the game. It was also a great day for my Anfield teammates Phil Neal and Ray Kennedy who also made their debuts. Kevin Keegan was the England captain and Ray Clemence was in goal.

I felt as if I was in good company, which was the case throughout my career. I was always surrounded by a good nucleus of friends. The Racecourse pitch was not in good condition and the game against Wales reflected the playing surface. It was awful and a goalless first half didn't go very well for the lads. As a defender I was happy with a clean sheet but the fans expected more from England. We then moved into a two-goal lead and that is how it stayed up to the last minute. Then Alan Curtis scored for them to pull one back. I was annoyed because I always wanted to keep a clean sheet, but I was pleased to start with a winning debut. I had won Under 23 and Youth caps, but they didn't mean the same as full international recognition.

Suddenly that 1975/76 season all came right and we battered Leeds 3-0 at Elland Road. I remember Ray Kennedy scored and Cally grabbed two.

This was a time when it was understood that new players coming to Anfield would sometimes have to be prepared to wait for their chance while they learned their trade under the famous Boot Room team. There were exceptions, like Kevin who burst straight onto the scene after joining us from Scunthorpe.

Others, like Ray Clemence and Phil Neal, had to wait for their chance. These days you hear fans asking why some foreign imports can't seem to fit in straight away, but in the past it was the Liverpool way to sign potential stars and nurture them. It happened to Ray Kennedy, Terry Mac and Joey Jones who all went on to become great crowd favourites.

One of Bob Paisley's great strengths was his knowledge of what players were capable of and how he might mould them. I suppose Ray Kennedy is the best example and I will come to that shortly. Bob's other big strength was his complete understanding of injuries. I can remember an occasion when Derby County's David Nish went down during a televised match. There were no immediate action replays or great close-ups then. Bob told us straight away that the lad had done his cartilage and would be out for some time. That's exactly what the doctors diagnosed the next day.

Bob had this trust in his staff and chief scout Geoff Twentyman knew exactly what the manager wanted in a player. Of course, Ray Kennedy had been Shanks' farewell gift as the club tried to freshen things up in the summer of 1974. He had not hit it off as a striker in his first season and looked uncomfortable with his back to goal. At Arsenal he had fed off John Radford who was great in the air.

Bob made what many thought was an astonishing decision at the time and switched Ray to the left side of midfield. They used a few reserve games to try him in that role. It was a stroke of genius. Ray used to have so many problems with his weight. We used to have a big roll of Johnson's cellophane in the Boot Room and the heavier players went in there to be wrapped up so they could sweat off some of the poundage. Bob got Ray to lose some weight and it helped him.

He had recognised the player's eye for a pass with that skilful left foot. He saw in Ray another attacking midfield player who could get you ten to fifteen goals a season. This was to give us the edge over our rivals. Coupled with the runs of Terry Mac from deep areas, it was a perfect set-up.

I suppose Ray was in the last chance saloon at Anfield when Bob pulled off his masterstroke. He could easily have moved on without the positional change.

Ray was an interesting character. After every game he would roar and complain that he was doing all of the running. Because there was no left winger, he was always tucked inside a three whereas Terry McDermott would always have an outlet with Jimmy Case wide on the right.

Ray would be diagnosed with Parkinson's Disease later in life and clearly some of the symptoms were affecting him while he was at his peak as a player, although no one knew what was happening at the time. Ray would be tired and sweat profusely. It made him irritable with himself. One minute he would be amiable and the next he would snap at you with real anger. His moods fluctuated. A specialist once told me that these could all have been the early symptoms of Parkinson's Disease.

Having mentioned the Kennedy positional switch as a masterstroke by Bob, I should add that another perfect example of his ability to see different qualities in a player related to my own situation. It was Bob who looked at this tall and skinny central midfielder and decided that my best position was at centre-half. Again, it was a stroke of genius on his part. It was also linked with his masterplan as to how the game should be played. Yes, he knew I could defend, but he also wanted people who could link play from the back and obviously realised that my midfield skills could help me in this respect. The end product was that he transformed my role and it led to England recognition, just as it did for Ray Kennedy.

People naturally point to Ray as the definitive example of Bob's tactical thinking, but I always think about my own situation and it is one of the reasons why I will never forget the boss. He helped to build and mould my career with this remarkable ability to see things in players that others could not.

Of course, this Liverpool side still had some experienced stars. Ian Callaghan was still a vital member of this team and Smithy would come powering back into the picture, but things were changing with the likes of Ray, Terry Mac and Joey giving us different options. We had the rock-solid people like Phil Neal who would turn in 42 league games, but then didn't he do that every season?

This would also be a campaign in which a young David Fairclough would burst onto the scene and he scored some vital goals in the run-in as the title possibilities improved with every game. One of these included the winner against Everton on April 3, 1976, when David struck at Anfield with just two minutes to go. What a moment that must have been for another local boy with real pride in the Reds.

Of course, he would get landed with the supersub tag that he absolutely hated. It lives with him to this day and yet people forget that David played in two European Cup Finals. I will never forget the Everton match because our win was secured on the morning of the Grand National meeting at Aintree.

The Evertonians thought their team had secured a draw when David suddenly picked up the ball from a throw-in out on the flank and set off on a mazy run. Sometimes his body used to go one way and the ball went the other, but he would somehow keep control. But if this style sometimes confused us as to whether he knew what he was doing, it certainly bamboozled the opposition and this day he finished by rattling the ball into the bottom corner. The fact is David was a very good player who was exceptional as a schoolboy and who would have made many more appearances if he had been at any other top-flight club. He suffered from the fact that Liverpool had quality in-depth and just to get into that team was a real achievement, let alone string together long appearance runs.

David ensured that we all went to the National feeling on top of the world. I remember that the team coach took us to Aintree where we had a fantastic day.

Three games out we beat Stoke City 5-3 at Anfield. Every victory turned into a scrap. We then beat Manchester City 3-0 and we were flying towards the title with one game to go at Wolves. Out of the last eight games we won seven and drew one. We had set ourselves up for one of the most incredible finishes to a season ever, needing just two draws from two games to win two trophies

– the Championship and the UEFA Cup. We had already set ourselves up in Europe by securing a 3-2 first-leg lead over Belgian side Bruges and so now every Liverpudlian was concentrating on the trip to Wolves on May 4 and the journey to Bruges on May 19.

The Wolves clash will go down as one of the most remarkable nights in Liverpool's history and not just because the club picked up its ninth title success. We travelled from the hotel to the ground on the team coach and hardly saw an amber scarf. Everywhere we looked was red and white.

The Liverpudlians had turned up in their droves and tickets were at a real premium. I had given my parents the comps I received for the game, but hundreds turned up without tickets, including my brothers Owen and Ian and a group of their mates. I was just hoping and praying they could buy tickets outside the ground and get in.

The dressing room at Molineux was right on the main road that ran in front of the stadium. You went through a swing gate in some railings and within three yards you were through a door and inside the dressing room itself.

I was starting to get quite agitated and kept popping outside, aware that the visitors' stand was already full. I thought: "I hope my brothers get in". They had been to every game, home and away.

I was panicking. We heard that desperate supporters had broken down a gate in the big end at Molineux. Many fans had got in before the police stemmed the flow. I looked across the ground. Their end was to the left, but the rest of the stadium seemed to be a sea of red. Then I got the message that my brother Owen was at the main door and couldn't get in. I was not even changed. We didn't warm up on the pitch in those days. Everything happened in the dressing room.

I was running about trying to find where Owen was. I went to the main entrance and he was there with the other lads. They were all distraught. I said: "Go down to the dressing room door and I will see what I can do." As I said, it faced right out onto the main road. I was preparing for one of the biggest games of my life, but I was worried about the army of fans still outside, not least my brothers.

I got back in the dressing room and said to Bob Paisley: "Boss, you must help me. My brothers have been to every game this season. Now they can't get in."

Bob immediately went out and grabbed the old steward who always looked after us. He demanded the key for the dressing room door that led into the road. He then turned it and said: "Get your brothers and their friends." I said:

"There's about eight of them" and immediately jumped up on a bench and peered out through a high window. I saw them amongst a mass of fans and shouted: "Get through the metal gate and come to the door." Bob opened it and Owen, Ian and the lads were suddenly inside our dressing room. They were shocked. They didn't realise the outside door led straight into this inner sanctum where we were preparing for this crucial title match.

The room was about 15 feet wide at the door end. When you went out of the door at the other end it was just about five metres before you were on the cinder track around the pitch. I grabbed a policeman and said: "You must make sure they get straight into the Liverpool end". He was one of the few people who had the authority to get them there. Suddenly Emlyn jumped up and said: "Bob, my mates are out there as well."

Bob eased the door open again and a procession of about 40 to 50 people poured through the dressing room carrying flags, banners and horns. They were screaming, shouting and chanting. It was bedlam in what should have been an atmosphere of organised calm. Bob now started to panic. He shouted: "What the fuck is going on? How many are there in your family? This has gone too far."

Legend has it that it was all my fault. Yes, I instigated it, but the rest was down to Emlyn. He shared a passion for the fans and, like me, had seen many supporters in tears outside. All this excitement was happening before a ball was kicked.

Eventually we managed to get changed and went out to a deafening roar from our supporters. It was unbelievable. They were everywhere. There must have been 25,000 of them there. Remember, we had not won the title for three years. They all desperately wanted to see us collect another Championship.

As the game flowed in the first half, Emlyn was beaten by Steve Kindon. He was not the most skilful player, but he had the speed of an Olympic sprinter. He got beyond Emlyn and myself and scored.

It was as important a night for Wolves as for Liverpool. They needed to win to stay up. Nerves were jangling and as the game went into the second half they were defending for their lives. Finally John Toshack and Kevin Keegan combined and Kev scored the equaliser that we needed to win that title crown. The game still had 15 minutes to go, but fans started to come off the big embankment and encroach on the pitch. They just wanted to celebrate and eventually retreated. Most times you could just shut up shop, but Wolves were desperate for the win and it was still on a knife-edge. Then Tosh swivelled and scored a second.

Now it seemed as if the entire Liverpool army had invaded the pitch. Our fans were everywhere and I started to panic. I realised the game might be abandoned and started to tell people to get off the pitch. They did, but only to the byline. Ray Kennedy now scored a third goal, smashing home a great left-foot drive.

Now all hell let loose with the fans back on the pitch. I was screaming at them. There was just a minute to go and there was still a chance of it being abandoned. I found myself squaring up to people and shouting at them in no uncertain terms.

They would suddenly realise what I was saying and run off the pitch, only for others to encroach. It seemed an age before the ref put his whistle in his mouth and blew for time. Now there really was a mass invasion and we were swamped as the fans lifted us high in the air and carried us towards the tunnel. Wolves were devastated. We were ecstatic. For a league season to start so badly and finish with such amazing scenes was incredible.

We had snatched the Championship away from the grasp of QPR. They had been watching the match at a BBC studio, sipping champagne at half-time. After our third goal went in, they all started to drift away. We had been head-to-head with QPR right to the end after playing and losing to them in the very first game. They would never hit such heights again.

In our dressing room champagne corks were popping. We wanted to go back out and see the fans who were refusing to leave. We went into a small stand running along the length of the paddock to give them a wave.

These scenes were sensational with the lads lined up the length of the directors' box surveying a sea of red and white in front of them.

We were singing and chanting along with the fans. Eventually, we got back in the dressing room and had a few more beers. Then we boarded the coach for the journey home. We got in a traffic jam on the M6 motorway. Everything had come to a halt. The next thing fans were getting out of their cars or emerging from their sunroofs as they saw our coach. They started to conga around the coach on the motorway with everything around them in deadlock. This could only happen with Liverpool supporters. It seemed to take an eternity to get going again, but we didn't care.

We had the Championship. Bob Paisley had his first title crown and the UEFA Cup Final second leg was still to come. This would turn out to be the start of the most remarkable era in Liverpool FC history.

We now had to prepare ourselves for the second leg of the UEFA Cup Final against Bruges. We knew that we only needed a draw to claim the trophy and were confident because of the manner in which we had reached the final.

In the first round we lost 1-0 at Hibernian, but came through 3-1 in the return for a 3-2 aggregate victory. John Toshack scored a hat-trick at Anfield. We then went to Real Sociedad in Northern Spain. It was a lovely town, but I remember that these were tense times because Spanish dictator General Franco was on his deathbed.

The Basques of Sociedad hated him and there was a suggestion that there might be tanks on the streets if he died. That never materialised although we did hear a cannon blast from the hillside above the city. It was traditional that when the home side scored there would be two cannon blasts to tell everyone in the region the score. When the opposition scored there would be one.

We were to win the game 3-1 in a tie in which I was to score my third European goal after the two against Stromsgodset. It was a headed effort that I was extremely proud of. I was delighted, but Ronnie Moran, in his wisdom, would give me a bollocking from the touchline. He was shouting: "Thommo. Concentrate. When you score a goal you go asleep. Forget about it and concentrate on the game." I thought: "There must be something in this. I have to keep my wits about me." In the end there were only five cannon blasts over San Sebastian that night and so I must have retained my focus.

I later asked Ronnie about his touchline rant. He said: "I have noticed that when you have scored a goal you can have five minutes of Looney Tunes." This was his phrase for anything that wasn't right. Ronnie added: "This could possibly lead to a mistake." I thought it was fair comment. It's a fact that the most dangerous time for a team can be straight after they score. You can relax and switch off. I always remembered Ronnie's advice, not least when I later became a coach myself.

In the return leg at home we beat the Spaniards 6-0 for an aggregate 9-1 success. This gave us real confidence for the next challenge against Slask Wroclaw. Poland was a depressing place. It was an Iron Curtain country at that time and these were always difficult places to go to. I remember that the changing room was in a big old house and contained just a few chairs and benches. We would take our legendary ice boots on this trip that the staff swore by on slippery surfaces. They had grips with big grooves in them rather than studs. No one else had these boots. The staff kept them in a big box. The first pair I received were not quite my size, but you had to wear them because they had this mystical quality about them.

We looked around this strange dressing room that was actually upstairs in this house. It was freezing, probably minus ten. We had seen that the snow was packed up on the side of a rock-hard pitch. There seemed to be military police everywhere. All of a sudden this old fella brought in a large pot containing tea and some manky cups. The players put the pot in the middle of the room.

Bob Paisley immediately shouted: "Put it back, you don't know what they've put in it." The environment just made you suspicious of everything around you and the boss was taking no chances.

We were disappointed because we were freezing and just fancied a cup of steaming hot tea. Bob just said: "They can't be trusted."

The magic boots were produced. When you were more senior, you would actually have your number on the boots. Numbers were rubbed out from years gone by. By now I had my own pair and that made you feel special. Probably these boots were not that good, but Bob Paisley convinced us of their qualities and this psychology worked every time we went out onto a tricky surface. Ronnie Moran would always say: "If you think you are going to fall, you will fall. Don't be negative. Think positive."

These were experienced men and we listened to them. We would be gliding across an icy surface without a care in the world. Our opponents would be treading tentatively as if they were on an ice rink. I honestly believe it was all psychology on behalf of the staff, but it worked. We beat the Poles 2-1 and followed up with a 3-0 success at home.

We then faced another Eastern Bloc country in the form of Germany's Dynamo Dresden. We had played them in the UEFA Cup in 1972/73 and so the club was going back to familiar territory. One incredible feeling was going through the famous 'Checkpoint Charley' that took you from the Western side of Berlin to the more sinister Eastern side, occupied by the Russians.

Of course, the imposing Berlin Wall stretched away as far as the eye could see on each side of the Checkpoint. We had all seen television images of people being shot trying to get across the no-man's land between the wall and the Western side. I remember driving from the commercial and colourful West Berlin into the drab and dreary environment on the other side of the wall. It was all quite frightening in a way.

Police looked under the bus with mirrors. I don't know why because no one would have been hanging on underneath to return to the East. It was all the other way. They checked the kit and the passports. Would they smile at us? Absolutely not. It must have been forbidden.

We knew that Dynamo Dresden were a very good team. We managed to get a goalless draw over there and won 2-1 at home thanks to Jimmy Case and Kevin Keegan and now we were flying towards a semi-final test in Spain.

Spanish giants Barcelona provided thrilling opposition in the last four. They had a sensational team at that time which included the legendary Johan Cruyff and his talented Dutch comrade Johan Neeskens. There was a big Dutch influence in Spain and this inspired technically outstanding football. We went to the Nou Camp for the first leg and while the stadium was magnificent I was disappointed. The attendance was only 70,000 in a ground that held 120,000. Unless it was the final, European football was no great shakes to the Spaniards while it was everything in Liverpool.

On a personal note it was wonderful to be able to pit myself against Cruyff. That was a great feeling. I always felt that the bigger the game, the better I played. We always felt that if we could score first, the opposition would not reply. This was a great Liverpool team and we had nothing to fear, even in Barcelona.

Kevin Keegan flicked this ball on in the first 15 minutes and John Toshack went in on it. As the ball bounced he lashed it into the bottom corner. It gave us the lead and we felt there would be no problems because we could defend with the best in the world. Barca hardly had a chance and when they did get through we had total confidence in Ray Clemence. In the second half the Spanish fans were upset and started to wave their white hankies, a traditional way of showing their disgust. The game went into the last ten minutes and suddenly we could sense a commotion on the touchline. After the game Bob Paisley told us what had happened.

The Spanish supporters had begun to rain down cushions from the high tiers in the Nou Camp. They were not aimed at our bench. It was just another way in which they signalled their frustration to their own team. As more and more came down Joey Jones got the wrong end of the stick. In his wisdom, he got out of the dugout and started whizzing them back into the stand as if he was throwing a Frisbee. Six or seven curved into the army of Spanish supporters on that side. Bob suddenly realised what he was doing and leapt up to scream at Joey. "What do you think you're doing? They're not throwing them at us. They're aimed at their own players. Get down to the dressing room before you cause a riot!"

I always smile when I think about Joey. I can remember a pre-season game in Holland. We all went to a corner cafe because the food was rubbish in the hotel. We couldn't understand the menu and then someone spotted the word omelette. We were trying to explain to the waitress what filling we wanted, be it cheese, prawns or whatever. Joey didn't want any filling in his.

He stood up, put his arms out and started making noises like the engine of a Spitfire. The waitress was completely bemused and so were we. Someone said: "What are you trying to say, Joey?" He replied: "Plane omelette!"

The place erupted into laughter. He was the most generous and lovely lad you could wish to meet. I felt proud to have come from the Kop to play for Liverpool. Joey was a player who was still a Kopite. It was as if we had dragged him off the terraces to play every week. He was not technically gifted, but he played from the heart. There were not many better defenders.

If a tackle was needed, Joey would make it. I remember a game against Middlesbrough. They had a player called John Hickton. Joey had a short fuse and hated losing. There was a melee in the box. I can remember looking at Joey and seeing that look in his eyes. Hickton pushed him which was not a good idea. Joey might have looked skinny but he would take on anyone. He nutted the Boro player right in the mouth and Hickton's tooth fell out. He was down on the floor searching for his tooth while Joey made the long walk to the dressing room, having been sent off. Later, our full-back was distraught, not for Hickton but because he felt he had let the team down.

All of these memories were in my mind as Bob related the Nou Camp touchline story in the dressing room. A 1-0 victory over there was a great result. John Toshack was writing poetry at this time. It was crap in fairness, but he actually had them printed. He penned this special verse on the plane flying home from Spain. Tosh must have been feeling inspired after scoring the winner.

The home leg wasn't as comfortable. I was to score, pushing Kevin Keegan to one side as the ball dropped in front of the posts. This put us one-up and as the crowd went mad I didn't hear a shout from Ronnie Moran who was just happy that we had extended our aggregate lead.

However, they hit back immediately and so I thought about Ronnie again and his words of caution about being vulnerable after scoring. It was a nervous finish, but we held on for a famous victory that would take us into the two-legged final against Bruges.

In fairness, they were not one of the great names of European football, but the Belgians had silky skills and were well organised. Maybe we got a wake-up call at Anfield because we found ourselves 2-0 down. This was a shock to the system, but we made a habit of fighting back and turned things round with goals from Ray Kennedy, Jimmy Case and Kevin Keegan. I can remember Jimmy's equaliser. It went in off his shins after the ball flashed across goal and hit the far post. Everyone was buzzing after that. Then Steve Heighway took on a defender and threw that famous jink. It led to him being brought down.

Kevin Keegan scored from the spot to give us a crucial lone goal advantage for the second leg.

With the league title in the bag after that famous win at Wolves, we now prepared ourselves for the final push and that UEFA Cup Final second leg in Belgium. Bruges was a beautiful city. Our fans were fantastic. The town had these small old-fashioned hotels and flags and banners were hanging out of every window.

In the game, Smithy gave away a penalty which was never his fault, of course. Nobody argued, but we were gutted and they were level with the away goals advantage. However, Kevin Keegan responded quickly, drilling home a free-kick from the edge of the box.

This time there would be no Molineux-style pitch invasion on the final whistle because they had fences all round the ground. The fans had also invaded the pitch following our previous UEFA Cup triumph in 1972/73. It had been impossible to parade the trophy that day and therefore difficult for those fans who had remained on the terraces to see what was going on. This time we could show off the famous trophy and revel in a success that had given us a memorable double. I remember that the giant UEFA Cup base fell off, but it was a great night and we were all hung over the next day following our celebrations.

I had to get myself together very quickly after our UEFA Cup triumph because I had to meet up with the England squad for the Bicentennial Tournament in the United States. This had been a hectic spell. Between the Wolves game and the UEFA Cup Final return there had been a two-week break during which I had played in the Home International Championships. These were still a key part of the football calendar at that time.

Don Revie had this vision of playing from the back, through the midfield and then forward. This is why he paired Brian Greenhoff and myself. Brian was smaller than me and he had also been a central midfield player before dropping into the back four at Manchester United. Don, like Bob Paisley, realised that we could play football from the back. It had become something of a Liverpool hallmark.

England won the games against Wales and Northern Ireland keeping clean sheets and this pleased me. We then went to play Scotland and this time I had a more experienced partner in Colin Todd although he was also a skilful performer as Revie maintained his logic. I could see how his mind was working.

We took an early lead at Hampden Park through Mick Channon. I can still see him turning away and swinging his arm like a helicopter blade. This was his distinctive goal celebration. However, we lost the game 2-1. This was the infamous match in which Ray Clemence let the ball slip through his legs from Kenny Dalglish for their winner. It was something that would haunt him because of the strong Scottish links in our squad. Of course, Kenny was still a Celtic player at this time. Don Masson had equalised for them from a corner. He was not the biggest and that annoyed me as much as the Dalglish goal, so two Liverpool players were not happy that day.

However, this was an amazing phase in my career. I had made my full England debut. I had won my second league title and begun to establish myself at full international level. I had won a second UEFA Cup medal and was now preparing for an exciting trip to the States where I had never been before.

I was thrilled to be going to America where some fantastic matches were lined up against the mighty Brazil and Italy, plus a game against Team America. This is what football dreams are made of. On May 23, 1976 we would meet the Brazilians in the fantastic Coliseum in Los Angeles. The crowd was made up of ex-pats and a decent Brazilian following, but it wasn't a big attendance. Nevertheless, it was tremendous to be turning out against men like the great Zico. I wonder if he ever told his kids that he played against the great Phil Thompson? Probably not, but who knows because I would later come up against Zico again when we played Flamengo in the World Club Championship of 1981, a 3-0 defeat in Tokyo that I don't particularly want to remember.

In '76 the Brazilians had an outstanding side that also included the likes of the amazing and moustachioed Rivelino who had a left foot that was like a magic wand. He would wiggle his left boot and pass superb balls with the inside or outside of his foot. You had to admire his ability, even in the heat of battle. He was absolutely fantastic.

We played ever so well in the game, but Trevor Cherry of Leeds missed an absolute sitter. We failed to take three or four more opportunities and this allowed the Brazilians to steal the game late on. Zico was being hailed as the new Pele at that time.

I have a Brazilian number 11 shirt from that match. Down the years I had forgotten who I swapped with. I always hoped it was Zico, but I have studied the records and if you count one to eleven on their team sheet, a player called Pinto Neto probably wore that jersey. I've therefore got a Neto shirt, although I don't think he gave it to me in a bag with Netto on the side. I wonder where Pinto is now? I hope he's not stacking shelves. Joking apart, it still remains one of my prized possessions and, to be clear, Pinto Neto WAS a great player as all of those Brazilians were.

We trudged off that day feeling very disappointed, although it had been an experience to play in a stadium that would later be good enough to stage an Olympic Games in 1984.

We then moved on to New York. As a boy I had heard all the stories about it and how dangerous it was to walk round. I can remember going for a stroll and looking at all the skyscrapers and not taking it all in. People had been going on about how dangerous it was supposed to be. They were saying: "Don't go down the backstreets. Beware of the Bronx."

I did not enjoy it because I was too nervous. Nothing happened, but people had built it up. My dad had travelled extensively and been there many times as a merchant seaman. I felt as if some of the sites were like a second home to me. To be in these towering, awesome streets was a wonderful thing.

I have vivid memories of the game against Italy. We were also paired with them in a forthcoming World Cup qualifier. Everyone was looking on this as a marker for that tie.

Don Revie made a few changes and left out Kevin Keegan who was extremely upset. Possibly Revie was trying to keep some knowledge away from the Italians. The biggest change was to bring in a young Ray Wilkins, a player who would later play in Italy. He did extremely well in the game.

The captaincy went to Mick Channon. The overlooked Keegan had the mindset of a Michael Owen. He never wanted to be left out, whether it was a tactical decision or for his own protection.

New York's Yankee Stadium is a baseball venue. Seventy-five per cent of the fans were Italian. They had more ex-pats than England and made a tremendous racket. The pitch still had the shale baseball diamond at one end and the grass was quite long.

We tossed up to see which end we were defending so we could choose our studs. We defended the grassed area in the first half. Being on the better attacking surface at this stage helped the Italians. They took a 2-0 lead with our goalkeeper Jimmy Rimmer being at fault for one of the goals on his debut. Revie immediately made a big decision and replaced him with Manchester City's Joe Corrigan.

We got a goal back through Mick Channon early in the second half. That gave us hope as we attacked on the better ground.

The Italians showed their nice side when things were going well. There were no incidents, but now it was tighter they changed their mood. This cross came over and somehow I found myself free from a corner. I headed the ball down in front of goalkeeper Dino Zoff and big Joe Royle tried to swing at the ball. It bounced between Zoff and Royle and into the net for my only England goal, but one I would savour to make it 2-2. Things got really heated. They had the famous Fabio Capello in their side, plus Franco Causio and a fella we would meet later in Franceso Graziani.

Giacinto Facchetti was at the back, a legendary defender. But it was the fair-haired Roberto Benetti in midfield who was their assassin. He was kicking everything that moved.

All hell broke loose when Mick Channon put us in the lead at 3-2. We couldn't wait for the final whistle at which point there was a lot of finger-pointing. Needless to say, I don't think there were many shirts exchanged. The World Cup was mentioned and the Italian crowd threw everything they could lay their hands on. It was chaos rather than a riot, but the most important thing was that our experienced team had beaten the heroes of Italy.

Our third game was against Team America in Philadelphia. They were a mix of homegrown players and experienced internationals from all round the globe. The venue was not as grand as the Coliseum or the Yankee Stadium, but some of the top players in the world played for Team America. I was disappointed it was not classed as a full international. My old mate Tommy Smith was in the opposition, having signed a summer contract for Tampa Bay Rowdies. Perfect club for Smithy!

The great Bobby Moore played for them, as did Italian legend Georgio Chinaglia. But the big draw was none other than Brazilian superstar Pele who played for New York Cosmos. We won 3-1 and it wasn't the most difficult of games, but that wasn't the point. I was on the pitch with some super heroes and it was more of an exhibition than a full-blooded clash. One thing sticks in my mind. One of the Team America players fired in a crossfield ball with real pace. It flashed towards Pele who could easily have stepped out of the way. Instead, he positioned his chest and killed the ball dead, immediately taking it under control. I just marvelled at how he took the pace out of the ball. It was a marvellous piece of skill and something that was worth the admission money in its own right. It was just a pleasure to be on the pitch with such legends, apart from Smithy, of course!

All this action was just a warm-up to the forthcoming World Cup qualifier in Finland. After this Bicentennial Tournament we were allowed to go home again before reporting back for duty in mid-June.

I can remember our Finnish headquarters was by a beautiful lake, although we had to go 30 yards down the road to the restaurant. Who turned up but Elton John, who had booked the penthouse suite in our hotel. All of the lads were invited up to look at his suite. We wondered at the expanse of it.

Elton was a real fan and was there cheering with the best of them as we made the perfect World Cup start with a 4-1 win. I played alongside Colin Todd with Paul Madeley of Leeds and Mick Mills of Ipswich completing an impressive defence. It wasn't the clean sheet I always craved, but it was nice to make a winning start. Our preparation with Don Revie in the Bicentennial Tournament had proved vital.

Revie had promised us that if we abstained from drinking any alcohol in the preparation, he would ensure we had a sensational party afterwards after being together so long. He didn't let us down. After the game we all went down to this big restaurant-cum-nightclub where there was an electric organ. I remember that all of these tables had reserved notices on them. Elton John's manager John Reid gave the manager hell, pointing out that we were legends in England. He said: "Get those signs off the table." It meant we could get together and have a great night.

A very young Ray Wilkins was up dancing on the tables. Good old Elton got up on stage for an impromptu jam session and gave us all of his hits. Peter Taylor, who had a decent voice, sang with him on a few songs. It was one of those evenings you never forget. I was proud and glad to be there. The whole squad almost drank the place dry and Elton picked up the tab which was a tremendous gesture.

We would later repay him at our North London headquarters with an England shirt signed by all the squad as a big thank you for a memorable night. It was a great finish to a fantastic season that saw me establish myself as a fully-fledged international.

I could also look back on two league titles, two UEFA Cups and one FA Cup success. The early days had been great, but now I was really up and running. I wondered if things could get any better, but the forthcoming 1976/77 season would actually be one of the most incredible in the history of Liverpool FC.

Injured by my own keeper and so I revel in the glory of Rome as a fan

E ven though we were champions and UEFA Cup holders going into the 1976/77 season, the Reds still felt it necessary to freshen things up with another big signing. It was the way they always worked. The staff believed that the best time to strengthen was when you were on top.

Some people might have been surprised when the name of the latest addition to the squad was revealed. Bob Paisley, looking to boost his fire power up front, invested £200,000 in Ipswich Town's David Johnson.

The surprise was only because David had previously been an Everton player and questions were always being asked as to whether he was a Red or a Blue. Of course, on the day he joined us he made it absolutely clear that he had always been a committed Liverpudlian. His arrival was clearly intended to give John Toshack something to think about.

David was drafted straight into the side for the opening eight games, but like other signings before him would now have to spend a bit of time in the reserves learning the Liverpool Way. That might sound strange, bearing in mind that he was an England international, but he wouldn't be the first or the last to have to be patient after joining the Reds.

Whenever we played Ipswich Bob Paisley had always been impressed by him. I always found Johnno a real handful. He forged a great partnership at Portman Road with Trevor Whymark and they always gave us a hard time, especially in the air.

Off the pitch, David was a great fella. He would gain the nickname 'The Doc.' He always had this little blue bag hanging on his peg at Anfield. As time passed, it became a bit of a laugh. He would always have 'flu, a cough or a rash and used these ointments and tablets that he produced from his bag as a cure-all for every ailment. It reached the stage when the lads looked to him whenever they needed something on the medical side, be it a simple Panadol for a headache or an anti-inflammatory tablet. They didn't need to go to Bob or Joe anymore. The Doc always had his magic bag.

After training one day we all returned to the dressing room to find that a red and white cross had been taped onto the bag to make it a true First Aid version. Everybody roared with laughter. The Doc tag stuck from that point and Johnno is still affectionately known by that name.

The team got off to a flyer, winning five out of the first six games. The Doc broke his duck during this spell and while it came in a 2-1 defeat at Birmingham he was still thrilled to be off the mark.

That season was to swing along with very few changes with the boss keeping the same team week in, week out. We blitzed Everton 3-1 at Anfield, scoring all of our goals before the interval. Although we were the top flight's in-form team and the club everyone was scared of, we then suffered a stunning reversal at Villa in mid-December where we lost 5-1. I remember that Andy Gray, Brian Little and John Gidman were all in the opposing ranks. What made it worse was that it was 5-1 at half-time.

I have never played in a game in which a team has had six shots with five going into the back of the net. Brian Little came forward and cut inside Joey Jones. He put in a left-foot shot that swerved past Ray Clemence and hit the inside of the post on the way in. It was a great strike and in all my life I have never heard the Villa crowd as ecstatic as they were that day. They were raising the roof and we were shell-shocked.

Bob didn't say too much at half-time. He knew it was just a pride thing for the second half. We kept a clean sheet and so that was some consolation, but not much. It gave us a kick up the backside and, incredibly, Bob kept the same side for the next game at West Ham with the exception of Tosh returning for The Doc. This showed the faith Bob had in his players. He would never panic and even though we then lost 2-0 at Upton Park, he still carried on without a single change.

We rewarded him with a rock-solid 4-0 Anfield win over Stoke in which yours truly scored the first goal. There is a great photograph of this strike. The ball came in from the left and I came flying through the air to direct the ball in the opposite direction past the great Peter Shilton and into the far corner. This was in the opening five minutes. A Phil Neal penalty and a Kevin Keegan effort put us comfortably ahead in the second half and The Doc came off the bench to finish Stoke off.

This was another season of home domination. We won 18 and drew 3 of the 21 league games at Fortress Anfield. This enabled us to accelerate towards another title success, even though our away form was patchy at times. However, in March, 1977 at the height of the campaign, I suffered another major injury blow playing against Newcastle.

It's amazing how things repeat themselves. Wrexham was a recurring theme for me internationally. Newcastle always seemed to feature heavily in my career. Of course, we beat them in the 1974 FA Cup Final. I previously broke my wrist against them and now I suffered another injury blow.

The game was at Anfield and we won 1-0 thanks to Stevie Heighway. Big Alan Gowling was playing up front for Newcastle and I tried to stretch round him with a straight left leg in an attempt to get a foot on the ball. As my leg made contact, it was as if it extended too far between the knee and the ankle. I had that sickly feeling again that reminded me of 1974 when I did my first cartilage. The leg didn't lock this time, but I sensed it was the same thing.

I went down and Clem said: "Get up Thommo, you're alright." I climbed to my feet, but almost immediately the leg twisted again and went from underneath me. I knew what it was. Maybe it was a bit of the Bob Paisley in me, understanding an injury situation immediately. What made it worse this time is that I didn't deal with it straight away. I went out that night to watch John Conteh defend his world light-heavyweight title crown against Detroit's Len Hutchins at the now demolished Liverpool Stadium.

It was a famous venue and the atmosphere was electric. I had been really looking forward to the evening and tried to put the pain of my knee injury to one side. Of course, John was a Kirkby lad like myself and I really wanted to support him. It was a controversial night because Conteh caught the American with his head, something that didn't surprise any of us. All hell broke loose. The whole crowd were on their feet although I could hardly stand because of my throbbing knee.

John was now in full flight and he took Hutchins out with a left hook to the chin. I was not so much grimacing for the American as they counted him out, but for the pain I was feeling. Even so, I still made a stupid decision and went on with Terry Mac afterwards to Flintlocks nightclub in the city centre. I must have been crazy. I should have been in hospital, not messing around in town, regardless of the importance of the night to a great friend and a magnificent Mersey fighter.

The first hours after any injury are the most important. The immediate after-care is crucial. Instead of seeking this early treatment I was sitting on a high barstool late into the night, which is not the most comfortable thing to do at the best of times. I'm sure it made things worse with the blood running down to my knee. I have no idea how I drove home. On the Monday I was back at Park House in Crosby and this episode was to finish my season, with 13 league games still to go and with an historic European Cup Final in Rome on the horizon.

I remember the doctor handing me a jar in 1974 containing my cartilage. He pointed to the split in it which had caused the problem. After this latest operation, they brought me a second jar. I actually thought they had given me a jar of cockles. Terry Mac would have been in his element.

Then the doctor said: "This is your other cartilage. It was in pieces when we removed it." The specialist added: "Your knee was in such bad shape that it was all mangled."

Every time I look at the two big scars on either side of my left knee, I think about those injuries and specifically that 1977 setback, the John Conteh fight and the nightclub folly. It's a lesson to all players. I wonder in amazement now when lads go in for cartilage surgery. It has developed into a keyhole procedure with just a little nick rather than the whole side of the knee being opened up.

Whenever I showed my knee to players when I was assistant manager at Anfield they would laugh and say: 'Who was the butcher?' It's just the way it was and it is why the word 'cartilage' used to fill players with dread. As it turned out, I was in hospital for two weeks as that 1977 season continued at pace. It was as costly an injury as a player can possibly get because this would turn out to be a glorious campaign for the rest of the lads.

My despair would actually open the door for a certain Tommy Smith and to say he seized the opportunity in every way is an understatement. The Anfield Iron, of course, would go on to score a famous header in Rome's Olympic Stadium as the Reds beat Borussia Moenchengladbach to claim the European Cup for the very first time. That was possibly the greatest night in Tommy's long and successful career, but before anyone could revel in the glory that was Rome, the title still had to be won and an FA Cup run had to unfold.

The Championship was wrapped up in the second-to-last game of the season at home to West Ham. We had been coasting to the title, but the lads finally secured it with a goalless draw. In fact, the team failed to win any of the last four games, draws against QPR, Coventry and West Ham, plus a final day defeat at Bristol City. It highlighted the fact that the title was all but won and that there were other things to focus on, with an FA Cup Final and a European Cup Final beckoning.

The FA Cup had run a similar course to 1974. The early rounds had been a bit of a stumbling block. Crystal Palace held us 0-0 at Anfield before we won the return 3-2. We then met Carlisle in the next round, a club that had figured in our '74 run. We beat them comfortably 3-0 and things were getting tasty. A 3-1 win against Oldham and a 2-0 win over Boro put us in the semi-final. It was great.

We had been quite lucky in that all of these ties had been at home, the replay at Palace apart. From the quarter-final I was now forced to leave the lads to get on with it themselves. I became a partisan spectator again. The team selection was fairly consistent, possibly with one or two changes up front from time-to-time. Then came a semi-final against Everton that would become part of Mersey folklore. Before the draw was made everyone was wondering if we would be kept apart to possibly set up the first-ever all-Merseyside final. It never happened and so we faced each other in the last four at Maine Road.

It was to be some game. Everton played out of their skin that day, but could only manage a draw. Terry Mac scored another goal of the season. It's worth repeating how he moved the ball from his right foot to his left on the edge of the box before chipping David Lawson with an unbelievable shot. I don't know why the Everton keeper even attempted to jump. He should have just turned round as soon as the ball left Terry's boot and walked back to pick it out of the net.

This super strike came after just ten minutes. Jimmy Case would be our other scorer while Duncan McKenzie and Bruce Rioch scored for the Blues. Of course, the whole game hinged on a highly controversial decision made by a man who used to win more headlines than the players in those days – the referee Clive Thomas.

Everton's Ronnie Goodlass fired in a cross and McKenzie helped the ball on. Northern Ireland international Bryan Hamilton, who had come on as a sub for Martin Dobson, turned the ball into the back of the net. The Blues turned away to celebrate while the Liverpool players just looked shell-shocked, convinced that the game had been snatched from them.

Everyone thought Thomas was pointing to the centre circle, but then it became apparent he was pointing to the edge of the box and that he had disallowed the goal. Was it offside? Was it handball? No one seemed to know and we didn't care.

Liverpool got the ball back into play quickly before Thomas changed his mind and a buzz went right round the stadium as the Evertonians screamed their disgust. Of course, sitting high in the stands, miles away from the action and talking to the guy next to me with no real focus on the pitch, I could tell straight away that it was handball! I suppose all you can say is: "That's football" although most people, including many Liverpudlians, would say: "That's Thomas."

He loved to be Mr Controversial and for once it worked in our favour. You take these things and move on. A funny thing happened on the way out of Maine Road. I bumped into my old mate Micky Lyons on the steps and, as you can imagine, he was still moaning about the decision. I just looked him in the eye and said: "Micky, you've had your chance. You know you've blown your chance now. You only get one chance against us and now it's gone. See you on Wednesday." In the replay, also at Maine Road, there was no controversy. We battered Everton 3-0. They were never going to get a second chance.

Funnily enough, many years later I would attend a dinner at Everton's 300 Club at which Clive Thomas was the guest speaker. There were touts outside selling tickets with people clamouring to get in to talk to him, or rather hurl abuse at him.

The Evertonians were snarling as soon as the Welshman, quite bravely in my view, walked into the room. Clive hammed it up when he heard the boos. It was a sound he was well used to hearing. The food went down in no time with everyone desperate to get to the main course of the evening – the baiting of Clive Thomas. Eventually we reached that point at which the fans could play their part in a question and answer session. Before the compere could even get through the formalities, an Evertonian leapt up and shouted: "Why the fuck did you disallow that goal in 1977?" Merseysiders like nothing better than to get straight to the point.

Thomas said: "Well, I'm just writing a book at the moment. If you want to know the real reason, you will have to go out and buy it."

There was uproar. I thought he was just joking for a minute and sat back waiting for him to give the real reason which, all these years later, none of us still had a clue about. People were screaming: "That's a disgrace. We've paid good money to get an honest answer from you."

He just repeated himself, saying: "It's a chapter in my book. Just buy it." He answered all of the other questions put to him, but every time someone slipped in a further request for the only answer that mattered, he just wouldn't respond to it. Of course, I did thank him on behalf of the Liverpudlians. Seriously, no one in Maine Road that day could understand why Bryan Hamilton's goal was disallowed.

At the same time, Reds' fans knew that, having got out of jail, Liverpool would not be found wanting in the replay and that's how it worked out.

We marched on with the treble in our sights and Manchester United now awaiting us in the FA Cup Final. This wasn't the United we know today. We were out and out favourites to win this game and secure an historic English Double. As it turned out, the final was quite tight and everything finally happened in an eventful ten-minute spell early in the second half.

Stuart Pearson grabbed the lead for United after 50 minutes when he took a pass from Jimmy Greenhoff and hammered the ball past Clem from 20 yards. Just two minutes later Jimmy Case had us all on our feet when, as cool as you like, he controlled the ball on his thigh and lashed a shot into the corner of the United net. I thought: "Here we go, we will take control from here."

It never happened because within three minutes United were back in front although the goal was a scrambling affair that only added to our bitter disappointment. Lou Macari was the scorer, ironically a player who once came to Liverpool and then turned down Bill Shankly.

There is a famous picture of him coming down the stairs at Anfield with Shanks fuming behind him. I can still see the goal as if in slow motion. Tommy Smith tried desperately to get his leg round the ball and hook clear under pressure from Jimmy Greenhoff. It fell to Macari whose deflected shot somehow found its way past Clem to make it 2-1. I remember Phil Neal's vain attempt to keep the ball out. He ended up tangled in the netting.

How we lost the game is beyond me. We totally dominated and the players were gutted at the end. I can remember Ray Clemence on the journey home. He suddenly chirped up: "We have a great day coming on Wednesday in Rome. There is no way now that we are going to be beaten in the European Cup Final. Let's enjoy ourselves."

It was just what was needed. Suddenly the drinks began to flow. They were a great bunch of lads. We had the jokers and the serious ones. From being down, we now partied the night away with a single-minded determination that Liverpool would now win the European Cup for the first time ever.

It was hard for me at this moment in time as I continued with my recovery programme. I had been trying to build up my fitness, but because of the extent of the damage it had taken me longer than expected. Those steps on the Kop were getting longer and steeper as I pounded up and down them in an effort to get fit.

Liverpool's 1976/77 European Cup exploits began against Crusaders of Northern Ireland. We could only manage a 2-0 victory in the first leg at Anfield, but cruised to a 5-0 success over there in the return two weeks later. Liverpool supporters were all over the place because the Reds have a fantastic Irish following. People were hanging from trees to try and get a view of the action in a crowd of below 11,000. It was an incredible sight and it helped earn us a second-round clash in one of the most dismal places I have ever been to on my Euro travels.

It was against Trabzonspor in the depths of Turkey. I can remember that the plane seemed to land on what was the edge of a cliff. We always used to hire an Aer Lingus plane in those days, probably because of our strong Irish links. They always provided first-class service. I remember this small runway and was glad when we finally touched down safely.

Tom Saunders had been out in advance to check things out. He selected the best hotel available, but it was still awful. The team coach had to negotiate a steep and winding street and the hotel itself just looked like a shop front. There were people all over the place waiting for us. It shows how passionate they are about their football.

When we arrived we saw some shops down the dingy side streets. We thought it would be worth a walk to stretch our legs, but all of these Turkish fellas started following us. They were giggling and holding hands and all getting close to one another. We were shocked to see these 17 to 18-year-olds cuddling up. It was the cue to get back to the hotel.

Of course, we took all kinds of food with us because Tom had warned us what to expect. You can imagine Terry Mac and me with our cases packed full of chocolate, crisps and rolls. The Turks must have thought the Seven Dwarves were coming. Our legs were hanging out of the end of the beds. I don't know how Alan Waddle coped.

These two guys used to travel with us, Alan Glynn and Harry Wright. They were two hoteliers who were good friends of the club. They used to come and make sure that all of the food was on time and prepared as well as it could be. The lads had been in the kitchens and reported back that everything had fat all over it. I woke up at 4am with terrible stomach cramps. I thought it might be an appendicitis problem and knocked the doc up, the real one, not Johnno!

He gave me some stuff to take, but I couldn't sleep. Clearly it was food poisoning and I couldn't eat going into the game although there was no way I was going to step down. We lost 1-0 after Smithy gave away a pen. Again, it was not his fault, honest! I was drained near the end. It was a warm day and I can remember my ears popping. The stadium could take 25,000 people, but it seemed more like 40,000. The noise was tremendous.

Because of the distance we were actually staying over after the game. When we got back to the hotel I was still not right. What followed was one of the most embarrassing moments of my life. My stomach was churning. I had wind and I farted, for want of a better expression. Instead of a mild explosion of wind, something else happened and I just grabbed my napkin and put it behind me. I had to go upstairs with the lads wondering what the hell was going on. Sorry if you are a bit squeamish reading this, but I had literally shit myself.

I couldn't get off the toilet and it just drained out of me. I don't know how I got through the match with this stomach bug. No one else had a problem, but I certainly did. After an hour I went down and told the lads what had happened, much to their amusement.

The Press lads had been to a nightclub. They said it resembled a scene from the movie Casablanca with Humphrey Bogart. They had a few drinks and the inevitable girls were trying to chat them up. They filled up with the local brew and then the bill came. It was enormous and they refused to pay. Suddenly these huge bouncers came over and they were frogmarched into a smoky back room. The boss man had a knife on the table. He said: "You will not leave here until you pay the bill." The lads scraped together as much as they could and felt they were lucky to escape with their lives. Of course, they thought it was not the time or place to ask for a VAT receipt.

I assume the Turks had a more pleasant stay in Liverpool although they were not happy to be on the receiving end of a 3-0 defeat that took us forward into a third-round clash with St Etienne. This, of course, would provide both players and fans with one of the greatest nights in our club's history.

St Etienne were the darlings of the French League. They had this player Rocheteau who was the Kevin Keegan of French football with his curly hair and fantastic skills. Many years later, when I was assistant to Gerard Houllier, coach Patrice Bergues told me that fans all over France had St Etienne as their second team. People travelled from all over the country to watch them. Patrice lived in Northern France and actually travelled to Liverpool to watch that famous European tie. Gerard Houllier was also there that night, but he was supporting Liverpool as a fan.

The away leg was first and I remember that the French supporters all had these fluorescent green and white curly wigs. They were a tribute to Rocheteau, although they could easily have been a tribute to Terry Mac if the French supporters had worn Scouse moustaches. Their famous chant was 'Allez Les Verts' – Come On The Greens. It was an incredible sight at the stadium. Their manager had a blond Afro hairstyle. The whole thing was very different from anything we had seen before.

They beat us 1-0 with a second-half goal and we did very well to keep the tie within reach. The return took place at Anfield on March 16 and it would go down as a legendary night, probably as famous as the 1965 Inter Milan game that was my all-time favourite as a fan. The only problem from my perspective was that I was in hospital having my cartilage out. I tuned into Radio City and listened to Elton Welsby's commentary. I can distinctly remember the excitement after just two minutes. Steve Heighway took a short corner on the left, finding Kevin Keegan 25 yards out. He angled a shot over the head of goalkeeper Curkovic and we were level. I could hear the crowd going mad.

I just shouted: "YES! GET IN!" It was the perfect start we wanted and I had to concentrate on this radio commentary rather than something like SKY Digital Interactive, which is how you would get the action now.

There was no Channel 433 or 'pay-per-view' in those days. But there is something that captivates you about a radio commentary because you also have to use your own imagination.

Five minutes into the second half the whole of Anfield was stunned when they equalised to go ahead on aggregate. Although the lads were clearly pushing hard, the chances were not coming as frequently as they would have liked. St Etienne were great on the counter-attack and Bathenay struck with a dipping 25 yarder.

It was an uphill task and the challenge would have killed off most teams. Then Ray Kennedy scored with a low shot after Tosh flicked on Cally's centre. The crowd exploded and I was as tense as anybody, sitting there in my hospital bed. Elton's commentary went up a notch as he got caught up in the excitement. I can remember his words as if he was repeating them. With just 15 minutes to go Bob introduced his famed supersub – David Fairclough. Elton picked up the action, and said:

"The game looks as though it has passed Liverpool by. It looks as though they have spent all of their energy. Ray Kennedy wins the ball. He plays it through to David Fairclough. DAVID FAIRCLOUGH IS IN SPACE. DAVID FAIRCLOUGH IS IN SPACE. IT'S A GOAL!"

I don't know if they were Elton's exact words, but they are the sentences that ring out in my mind and take me back to a moment of real magic as I nearly leapt out of my hospital bed. I screamed 'YES!' and punched the air. I could hear people running down the corridor. Two night nurses burst in. I must have woken up the whole ward. My only regret was not being there, but for just a couple of minutes it was just sheer delight.

What was best about the Radio City commentary was that after the final whistle they immediately played 'You'll Never Walk Alone' over Elton's commentary as they replayed the final goal. It made the hairs stand up on the back of my neck – and this was only the quarter-final.

When you see it on TV later, it doesn't do it justice. It was a superb night and it made Davie a legend forever and a day. I can still see him in my mind's eye, spinning in the air with his arms outstretched after his goal, just like my hero Roger Hunt used to do back in the Sixties.

Our European Cup semi-final opponents would be FC Zurich, which was a fantastic draw for the lads. It was not a problem. We won the first leg 3-1 in Switzerland with a Phil Neal double and a second-half clincher from Steve Heighway. You can never guarantee anything in football, but we all felt a place in the final was now assured. I could not believe it. We were going into the second leg of a European Cup semi-final with a tremendous lead. The Swiss were never the strongest and I had total confidence in the lads to finish the job.

However, it gave me a real dilemma because by now I was the well-established manager of the mighty Falcon FC in Kirkby and we were playing in a cup final that night!

The season before they had made me the youngest manager in the Kirkby and District Sunday League. I had gone to watch a pre-season friendly in which my brothers Owen and Ian were playing for Falcon, a local pub team. The manager was a great lad called Terry Campbell who had just been chosen by the players as their new boss. However, at half-time they all trooped over to me instead of Terry who was on the other touchline. Naturally, Terry didn't take that too well and so he resigned just 45 minutes into his 'career.'

I would have felt the same if I had not been shown the respect I felt I deserved. After a few jars in the pub the lads must have been talking and discussing the situation. Owen came over and said: "Phil, we would like you to be manager of the team."

I immediately thought: "Do I really want to do it?" My second thought was: "It might be good, something to take my mind off things on a Sunday."

I accepted on the spot and was manager for the next 12 years! Here I was, playing at Highbury or Old Trafford one minute and then focusing on the Kirkby and District League the next. We moved up to the Kirkby Newtown Combination a few years later. We were the only team to win the treble in that League.

You might wonder why I am so proud and enthusiastic about that time in my life when I was winning Championships with Liverpool and playing in European Cup Finals. It's all to do with respecting your roots, enjoying being with your mates and having a real passion for football at every level.

There were some great Sunday teams around at that time and there still are, sides like Woodpecker, Kingfisher and the Windmill, all pubs of course. They might not have the same ring about them as Real Madrid, Barcelona or Inter Milan, but all of those local teams had some great characters.

When Falcon won the treble it cost me a few quid. I used to buy the booze to fill up the cups. This brings me to that night in 1977 when I was injured and therefore not playing in Liverpool's European Cup semi-final, second leg at Anfield against FC Zurich. As I said, the Reds had a powerful first-leg lead and I knew we would not surrender it.

When I found out that my other team, Falcon, had a cup final that same night it was a bit of a dilemma. We were playing the famous Fountains Abbey (another pub!). What should I do? Enjoy a European Cup affair at Anfield or take charge of Falcon at Prescot Cables' tiny ground on an atrocious night. If Liverpool had faced any kind of a serious challenge for their European Cup Final spot, I would have been there cheering them on. However, I opted for the Falcon challenge on a pitch that was six inches deep in mud and which would have done Derby County's Baseball ground justice in its heyday.

What a game it turned out to be. Fountains Abbey had this centre-back called Big Joe. He was a nice bloke, but he was really up for this game. It was 2-2 and in the last couple of minutes we were just hanging on. Then one of our lads, Nick Cochrane, scored with a diving header to win the game. He's always reminding me about it. I can't remember what the hullabaloo was all about. I suppose Fountains Abbey might have been just a little bit upset because Nick was a mile offside.

We had this young referee, Colin Bascombe, who gave the goal. He overruled the linesman who was flagging. That was a bad mistake in a Sunday League Cup Final. I have this image of 'Big Joe' standing over him. We thought: "The young lad is going to give way."

He didn't. He stood his ground and during the closing moments we were kicking it anywhere to survive. That gave me my first cup final success as a manager. I'd organised a coach to take us the short distance from Kirkby to Prescot. Our match kicked off at 6.30pm and so we were able to listen to the remainder of the Liverpool match on the radio.

My brother Owen, who didn't play in Falcon's final, had gone to Anfield. I had to make big decisions for the game, as every good manager should, and he wasn't selected. However, you will already know by now that he is a fanatical Red.

Cross country was an early passion. Here I am pictured on the track (I'm the one in the middle).
Above right: A picture of my mum and dad during happy times in Kirkby

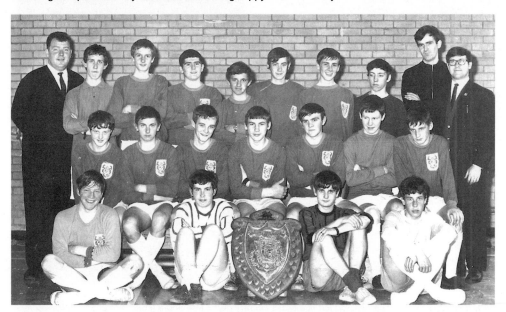

Where it all started with Kirkby Boys after winning the Welsh Shield in 1969 with our manager Vin Kelly
and coaches John Channel and Terry Duffy. That's me, third from the left, back row

THE WEST BANK
HIGH SCHOOL
SKELMERSDALE

WEST BANK

COMMENDATION

AWARDED TO Phil Thompson

FOR An Excellent Speech
(Definitely a born teacher)

SIGNED Staff & 1st & 5th pupils.

Headmaster

DATE 3rd July, 1975.

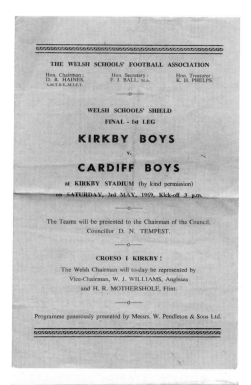

THE WELSH SCHOOLS' FOOTBALL ASSOCIATION

Hon. Chairman: Hon. Secretary: Hon. Treasurer:
D. R. HAINES,   F. J. BALL, M.A.   K. H. PHELPS.
A.M.T.B.E.,M.I.E.T.

WELSH SCHOOLS' SHIELD
FINAL - 1st LEG

KIRKBY BOYS
v.
CARDIFF BOYS

at KIRKBY STADIUM (by kind permission)
on SATURDAY, 3rd MAY, 1969, Kick-off 3 p.m.

The Teams will be presented to the Chairman of the Council,
Councillor D. N. TEMPEST.

CROESO I KIRKBY!

The Welsh Chairman will to-day be represented by
Vice-Chairman, W. J. WILLIAMS, Anglesea
and H. R. MOTHERSHOLE, Flint.

Programme generously presented by Messrs. W. Pendleton & Sons Ltd.

Patron:
HER MAJESTY THE QUEEN

President:
H.R.H. THE DUKE OF KENT

Chairman: Secretary:
DR. A. STEPHEN   D. FOLLOWS, C.B.E., B.A.

INTERNATIONAL
YOUTH
TOURNAMENT

To be played
in Spain
11th—23rd MAY, 1972

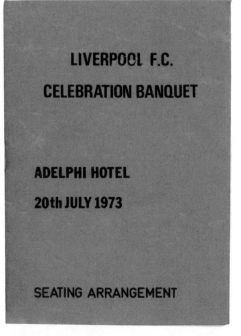

LIVERPOOL F.C.

CELEBRATION BANQUET

ADELPHI HOTEL

20th JULY 1973

SEATING ARRANGEMENT

Early souvenirs from my career. Top left is a cross country certificate and a 'commendation' I received for a school speech during my playing days. There's also a programme for Kirkby Boys, one from an international tournament in 1972 – and even the seating arrangement from our 1973 celebration dinner!

*At Picton Library in Liverpool after our famous 1972/73 Championship success.
You could tie up a tug boat at the Pier Head with the knot in my tie!*

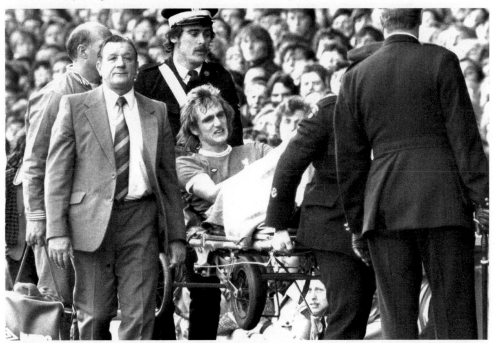

*After my first real injury in 1974. I needed my cartilage out after this. I must have been important to the
side in those days because Bob looks upset*

The Rolling Stones starring Phil Thompson, the night before a Scotland v England game in Glasgow. Also pictured are Russell Osman, Terry Butcher, Trevor Francis and Viv Anderson. Below: Celebrating my only goal for England against Italy in New York with Mick Channon trying to catch me

In front of the Shankly Gates with my first Championship plaque, my UEFA Cup medal and my Central League winners trophy – a unique treble I achieved in 1973

THE FOOTBALL ASSOCIATION

LIMITED

Patron: HER MAJESTY THE QUEEN
President: H.R.H. THE DUKE OF KENT
Chairman: SIR HAROLD THOMPSON, C.B.E., F.R.S.

Secretary:
E. A. CROKER

Telegraphic Address:
FOOTBALL ASSOCIATION, LONDON, W2 3LW
Phone: 01-262 4542
Telex: 261110

16 LANCASTER GATE, LONDON, W2 3LW

Our Ref: HNB/ST/1347   *Your Ref:*   28th April 1978

P Thompson Esq
c/o Liverpool F C
Anfield Road
Liverpool
L4 OTH

Dear Sir

I am writing to confirm the decision of the Disciplinary Committee that
was given to you and your Club representative at the meeting in Birmingham yesterday, as follows:-

"Having considered the evidence the Commission is satisfied that you
were guilty of a breach of F A Rule 35(a)(viii) and it has been
decided that you be fined a sum of £300".

In reaching its decision the Commission has taken into account the apology you have tendered and your very good record over a long period.

Please note that the amount of the fine must be remitted to the above
address within the next 21 days.

Yours faithfully

for Secretary

c.c.   The Secretary, Liverpool F C

Despite Bob Paisley's best advice, I ended up in hot water for THAT tackle. Here's the FA letter confirming their decision to fine me – and the receipt to confirm I paid up!

No. 10473   RECEIPT

THE FOOTBALL ASSOCIATION

16, LANCASTER GATE
LONDON
W2 3LW

VAT. Reg No. 238 9230 47

DATE	RECEIVED WITH THANKS FROM		THE SUM OF
30 MAY 78	P.B. THOMPSON FINE	TOTAL:	300.00 300.00

Burroughs 28437/7020.

FORM No. 08

Secretary

The FA Cup semi-final versus Manchester United in a replay at Maine Road on March 31, 1979. We drew 2-2. I'm tackling my old England colleague Brian Greenhoff

Lifting the Charity Shield at Wembley once again. Never mind the perm, where did those double or treble chins come from?

THE GLORY OF ROME

It was always doubly difficult for the Falcon lads with me as manager. Other teams would raise their game against us. The number of times I nearly got in a scrap for Falcon was nobody's business. Even then I was quite vocal on the line. Some of those lads in the opposition were hard boys. Many of our games were becoming a kicking match and I said that I wanted to pack it in. I told the boys: "You all have to go to work on a Monday." They held another meeting and said: "We want you to continue. We don't want to duck out."

I can remember this opponent Gerry Reid who was a hard lad. I had a few words with him in one match. He was kicking hell out of our lads. When the final whistle went he came marching across the pitch in my direction, looking as angry as hell. Our Owen later said: "I stood behind you. I was not going to back down." As Gerry got up to me he suddenly thrust out his hand and said: "Well done, you deserved to win." Owen thought: "Thank God for that." I'm good friends with Gerry now. It's great when lads get stuck in, give and take stick and then walk away at the end, having enjoyed the battle.

It's no different being on the line at Liverpool. It doesn't matter what happens during the game, you shake hands on the final whistle.

I had some great times managing Falcon. Let's just say I used them as practice for when I would ultimately become Liverpool's caretaker manager following Gerard's shock illness.

I can remember one game against a team called Woodpecker, who had won the League the year before. It was a summer game and many people were away on holiday. I only had ten men and I said: "Where's Bernie Harrison? I've seen him."

The lads said: "He's outside, but he's a bit worse for wear." I looked all over the playing field and then spotted a body lying down. It was Bernie and he was fast asleep. I shook him, but he said: "Sorry, Phil. I can't play. We had a party last night. Everybody stayed and took the beds and so I was up partying all night." I said: "You must play. I know you normally defend, but just hang around up front and play as long as you can."

Bernie looked at me through eyes that looked like piss holes in the snow. He was white. He picked himself up and trudged towards the dressing room. Guess who scored the winning goal in a 3-2 victory? Bernie, of course, and he never lets me forget it.

This was the thing about the lads. They always listened. I said: "If you give me respect I will manage the team." I must have been a pain in the arse at times. I shouted and I screamed, but they always showed that respect. We stuck together. The lads are still playing, but it's not the Falcon any more. Take a bow the 'Grey Haired Big Belly Crew', who now play in the Over 40's League. Great times and great memories.

We were now on our way to Rome for the European Cup Final. It was just 'Dreamsville' because we were so confident. If we had beaten Manchester United in the FA Cup Final maybe we would have been on too much of a high to lift ourselves again for another massive game because of the celebrations that would have obviously followed. The defeat and the manner in which it happened actually made us doubly determined to finish the season on an all-time high. The lads didn't have too much time to regroup after the agony of Wembley, but there was a steely determination about everyone in the squad and I could see that there was no way we were going to lose against our old adversaries Borussia Moenchengladbach.

We stayed in the Holiday Inn in the centre of Rome. John Toshack and myself were resigned to sitting out the most important game in Liverpool's history. That was a blow, but we were with the lads in every way. When it came to the team selection Bob Paisley chose to go with the vastly experienced Ian Callaghan and that meant there would be no place for David Fairclough who had only missed four of the last 12 league games that season.

There was a real togetherness about the squad, and for my part it was still great to be a part of an historic occasion, even though I was hurting inside because I could not play in the match. Tosh and I travelled with the team and Bob Paisley ensured we were involved in every way. The atmosphere amongst the lads was tremendous.

Nothing ever fazed this Liverpool team because of the self-belief we had. There was always a lot of humour in the dressing room and the players revelled in a challenge. We would always be focused, but relaxed and this was the mood as Bob led everyone out to inspect the Olympic Stadium pitch. I will never forget what happened next. As soon as we entered the tunnel area, a wall of noise swept over us. Then we caught our first glimpse of the terraces and it seemed as if the whole arena was full of Liverpudlians. Red and white chequered flags were everywhere. Someone must have made a fortune outside the ground. Liverpool's travelling army exploded when they glimpsed the players. It was the kind of deafening roar that made the hairs stand up on the back of your neck. As a Scouser and a Liverpudlian, I was so proud.

This was the moment Bill Shankly had dreamed of. This was the culmination of years of hard work. We had won two UEFA Cups. Now we were on the verge of claiming our first European Cup and it was as if the whole of Merseyside had invaded the Eternal City of Rome. As a Kopite myself, I just looked in awe at the greatest fans in the world. They were all wearing red. The German supporters were just sitting there, many of them taking photos of our massive travelling army as they partied on the steep terraces of the Olympic Stadium. If you were one of the lucky ones to be there, it is surely an experience that you will carry with you for the rest of your life. Just to be able to say: 'I was in Rome' is a badge of honour, the football equivalent of the VC.

Of course, I had read all of the newspaper stories of the sacrifices many supporters made to make the trip. People had sold their cars, bits and pieces of jewellery, anything they could get their hands on just to be a part of the glory that was Rome. Many travelled overland, by car or by train. Fans told me later that most of the trains had no running water and no working toilets. People were sleeping in the luggage racks. Some Scousers even managed to get from Lime Street to Rome's famous Termini Station without a ticket.

That takes some doing, but Scousers are the best in the world when it comes to improvisation. It sums up just how desperate many were just to be in Rome on this night of nights. Of course, many people travelled without match tickets, but just getting there was the first challenge.

I've said that we were up for this game after the United cup final defeat, but having experienced this truly remarkable show of fan passion, I had no doubts at all about the outcome of the European Cup Final. How could we lose? The fans themselves gave us a feeling of invincibility. I'm not sure if the most famous football banner of all time had been unfurled at this stage, but more about Joey Jones later.

For now the lads returned to the comparative quiet of the dressing room, but I can tell you that the mood in there was electric. We couldn't wait to get out and see the fans again. Everyone was saying: "That was only the rehearsal. What's it going to be like when the curtain goes up for real?"

We couldn't wait to get down that tunnel. We couldn't wait to hear the singing and the chanting and see those red and white chequered flags held high. It got to 7.30pm and we were really hyped up. If Jim Carrey had been in our dressing room, the team talk would have been just three words. "It's Show Time!" Oh yes, and then we had the game!

It was lovely. I walked out behind the lads and made my way to the bench I remember being surprised to see the BBC's Stuart Hall sitting alongside us. I don't know how he got there, but it got me thinking about how Stuart might describe what was going on all around us. He had this colourful, descriptive way of capturing the moment. His words that night would have been worth their weight in gold, or at least worth the same as the trademark gold medallion he always wore round his neck.

Then I turned round and saw THAT banner. 'JOEY ATE THE FROGS LEGS, MADE THE SWISS ROLL AND NOW HE'S MUNCHIN' GLADBACHS.'

What a masterstroke by the fans who made it and what a source of pride for Joey Jones. It made him feel ten feet tall and was a fantastic tribute to his special relationship with the Kop. To have a banner like that created in your name is something really special and it would be carried into battle for years to come, even after Joey had long gone. Fans don't often make banners in the names of defenders.

It's usually the superstar strikers who get all the focus of attention. But this was their way of saluting a lad who came from their midst and carried their dreams. Joey was a very good player and a great guy and I know that he still cherishes this tribute.

He was later given the banner and it is on loan to the club. Sadly, it is so big that there is no space in the present Visitors' Centre to permanently display it, although it comes out for special exhibitions and events.

We shouldn't forget the match itself. It turned out to be a very good game of football, possibly the best European Cup Final of that era. Most of the previous games had been tight and finished 1-0. This one ended 3-1 in our favour and it was a great advert for football.

My good mate Terry Mac was soon found by Steve Heighway and rattled a shot into the bottom corner of the German net to give us the lead. I remember those nets. They seemed like something from a Sunday League game, stretching no more than two feet over the line. The nets just flopped as if they had not been tied back properly. We retained our advantage until half-time.

Moenchengladbach's best player was Allan Simonsen who was good enough to win a European Footballer of the Year accolade. He had great skill and latched onto a mistake by Jimmy Case, flashing the ball beyond Clem into the top corner to give Borussia a lifeline. It was the only time in the game that the Germans came to life and it stunned the Liverpool fans, well at least for about a minute!

Then the fairytale took over. It was almost as if it was meant to be. It was supposed to be Tommy Smith's final season. He had a testimonial game looming at Anfield before finally ending a fantastic Liverpool career. Tommy was playing in my position in this game. We won a corner on the left and I can still see Steve Heighway's cross. Some balls are made for heading. You don't need to move your neck muscles. This centre had 'head me' written all over it, and Smithy obliged. He caught it square on and the ball flashed high and wide of goalkeeper Kneib's right hand with the defender on the line also rooted to the spot.

I was sitting on the bench thinking: "Who was that?" It was the most perfect header. Then I saw Tommy running away toward his left with his arms beating in front of him. It was brilliant. It was as if someone had waved a magic wand over the Olympic Stadium.

It was the same for Kevin Keegan. This was also his last game. Kev had been heavily criticised for his performance at Wembley in some quarters. People used the fact that he was leaving as a stick to beat him with.

It was completely out of order. It was fitting that our super hero put on an astonishing display in Rome to remind every one of those critics what a wonderful player he was. Berti Vogts had been given the challenge of man marking him. The German international was led a merry dance.

Kevin was going on runs to open up space for other people. He looked dangerous in his own right and it was like a Mini trying to mark a Rolls Royce. That's no disrespect to Vogts, who was a great player. It's just that Kevin was unstoppable on the night.

Kevin turned his marker and set off for goal with Berti in his wake. I was screaming: "Go on Kevin, score!" The German threw in a lunging tackle and Keegan went down in the box. There was no controversy. It was a penalty. The best man to take the kick was our specialist Phil Neal. He was ice cool under pressure and immediately stepped forward to pick up the ball. The problem was, goalkeeper Kneib was an absolute giant. He'd looked seven feet tall before the game and now he was growing with every second, his frame seeming to fill the entire goal. Where would Nealy place it? My fears were all unfounded. Our full-back slotted his shot right into the bottom corner. I don't think Kneib even dived.

From that moment the stadium was rocking and I enjoyed every minute of it, although there was naturally an inner disappointment that I was not out there with the lads. My loss had been Smithy's sensational gain, but I was never going to resent that because he had been one of my boyhood heroes. I was given a medal because I had played in previous games, but it never means quite the same if you don't finish things off in the final.

Still, this was truly a glorious night for the Reds and the after-match celebrations are part of Anfield folklore, not just for the players but also for the fans. Even now people still remind me about that night. There was not much security at our Holiday Inn base in Rome's city centre. It became a focal point as people found out where we were.

It was always going to be impossible to keep the Scousers out. Can you imagine even an army of hotel staff trying to stop them? We were in a large room not too far from the bar. They had put on an open buffet and this big oblong table was full of food. Inside this table was another that held the gleaming European Cup. We began the party and it was sensational. The bar staff had been told to give us what we wanted. Beers all round, some bottles of wine, a bottle of gin, a bottle of Scotch, some champagne. Yes, let's have a quick one to get us going.

As the evening wore on, I began to look round this VIP room. Amongst the suits and beautiful dresses of the ladies there seemed to be a growing number of people stripped to the waist with Union Jacks and red and white chequered flags draped over their shoulders. The Red Army had arrived, one by one at first but building into a multitude. They had infiltrated the official celebrations, but we didn't mind and no one said anything.

The first challenge achieved, the fans now turned to their second task. Suddenly people were on their hands and knees, lifting the white cloths that hung to the floor on the buffet table. They would disappear and then emerge on the other side to touch the European Cup and have their pictures taken with it. There must have been 700 people in this room by now and the majority of them were not with the official party.

We just laughed at the ingenuity of our fabulous fans. They had cottoned on to the fact that the waiters had been primed to bring free booze to anyone who wanted it. People were walking round drinking from bottles of wine and toasting a famous victory.

No one in the official party was bothered. Those fans had been as much a part of this famous victory as the players. However, as the evening wore on and the demand for pictures and autographs became intense, we finally decided to move upstairs into one of the rooms. We got this trolley and said to the waiter: "Ten bottles of wine, ten bottles of champagne and a couple of bottles of Scotch." We loaded it up and about 30 players and wives went upstairs to continue the party.

Of course, we were singing and making a tremendous din in this room. Suddenly there was a knock on the door and the hotel manager came in to say that there had been some complaints about the noise. Of course, he got dog's abuse, but he was only doing his job. We took our trolley and piled it up again with the booze and followed the manager to another side room where we partied a little more quietly for the rest of the night.

The next morning Terry Mac and myself did not surface as early as some of the lads. Many had gone down to gather around the big swimming pool and it was here that a now famous incident happened. The reports had begun to spread that Jimmy Case or Tommy Smith had given Kevin Keegan a black eye as a farewell present after the FA Cup Final because he had played so badly. No one thought about the fact that from the Saturday through to the Thursday morning, Kevin didn't have a black eye, but you know how rumours grow with every new telling.

The truth is that everyone who came down was being thrown into the swimming pool fully clothed. Phil Neal was wearing this new pair of shoes and he didn't want to go in. He flailed his arm back as they grabbed him, giving Kevin the shiner. Sorry to disappoint everyone about the myth. That was what happened.

The homecoming was incredible. For us to have won the European Cup for the first time was magnificent. Bill Shankly had started the dream. He had built the rock-solid foundations that took us on the first part of our journey. Bill won Championships, the FA Cup and the UEFA Cup. He made us believe in our dreams and the intentions were clear. Nothing would stop us ultimately winning the European Cup.

Bob had picked up on the challenge and carried the banner forward. It was brilliant and now we were reaping the reward with a sensational tour around the city that was, I have to admit, something of a blur, but a wonderful blur. If it was tinged with sadness it was because we were saying a final farewell to the legend of Kevin Keegan. He will always be one of the greatest players ever to star for Liverpool and England.

I know he upset some people by announcing his intentions to leave months before he eventually departed for Hamburg, but that simply reflected his honesty. He was the best ambassador Liverpool has ever had. Yes, we rightly salute the legend of men like Billy Liddell and 'Sir' Roger Hunt, but Kevin was different. He would sit or stand and sign autographs forever and a day.

He had come from a humble background like many of us in the squad and recognised and appreciated the trappings in life that the game had brought him. He would never snub a supporter in any situation. Kevin had been the new generation. A club like Liverpool always needs an idol like that, someone with real star quality to carry the great traditions forward. He had good looks. He was a pin-up.

He was like a popstar, but he could also play. Kevin Keegan was a bundle of energy and he scored some vital goals for the Reds down the years. He had been a part of the finest chapter in the history of the club up to that time and his input should be remembered forever.

It was an extra special time because we were achieving firsts, not least that first European Cup triumph. Even though I didn't play in the final that night, it was probably the greatest of our European triumphs, although Istanbul 2005 would run it close because of the incredible nature of the fightback.

THOMMO

Chapter 6

A European Cup medal in my own right and the captaincy follows

We now moved into season 1977/78, which has special significance for me. The Chinese have their 'Year of the Lion' or whatever. This was the 'Year of the Scouse Perm.' It was also the 'Year of the New Super Hero.'

More about our hair-raising antics shortly, but first some thoughts about another Bob Paisley masterstroke. We have spoken about Bob and this ability to make people better players by seeing different strengths in them. He also knew that a club like Liverpool needed special stars and, having lost one in Kevin Keegan, there was an urgent need for an immediate replacement. Bob pulled off a coup by bringing in the legend that was Kenny Dalglish. In the previous season he had nutmegged our goalkeeping giant Ray Clemence in that famous Scotland v England clash at Hampden Park. We all knew Dalglish had special qualities, but we didn't have a complete understanding about his ability because we simply did not see enough of Scottish football at that time. It was very rarely on our TV screens and while we knew Kenny was star quality north of the border, the big question was whether he could translate that in the English top flight.

It took about 30 seconds in pre-season to grasp that here was a very special footballer, someone who was blessed with unique skills. He was also humble and had this work ethic, which was the hallmark of all great Liverpool players. You couldn't come to Anfield full of your own self-importance.

That would soon be knocked out of you. Kenny was as modest as he was magnificent and we all looked forward to his debut in the Charity Shield against Manchester United, a game that offered us the chance to extract revenge on the side that had beaten us in the FA Cup Final.

Of course, they were determined to try and put one over on the new European Cup holders. It was never going to happen. Kenny immediately swivelled on a ball and lashed it over the bar, but we saw something special that day and all of the fans were looking forward to our opening day league game against Middlesbrough. I can remember Ronnie Moran shouting: "Just play it in to Kenny's feet." He kept repeating it.

Kenny had the biggest arse in football, or it seemed that way to defenders when he leaned forward and pushed it back to prevent them getting anywhere near the ball. It gave him the space to guide the ball right or left. When he had made his mind up, the pass was perfect, or he would turn people on a tanner, to use an old expression, and then bend the ball into the back of the net. Straight away everyone knew this boy was special. Memories of Kevin disappeared all in the space of 90 minutes against Boro. Here was a new star for the next few years in more ways than one.

Kenny was an absolute pleasure to play with, to train with and to have a laugh with. Like many of the lads, he came from a modest background, and it seemed to make him doubly determined to succeed. Dalglish scored in five out of his first six league games. Immediately he was dubbed the new 'King of the Kop.' It was a love affair that has lasted to this day.

Meanwhile, Tommy Smith had been persuaded to defer his decision to leave the club. Smithy signed a new contract. I only played in the first game and then did not play for a while. Our defensive options had also been increased in the summer with the fairly quiet signing of a boy from Partick Thistle who, in his own way, would eventually become as legendary as Kenny. His name was Alan Hansen or 'Big Jocky' as he became known.

I can remember his first training session. I was amazed at how high he could leap. He also had these silky skills and looked as much a midfield player as a centre-back. Here was a young lad who was destined to become a truly great player. He was also extremely lucky because two highly disciplined young men would now take him under their wing. Thommo and Terry Mac would show him all the delights of the city centre.

Being a Scotsman, we thought he would be like the rest of us. We asked him what he wanted to drink and in this heavy Tartan accent he replied: "Canadian Club." Yes, we said, but what would you like in it?

"Canadian Club," he repeated and then, as if he had finally understood the question, he added: "With ice."

We did not drink spirits, but we taught him that he would never become a player without getting a few pints down his neck. It's funny, but he seemed to learn quite quickly and became a good friend of ours. He was still like a little boy lost, but we took care of him.

Even big Al did not expect to get his chance as early as he did, but everyone could see the potential in him. With the arrival of Dalglish a new breed was coming through with the likes of Sammy Lee starting to show things in the reserves. Later that season Graeme Souness was to join us. More about him shortly. John Toshack's games were getting fewer and while I started the season against Boro I was to have a recurrence of my knee problem and I only managed one appearance between that point and early November. I was then to re-establish myself in the team.

A quirk of fate would set up a fascinating showdown when the European Super Cup paired Champions Cup holders Liverpool and Cup Winners' Cup holders Hamburg in November 1977. Of course, it meant an early opportunity to see how Kevin Keegan was settling in with the German side. It also gave us a chance to remind him that he had left the best club in Europe, albeit for a different type of challenge.

The Super Cup was over two legs and the first game was in Germany. We realised quickly that the Hamburg fans idolised their new hero. Kevin had made a massive impact in his early games in the Bundesliga, as we always knew he would. Kevin could have gone to one of the traditional giants like Real Madrid or Barcelona. The fact that he had chosen to join one of the less fashionable of the European clubs only served to make the Hamburg fans respect him even more. It was a major decision for the former Anfield super hero, but as usual Kevin got it absolutely spot on. Not only did he go on to make a major impact in German football, he also won the European Footballer of the Year award twice as a Hamburg player, a sensational achievement.

However, we were determined to make a point of our own in Germany to prove that there was life without KK. We would draw that first game after being 1-0 down at half-time. Our team was: Clemence, Neal, Jones (Smith), Thompson, R. Kennedy, Hughes, Dalglish, Case (Johnson), Heighway, Fairclough and Callaghan.

We called Fairclough 'The Whip' because of the shot he had with his left foot. Some persisted in calling him supersub, but Davie was better than that and scored some crucial goals for us. His effort meant that there was everything to play for in the return at Anfield. Of course, Kevin's return dominated all of the headlines in advance of the game. We were up for it. The crowd was up for it. I have no doubt that Kevin was up for it, but a couple of Kirkby kids stole the show in a sensational 6-0 victory. I opened the scoring after 21 minutes and Terry Mac scored the next three to ultimately earn himself a fantastic trophy as man-of-the-match. Fairclough made it five and, fittingly, the new King of the Kop, Kenny Dalglish, grabbed the sixth. Kevin was to leave Anfield as sick as the proverbial parrot.

After not playing in the European Cup Final in Rome, I made a pledge to myself that I would win a medal in my own right. I had been given one in 1977 for playing in the earlier rounds, but I've explained that it wasn't quite the same. Although playing again after my long lay-off was a priority, my main aim was to fulfil a lifetime's ambition and play in a European Cup Final.

Having got back in the team in the November, I linked up again with Emlyn Hughes in the heart of the defence. Alan Hansen then came in when Emlyn got injured, but he was still going through a learning process. We also had Smithy vying for a place because he had deferred his retirement after playing such a memorable part in the European Cup Final.

I remember Al getting a chance to show what he could do when he made his debut against Derby County in a 1-0 home win. People were amazed by the silky skills he showed for a centre-back, but it meant he took chances at times. That was slightly frowned upon by the staff, but they had this way of teaching you your trade. They would tell Al to do his tricks in the right areas, but he was still prone to the odd mistake.

I recall that the game after his debut was against Manchester United. It was "Welcome to the English top flight, Al." He tried one trick too many and Old Trafford was not the place to take risks. Although he did quite well, it set a few alarm bells ringing. However, it was only the learning process and the staff still had faith in him. He was kept in the side the following week for another daunting test at Arsenal. As the years went by he began to understand more about the game. Things register when Ronnie Moran is constantly bawling at you. Ronnie used to say: "If they don't understand hit them hard. If they still don't understand hit them harder."

The staff did not want to take away a defender's instinct to play from the back. At the same time, they wanted you to do it at the right time. Alan Hansen became one of the best defenders in the world, far more appreciated by Liverpool supporters than his own countrymen who always seemed to prefer the more robust and aggressive style of Willie Miller and Alex McLeish. We couldn't understand it.

At last my own injury situation had settled down and I was more or less ever-present. I missed two successive games in the middle of February, but the rest of the time was fantastic. I was even to score a couple of goals. I was never prolific, but I enjoyed scoring. One came against Sunderland, a good header at the Kop end that always filled me with joy. I'd already scored in a 4-2 FA

Cup defeat against Chelsea at Stamford Bridge, a result that was a bitter blow after our great run of the previous year. However, it made us all the more determined to work hard on every other front.

I had seen a great pre-season photograph of Kevin Keegan in action for his new club Hamburg. This little guy was sporting an Afro cut and was looking like Michael Jackson in his early days. It was called the bubble cut. In simple terms it was a perm. Kev had started a fashion that was to really catch on. I saw it as a dare. It was around mid-January and many of the lads had been discussing the pros and cons over a few beers at a European game. "Should we all get our hair done?" It wasn't the usual topic of conversation.

I may shock a few people when I reveal who was the instigator of the perm dare. It was none other than the mighty Tommy Smith. He was saying: "Let's all get a perm," although it didn't seem to fit Smithy's image. As it turned out, nothing happened. It was coming up to my birthday and I thought: "I'm going to take the plunge. I'm going to be the daredevil." I went to Charlie Wynn's Chopping Block hair salon in Kirkby. I wouldn't have it done downstairs in the main room. The styling was done upstairs, but I actually had mine done in the attic so nobody could see. I looked in the mirror and saw this bubble cut looking back at me. There was no turning back.

I'd had it done between the Saturday and playing Wrexham in the fifth round of the League Cup at the Racecourse Ground. You can imagine the stick I got from the players. That was bad enough, but how would the fans react at the Racecourse? I believe they call it the 'big reveal' in the makeover business.

I ran out with this bubble cut and immediately people were screaming: "Look, Liverpool have signed Shirley Temple." The catcalls were relentless. I just laughed, or was a giggle more appropriate with a perm? Anyway, everybody slaughtered me, as you can imagine. I had bought one of those little brown Afro fork combs and that became an ever-present in my jean pocket. Although Kevin Keegan had started it and I had followed, not many imitated at first. It didn't help that every time I got the ball, someone would shout: "Hit the big pufter."

However, then it started. Terry Mac and Phil Neal had it done. Mick Lyons and Bob Latchford followed suit at Everton. It was amazing and it changed the conversation when you met up with other players. Instead of: "Alright mate, how are you, how's the family?" it became: "How's the perm? Where did you get it done?" But there was still no Smithy!

Our dear friend Graeme Souness used to say that his was natural. We'd say: "You must tamper with yours", and he'd reply: "No, it's natural." No one ever found out. Of course, all of this would lead to the national image of Scousers all having perms and Terry Mac-style moustaches. Those famous Harry Enfield sketches were borne out of those days at Anfield Road and Melwood Drive and we never got any royalties for it!

They were great times and funny times, especially when the fans started copying the style. One of the newspapers ran a big article under the headline: 'New Wave Of Footballers', or to use the phrase of the lads: "Tampering with your hair." It had about 12 players lined up and my picture was spread across two pages, presumably because I was the instigator in England. I must have been an icon for the perm in those days.

I remember a young Bryan Robson 'tampering' with his hair. My wife Marg, my girlfriend at the time, will tell you that she had hers done before me. We must have looked a hell of a sight going into town. Her perm and my perm used to get tangled up. I would get really angry with her when she pinched my brown Afro comb. It was a real laugh.

Whenever I attend sporting dinners and there is a question and answer session, it always comes up. I always say: "Okay, put your hands up if you ever had a perm." Often 60 per cent of the lads in the room respond.

Maybe all this 'tampering' brought us luck on the pitch. We finished the season with a 12-match unbeaten run in the league, winning nine and drawing three although it was still not quite good enough for us to recapture our title, which was won that year by the up and coming Nottingham Forest under Brian Clough. We had a long and successful run to the final of the League Cup beating Chelsea, Derby, Coventry after a replay, Wrexham – where the perm made its debut – and then Arsenal over two legs. It took us into the final where we were looking to claim the trophy for the first time. Forest stood in our path. Of course, the Evertonians decided that the League Cup was the Mickey Mouse Cup. My brother-in-law Jimmy Dutton, a Blue, decided to make a special mascot for me.

He got a Fairy Liquid bottle, attached two arms and stuck a Mickey Mouse head on the top. He painted it and added two Mickey-style legs on the bottom. "Here you are," he said with a twinkle in his eye. "You've now got a real Mickey Mouse Cup even before you play Forest."

I thought: "This will be my lucky omen." Jimmy was also a bit of a poet, and a special verse accompanied Mickey. It said:

This cup is sent to you dear Phil
It's the one you've never seen

It's presented down at Wembley
By Her Majesty The Queen
But not the Queen of England
I'm sad to say hard luck
But by the Queen of Disneyland
And her husband Donald Duck

Jimmy was always writing sarcastic poems. I thought: "Eat your heart out Jim. I'm going to turn your Mickey Mouse Cup into something positive." He gave it to me the day before we travelled for the final and I took it all the way to Wembley in my bag as my lucky mascot.

Of course, Forest were looking for a double of Championship and League Cup. They had some good players, but their England goalkeeper Peter Shilton was ineligible. His place was taken by a talented youngster, Chris Woods. The rest of their team was: Viv Anderson, Frank Clark, John McGovern, our old centre-back Larry Lloyd, Kenny Burns, Martin O'Neill, Ian Bowyer, Scouser Peter Withe, Tony Woodcock and John Robertson.

Our team was: Ray Clemence, Phil Neal, Tommy Smith, yours truly, Ray Kennedy, Emlyn Hughes, Kenny Dalglish, Jimmy Case, Steve Heighway, Terry McDermott and Ian Callaghan.

Clough was naturally disappointed to be without Shilton. When he bought him, he stated: "Peter will save us 12 goals a year which will guarantee us 12 extra points." He was right, but Peter couldn't play in this tournament. As it turned out, his young replacement Woods had an inspired afternoon.

We battered them at Wembley, but had to settle for a goalless draw and it went to a replay at Old Trafford four days later on March 22. My lucky Mickey Mouse Cup omen went with me again.

He had his place of honour under my peg in the dressing room. We battered them again, but they suddenly snatched a penalty. A ball was played through and John O'Hare burst down the middle. He was just on the 'D' and outside the area when I tripped him up.

I thought: "He still has Clem to beat," but you were not sent off for a tackle from behind in those days and I decided to take no chances for the good of the team. Referee Pat Partridge must have been 25 yards away. The break had also caught the linesman out. I was absolutely gobsmacked and amazed to see Mr Partridge pointing to the spot. O'Hare had been two yards outside the box when contact was made. I was astonished how two officials could get it so wrong when the entire stadium saw what had happened.

Robertson despatched the penalty and I held my head in my hands. I was furious and what I said to the referee would have earned me a massive fine these days.

We had been in complete control. A Terry Mac goal had been disallowed after taking it down on his shoulder and then lashing it past Woods. It was to be the only goal 'scored' in open play over the two games, with young Chris in inspired form. We wanted to claim our first League Cup and while we put that right big style in the years to come it was still a bitter disappointment to miss out.

When we got back into the Old Trafford dressing room I got hold of that Mickey Mouse Cup and booted it all over the place. Its head fell off, then its legs. I was so angry. TV were knocking on the door for a comment from me over the penalty. Both Bob Paisley and Emlyn Hughes told me to be careful in the heat of the moment. They said: "Don't go out there Thommo," but I was determined to go on and put the record straight.

I stood in front of the camera and in my Scouse brogue I slaughtered the ref. It was possibly the first time the phrase 'professional foul' was ever used on air to describe this type of incident. I would have got stick if I had not made the tackle and O'Hare had gone on and scored. I know it was wrong, but the laws of the game told me that they would get nothing more than a free-kick on the edge of the box. It doesn't matter that the tackle was worthy of a pen. I was angry and aggressive on camera and Bob and Emlyn were right.

I was charged with bringing the game into disrepute at a hearing in Birmingham. Bob went down with me. Terry Mac used to take Bob off to a tee. In that North Eastern voice, Terry was saying: "You are going to get imprisonment for this if he tries to defend you."

I remember the hearing. Bob's words were ringing in my ears as we went through the door: "Phil, when you are in there be humble. Apologise. The ref is always right. It will never happen again. It was out of character. This is the only time I've ever been in front of a disciplinary panel."

I probably bored them so much with my grovelling apology that one of them interrupted me. He said: "Mr Thompson, you say you won't do it again."

"That's right," I replied. "I recognise the error of my ways."

He immediately pushed this newspaper cutting across the table at me. Bob winced as he read it out.

The headline said: 'I would do it again to save my team.' I was fined £300, but not suspended because of my previous good conduct. I had never been in this situation before and assumed the club would pay the fine, but they just said: "We'll take a cheque from you and send the money off."

It was a right kick in the goolies, but you put it down to experience. Looking back, I just wish I hadn't taken it out on Mickey Mouse. It would have been nice to still have the Mickey Mouse Cup because I could have hung my runners-up medal on him.

This was the emergence of a very good Nottingham Forest side that would become something of a bogey team to us for a few years. We had some fantastic struggles against them. I remember one newspaper photograph, taken at one of our games. People talk these days about Arsenal or Manchester United melees in the heat of battle. They had nothing on this. The picture showed Graeme Souness holding Ian Bowyer by the throat. He has got him by the Adam's Apple and is pushing him away. It summed up the togetherness of our team and the fact that we did not back down in any situation.

We might have lost the League and been edged out of the League Cup by Forest, but our 1977/78 European Cup dream was still alive. Our first-round challenge took us back behind the Iron Curtain although this time we were fortunate to fly straight to Dresden whereas on our previous visit we had been forced to go via the notorious Checkpoint Charlie in Berlin. The first leg was at home on October 1, 1977. We gave one of our best Euro displays ever against a top-class team. The 5-1 scoreline at Anfield emphasised the fact that we murdered them. It was an awesome performance.

We were defending the trophy and that gave us an extra incentive. The previous year we had strolled through at this stage against Crusaders. Now we did the business against top-class opposition and we were full of confidence for the return, especially as the journey was much more straightforward than it had been before.

Naturally, we felt that at 5-1 the game was effectively over, but we had an experience that I will never forget. You can never suggest that opponents have taken performance-enhancing drugs, but I looked deep into the eyes of the Dresden players that night and they were on stalks and shining. This time they came out and murdered us in the first 45 minutes. Ray Clemence was inspired and the defence had to work like Trojans to keep the tie goalless at half-time. To get into the dressing room 0-0 was a miracle.

Ten minutes into the second half we were 2-0 down and now leading 5-3 on aggregate. Gradually their energy began to wane. There is no way they could have kept that up, with or without help. After 75 minutes the game finally began to turn and Stevie Heighway grabbed a goal to put things well and truly out of their reach. It was as if they were in an inflatable boat and someone had suddenly pulled out the plug. They were sunk in the last ten minutes, but it had been possibly the most frightening football experience of my life.

We then came up against the mighty Benfica and I was delighted to be able to play in the magnificent Stadium of Light in Lisbon. We came through this round quite comfortably, which was a tribute to our quality.

As fate would have it, we were then drawn against our old adversaries Borussia Moenchengladbach, who we had beaten in the 1973 UEFA Cup Final as well as seeing them off just months before in the majestic surroundings of Rome. I always fancied our chances over two legs.

They were to beat us in Germany, but Craig Johnston gave us a lifeline with a goal in the closing minutes, which deflated them. At 2-0 it would have been a tall order, even at Anfield. Now we had the crucial away goal. As it turned out, we gave them a 3-0 drubbing at Anfield to win 4-2 on aggregate. An early goal from Ray Kennedy set us on our way.

It was onwards into the final and it was strange how we met old rivals every inch of the way. First it was Dresden, then Benfica, then Borussia Moenchengladbach and finally Bruges who we had met in 1975/76. They were a well-organised and disciplined team with some good individuals. I was thrilled that the final was at Wembley, the original Anfield South. This was a win-win situation from our perspective. Of the 92,000 spectators present, probably 75,000 of them were from Merseyside.

It was never a great game. It just never took off. We should have won by four or five. David Fairclough got through on goal. So did Terry Mac. Their keeper did well for them and at 0-0 I'm thinking: "This can't be right. This is not how the script should go."

It was down to the defence to make sure that we did not concede a silly goal. We did our job and Clem, for the most part, was unemployed. Then came a piece of action at the other end that was to shape Kenny Dalglish's career. This was to be the famous 'Dink.'

Kenny sussed their goalkeeper out. He had sprawled at the feet of Terry Mac earlier and Kenny remembered that when he also got through on goal. As the keeper advanced toward him, Kenny's delicate little chip sailed over the Bruges man and into the far corner. I would see him do it umpteen times in the future, but to watch him perform such a wonderful piece of skill in the high-pressure atmosphere of a European Cup Final emphasised that we had someone in our ranks who was truly special. Kenny carried on running towards the Liverpool fans at that end with that beaming smile across his face and his arms held high in the air. How he got his arse above those advertising hoardings I will never know! I thought he was going to scrape it on the top of them, but what a moment.

Prior to this game, Tommy Smith had suffered a massive blow when he dropped a lump hammer on his foot while doing some building work at home. His fairy-tale from the year before had turned into a nightmare a year later. He was unavailable for the final. Smithy had been playing at right-back with Phil Neal on the left. Alan Hansen, whose season had been up and down while still showing his quality and his potential, was the man who filled the gap left by the Anfield Iron in a defensive shuffle with Emlyn going to left-back and Nealy to the right while the young Hansen slotted in alongside me.

After Kenny's goal, big Al picked up a through ball. I had this nose, of course, for reading situations. I could always sniff out danger and I was extra cautious as Alan played a backpass towards Clem. It dropped short and the Bruges attacker was round him in a flash. I raced back onto the line.

The striker hit an angled shot and it was going in. I stretched out a long leg and prayed. I've talked about your life flashing before you in moments of danger. I thought about Rome and my frustration at missing out. I desperately wanted that winners medal in my own right. My foot was almost on the chalk line between the posts, but I managed to turn the ball away to save us the embarrassment of an extra-time period Bruges just did not deserve.

It meant I got my wish. I had won a European Cup medal in my own right and it meant everything to me. I now had two in my possession, one cherished a little more than the other but both very special. Once again we were celebrating in a Holiday Inn, this time in Swiss Cottage rather than Rome. Believe it or not, the security was a lot tighter this time. No one was going to get in and so those scenes of the previous year would not be re-enacted. However, nothing was going to stop me having a night to remember and I was up on the mic with Sammy Lee singing all the Scouse songs. It was another great end to an eventful season. We had retained the European Cup and ensured the squad was stronger than ever with the acquisition of Kenny Dalglish right at the start and another Scot, Graeme Souness, in the January.

Let's just call it Bob Paisley's belated Christmas present. Souness was a tough tackling midfielder. He had to wait a bit of time to play, but he would then make his mark on the team and no one was going to stop him. Kenny and Graeme were roommates. They were always together along with Jockey Hansen. The Kirkby pair, Terry Mac and myself, were always in and out of their room or they had long sessions in ours. Graeme said to me: "It's so different at this football club." He had previously been with Spurs and Boro. I said: "Hey, now you are playing for keeps. What you did before was training for it. This is where the big boys hang out."

Maybe he laughed at my words a bit, but when you are at a club like Liverpool the pressure is at boiling point, week in, week out. Success was a must for us because of what we had already achieved. We didn't think about anything else. I reminded him what the great man said: "First is first. Second is nowhere."

There is no doubt that Souness had the required ability, passion and never-say-die attitude every Liverpool player needed. He was to play a fantastic part in the success that was to beckon. Later I will tell you about what happened between us to open up a massive rift, but for now I'm happy to say that Graeme Souness was the greatest midfield player this country has seen, including the likes of Bobby Charlton and Bryan Robson. That's as big a tribute as I can pay Souness the player. He was different class and when I speak about Souness the footballer, I never knock him.

We felt things were really coming together as we entered the 1978/79 season as European Cup holders. The players were peaking at the right time and they were in the right age groups. We got off to a flying start with a 2-1 opening day win over QPR and then went to Ipswich Town where Dutch star Arnold Muhren had just been signed to slot in alongside countryman Frans Thijssen. Manager Bobby Robson was convinced this skilful Dutch influence would give his side a new fluency. Muhren was described as this great box-to-box player who was a high-energy performer. All this hype clearly focused Terry McDermott in our midfield.

There was no way Terry was going to be overshadowed and he produced an unbelievable performance in a terrific 3-0 win. Muhren was told to mark him, but Terry was making these surging runs for which he was famous and the Dutchman didn't know how to handle it. Every time Ipswich tried to regroup Terry would get back into position and then go again. Muhren was on his knees, out for the count. Although Terry lived life to the full, he was one of the fittest men at the club.

A few days later, on September 2, we produced one of our greatest-ever performances when we entertained a high-profile Tottenham side featuring the newly-crowned World Cup winners, Argentinian stars Ossie Ardiles and Ricardo Villa. It had been a real Spurs coup to bring those two world-class stars to England and they had looked the part in their opening games. We crushed the Londoners 7-0 on a day when Kenny Dalglish and David Johnson both scored doubles. It was one of our most inspiring performances ever and we seemed to be able to score at will. Of course, it was Terry Mac's final goal that everyone still talks about because it epitomised our free-flowing play.

The ball came out of the right-hand corner of the Kop goal half and was swept into the middle of the pitch. Johnno played it to Stevie Heighway on the left. Terry, who moments earlier had been in our box when the ball was won, had immediately set off on a surging forward run. He reached the opposing box without breaking stride as Stevie's perfect cross came in. Terry hated heading the ball. He said it affected your brain cells. But he directed a superb header into the roof of the net and wheeled away in one movement to what was then the Kemlyn Road side, now the Centenary Stand.

It was a fantastic way to end a brilliant game. I was so proud of our display I took cuttings from all the newspapers and I still have them today. The Sunday People would give individual ratings from 1-10 for the players. When you got 8/9 you were well pleased. When you got 5 the reaction was: 'Bastard!' This was possibly the first and only time every single player got a perfect 10. The reporter was a great judge that day.

Emlyn Hughes got injured in this game and missed the subsequent trip to Birmingham where there was no resting on our laurels. We won 3-0 and this made it 19 goals in five games. The good thing was that they were all spread round. The team was really taking shape and those who made over 30 appearances were: Clemence, Neal, Alan Kennedy, Thompson, Hansen, Ray Kennedy, Dalglish, Case, Souness and McDermott. Heighway and Johnson made 28 and 30 appearances apiece, the fading and injured Hughes 16 and Fairclough and Lee just a handful.

Alan Kennedy was the new boy that season. He was a great lad and had a succession of nicknames. In fact, it all got quite complicated in the end. Because of his character, he was often the butt of the jokes, but he always took it in good heart. We knew all about him because, like Terry Mac, he had played against us for Newcastle in the 1974 FA Cup Final. Alan came in as an orthodox left-back who was always ready to get forward, although it was often head down and full pelt. We always used to say that while Al didn't know where he was running, neither did the opposition and so it could cause a bit of havoc. When he went on one of his runs we used to say 'open the gates,' but he was all part of that great blend.

I mentioned his nicknames. Of course, the fans would call him 'Barney' after Flintstones character Barney Rubble. It was to do with his broken nose and rugged looks. We called him 'Bungalow' at first 'because he had nothing upstairs.' Then it became 'Moony' because the Moon is a balloon.

Then someone noticed a columnist in the Daily Mirror called Belle Mooney and so Al became Bell. Then it was extended to 'Belly'. Confused? Football is full of these strange little quirks. I'll give you an insight into some of the other nicknames later. Alan was great in the dressing room where he was always a good natured and likeable lad. He was an excellent defender who used his pace to good effect. Later, of course, he would become part of European Cup folklore in his own right.

We had a great squad and we were scoring goals galore. The Sun newspaper, later to become reviled in Liverpool after Hillsborough, put up a £50,000 challenge that season for any team who could score 85 goals. Of course, that became something for us to aim for. We went on an unbeaten run of 11 games. The next match was against our arch-rivals Everton. They were to stop us in our tracks at Goodison. It is a day fans will remember for one famous incident at the end of the game. Blues' goal hero Andy King was on the cinder track on the final whistle, being interviewed for that night's Match of the Day. An over-zealous policeman grabbed him and threw him down the tunnel because he had been told to keep that area clear. This was our first derby defeat for seven years. It used to give me great delight on derby day to hear the Liverpudlians chanting: 'You'll never beat the Reds.'

I used to give tremendous stick to Everton's Mick Lyons, who was a mate of mine. We always used to have a friendly fiver on the derby and I was quids in. Sadly for Mick, he didn't play in the game in which they finally ended their hoodoo and so we didn't have the usual wager. He was gutted.

After this setback we played Leeds at home and it took a Terry Mac pen in the last ten minutes to give us a draw. These were unusual blips in an otherwise outstanding league campaign. We were straight back to winning ways after that with a 3-1 win at QPR. I remember a fantastic Boxing Day at Old Trafford where 55,000 people saw Ray Kennedy score after just five minutes. We were in complete control and won 3-0. It showed the capabilities of the side we were becoming.

After the Everton game we would only lose two more league games to the year-end, against Arsenal on December 2 and Bristol City on December 18. They must have been a decent top-flight team at that stage to beat us. It was in the middle of all of this that the club named a new captain with Emlyn Hughes in and out of the team. They turned to Kenny Dalglish and I must admit that I was a bit miffed. So were some of the others. Terry Mac could not understand the logic and nor could Phil Neal who said: "I just can't understand it, Thommo. It is your right to be captain of this football team."

I suppose no one has a right. You have to earn it, but I had worked hard and had hoped that my chance would come with Emlyn's games few and far between. I don't think Kenny took to being skipper, but I still began to question myself and wondered if it was to do with my lifestyle. Bob Paisley was a wily character and I wondered if he had heard all the stories about our nightlives. We were young and we loved to have a great time. Bob would say that when things started to interfere with your game then he would come down hard on the individuals concerned. I was thinking: "Maybe it's my lifestyle that is stopping him from trusting me with the captaincy."

I remember one specific incident in the dining room at Anfield. We had been out the night before and I can distinctly recall picking up this spoon and trying to eat some tomato soup. It's strange how a bowl of soup can provide a defining moment in your life, but it happened that day. My hand was shaking as I tried to lift the spoon to my lips. It was the first time I had realised that I was not getting the balance right between football and the social side.

I had met Marg, my wife, in the summer of 1976. We began courting and gradually got closer. It meant I was not going out as much with Terry Mac and the lads. The 'shaker' with the soup had made me look closely at myself and I thought: "I can't carry on like this. It's wrong for a professional footballer. It's definitely wrong for a potential captain who has to be a good influence on people. This is not what a captain does".

I decided to do something about it. I had a good girlfriend and said to myself: "This is where I want to go. This is the direction I want to take." Things didn't change overnight, but my life started to come together in a different way. I was 25 and finally settling down. Instead of more nights out with the lads it was more nights out with my girlfriend. It's funny how things stick in your mind. I later relayed this story to Gerard Houllier. He knew that I could look some of our young players in the face and know if they had been over-doing the social bit. Not too much passed me by. When I saw lads over-indulging it was like looking in a mirror and I felt I could speak to them in a way they would understand.

We were powering to another title and a significant day in my life suddenly arrived. It was quite unexpected. Emlyn had been back in the side for another spell, playing at left-back with Phil Neal on the right and Jocky Hansen and myself in the middle. Then Emlyn succumbed to another injury that was to finish his career with Liverpool. It was April 7, 1979. An hour before our home game with Arsenal Bob Paisley started to name the team. I was fully expecting Kenny to be captain, but Bob turned round and said: "Phil, you will lead the team today."

I was stunned. I always thought my chance would come, but not on that day. I never asked Bob or Kenny about the change of heart. Certainly, Kenny was not one for talking to the Press or doing things like that. He kept to himself. I was so proud and I will never forget what happened next. The lads knew what it meant to me. I couldn't get in touch with my family to tell them the news although I knew my brother Owen was in the Kop while my other brother Ian and my mum and dad were in the stands. I felt like saying to Bob: "It's about time too," but I just beamed because I was so thrilled.

I couldn't wait for the call to go out and when it came I bounced to my feet to lead the lads into the tunnel area. I was feeling ten feet tall and had no problem reaching up to touch the 'This Is Anfield' sign, feeling extra special as I did. I glanced at my captain's armband and then it was up and out on the pitch. I had made sure we were out before Arsenal and sprinted towards the Kop where I knew Owen would be thrilled to see me making my debut as skipper. I tried to pick him out in that same position where we always used to stand together in the early days. There were loud cheers, but the crowd were also laughing and I thought: "What's going on?" Then I spun round, suddenly realising that I was the only one on the pitch. The lads had held back in the tunnel and were all killing themselves laughing. I was so excited I hadn't noticed. It was one hell of a wind up, but I was happy to be the butt of this particular joke. More to the point we won 3-0 and so that made a wonderful day even better.

We were to lose just one other game between then and the end of the season. It was at Villa Park two weeks later. Incredibly, they beat this masterful Liverpool side 3-1 and that proved our biggest defeat of the season. No one had done that to us before. After the game we came into the dressing room defeated and gutted. I was really down because I had scored an own goal. Bob had a bit of a go at the team. Then he turned to me and in front of all the lads said: "Is the captaincy too much for you? Is it getting to you?"

I was stunned and came back with two words. "Fuck off." He said: "What do you mean, fuck off?" I said: "If you don't think the captaincy is right for me, take it back!" Bob had this way, now and again, of stirring you up. He was looking for a response and he got it. The lads were all smiling later and Terry was doing his famous Paisley impersonation. "Is the captaincy too much? What do you mean, fuck off?" Knowing how the staff worked, they liked you to show spirit. They never wanted you to just accept things. Whenever there was a ruck, it was soon quickly forgotten as we got on with the challenge of winning matches. Having the captaincy was the best thing that ever happened to me and, despite my response to Bob, I wasn't going to suddenly give it up without a fight. I wanted to hold trophies above my head.

As a local boy and a Liverpudlian, that meant so much to me. I also felt I was right for it. I was vocal. I was motivational. I hated defeat. I felt I could read the game and was in the perfect position for a captain. I even thought it was my right and my destiny to skipper the Reds. That may sound big-headed, but anyone who knows me will tell you that I'm not like that. I'm the opposite.

That is why Bob's retort hurt me so much. To support the club as a kid, to come from the Kop, to come through all the teams and then to be made captain was very special to me.

I would keep the armband and after the Villa reversal, we got back to winning ways the following week with a 1-0 win over Bristol City. It was not the most inspiring of games, but the victory was crucial. We then had a couple of away draws before finishing the season with a real flourish, winning the five remaining games with 13 goals for and only one against. We were champions with a couple of games to spare and fittingly beat Villa 3-0 at home to claim the trophy.

This capped an unbelievable League campaign. I had never felt so good and so confident before every game. I felt we could score at will, home and away.

How my wife Marg caused a Sunday League riot – and the pride of England

After winning the League title against Villa I was chatting to a couple of friends, Paul Orr and his brother Joe, about their Sunday League team in Kirkby called Fantail. They were a very good side and had reached the final of the National Sunday Cup, a major achievement. They were due to play another pub team, Twin Foxes, at the Hitchen FC ground near Luton. My interest in Sunday football is well known and I was still involved with my own team, Falcon, at this time.

We had won the Championship and had a bit of a celebration and so I thought it would be a good idea to go down and support Fantail. My wife Marg wanted to come as well as my brother Ian. We thought the journey would take two-and-a-half hours but it took over four in the end as we tried to find this small ground that had an embankment on one side.

It was a nice grassed area and as it wasn't too packed the three of us, plus Joe Orr, sat down to enjoy the game in the sunshine. It was all very enjoyable and I was admiring the midfield skills of John O'Leary, who is something of a Sunday League legend. People were saying: "Look at the size of him" and it's a fact that John does resemble the image people have of a typical Sunday League player. However, he is a class act and was giving his usual masterful performance in midfield, just sitting in there without any need to run around while pinging these passes all round the pitch.

People around us were making the usual jokes about Scousers and the ale was flowing with no real sign of a problem. Then Fantail scored, much to our delight, and the banter began to get a little bit nearer the knuckle. With five minutes to go Joe thought it would be a good idea for us to make our way down towards the clubhouse. People had spotted I was there and a lot of people were gathering round with the atmosphere deteriorating rapidly.

We stood up and all of the opposing supporters started to throw abuse in our direction. One close to me shouted: "You big-nosed Scouse bastard!" My wife Marg had a telescopic umbrella in her hand which, when closed, resembled a handy truncheon. She whacked him over the head with her brolly. It was an instinctive thing, but it was to cause mayhem.

We had to run with a hundred people chasing after us. Young Joe was trying to push us on towards the clubhouse as bottles and glasses began to rain down. We swept round the corner, Marg still clutching her truncheon, and shouted to the stewards to let us in. I looked at Marg and she looked at me. We were untouched. Then we looked at young Joe and he had blood running down the back of his head. A bottle must have caught him.

It was meant to be a tranquil, relaxing day out. I said thanks to my wife. She was defending my honour, but let's just say it all got out of hand. We had to stay in the clubhouse for hours after the game. We ended up celebrating with the Fantail lads and it got so late that we booked ourselves into a hotel that was not the best, but which provided a bed to sleep off a remarkable afternoon

I did not get back into training the next day until noon, a couple of hours late. I looked at Joe Fagan. He knew where I had been because his son had played in the game against the Twin Foxes and he had told him. It was not a problem and Joe just said: "Get your kit on and have a run round the track." It was another bit of Sunday League folklore and one that people in Kirkby, the home of Fantail, still recall.

We had the League won and then went up to Middlesbrough on May 11. We had agreed to help out one of the old Boro players, Willie Maddren, who was a friend of Graeme Souness. Willie was opening a sports shop and Bob agreed it would be okay, especially as it was midweek. The shop was packed and we were happily signing autographs and mingling with people. It must have been a massive attraction and more and more fans piled through the door. Willie was overjoyed, or so we thought.

After about an hour, with about 150 people in this small shop, the floor suddenly gave way and everybody dropped about eight feet. There was David Johnson with his arm up in the air shouting: "Don't panic."

Kids were screaming and everybody was shocked as this hole opened up that was about ten feet square. Of course, we had the perfect man for this emergency. The Doc was administering plasters for any cuts or bruises, being the First Aid medic that he is. I suppose it could have been really nasty. What would have happened if any of the lads had broken an ankle? The Doc would have been in his element, but Bob Paisley would have been fuming. We went back to the hotel and it was all over the news. Willie Maddren's shop got massive publicity for all the wrong reasons. We just had to focus on the game and it was fitting that The Doc scored the only goal in a 1-0 win.

We now needed three goals in our final game to rip-off The Sun and claim that £50,000 prize for scoring 85 goals. It was a tough test at Leeds United. Bob decided we would drive up by coach on the morning of the game because it was fairly close. We produced a fabulous performance to win 3-0 and achieve our aim. Johnno was on fire and he scored a double, with Jimmy Case getting the other goal. I can remember Jimmy's celebration. He had his hand outstretched indicating five for fifty grand. It was just a laugh then.

Of course, much of the focus was on our goal feat, but what was also significant was the landmark record we set for goals conceded, a miserly 16 in 42 games with just four at home and 12 away. The back four of Phil Neal, myself, big Al or Emlyn and Alan Kennedy can reflect on that with real pride, not forgetting the magnificent Ray Clemence in goal. He was the best in the First Division, despite the claims of his England rival Peter Shilton. Clem was majestic, acting as my eyes and ears in the box. He could be unemployed for 80 minutes and then pull off a world-class save. What was amazing was that he was the worst trainer in the world. Shooting practice was a complete waste of time. I might as well have gone in goal. He just saved himself to play out in the five-a-sides.

We didn't mind. We knew what he would be like on the Saturday. As I said, I played in front of both Clem and Shilton for England, both great keepers, but I always preferred Clem. He played his part in that record 16 goals against achievement that will never be beaten because it was achieved over 42 games.

Incredibly, despite our dominance, we had gone out in the second round of the League Cup to Sheffield United and the first round of the European Cup to Nottingham Forest. The Blades hit us with a real sucker punch in a tie that was played almost entirely in their half.

Forest were not seeded by UEFA in the European Cup and that opened up the possibility of us being drawn together. We went a goal down at the City Ground. Normally, we would just retain our discipline. We never used to panic. However, we started to chase the game, possibly because we were up against another English team. Colin Barrett caught us out and we were 2-0 down. They held us 0-0 at Anfield and so the Forest jinx ended our hopes of three successive European Cups.

These setbacks definitely focused us on the two main domestic challenges, the League and the FA Cup in which we would reach the semi-final. We opened our Cup run in the January with a game at Southend. When we got to

Roots Hall there was six inches of snow on the pitch. The tie should never have been played. It ended up a bit of a lottery and we got away with a goalless draw before comfortably winning the return 3-0. We then beat Blackburn and Burnley before securing a tremendous 1-0 win at Ipswich Town where Bobby Robson had developed an excellent team.

This took us through to a semi-final challenge with Manchester United at Maine Road. Kenny Dalglish gave us the lead, but United hit back to equalise and then go in front. With just eight minutes left we were pushing for the equaliser and I suddenly found myself making a forward run in the inside-right channel after Terry Mac played me in. I slid and crossed this ball in about a foot off the floor. Instead of goalkeeper Gary Bailey dealing with it, he palmed the ball up. Who should be running in but my defensive partner Alan Hansen and he put the ball in the net with a side-foot volley, running to our fans on the Kippax side with us trying to catch him.

We now pressed for the winner, but just couldn't finish them off. In the dressing room afterwards, Bob Paisley just laughed and said: "What were my two centre-backs doing up there in the opposing box? I don't mind today, but don't do it again."

The replay was at Goodison Park. We were confident that we would not give United another chance, but Jimmy Greenhoff scored the only goal of the game to knock us out. It was to be a significant day in more ways than one. Emlyn Hughes played in the match, but it was to be his last for Liverpool. It was after this defeat that I was handed the captaincy.

Bob had made it clear that his first choice centre-backs would be Alan Hansen and myself. They must have sounded like harsh words to Emlyn, but as we all learn in football, reputations count for nothing. The man the fans had dubbed 'Crazy Horse' because of his surging runs would move on to Wolves, where he would have one last moment of glory by winning the League Cup.

For our part, we had to settle for the Championship, but what a famous success it was. On a personal note I returned to the international scene, albeit only for an England 'B' game against West Germany. It was still an important game with a lot of senior players involved. Bobby Robson was the manager and I was proud when he asked me to be captain. The pitch was covered in snow and the Germans compressed it with a roller to make it two to three inches thick. We could wear our boots, but we were told to blacken the bottoms with boot polish to give them more grip. I don't know if it was an old wives tale, but it helped us psychologically.

Terry Mac and David Fairclough were also in the side, along with John

Gidman who had signed for Liverpool before me, only to be released. We won 2-1 and the bonus was that Terry and David were the goalscorers, a great night all round for the Anfield lads.

We went into the 1979/80 season looking for our fourth Championship triumph in five years. The season didn't get off to a blistering start. Bolton held us to a goalless draw at Anfield on day one, but as things developed we would become untouchable again. The team was at its peak and we were so confident. We had a tight squad and very few of the established players missed games. I was delighted to complete all 42 league games for the first time. It meant my injury problems were behind me. I was one of three players with a full complement of league games along with Phil Neal and Kenny Dalglish. Ray Clemence and Graeme Souness missed just one and Ray Kennedy two. Alan Hansen played 38 games, with four players – Terry McDermott, David Johnson, Jimmy Case and Alan Kennedy – all on 37. To have 11 players each contributing 37 games or more indicates that the team was more or less picking itself. As supremely talented as Bob Paisley was, we almost didn't need a manager for league games. We were just cruising in the top flight.

David Johnson was quite prolific in this season. He scored 21 league goals and developed a fantastic understanding with Kenny Dalglish. What a dream opportunity it was for The Doc to be playing alongside Kenny, but no one should underestimate Johnno's ability. Bob was always going on about the importance of defending from the front. The Doc did not give defenders any time at all to dwell on the ball. He could tackle as well as any centre-back. It also didn't take him long to get wound up if people started kicking him.

In one game he was knocked out after taking a bash on the nose. He was dazed and groggy, but came straight back on with 20 minutes to go. The lads gave him stick because we had never seen The Doc looking so controlled and skilful. We were saying: "You should get concussed more often, Doc."

Of course, the old joke was being re-written that originally featured another Anfield striker, Tony Hateley. Tony was great in the air, but not too clever on the ground. In one game he was knocked out and when he came round, he asked: "Who am I?" Bob Paisley, as quick as a flash, said: "Tell him he's Pele." I'm not sure if it's true, but it was a little bit of Anfield folklore.

As the season progressed, the team was scoring goals for fun. We always used to talk about wobbly November, but we went on this run through to January without too many problems. In the October we had played a league game against Everton at Anfield. It wasn't a particularly good result, finishing 2-2, although I suppose that was a great result for our arch-rivals at that time!

I remember it for one big reason. I loved playing in derby games, probably because I hated watching them. I had some of my best moments in derbies, but I always had this fear about scoring an own goal. As a kid I had vivid memories of Everton's Sandy Brown scoring a classic o.g. with a full-on header. After that, every own goal on Merseyside, be it at Anfield, Goodison or in a Sunday League game, was referred to as a 'Sandy Brown.' What a tag to carry round with you. It was particularly cruel for Sandy because no one remembered the fact that he once scored an excellent derby goal for Everton at the other end. The other irony for Sandy was that his famous own goal came at Goodison in a famous Championship year for Blues fans, 1969/70.

I was at Goodison that day, standing with the Red Army in the Park End as Emlyn, the unfortunate Sandy and then Bobby Graham scored the goals that would give us a comprehensive 3-0 victory. I had played for the Liverpool 'A' team in the morning and was thrilled with our triumph. However, the image of Sandy's pain was something that was always in the back of my mind whenever I subsequently played in these high-profile matches.

An o.g. would be scored in this latest derby, played on October 20, 1979. The man who had that look of anguish on his face was none other than my best mate at Everton, big Mick Lyons. I remember that Terry Mac and myself used to meet him at a pub in Hanover Street in Liverpool city centre. The manager would give us a stay-behind and we had some great times. We became really good mates with Mick. He was the nicest, most polite guy you could ever wish to meet, but when he pulled on that blue shirt he turned into the Incredible Hulk. His muscles would start popping out of his shirt. Micky was a Blue through and through. They used to say he would run through a brick wall for Everton. That own goal was a massive personal blow for him, although the draw possibly helped him get over it.

Mick was a very good player. He could play at centre-back or centre-forward. He was inspirational enough to become club captain and was what we would call a player's player. Of course, many Evertonians preferred the flicks and tricks of people like Duncan McKenzie who were prone to giving the ball away, forcing lads like Micky to fight to get it back. There were times when people like Mick and his great mate Terry Darracott became the whipping boys when things went wrong, but here were lads who loved their club and I could never understand it.

I'll tell you what. Mick Lyons was a top-class defender. The fact that Everton did not win a major trophy at that time had nothing to do with his effort and commitment. He was as good as men like Dave Watson and Derek Mountfield, who would later win Championship medals in Everton's great team of the Eighties.

In the Anfield camp, we showed consistency in all positions during that 1979/80 campaign. Kenny Dalglish would finish with 16 league goals to back up Johnno's excellent 21.

Terry Mac contributed his normal tally of double figures from midfield and that figure did not include cup goals. The Championship would be ours once again and there was a regular debate about this possibly being the greatest Liverpool team of all time because of the things we had achieved.

In November 1979, I would go on to captain England, which I looked on as a wonderful honour. We were playing against Bulgaria at Wembley on November 21, but when we turned up the stadium was shrouded in fog. You don't see so much of it these days, but on this night you couldn't see from box to box. The match was postponed. If it had been a friendly, that would have been it, but it was a European Championship qualifier and so we gathered again on the Thursday. We had more or less qualified for the Finals in Italy and there was not much at stake, but any big match at Wembley is important.

We were in the hotel on the morning of the game and I heard that Kevin Keegan had been allowed to return to Germany because Hamburg had a crucial game on the Friday night against Stuttgart. Kev felt he wanted to give something back to Hamburg and manager Ron Greenwood did not stand in his way. I thought: "I wonder who will be made captain?" There were a few more experienced players than me in the squad, people like Dave Watson, not the Everton one but the big centre-back who used to play for Southampton. We were top of the First Division at the time and I hoped that might influence Ron Greenwood's decision.

He called me to one side and said: "Liverpool are going well Phil. You deserve to be captain of England tonight." I was buzzing, but I didn't know if I should tell anyone. On the coach going back from training Ron called for attention and announced: "The captain tonight, for the first time, will be Phil Thompson." There was a big roar from the lads, who knew how much it meant to me.

There was no instant SKY Sports News at that time to break the news. I managed to ring my family to make sure they were all coming down. I remember the occasion because Glenn Hoddle was making his international debut. It was a big night for both of us. For me to walk out at Wembley in front of 72,000 people carrying the plaque to exchange with the opposing captain was fantastic. The game was on TV and when I got home, people said to me that there was real elation in the local pubs and clubs when they saw me leading out the team. It was a proud moment for my family, including my mum and dad. I had now skippered club and country. I would be captain of the Reds for three seasons and this was wonderful. England won 2-0 that night and Glenn scored on his debut, so there was a lot to celebrate.

Behind our elation at winning another Championship was our total frustration in the European Cup, a competition we had won twice in a row in 1977 and 1978. We would follow that by going out twice at the first hurdle, which was a massive blow. It was no consolation that we were knocked out this time by one of the great Georgian teams, Dynamo Tblisi. They had this huge stadium and while we had secured a 2-1 first-leg lead at Anfield, we knew it would be tough away from home. We remained confident, but they proved unstoppable and murdered us 3-0 in front of 80,000 people. It was a massive blow to our pride because we did not believe lightning would strike twice in this competition.

The FA Cup that season would produce one of the funniest incidents I have ever witnessed at Anfield. We were paired with Grimsby in the third round. We would romp home 5-0 and it ended up like a testimonial. The Kop had one of those days for which they are famous. How and where these songs and chants come, I have no idea, but it always seems instinctive. I think the Grimsby fans might have started it by chanting: 'We only sing when we're fishing.' This triggered something in the imagination of the Kop. It started with 'Oh Jimmy, Jimmy. Jimmy Jimmy Jimmy Jimmy Jimmy Plaice.' We were all laughing. Sometimes you are so focused on the pitch that you don't hear things, but this was different. The next chant went up: 'Phil Seal, Phil Seal.'

It was like a challenge to the Kop and they began to work out some more fishy thoughts. We had 'Kenny Dogfish' and then 'Sting Ray, Sting Ray Kennedy.' When they started on the swordfish, Clem, The Doc and myself all looked round, not that our noses had anything to do with it. I thought: "We are not going there, surely."

It was a great night and the fact that 50,000 fans had turned up for the opening round of the cup against lower league opposition was astonishing. After this we were to play our old foes Nottingham Forest. Ironically, we would face them twice in a few days, the other game being the semi-final of the League Cup. The latter came first.

Forest were our jinx team and they had players who could wind you up. They could also be physical and we lost our first-leg game 1-0 at the City Ground on January 22. Four days later we gathered again at the same venue for our FA Cup confrontation.

We had a meeting and it was clear that we were determined to smash this so-called jinx. I have to say that we took gamesmanship to the brink. There was no way we were going to lose. We pressured the ref. We pressured the linesmen. Kenny Dalglish scored and Terry Mac netted a pen to make it 2-0. We thought that was the end of the Forest hoodoo, but they would hold us 1-1 in the League Cup return at Anfield to claim another place in the final.

People ask why they were so dominant over us at this time, despite the fact that we were all-powerful in the top flight. Let's be clear, they were good enough to win the title and the European Cup in their own right. They had a very good manager in Brian Clough who worked out a formula for beating us. It was like a boxer who defends and looks for the sucker punch. They defended deep against us with the logic that we might tire ourselves out and be vulnerable to a goal on the break.

Clough was not just a good manager, he was also a controversial character who could be outrageous at times as we would ultimately find out with his comments after the Hillsborough Disaster that I will deal with later. I remember following him once into the players' tunnel. Big Alan Hansen was a quiet lad in those days. Clough was just behind him and kept clipping our defender's heels. I told you that they liked to wind people up. Al kept looking round, but it didn't stop Clough. I started saying: "What the fuck are you doing?"

He never flinched, turning into their dressing room without a glance back. We heard stories after the game that he had possibly had one too many. Cloughie's problems in that area have been well documented. I have never seen anything like that tripping incident before or since. Clough felt he could do as he pleased in the game. He was a maverick character who was a good manager, but who over-stepped the mark in many areas.

Our League campaign was to tick along. We lost seven games that year against just four the previous year and only picked up 60 points, but it was good enough to polish off the title. What was particularly nice was to win it at home. We needed to beat Aston Villa on May 3, 1980 to clinch things and The Doc netted after just three minutes to give us the perfect start. Bob Paisley had always signed someone each summer to give us a further lift. This year had been a bit of a strange one because he had gone to Israel to sign international Avi Cohen. That was our first-ever contact with famed super agent Pini Zahavi. Avi was his first player.

Avi spoke excellent English. He was a real gentleman and found the hustle and bustle of the English game difficult at first, but he was a magician with the ball from left-back. In all, the Villa match was only his second full game and he was absolutely devastated when he scored an own goal to bring Villa level. However, he made amends after 50 minutes when he scored what could be described as the winner, even though The Doc added a third and Villa scored an own goal of their own to put us 4-1 in front.

Avi's wife Dorit was in tears when the Kop chanted his name after he wiped out his own goal with that crucial effort at the Villa end. David Fairclough and his girlfriend were going out with some other people that night and they took Avi and Dorit along with them. After a good night out they went back to Avi's house and because all the lads had been watching a cult TV series that featured a fat Australian cop called Bluey, they asked if it could be put on.

Avi looked a bit doubtful, but turned to Dorit and said: "Put the Bluey on for the boys." She said: "I don't think that is what they mean," but Avi said: "They are guests. Put it on." The lads suddenly realised that it wasn't the fat Aussie cop they were talking about. It was a Bluey of a different kind, but things must have got lost in the translation and they all roared with laughter as they explained who Bluey really was.

Another player who came to the fore at this time was a local lad who, like myself, had this tremendous pride in playing for the club he had always idolised. Little Sammy Lee was an absolute bundle of energy and passion who loved the club and loved his football. I can remember him playing in the staff games when he was just 16. Bob, Joe and Ronnie always wanted him in their side because he would run and run. The jokes about Sammy's height were inspired by himself. Like me, he learned that it's better to poke fun at yourself rather than letting others have a pop at you. Of course, the famous chant was: 'He's fat, he's round, he bounces on the ground, Sammy Lee, Sammy Lee.'

When Sammy was our first-team coach at Liverpool I remember Patrik Berger going down with a knee injury right in the bottom corner in a game at Upton Park. Gerard Houllier said: "Sammy, go and help the physio." Sammy sat there. Gerard repeated: "Sammy, he needs help and we need to know what is happening."

Sammy stood up and set off to try and reach Patrik. He had to go down one side, across the back of the goal and down the other side. Suddenly every West Ham fan in the stadium started the chant: 'He's fat, he's round, he bounces on the ground, Sammy Lee.' I was to get my come-uppance later when fans caught on to the 'Pinocchio' thing, but we had not heard the Sammy chant for years and we all roared with laughter. He was a top guy, a super player and an excellent coach. Later he would become a very close friend.

In that 1980 Championship season it was Lee the player who was beginning to emerge and I was delighted for him when he played in the last five games as we secured our crown. With Steve Heighway dropping out of things with just a couple of starts and several appearances as sub, the manager now had a new nucleus of players who would help him drive things forward. These included Terry Mac, David Johnson, Ray Kennedy and Alan Kennedy who had each had their settling in period but were now key members of an outstanding team. It was all bearing fruit.

We continued our FA Cup run after seeing off Grimsby and Forest, beating Bury and Tottenham before having four semi-final games against Arsenal. We battered them at Hillsborough, but it finished goalless. We then drew twice at Villa Park, again having great chances to go through. Finally they beat us 1-0 at Coventry's Highfield Road where Brian Talbot scored their winner.

We were gutted because the final should have been within our grasp. These were the days when games went to a replay after extra time. You will never see four games played now. Possibly that marathon encouraged the FA to look at alternatives like penalty shoot-outs.

I was to finish that 1979/80 season on a high. I was now established in the England set-up and heading to the European Championships in Italy. We got some good scalps that year. After being captain against Bulgaria we played the Republic of Ireland at Wembley and won 2-0 in a qualifier. We then played a couple of friendlies before we set off for Italy. We beat Spain at the Nou Camp where I had once scored for England in the Mini World Cup. It had been a lucky venue for me because Liverpool had beaten Barca there in the '75/76 UEFA Cup semi-final. It was fate that I would have another happy day there and we beat Spain 2-0.

Then, on May 13, we played against world champions Argentina. It was my first sight of a young boy who would become one of the best players in the world, Diego Maradona. He was only 18 at the time, but he had previously ripped the Scots to pieces. Because Argentina were such a big name, we were really up for this friendly. England had a good sprinkling of Liverpool players – Clem, Phil Neal, David Johnson, Ray Kennedy and myself as well as ex-Red Kevin Keegan.

Maradona was short and stocky, but he could leap like a gazelle, had immaculate ball control and was so quick off the mark. He danced past four of us and only had Clem to beat. In one movement he knocked the ball past him. The ball went inches wide of the far post. If it had gone in, it would have been as good as the goal he later scored against England in the World Cup, the famous Hand of God game. After the match, a tremendous 3-1 win for England, he was probably rushing to get my shirt, but I'd already swapped with Leopoldo Luque of River Plate who I had been highly impressed with in the 1978 World Cup. Johnno had been on fire in the game and he scored two. I don't know if he got Diego's shirt.

We then went to the Home International Championships, only to be brought down to earth by Wales at the Racecourse. I was captain again in a side that showed several changes. Joey Jones, who by now had returned to Wrexham, was in the Welsh side. I sliced the ball past Clem for an own goal and Joey was highly delighted. It was a game in which Larry Lloyd, now at Forest, made his only England appearance. I was not too concerned about that, remembering his famous shout to Bob Paisley at Melwood when I was only a kid and a ball sailed over my head. "A real centre-half would have got that," said Lloyd cynically, annoyed that he was out of the first team. I never had much time for him and I wouldn't lose any sleep about his one-game England career, even though I lost a bit about my own goal that night.

We then had another disappointing result when we drew 1-1 with Northern Ireland at Wembley. Because of those two results, everyone was thinking that the game against Scotland at Hampden Park could relegate us to the wooden spoon position, especially with 85,000 Scots baying for our blood. But we were fired up and ready for the challenge. Ray Wilkins came into the side and The Doc partnered Paul Mariner of Ipswich Town, who was an aggressive bugger. I remember we were banging on the dressing room ceiling and walls to tell the Scots we were ready. I was thrilled to retain the captaincy and we beat them 2-0.

Kenny Dalglish was playing for Scotland and Ron Greenwood said to me: "You know how to play him. Don't get too close to him. Stay far enough away to see what he is doing." I understood Ron's logic. Kenny loved it when defenders got right behind him. He would stick his backside out and lever the space to turn them. My solution to the big arse syndrome was to give myself enough space not to allow him to turn and play passes behind me. Ron had emphasised this to us all, but he said to me: "Thommo, you know what he's like. Get round him in the box."

Trevor Brooking and Steve Coppell scored our goals and we were flying. I remember Andy Gray coming on for the Scots in place of Roy Aitken. What I still couldn't understand about the Scots was why they continued to overlook Alan Hansen for Miller and McLeish. All the talk at that time was about the

Anglos and the Scots and the problems in the squad. More about that later.

We went on to the European Championships in Italy and set up base in Sorrento near Naples. A number of the wives and girlfriends had planned to come out and stay not far away. We had used the England Travel Club to book the girls' accommodation. We had been training for about six days when they arrived and wanted to go down and check they had settled in okay. Their hotel was supposed to be about ten minutes drive away, so we got a taxi and set off.

The driver took us all round the backstreets. We seemed to be going for ages, right into the heart of the old town. Finally, he dropped us off in front of a load of terraced houses. We looked at this poky little hotel. If it had been possible, it would have been graded minus one star. We couldn't believe this is where the girls were and went inside to enquire about them.

We went through a tiny restaurant that had food all over the floor and eventually reached the rooms where the girls were all gathered. You couldn't swing a cat in any of them. We were disgusted, but Marg and the other girls tried to make light of it. They played things down because they didn't want to upset us. The England team hotel we had left behind was five-star and built into a cliff. In the distance was the beautiful Isle of Capri, but there was nothing glamorous about this hell-hole. This was supposed to be a holiday for the wives and girlfriends, but there was no pool and nowhere to sit and relax.

We went back and told the other players what it was like. Some of the staff found out and Ron Greenwood called us together. He said: "Boys, I hear you've got a bit of a problem." We explained that the girls were in this ramshackle hotel that was booked through the England Travel Club and said it was scandalous that this should have happened. I said that the only bonus was that Rigsby of 'Rising Damp' wasn't on the reception. Ron just said: "Leave it to me."

We went training, but I was worried about Marg as well as Phil Neal and Clem's wife who were also there. Later Ron called us together again. He said: "Tell the girls to pack their bags. They are coming over here to join us." To be fair, the girls had not complained. They just wanted our minds to be on the football, but Ron knew the importance of the players being totally focused. He insisted that the girls join us in our five-star accommodation and they stayed there for the duration. It was a fantastic gesture by Ron and the FA.

We played Belgium in the first game and drew 1-1. It was probably more famous for the police firing tear gas canisters into the crowd. The gas wafted across the pitch and Ray Clemence was down on his knees with his eyes streaming. The match had to be stopped for ten minutes. Later UEFA selected two players to undergo random drug tests. Who should get called but Messrs Thompson and McDermott. The heat was oppressive in June. I was really dehydrated and struggled to provide a sample, especially with two officials standing over me. Of course, 'T' had no problems in the urine department. After all, he once managed to do it in front of 60,000 fans on the steps of Picton Library, a story we have already recounted.

He was out of the door in a flash, saying: "See you Thommo." I continued to sit there. They had the taps running to try and encourage me. Not a dribble. I was four hours in an empty stadium and in the end was walking round with bottles of beer in my hand, still tracked by these officials. I ended up half pissed before I finally produced my sample four hours later. Everyone had gone. The lads thought it was hilarious when I eventually surfaced.

The result was disappointing, not least because we had to play host nation Italy in the next game. They beat us 1-0 in a very physical encounter. We then played Spain and I think we had to win 7-0 to stay in the tournament. As it was, we won 2-1 and so that was the end of our Championship.

The girls were still at the hotel when the team flew home. We asked the FA if we could stay on and they agreed. We were there for another three or four days. The thing that sticks in my mind is that Terry Venables and Bobby Robson, who were scouting for England at that time, were also there.

I was in the pool with Marg and we were playing keepy-ups with our heads with a ball. We were getting up to 30 or 40. Terry was impressed, not with my skill but Marg's. He didn't realise at the time, but I had actually met her when I was reffing a women's charity game and she was playing for one of the teams, Leeside Ladies from Kirkby. She was actually a midfield player and her team was quite good. They were leading 7-0 in this match, so I handed over the ref's whistle and started to play for the opposition who were less experienced. Marg's sister Pauline was having a go at me for playing for the other team.

This was the first time I had set eyes on my future wife. It must have been her dribbling that impressed me! Anyway, whenever I meet Terry Venables his first question is always: "How's your wife's heading ability?" People always wonder what the hell he is talking about, but it always brings back memories of that European Championship, Rigsby's Hotel and Marg's obvious talent with a football. Shame Terry never mentions my ability!

We started the 1980/81 season with a trip to Wembley for a Charity Shield clash with West Ham. In those days we travelled to London the day before by train and on the way down I began to get a throbbing pain in my jaw. As the night wore on it became increasingly painful and at midnight I was forced to call Ronnie Moran and Joe Fagan to my room because I couldn't get asleep.

They realised that something would have to be done straight away and contacted the hotel reception. Around 1.30am a taxi pulled up outside and the three of us clambered in for a journey through the dark streets of London that took about 25 minutes. Eventually we pulled up in this mysterious tree-lined street that had houses on either side resembling those in the Addams Family TV series. We were driving slowly trying to spot the right number. We must have looked like kerb crawlers.

Eventually we spotted the address we had been given and told the taxi driver to wait. It was quite spooky walking up to the front door and ringing the bell. We tried to make a joke of it and someone said they expected Boris Karloff to answer. Eventually we were allowed in and went into this room that was as dark and dismal as the exterior of the building.

In the middle of the floor was a dentist's chair and to the right was a rough looking sofa on which Joe and Ronnie perched themselves, giving me that look that suggested we were about to play a lead role in a horror movie. I assumed the dentist's chair was for me and sat down. Years later Gazza would make the 'dentist's chair' famous as an England goal celebration, laying back while the lads poured liquid into his mouth. My experience was clearly not going to be based on elation, but something very different.

This guy appeared wearing a white tunic that only had the top three or four buttons fastened, simply because his pop belly was protruding from below that point and hanging over his belt. I looked at Joe and Ronnie and they didn't need to say anything. Their wide eyes were declaring: "It's Boris!"

Dr Karloff, or whoever he was, said: "I need to look in your mouth," and he started probing with these steel utensils. "Looks like an abscess," he added quickly. "It will have to come out."

He looked at Joe and Ronnie as if to seek their permission and they just nodded. I don't think any of us had said a word. I muttered: "I just need to get it sorted," and he immediately started to scramble around in this draw, pulling out a large needle that he proceeded to jab into my gum. Nothing was sterilised. He went back into what looked like an old toolbox and I looked again at Joe and Ronnie. They were trying to look calm so as not to frighten me, but I was getting increasingly worried.

Boris tested the gum to ensure it was numb and then started cracking my tooth with what looked like a pair of pliers. Within seconds the tooth was out and I saw what looked like a large blob on the end. I assume this was the abscess. I then started thinking: "Has he taken the right tooth out?" Clearly my confidence wasn't high.

I was still in agony when Boris got this gauze and stuffed it into the hole in my gum. No gloves or anything. I was like a rabbit caught in headlights, but I managed to splutter out a few words. "Have you got the tooth?" I asked. It wasn't that I needed it to put under my pillow for the fairies although the thought did cross my mind. I don't know why I asked. Possibly I wanted it for evidence at the inquiry I was sure would follow. Anyway, this guy starts scrambling through his drawers trying to find the offending tooth without any success. Then he looks on the floor and under the chair without success.

"Sorry about that," he says and disappears with all the skill of a vampire rushing to get back to the coffin before the sun comes up. We headed for the door and the waiting taxi. It was not exactly the kind of preparation you would want for a Wembley appearance, but we were soon back at the hotel where I finally managed to get a few hours sleep. I have to say that Boris had done a good job. When I awoke the pain had all but gone although I was a bit groggy because of the tablets I had been given.

I still played in the game and we beat the Hammers 1-0 in front of 90,000 people with a goal from Terry Mac. It was exactly the start we wanted although that 1980/81 campaign, while being legendary in its own way, was one of mixed emotions.

We started well enough with a 3-0 home success over Crystal Palace. However, this was to be the year of stalemates and 17 draws in the league were to prove costly as we fought to retain our title. It was also a season in which we used a lot of players, 23 in all, because of a multitude of injuries. Only Phil Neal managed a full complement of 42, which was the expected norm for him.

Sammy Lee would come in and make the number eight shirt his own with Jimmy Case in and out of the side. Names like Avi Cohen, Richard Money, Colin Irwin and Howard Gayle would appear on the team sheet. Kevin Sheedy made his debut and Ronnie Whelan played his first game for the club.

In mid-November we went to Crystal Palace, having hammered them at Anfield. I was looking forward to the game. I remember their goalkeeper kicking the ball deep into our half. It caught in the wind and looked as if it would clear me. Clem's positioning was always perfect in these situations and I expected to hear him. Then I'm thinking: "Where are you, mate?" He must have back-peddled and then suddenly realised he needed to come for the ball. In doing so he absolutely clattered into me as the ball went out for a corner.

I was off my feet when contact was made with my eyes focused on the ball.

I landed on the corner of my shoulder and felt this almighty crack. I looked up, saw Clem and said: "Just leave me." Straight away I instinctively brought my other arm up to protect the damaged shoulder. Ronnie Moran came on and put his hand under my shirt. Almost immediately I felt the collarbone slip out of place. I was in agony as they carried me off on a stretcher.

Joe Fagan took me to the nearest London hospital where I had to sit in the public waiting room with everyone else who was waiting for treatment.

The pain was still excruciating. I was a bit conspicuous to say the least, in my red kit and football boots.

People were looking at me and then this male nurse came over and said: "Phil Thompson of Liverpool. Can I have your shirt?" Joe Fagan said: "Fuck off, you idiot. Can't you see the boy is in agony and you are asking for his shirt."

They took X-rays and it confirmed the dislocation. All they can do in this situation is put your arm in a sling. I walked out, still in my kit, and we got a taxi back to the Palace ground where the game had just finished. We then boarded the coach to try and make the 6.30pm train. The coach was flying round these minor roads to beat the traffic. Every time we went round a corner I could feel the bones grinding together. We made it with ten minutes to spare.

The injury was a real setback for me. I was hoping all of my problems were all behind me, but it was symptomatic of the club in general that year. We had a lot of injuries. Colin Irwin would come in and partner Alan Hansen at centre-back. Phil Neal played in that position. I returned and started with Colin Irwin. The team was in turmoil and we ultimately finished fifth, our lowest position for ten years.

I remember the derby game that unfolded at Anfield in March, 1980. With 13 minutes to go Everton's John Bailey glanced a header into his own net from a corner. Jimmy Case saw 'Bails' in a club that night and shouted: "Okay John which way are you heading?" John was not amused.

I was to make my comeback from the collarbone injury at Manchester City in the semi-final of the League Cup in January. It was successful although I can remember going to take a quick throw-in and having to leave the ball because I realised I could not get my arms right over my head.

I played just two more games and was ruled out again with a thigh strain. I couldn't shake things off and was in and out of the team. The draws and inconsistency continued and the fans were naturally unhappy, but the all-round injury situation was significant.

However, we would reach the League Cup Final and this was pleasing because it had been something of a jinx competition for us. The date was March 14 and I was still out injured, leaving Ray Kennedy with the chance to become the first Liverpool captain to pick up this particular cup.

I was gutted to have to sit on the sidelines at Wembley, especially as I had been so close to a return. With neither side able to break the deadlock, the game went into extra time and I wondered if it might go to a replay.

Then Alan Kennedy scored and I thought my chance of being involved in a second game had gone. Incredibly, Ray Stewart snatched a late penalty for the Hammers, forcing a replay on April 1 at Villa Park.

I was thrilled to be back and leading the side although I wasn't quite so happy when Paul Goddard gave West Ham the lead.

However, for the next 40 minutes we produced some top-class football and turned things round to win 2-1 with goals from Kenny Dalglish and Alan Hansen. Big Al's was a bit of a deflection and some suggested it was an own goal but being a centre-half, we were kind to him. Even Hammers' manager John Lyall admitted that he had never seen a display like it for a long time. It meant a lot to us after the season we had endured.

The result gave us our first League Cup triumph, but it would be the first of many. I would no longer call it the 'Mickey Mouse Cup' and put memories of that spoof trophy, made years earlier by my Evertonian brother-in-law, firmly out of my mind as I led the lads forward to collect the trophy. However, I was faced with the Mickey Mouse scaffolding platform instead.

This had been erected to enable the players to get from the pitch at Villa Park to the stand where the presentation would be made. It stretched over the paddock.

As soon as we stepped onto it, the plywood below our feet started shaking. I thought it was going to collapse. However, I soon had the cup in my hands and was really proud to be the first Liverpool skipper to achieve that.

A young man by the name of Ian Rush had played only his second game. He had taken some time to settle after joining us from Chester. He finished up with nine starts, but incredibly he never scored in any of them.

Even though Ian had joined us from the lower divisions, he still came with a great reputation for finding the net. Like many before him, he had to spend time in our reserves finding his feet.

I knew we had a very good player on our hands as I watched him perform that night at Villa Park.

There was one through ball that he turned on in one movement before crashing in a shot that came back off the crossbar.

All of a sudden, any nerves he might have had seemed to disappear. I thought: "This boy can play."

He finished the season wearing the number nine shirt that would become his own. In a wider sense we had the League Cup in the bag, but something more fantastic would follow.

It was the glory that was Paris, not Rome!

THOMMO
Chapter 8

European Cup ecstasy – then chasing the victory parade in an ice cream van

O
ur 1980/81 European Cup run started in style with an 11-2 first-round aggregate victory over Finnish side Oulu Palloseura.

It was embarrassing in as much as the first leg finished 1-1. Then we hammered them 10-1 at Anfield. Hat-tricks in the European Cup always look good on your c.v. and Graeme Souness and Terry McDermott both achieved that feat.

We then faced the so-called 'Battle of Britain' against an Aberdeen managed by Alex Ferguson, who had not yet achieved knighthood status at that stage. Nevertheless, he was idolised in the Granite City where he had developed a team good enough to win the title ahead of Rangers and Celtic.

He relished the prospect of trying to knock Liverpool out of the biggest of all cups. What he didn't realise was this was not just an England v Scotland club affair. We had three extremely proud Scots in our team and Messrs Dalglish and Souness had brought back the stories of the divisions in the Scotland international dressing room between the Anglos, the Scots who played in England, and the Scots who stayed north of the border. It was mainly Alex McLeish and Willie Miller who were proving to be a thorn to our lads at get-togethers. They were also helping to keep out Alan Hansen and we thought they were not fit to lace his boots.

We therefore had these lads who were so intent on winning over the two legs. Graeme used to have a lot to say in the dressing room. Kenny didn't say much. Big Al hardly said a word at that stage. He did all of his talking out on the pitch, yet he was going round shouting: "Make sure we beat those Scottish bastards. We must win."

I couldn't believe it. This was a sign that we simply could not lose. Barring an early flurry by Aberdeen at Pittodrie, there was not too much to worry us and Terry Mac again scored one of the goals of the season. I have already described it earlier, but I'm happy to repeat that it was a classic in which he chipped Jim Leighton with his weaker left foot from the angle of the six-yard box. As a goal it was technically as good as you will ever see, but Terry had a habit of doing that. It gave us a 1-0 advantage to take to Anfield that demoralised Alex and his team.

There was no let-up in the return leg. Big Al, Kenny and Graeme were even more up for it before the game and they wanted a top performance from everyone. I found it quite funny. I was vocal, but Alan was putting me to shame. I was amazed by Al. He even scored the fourth goal in a 4-0 victory. Willie Miller's own goal fittingly started the rout after 37 minutes and Phil Neal scored just before half-time. Kenny popped one in midway through the second half and Al polished them off with 19 minutes left. The Anglos and the English were elated.

We met CSKA Sofia in the third round and blitzed them 5-1 at Anfield in the first leg with another Souness hat-trick. Sammy and Terry also scored so it was a good day all round for the midfield lads. A David Johnson goal away confirmed our superiority.

All this was going on against the backdrop of our mixed league form. Possibly this focused us more on the European Cup, which we desperately wanted to win for a third time. Bayern Munich stood in our path in the semi-final and it was a goalless stalemate at Anfield, a result that must have lifted their spirits. However, their failure to score away from home actually gave us the edge, backed up by some ridiculous comments in the German press made by Bayern's international star Paul Breitner. He could have been a Scouser with his perm and moustache! He said that we lacked technical ability and that this lack of creativity meant we had no chance of coming out on top in the Olympic Stadium.

It was a red rag to a bull. It was always going to be a huge game, but his words really fired us up. The one problem was that we still had injury worries. I did not play because of a thigh strain and Alan Kennedy was missing. Richard Money came in at left-back, while Colin Irwin played alongside Hansen in my position and was outstanding on the night.

The Reds would grab a 1-1 draw that would see us though on the away goal, but it was the performance with comparatively inexperienced players slotting into the back four that was really encouraging. As I said, Colin was cool, calm and composed. Nothing used to ruffle him. Sometimes you wanted him to get a little bit angrier, but he could look back on this display with pride.

There was a moment of real hilarity on the bench in the build-up to Ray

Kennedy's crucial 83rd-minute goal that proved the match winner. We got a bit of a breakaway and the ball went to The Doc who was limping at the time. Bob Paisley screamed: "Has anyone got a gun? If I had one I would shoot him now and put him down." Bob had these little sayings, not least for players who limped which he didn't like, even when you were genuinely injured. He would say: "I'm not kidding, if he had shit in his eye he would limp."

Thankfully, there was no gun to hand and The Doc had nothing in his eye because he found Ray who promptly stuck the ball in the back of the net. The Germans stepped things up to grab the equaliser, but we were home and dry.

Of course, this night would be legendary for another Paisley masterstroke that was rewarded with a sensational substitute's performance from winger Howard Gayle, who came on to replace Kenny Dalglish who was injured. It took a lot for Kenny not to finish a game and he was almost impossible to replace. However, Bob realised that Howard could run the tiring Germans ragged on the flank. He was a player who could catch pigeons, he was so fast. Howard also had an aggressive edge to his game. His introduction changed the whole course of a tie that might have gone the Germans' way.

Howie took the game to Bayern. He was getting the ball and running 50 yards with it, leaving two or three players trailing in his wake. The methodical Germans only had one solution and that was to kick him. He didn't mind the first couple and got on with the job in hand, but the more they tried to boot him, the more he started to react. Howard, as was his way, started to take revenge. He'd done a great job to rattle the Germans, but the wily Bob knew that if he didn't take him off he might be sent off. Howard the sub was subbed himself by Jimmy Case, but he had done himself proud and no one will ever forget his impact that night.

On the team coach we were singing all the Liverpool songs as the Bayern players walked past. We made sure we raised the volume when Breitner walked past. It was a fantastic experience, even though I was sidelined.

The 1981 European Cup Final was probably the greatest personal football moment of my life. It was the all-whites of Real Madrid versus the all-reds of Merseyside. What a confrontation. The Spaniards had built up a sensational European Cup record, but now we were the dominant force. I was talking to my brother Owen and kept saying: "Do you think it will be me picking up the trophy?" He just replied: "There won't be any other outcome."

Having given it the great build-up, the match itself was awful with both defences dominant, but in these games it's the winning that matters. As Shanks used to say: "First is first and second is nowhere." His famous words always drove us on and Bob and the other staff had carried this logic through. Madrid had bought England's Laurie Cunningham who was a skilful winger. He took in-swingers from the right-hand side with his right foot. This entailed him clipping the ball with the outside of his boot to bend them into the defenders. Normally, you would use a left footer to do that. This had become a big talking point in Spain where he was making a name for himself.

I always said we enjoyed ourselves, even in the heat of battle. I remember David Fairclough taking a corner once against Crystal Palace and kicking the bottom of the corner flag. He made the slightest contact with the ball that rolled over the line for a goal kick. Terry Mac was howling with laughter and we had players on their hands and knees. The Whip went as red as his hair.

Something happened in the Parc des Princes in Paris that caused a similar reaction. Ironically the pitch was awful. They had rolled either side of the lines all over the pitch and they were subsequently raised. This ball came to me and I prepared to clear it with my right foot. It suddenly hit the line of the box and jumped up about three feet. I headed it and ran through a couple of startled Madrid players. Alan Hansen was roaring with laughter to the side of me.

As it turned out, it would not only be my day as captain, but Barney Rubble's day, as the fans called Belly. He raced through onto a throw-in from Ray Kennedy. I'm sure the stewards, in anticipation, opened the gates at that end of the ground. Alan could have passed inside to David Johnson, but he took the decision to shoot which was a good one. Who in their right mind would pass to The Doc that far out?

Alan hit the ball perfectly and as it hit the net he kept on running towards the Liverpool fans at that end with the rest of us taking chase. I immediately started to think about my dream of picking up the European Cup. The sight of the Liverpool fans celebrating was incredible. It could have been tense, but we saw out those nine remaining minutes with ease.

All the lads used to laugh and joke that the staff only had three substitute numbers – 10, 9 and 5. Bob would get out his fishing rod and more often than not it would be Terry Mac. We could see Jimmy Case warming up on the touchline. Sammy Lee had done a great man-to-man marking job on Uwe Stielike in midfield. He was going to stay on. We were all looking at The Doc and wondered if Bob would sacrifice an attacker to accommodate Jimmy. Then the number 7 went up and everyone thought it was April 1. He was taking off Kenny Dalglish. Even to this day Johnno can't believe it. He is thrilled that he was given the chance to stay on longer than King Kenny in a European Cup Final.

I went up to get the trophy. It was a proud moment and I was desperate to get my hands on that most famous of trophies. The official who was up there started to talk to me. He suddenly got hold of the cup and I thought: "He's going to lift it." I gestured with my hands as if to say: "Just give me the cup." I had managed to get tickets for all the lads from my Sunday team, Falcon. They were all in a row at the front with their flags. When I lifted up the European Cup, they were the first I showed it to because I knew exactly where they were.

It was a superb trophy, a real cup and not like some of the others we have seen down the years like the dreadful Canon League thing that once replaced the magnificent League Championship trophy for the benefit of the sponsors. The European Cup was world-renowned. To get the opportunity to lift it was amazing. The scenes of joy as we came down the steps were remarkable.

It makes me giggle when I see our celebrations. We had to put stickers over the Umbro sign on our shirts and shorts because of UEFA rules. They had put no money in the UEFA kitty and so we were told we had to blank out the logos. The lads used to get a few quid for featuring those logos if we won a trophy and some were not going to miss out. They ripped off the patches, even from the start. I had to leave mine because I knew I might be pictured with the cup.

The celebrations afterwards were superb and we all went back to a hotel in the centre of Paris. Some of the lads took the trophy to the famous Moulin Rouge, but I stayed at the main reception with my family and we had a tremendous evening.

It had been agreed that we would tour round Liverpool on an open-topped bus on the Thursday, something we always looked forward to. You look at images from these nights and they are truly remarkable with fans stretching as far as the eye can see.

Terry Mac and myself used to always position ourselves upstairs at the back with a crate of beer for us and bottles of wine for the girls. It was a party on wheels. I always felt the bus would sometimes go too quick for the fans to get a proper view. If we stood at the back it meant the fans could see us even as we disappeared into the distance.

We were well round the circuit and approaching the junction of Queens Drive and Utting Avenue, the turn that leads up to the stadium. This point was always heavily congested with supporters. Obviously there were no toilets on the bus. The lads could use a bucket, or whatever, but the girls and wives had to cross their legs. Marg was desperate to go at that point and I said: "As we make this turn and the bus slows, we are going to jump off and ask if we can use a toilet in one of the houses along Utting Avenue." It was chocker leading up that stretch to The Clarence pub.

We got off and Colin Irwin's girlfriend followed us. We saw these people in a garden, cheering the lads. They were shocked to see me off the bus and even more surprised when I asked if we could use their toilet. Of course, it wasn't a problem. They said: "Upstairs, second on the left." I don't know if the girls were powdering their noses, but it took quite a while and when we got back outside the bus was disappearing under the railway bridge in the distance and out of sight.

I had to think what to do. Suddenly an ice cream van came along the road and I jumped out in front of it. It was like a scene out of a 'Carry On' movie. The driver was stunned to see the Liverpool captain waving him down. I said: "Do us a favour mate, give us a lift." He said: "No problem, but you'll have to climb in through the hatch."

Now if you've ever bought an ice cream you'll know that the serving hatch is quite high up and about four feet square. My missus was wearing a pair of trousers. No problems there as I pushed her up onto the counter and the guy pulled her through. It was a bit more difficult with Colin Irwin's girlfriend. She was wearing a short skirt and the crowd that had begun to gather gave a cheer as she was hoisted in. Then I had to climb through the hatch myself. It was a bizarre moment as I shouted: "Follow that bus."

So it was that Mr Whippy roared up Utting Avenue with his chimes going like some sort of comic police car in pursuit of the European Cup. We needed to get ahead of the coach and so when it went straight across towards Walton Breck Road and the Kop, we turned right down Anfield Road and then took a left on two wheels with a full load of lolly ices crashing round in the freezer.

Having got back onto Walton Breck, I stood in the middle of the road with my hands in the air and the police escort looking totally stunned. The lads on the top of the bus shouted: "Where have you been?" They would never have believed me if I'd said: "For a number one, a number two and a ninety-niner!"

Instead, I waved to my unlikely travel companion in the nearby van and as the team bus and the European Cup went on its way towards the city centre, Mr Whippy went in the opposite direction doing a roaring trade.

We settled down upstairs at the back alongside Terry. I just said: "Don't ask," but it was a fantastic story and we roared with laughing as we continued down Everton Valley. Marg was constantly grabbing hold of my belt to stop me going over the top as we continued to lean over and wave to the crowd along the route. I kept seeing lads from the Falcon, the Kirkby pub whose

Sunday League team I managed. I kept shouting: "See you back there later." This would lead to a remarkable incident in its own right.

After we had won the League Cup in the April, chief executive Peter Robinson said to me: "Do you realise the trophy was left on the bus last night? You are the captain. You should have taken it home with you."

Those words were ringing in my ears as we stood on the steps of the Picton Library holding up the European Cup to thousands of Liverpudlians gathered in the city centre.

We'd completed the tour and hailed our magnificent fans. Now the coach was taking us back up to the Melwood training ground to get our cars. The lads asked if I'd prefer an ice cream van for transport, but I settled for the team bus.

When I got off I picked up the European Cup. There was no box for it, just a big velvet bag. I walked across the car park and lifted the boot of my Ford Capri. There were no Mercedes then, no Daimlers or giant Four Wheel Drives. I drove the car and the cup straight to the Falcon, opened the boot and walked into the pub clutching this big velvet bag. There were lots of families in there and most of my mates.

When I took out the European Cup the place was in uproar. Of course, no one expected it. They had a couple of our Falcon Sunday football trophies behind the bar and they edged them to one side so that I could give one of the world's most famous football trophies pride of place. People were ringing their friends saying: "They've got the European Cup at the Falcon." You can imagine being on the other end of the phone saying: "How much have you had to drink?"

I was rather drunk myself, having partied throughout the tour of the city. People were picking up the cup and having their pictures taken with it. It was soon closing time and I said: "Bring the kids down tomorrow and they can all have their photos taken with the trophy."

I then held the European Cup above my head and walked out to another roar from everyone in the pub. When I got home I put it on the sideboard. It looked fantastic. Then I went to sleep. The next thing the phone is ringing. I felt really rough and said: "Who is it?" A familiar voice said: "Phil, it's Peter Robinson. Have you got the European Cup?"

I closed one blurred eye and saw the gleam of a trophy. Peter said: "The world's Press are waiting. We need it straight away." I just said: "Yes, Peter," but I still took it down to the Falcon at 11am as I'd agreed for a more important photo call. There were babies sitting in the European Cup. Some of those babies will be 25 now, but I bet there are some fantastic souvenir pictures out there.

I finally got the trophy back to Anfield at noon. Peter Robinson was fantastic. The Press and the TV cameras had been forced to wait, but he fully understood. We had some more official pictures taken with the cup. As I said, just holding it made me feel the proudest person in the world.

I had been involved in some great team performances in my time, but this was the pinnacle after a traumatic season with injuries. During that campaign I had played in two World Cup qualifiers for England. We beat Norway 4-0 at home and lost to a ridiculous penalty in Romania. I had then been ruled out through injury and it had been a dodgy time to see if we could qualify for the World Cup Finals in Spain. After Liverpool won the European Cup, England had a game on the Saturday against Switzerland. I was not involved and when the team lost 2-1 there was more criticism from a disenchanted public.

The squads had been confirmed for Switzerland and the following match against Hungary. My name was not included, but then Ron Greenwood came on and asked me to join them for the crucial Hungary clash. It was a special occasion for English football in the famous NEP Stadium. Ron took me to one side and said he wanted me to operate in a sweeper's role and so I had to change my game slightly. It turned out to be a fantastic night for me.

Ron had brought back a lot of experience, using his old guard to try and qualify for Spain. We beat Hungary 3-1 in their own backyard where they were usually rock-solid. Trevor Brooking scored a famous goal in the top corner, his shot sticking between the stanchion and the back of the net. Many papers gave me the man-of-the-match plaudits and I was thrilled to have come back and made such an impact.

However, all of this elation suddenly disappeared when Ron made a shock announcement to the lads on the plane that he was packing up. He had taken a lot of criticism in the battle for us to qualify. Kevin Keegan was very forthright. He got all the players together and we told the manager that if he packed in, so would we. We had respected what he had done for us, both on and off the pitch. He was a special man and he would do anything for his players. He was also a very good tactician. Our stance moved him and he decided to stay on.

It was a good end to a memorable summer after a topsy-turvy First Division season. I then had an even bigger match on June 20 – my marriage to Marg. We had been courting for five years. She had mended the error of my ways and become my soul mate. She put me on the straight and narrow and it's the same to this day. We were married at St Joseph's Church in Kirkby by Father Jimmy

Collins, who was a great Liverpudlian. It was a special day in a special year.

We had no distractions going into the 1981/82 season in the shape of the Charity Shield. The year before had been unusual in that we had won the European Cup, but failed to make an impact in the League and FA Cup.

In his usual way Bob Paisley would set about keeping people on their toes with some additions to the squad. One signing that set things running in my mind was the acquisition of Mark Lawrenson from Brighton. Mark was a versatile player who was comfortable in a number of positions. However, his best role was probably centre-back and Bob's logic was probably linked with the injuries that Alan Hansen and myself had both suffered although the focus was more on me – despite the fact that I had recently lifted the European Cup. This was a bit of a wake-up call, but I have to admit that it was a shrewd signing on Bob's part as most of his transfer dealings were.

In the first game the boss pulled a bit of a surprise at Wolves. Al and myself were retained in the middle with Lawro at left-back. Alan Kennedy was the one to miss out and he was not happy. At least it indicated to me that Bob was ready to give me a chance to prove I could maintain my productive partnership with Big Al without any further injury problems. This defensive set-up was only to last three games before Alan Kennedy came back with Lawro dropping out. I was to hold down my position although I had mixed emotions about the start of the season.

I felt my performance level was not great, even though I did not miss a game right through to January. Lawro apart, there had been another significant bit of transfer activity in the summer. We had signed a new keeper in the shape of Bruce Grobbelaar from Vancouver Whitecaps.

After the European Cup Final, Ray Clemence had made a significant early statement that he wanted to move on. A deal seemed to be done very quickly with Tottenham Hotspur. There had been speculation about Grobbelaar even before the European Cup Final and I believe a newspaper reporter told Clem that the Zimbabwean international was coming to Anfield as the number one.

There was no way Clem was going to play second fiddle to another keeper at that stage of his career. Possibly before Bob was given the chance to explain, Clem was off. He had been one of the elder statesmen within our team and someone I looked up to. It left a big hole in the squad as far as I was concerned. Ray Clemence was as much a legend as a Liddell, a Hunt or a Keegan in my book. He was immense as a goalkeeper and got on with his day-to-day routine without any fuss.

Defenders, particularly those in the middle, require a telepathic relationship with the man between the posts and vice versa. You rely on each other in a massive way. Clem's transfer would prove an even bigger blow as the season wore on. I had to forge a new understanding with Bruce which was difficult. Let's just say he was eccentric where Ray was rock-solid. That doesn't mean he wasn't a good keeper. He was just different.

I knew Clem's game inside out and he knew mine. Bruce was certainly agile and could do some unbelievable things, but he could also be erratic. This uncertainty did not help the defensive unit. It was strange because Clem was not over the hill by any means as his subsequent career with Spurs would prove. It was difficult to find out what was going on in the Boot Room at that time, even for the club captain. I had my own worries over Mark Lawrenson. Maybe Clem had seen something and realised it was time to move on. He was older than me.

The change between the posts certainly caused a fundamental change to how we operated as a back four. To say the first six months were difficult is an understatement. I have to say that Bruce became a great friend. He was trying to understand how we did things, but during that spell I spent more time on the goalline than I had ever done before which was very unusual for me. At times, on the edge of the box, I would get bowled to the ground, not by some strapping centre-forward but by my own goalkeeper. It was this confusion that brought a certain amount of instability to the side, although Bruce would go on and win countless honours in his own right in the end.

Of course, another view could be that I was not playing well or the back four was not performing as a group. It just seemed coincidental that the change of keeper had caused this uncertainty. The team was up and down. I had retained my place alongside Big Al, but was going through the worst time in my whole career during this spell.

It didn't help that we had the shattering news on September 29, 1981 that the great man, Bill Shankly, had died. I have already explained how I felt when he left the club, but this was something else. Shanks had been everything to me. I was always his protégé as the last one he brought through the ranks. After he retired he used to ring me. When I had injury problems, I would get a nice phone call and after a short chat I would feel a million times better,

I remember coming into Melwood after he died and spotting that Sammy Lee had been crying. He only knew Bill as a fan, but it summed up how the death of a legend had rocked the whole football club. It was strange because we were to play Swansea in our next home game on October 3, managed by John Toshack, who had been one of Bill's most successful signings. The teams lined up at Anfield before the game for a minute's silence as a mark of respect. As the ref blew his whistle to signal the silence, Tosh peeled off his top to reveal his old Liverpool shirt underneath. It was a wonderful gesture and one that was recognised by the whole crowd.

These days I tell Shanks stories to my kids. I tell them of the legend and what he did for Liverpool FC. All that came from a humble background as he brought us from the old Second Division to become one of the most respected clubs in the world. It's nice to see Shankly banners at Anfield even now. People will never forget him.

Back on the field of play we had a diversion from a mixed league spell when we went to Tokyo to play Flamengo in the World Club Championship that was always between the South American and European Cup holders. It was a marathon journey to Japan, broken by a stopover in Alaska. To beat the boredom on the plane, we played shoot pontoon from start-to-finish. The other passengers thought we were crackers. I remember that Terry Mac and Alan Hansen were sitting together. We were all having a few drinks on the plane when the food arrived, plus a pouch containing the cutlery.

Big Al started putting carrots and cauliflower in this bag and laying it on the baldhead of the man in front, who was fast asleep. It was a bit mischievous and Bob Paisley saw what was going on, even though he was further down the plane. He didn't miss much. He was screaming: "You are going to get us thrown off!" That was rich at 40,000 feet above sea level! Joe Fagan still had to tell the lads to behave. Bob had made it clear that he wanted no controversy on or off the pitch. He wanted nothing to damage our credibility or reputation.

I remember the game very well. This would be the first time ever that we wore our names on the back of the shirts. The pitch, however, was brown and looked burnt. Nottingham Forest had previously played for the World Club Championship in Tokyo and Brian Clough had commented: "The Japanese are amazing people. They are the most technically gifted workers in the world. They can make the smallest radios and the smallest TVs, but they can't make grass!" It was a fair point.

I remember Bob asking me if I was fit. I was carrying three stitches in a foot injury and he had Ronnie Moran testing me to ensure I could kick the ball right on the stitches. I was still captain at this time and determined to try and pick up another piece of famous silverware. I was never going to pull out.

We played well for 20 minutes, but then Flamengo clicked into gear, inspired by Brazilian superstar Zico, who was called the 'White Pele'. They ran   out

3-0 winners and it was a demoralising defeat. Bob Paisley admitted that he got our minds wrong for the game and that we had treated the whole affair like a bit of a break.

I remember we went to this three-tier golf driving range. They are built this way because of the lack of open space in Tokyo. It was an incredible sight and we all went with a bag of 'bats' to show our skills. Of course, we were on the top tier and Big Al, a great golfer, was driving the ball hundreds of yards. Some of the lads had been to the joke shop and bought these balls. When you made contact smoke would come out of the back like an Exocet missile. The Japanese didn't see the funny side because they take their golf seriously.

We went back the next night and took Howard Gayle, who wasn't a golfer. He swung at this ball and it rolled a few feet and then dropped off the edge of this high platform. What was more hilarious was that his driver went about 20 yards off this third tier and landed on the range. We carried on lashing these balls as far as we could and the next thing we see Howard down below us on his hands and knees, crawling like a commando to try and retrieve his club with all these golf balls whizzing past his head and the Japanese going berserk.

We definitely went out there with the wrong attitude and we got punished for it, but the fun did not stop. Terry Mac had bought this other trick in the joke shop. It was a piece of wire with a ten-dollar bill attached to one end. You had this little button in your hand and when you pressed it the wire recoiled like lightning to pull in your note.

We watched in Alaska Airport as Terry caught out one sucker after another. We were all in bulk. He would sling the bill ten yards away. You could not see the wire because it was so fine. Someone would stroll up, see the bill and casually try to pick it up. Terry would press the button and it would disappear. It's amazing how such a simple toy kept us all amused for about two hours. This Japanese businessman was caught out and he thought it was hilarious. He sat amongst us as Terry set the trap time and again. My kids have just bought one and every time I see them use it, I see Terry and hear the squeals of laughter coming from every player in that Liverpool squad.

Back home our mixed league form culminated with a 3-1 home defeat against Manchester City on Boxing Day. We never played well as a team, but I had a nightmare day. It all went wrong. The next game was an FA Cup clash at Swansea, who were in the top flight at that time, having been inspired by Tosh and a couple more Liverpool ex-players in Cally and Smithy.

We were determined to get going and I was looking forward to the game. It was the usual preparation and I can well remember being on the team bus on the Friday morning going from Melwood to Anfield after the final training session. I was sitting halfway back with Terry Mac and Joe Fagan came back to say: "Phil, the boss wants to see you in his office when we get back." Ray Kennedy overheard this and said: "I know what it's all about." I said: "Tell me now if you know." Ray said: "They are going to take the captaincy off you."

It was not a nice way to find out something like that. Ray was like that. If he had some info he couldn't keep it to himself and he added to the intrigue by saying: "I know who the new captain is going to be." I replied: "Are you going to tell me?" The truth was, I didn't need telling and didn't flinch when he said: "Graeme Souness." My cynical reply was: "There's a shock."

I remember Terry Mac saying Graeme wanted the captaincy to make the most of it for himself. I had my own thoughts and as soon as I got changed I went to Bob's office. I didn't bother with the small talk, pinning him down straight away. He said: "I'm taking the captaincy off you for now. I think you need something to help you with your game. You are taking too much responsibility on your shoulders."

It was true that when we conceded a goal, I would put my hand up and say: "If I was in that position we could have done this or that." However, my response to Bob was: "I don't agree with you, but because you are the manager I will accept it." The way he had phrased it, the situation was not cut and dried but there was no way he could take the captaincy back off the new man which brought me to my next outburst. I said: "Who are you giving the job to. No, let me tell you. It's Graeme Fucking Souness isn't it?"

Bob was not a great communicator and he choked on his words. I said: "I knew it was him", and stormed out of the office. I was furious. He knew what it meant to me. He had a real understanding of my pride in being skipper. I had held aloft the European Cup only months earlier. Not only was the captaincy taken off me, but I had to find out from a teammate.

Let's just say the season was not going well. You get bits and pieces of grumbling at any time, but this was different. I had this idea that things were going on behind my back. Bob's words kept ringing in my ears. "I think it will do your own game a lot of good without the pressure of the captaincy. Concentrate on getting your own game right and that will benefit the team."

Bob was clever and knew what my reaction would be. I would be positive and aggressive. This is what happened although for two months I just ignored Souness. One day the lads were going for a walk. We were in two groups and I was walking with Terry, 20 yards behind the Graeme Souness group. He came back and started to walk alongside me, saying: "We need to talk." He said: "I had nothing to do with you losing the captaincy." I said: "Okay" and he repeated: "I wanted you to know it had nothing to do with me."

That broke the ice. On the pitch I just got on with it, which brings me back to the Swansea game. All week the papers had been full of the captaincy business. You can imagine what that was like for my pride. I focused on the game because it was a potentially tricky tie. Many people were tipping us to go out, but we produced a majestic performance.

I can remember sitting in the dressing room and Souness standing up to lead the lads out for the first time. Instead of being first, I decided to go out last. Joe Fagan was still in there and he just looked at me with that familiar gaze, and said: "You have got to make sure you do a great job."

I glanced back and said: "You'll get 100 per cent. When I'm out there with my teammates Souness will get my full backing, but don't ever tell me what to do when I'm off the pitch."

As it turned out, I had my best game of the season. Bob Paisley got it spot on. It had bucked me up and bucked up the team. We won 4-0 and then it was back to league affairs. We were 12th at Christmas and from that point won 19 of the last 20 games to win the League title.

However, my problems were not over. We met Barnsley in the newly-named Milk Cup and they took us to a replay at Oakwell. Two minutes into this game I collected a ball about six yards from the touchline. I took it further out to clear and their striker Colin Walker dived in from five yards and took me late. His studs hit me right in the calf.

Straight away I knew something was wrong. I put my hand to the back of my leg and Ronnie Moran ran on to ask: "What's up?" I said: "I think it's cut." Ronnie moved my hand and that revealed a massive rip in my sock. I put my middle finger in there and it was embedded in a gash about an inch long and four inches wide, just above the Achilles. There was no blood. Ronnie said: "We will have to get him off the pitch." They took me to this cramped treatment room and this big doctor came in. He looked at the wound and said: "This is a nasty one. Just lie down there."

I thought about 'Boris Karloff', who had taken out my abscess and was relieved to see that this doctor at least had some sterilisation stuff. I saw him take out some material to stitch the wound and I asked the obvious question: "Are you going to inject me?"

He said: "No need, you won't feel a thing" and he was right. I received ten stitches and all I could feel was a slight tug as he pulled it all together. I found out later that the lad who did it was a binman in his previous life. Of course, I had a right go with the Press and was a bit disrespectful, but it was not very good for me to be facing a lay-off, especially with the team getting back on its feet. The World Cup was also not too far away. At that moment in time I didn't know how bad it was or how long I might be out for. My injury gave Bob the opportunity to bring Mark Lawrenson and Alan Hansen together. I was looking at it and thinking: "Is this the shape of things to come?"

My treasured number four shirt had actually gone to Alan Kennedy, who had returned at left-back. Swansea would get their own back against us in mid-February with a 2-0 win at the Vetch Field. I was watching from the sidelines trying to recover from my injury. However, the team would only be beaten once between then and the end of the season. We were also making good progress in the Milk Cup and a semi-final victory over Ipswich Town set up a final challenge against Tottenham on March 13, 1982.

A week before the final I played a couple of reserve games on the comeback trail. The staff would always say: "Keep yourself ready just in case," but you tended to think this was just toffee to keep your spirits up. However, never a truer word was said because Alan Hansen damaged his ankle in a 5-1 league win over Stoke City and straight away he was out of the final.

Talk about someone throwing you a lifeline! It was astonishing. I took my place in the side at Wembley, but we were losing 1-0 at half-time. Then Ronnie Whelan scored a very good equaliser, his first goal of the season. It is part of Anfield folklore that Bob told all of our lads to stay on their feet in the moments before extra time, with the Tottenham players all sitting or lying down. If you look at the video you will see that I started that logic. I thought: "There is a huge psychological opportunity here." I went round and said: "Don't sit down. Look at them. They are knackered. They are finished."

We always felt we were the fittest team around. Shankly had also taught us to make the ball do the work. He would say: "Save your energy." That is what happened at this crucial moment. We could not wait for the game to get underway again. Ronnie was to score his second and Ian Rush polished Tottenham off. Having struggled for years in the League Cup we had now won two successive finals.

Bob Paisley made it even nicer when he came up to me as we gathered to go up for the trophy. Because the competition had become the Milk Cup two trophies were up in the Royal Box, including the original silverware. Graeme went up to collect the sponsors' Milk Cup and Bob told me to collect the League Cup I had lifted the year before against West Ham. It gave me a tremendous lift and from there until the end of the season I remained in the side, but wearing the number six shirt. Alan Hansen found himself wearing the eleven with Alan Kennedy pulling on my old number four. It was a very strange numbers game at the back, but I was just thrilled to be injury-free again and in the side.

Lawro's versatility came through when he played in midfield and it all came together as we put our previous season's league form behind us to regain the title. Our final home game brought us up against our Milk Cup opponents Tottenham and we conjured up the same scoreline. It was strange to see Ray Clemence in the opposing goal.

I remember that Glenn Hoddle scored a sensational goal at the Kop end that day, but Lawro's header in the 51st minute gave us a lift before Kenny grabbed the lead soon after. Ronnie Whelan tied it up with three minutes left and the stadium erupted as we celebrated another famous Championship win.

The first person I went to was Clem at the far end of the pitch. It had been a big decision for him to move on. Bruce Grobbelaar had secured his first Championship medal and there is no doubt that Ray could have continued and claimed another one for his collection.

It had been a strange season and one that got my mind scrambled about what was happening and what was to come. It was also a year when a couple of new lads started to make names for themselves, two in one position. Ronnie Whelan and Kevin Sheedy were both looking to claim the left-midfield berth that had once been the undisputed property of Ray Kennedy. Ronnie and Kevin both had great ability. Possibly Sheedy was ahead in the pecking order, but Ronnie took his chance when it came with his rival injured. Kev was always more left-sided, but Ronnie had special qualities of his own and came into the side at the same time as a young Ian Rush. Both would be almost ever-present from mid-October.

They became and remained great friends. It was nice to see and they would become a great part of the Liverpool set-up. I had experienced the peer factor and the unwritten rules that young players have to observe. These were two up and coming stars who looked to see how things were done in the first-team dressing room.

We nicknamed them 'Tosh' and 'Vitch'. Naturally Rushie was Tosh. He couldn't score a headed goal at one time and then got four on the run. I remember he scored against Athletic Bilbao and because he was Welsh we tagged him with the famous name of the great John Toshack. He still gets it even now. Irishman Ronnie had this habit of saying 'dust' instead of 'just.'

Because of that he became 'Dust' and then 'Dusty'. We changed it depending on the foreign opposition. When we were playing in Romania or Bulgaria he would become 'Dustovitch' or 'Dustovan' if we were in Holland. It all started going like that. Dustovitch stuck and then he became 'The Vitch' although it would change to 'Dusto' if we were in Spain. I told you football nicknames were strange.

What great players they became. Ronnie Whelan had that classic desire to win. He was a great athlete and scored loads of goals from midfield. We had generations of players who could do that, like Terry Mac and Ray Kennedy. Ronnie was equally prolific.

Then there was the young and gangly Rush, who couldn't score in his first nine games and then couldn't stop. He was a fantastic player who was always cool under pressure. He had this telepathic relationship with Kenny a la Keegan and Toshack. It's fitting that 'Tosh' lived on in the Liverpool team.

Kenny never seemed to play the ball to feet. He would play it into the space ahead of you and it was inch perfect to run on to. Rushie could take the Mickey and give it back and it was nice to see another couple holding their own in the dressing room and continuing the legend.

We beat Everton home and away that season. Although we dominated them down the years, we had not claimed a league double over them since 1972/73. This was also Craig Johnston's first season after joining us from Middlesbrough. He was a strange but likeable lad. He was into his cars, music and photography. That has gone on into his life. He came up with the idea for the Predator football boot and hundreds of people must have laughed at him. Craig had the last laugh and he must have made a fortune from that project. He could be quite eccentric.

There were all these stories of how he paid his own way from Australia to go to Boro. Now here he was, playing for Liverpool. He was a bubbly character and you could never knock him down. Craig had a lot of confidence in himself and he needed that as he bided his time to get in the team. It wasn't until the March that he finally had a run in the side.

Through all the turmoil of this year Johnno was to make way for Rushie, which was not a bad swap when you put it in the context of what was to come from Tosh. The Doc and Rushie actually became great friends and they are still big mates.

The European Cup was strange that 1981/82 season. We were paired with the same team we had demolished 11-2 on aggregate the previous year in Oulu Palloseura. This time we only managed a 1-0 win away, but stuck seven past them at home. We then played AZ '67 Alkmaar from Holland in the next round. They had a great Dutch player called Johnny Metgod and it was a good result to draw 2-2 over there with goals from Johnson and Lee.

We made hard work of it at home where the score was 3-2. Things were not going too well at that time and this match epitomised that six-month spell. The ball came in high from the right on the edge of the box. Bruce did not collect it, but punched clear and the ball fell to Metgod some 30 yards out. He was very dangerous in these situations and with the keeper out of position I sprinted back towards the Kop goalline as Metgod struck this shot. It was a dipping volley and I was face-to-face with the Kopites as I ran towards goal.

The ball hit the underside of the bar, came straight down and hit the laces of my boot, rebounding straight into the net. I was looking at the faces of the fans as this unfolded. I couldn't do anything about it, but I was devastated. Alan Hansen got a goal with five minutes to go and we won on aggregate, but it was not the best of nights for me.

We then met up with CSKA Sofia again. The year before we had given them a 6-1 aggregate hiding. It was not to be this time. We won 1-0 at home, but lost 2-0 away after extra time and there were murmurings of discontent with people pointing the finger as our European Cup dream came to an end. Our League and Milk Cup double would turn things round, but it highlighted the standards we had set ourselves.

Of course, things happen that put everything into perspective and just before we beat Tottenham to secure the Milk Cup, Marg gave birth to our first child Philip. With Marg in labour I missed training. Nothing was going to make me miss the birth. People say: "What is it like? Is it the same as winning the European Cup?"

The birth of your first child is incredible, especially if you are fortunate enough to be there. I'm not ashamed to say that I broke down in tears when I saw him. He was breech birth as well, which can be difficult and you are helpless. I just wanted to be there with Marg and it was an emotional roller coaster ride seeing her go through the labour.

That night I went to bed early and was up at 6am to catch the train from Lime Street to London to link up with the lads. I got there as they were starting lunch and obviously they wanted to know what we had called the baby. I proudly declared "Philip Glen" and Ronnie Whelan immediately said: "Oh, Little Teabags." Ronnie saw my surprise expression and added: "PGT, PG Tips!" Typical of the mindset of footballers and all of those nicknames I have talked about.

With the 1981/82 title won, I set off to join up with the England squad for the World Cup Finals. The home internationals had been staggered in the build-up. We played Northern Ireland in the February and Wales in the April. As the build-up continued we had a convincing 2-0 victory over Holland before we prepared for the historic 100th game between England and Scotland. That was great and the game saw the coming together as a partnership of Terry Butcher and myself. I was unsure who I might play with. Southampton's Dave Watson had been edged out and I had been paired with Steve Foster. Manager Ron Greenwood was asking me who was the best one for me to partner.

I found this strange, but I went through the merits of the various candidates. Terry was this up and coming centre-back who was a left-footer while the others were all naturally right-sided. Terry had that aggression I liked and he loved heading the ball. I felt I could work off him and he got the most plaudits from me. We played a Scotland team that featured Kenny Dalglish. Once again Ron Greenwood said: "Same again. You know what to do. Don't get too tight on him."

Big Al and Graeme Souness were also in the Scotland side and both countries were going to the World Cup in Spain. Although this was part of the Home International Championship with more important games to come, we were still fired up. We had learned to look the Scots in the eye and be as aggressive as them. We claimed a fantastic 1-0 victory with a goal from Paul Mariner. We now had strong characters in the side like Mariner, Butcher, Bryan Robson and Kevin Keegan. A 1-1 friendly draw with Iceland followed with more of a second team out. We then met Finland in our final game before the World Cup and produced a resounding 4-1 victory.

Prior to the tournament itself Kevin Keegan was having problems with a back injury. A couple of days before we left for Spain he was not at a training session and it transpired that he had taken a private plane back to Germany to try and sort things out. I started to think: "Who will be named as captain if Kev is missing?" It continued to spin round in my mind.

The FA had done really well in organising things and we were stationed in Bilbao where everything was right. However, because of the Basque security situation there were police everywhere as we moved about. When we went on the bus to the training ground we would have four security vans in front and four behind with motorbike outriders on either side. On one occasion we got stuck in the centre of a jam in town. The police piled out of the vans and surrounded our bus with their guns at the ready. It was quite a sight.

Of course, we just got on with our preparations at what was a quaint training facility in the hills above the town. We could still see tanks with people looking out of the turrets while clutching machine guns. When you went over by the fence to collect a loose ball, you could see the heavily-armed security guards. It was like being in an eastern European country, but we got used to it. The Spanish government did not want to take any chances with such a high-profile tournament taking place in their own backyard.

We were to meet France and it was lashing down ahead of the game. Then we woke up on the day and it was clear blue skies and a truly fantastic day in the middle of June. Kevin had still not returned and Ron Greenwood came up to me and said: "Phil, I've had to make a big decision about the captaincy between you and Mick Mills. You are two of our most experienced players. I am going to make Mick skipper."

I had always taken that honour before and Ron saw my disappointment. He said: "This will probably be Mick's final big tournament for his country." I thought: "Why should that make any difference? It should be about the right person doing the job."

No disrespect to Mick, who was a great player but it was one of the few times that Ron had disappointed me. Mick led the team against the French who had real quality with the likes of Michel Platini orchestrating things in their side. At our final training session we were practising set pieces. Full-back Kenny Sansom had this enormous long throw that could penetrate deep into the box for the big lads like Butcher to meet. Bryan Robson suddenly said: "Stevie Coppell can also launch them."

Lo and behold, just 27 seconds into the France game Bryan was to score the quickest goal in World Cup history. The ball was played straight into the corner where the French conceded a throw. Coppell sent in this long throw and Bryan turned Butcher's flick over the line. What a dream start.

Just before half-time they got an equaliser when Soler raced through to score. That brought them back in the game in the intense heat of the San Mames Stadium, which was very much like an English ground. We went on to claim a memorable victory, but I recall that my ears popped in the last ten minutes and we were all absolutely drained because of the heat.

The staff had weighed us before the game and we were put back on the scales at the end. Paul Mariner actually lost a stone-and-a-half just in fluids. I lost half a stone. The medical staff were astounded. They were getting cold water down us and putting cold towels over our shoulders and heads. I don't know who got called for the doping test that night, but it would have been

Perm any one from three, but notice the one in the middle, taken after our Christmas night out with a white-faced squad. Three great teams

With mum who is giving me that look that means she is very proud of her lad. Miss you mum

Great scenes in the dressing room with a formidable team after clinching the League title in 1976. Notice the bottles in our hands – all lemonade!

With Bob and Sir John Smith after winning the League Cup against West Ham at Villa Park.
I was injured for the first game, but thankfully there was a replay for me to lift our first ever League Cup

Hang on Barney, let me have a go. The hero of the night, Alan Kennedy, runs off with the European Cup in 1981

Jogging alongside Anfield teammate Ray Kennedy and manager Don Revie during an England get-together

With Terry Mac after exchanging shirts in the 1974 FA Cup Final. Maybe I just had a little whisper in his ear to say: "See you in a few months 'T'!" Below, we celebrate in style. Someone gave me a Geordie bowler hat, not quite matched by Stevie's bobble hat and Ray's cap

Playing in the Bicentennial Tournament in the States in 1976 for England against Team America whose side featured Pele and Tommy Smith. I am pictured up against legendary Italian Georgio Chinaglia who actually hailed from Wales!

Famous photo on the fields of Kirkby overlooking the Sports Centre and the beautiful River Alt. This photo won an award for photographer Stephen Shakeshaft

During better times and clearly before my Souness bust-ups, this image proves we did actually get on at one time, as we celebrate a goal

A flying header at Anfield

Where have I seen that perm before? With my mate Phil Neal

impossible to give a sample.

The English Press had been speculating about the make-up of our squad and if it was good enough. They had identified the defence as a weakness and the attack as a strength. However, we had defended well against the French and kept a clean sheet as we beat Czechoslovakia 2-0 and so that pleased us. We then beat Kuwait 1-0 to top the group.

We then got West Germany and the host country Spain at the next phase, which was always going to be massively more difficult. We had to travel to Madrid to play two games in Real Madrid's famous Bernabeu. The game against the Germans was very tight. The defence did well again and we kept a clean sheet. Karl-Heinz Rummenigge hit the bar, but that was as close as they came. Germany then beat Spain 2-1 before we met the hosts at the Bernabeu, needing to win and score two goals to go through. Kevin Keegan and Trevor Brooking were fit, but both were named as subs. Eventually they came on to replace Graham Rix and Tony Woodcock. I can remember Trevor shooting wide and Kevin missing a simple header that he would normally have buried. These were two glorious chances, but it wasn't to be. The two 0-0 draws meant we were out with the Germans progressing.

The only positive was that the defence had done itself proud after being named as the potential weak link. I have to say that playing in those World Cup Finals was one of the highlights of my career. To turn out against countries like France, West Germany and Spain was a tremendous experience because they all had world-class players. Of course, I would now have to turn my attentions to the club challenge that lay ahead.

Football's most amazing wind-up, but no smiles in Rome as Joe rocks me

1982/83 was a massively important year for me. I had been granted a testimonial season and plans had been put in place months before with the appointment of a committee of dedicated individuals who would work tirelessly to help make it a success.

I joined Liverpool in 1969 and made my debut at just 18. I was therefore well over the ten-year qualification rule. I was not one of those to seek help from hordes of businessmen. The committee was made up of people I had known for years and included many fans. My good friend Peter Bradley let me use his 'GO GAS' premises on Knowsley Industrial Estate for meetings. He was on the committee, as was my brother Owen.

Then there was Fred Hook, who had helped Ray Clemence with his and photographer Alan Sinclair. Teacher Geoff Roberts, another good friend, offered his support. Geoff was also centre-half for my Falcon Sunday League team. Another great mate who sadly died a few years later was Terry McEvoy, who was a fantastic Reds' fan. My chairman was Alan Brown, who I had known for many years. Alan had helped with a couple of other testimonials and that kind of experience is crucial. Then there were two individuals who were 'Clerks of the Court', Dave Gregg and Gerry Fenlon.

I have to say that Gerry was a real driving force and helped to bring everything together. He pushed and shoved people to commit their time to a lot of functions and this is crucial to the success of any testimonial year. Dave was a great organiser. Both Dave and Gerry were friends of solicitor Kevin Dooley who couldn't help personally because of business commitments, but who put forward the kind of people you instinctively need. A lot of people say they will help, only for that support not to materialise. Gerry was someone who pushed everyone to deliver.

Behind all of the hard work my committee also had a fantastic time because we made sure that every event was an occasion you could really enjoy. It didn't matter whether it was a small event in a pub, a social club or a giant black-tie dinner at St George's Hotel, we treated every gathering in the same way. Len McCormack was a buying director for Asda and got their support for the latter.

As I launched my testimonial, Liverpool revealed that they were offering me a two-year extension to my contract to take me through to the age of 32, which was a fantastic gesture when you consider all the injuries that had hampered me and the fact that new players were being added to the squad. The new deal gave me peace of mind.

I had won six league titles with Liverpool and wanted to win more although I was aware that a testimonial year takes a lot of hard work and can take your mind off football. As the year wore on there were a lot of comments, especially from Bob Paisley, who was worried that my mind was elsewhere and not on the football.

You have to strike a happy medium. People on my committee were giving it everything and it was all free time they were putting in, but I knew that my day job had to be the biggest priority. Having a new-born baby, as everyone will realise, can also add to the pressure and there is no doubt that it was an extremely hard spell trying to keep on top.

When the football side got underway it was an unusual experience because the boss decided to try something completely different when we came up against Tottenham at Wembley in the Charity Shield. He came up with this idea of playing three at the back with each of us in our best position. When you looked at it, we had the three best centre-backs in the country at that time with Alan Hansen, Mark Lawrenson and myself all up for the challenge.

This brings me to a nice story. I was doing an after-dinner speaking engagement in Manchester, of all places. I didn't think they had such good humour. This guy sidled up to me on the top table and said: "Phil, all these strange formations that people play now. Terry Venables with his Christmas Tree formation, 4-3-3, 4-4-2, 4-4-1-1. I remember seeing you playing in the best back three I have ever witnessed in my life. There was Alan Hansen, there was you and there was Mark Lawrenson. You were like a nose between two thorns." At this point I just burst out laughing and couldn't believe it. I asked him to stand there while I added it to my after-dinner stories.

The formation certainly worked against Tottenham. I could stride from the back and slide balls forward for the likes of Ian Rush, who went on to score the only goal of the game from one of those passes. Bob persisted with this system early on, but all three of us had injuries every now and again and it encouraged the boss to go back to the tried and trusted 4-4-2 with Lawro in midfield or slotting into the back alongside Big Al or myself.

Everything was going well and we were unbeaten in the first seven games. Bob had made his usual summer investment in the future by bringing in Dave Hodgson from Middlesbrough. We now had quite a Boro cast in Hodgy, Craig Johnston and Graeme Souness. Dave scored in his third and fourth games to make an immediate impact and things looked bright for him. He was then to get a bit of an injury in a 3-0 win at Swansea that was to keep him out for a few months.

Hodgy loved his clothes, not least his leather trousers. He had this guy in Middlesbrough who could make them in any shape, size or colour and was taking orders from all the lads. Although his Liverpool playing career started well, he then went through a period when he just could not hit the target. His confidence was affected and he started to pass instead of shoot. The lads started to take the Mickey in a fun way, but in the end the staff had to tell us to lay off because it was affecting him so much.

We signed another lad with Hodgy, an unassuming young man from Ayr United by the name of Steve Nicol. He needed size 13 boots and so you can imagine the Mickey-taking that went on when he was introduced to the lads. Stevie would take some almighty stick about all manner of things. He became an easy target for the lads to wind up. When the Scottish lads were joining up for international duty, they would be travelling up the M6 to a bleak Carlisle. The back window of the car would be full of snow and Stevie, as the young one in the group, would be told to get out and clean it. As soon as he reached the back of the car, the lads would drive off, leaving him standing in the snow in a short sleeved t-shirt. He could never get a grip of it.

He once went on a cruise to Norway. You get off the boat at various points to look at these beautiful little ports. Steve loved his crisps and lemonade and stored them in his cabin. He was with his wife and on one trip ashore he spotted this weighing machine. He climbed on and shouted in horror at his wife Eleanor that he was nearly a stone overweight. She was roaring with laughter and pointing out that he was holding two large bags full of bottles of lemonade and all kinds of stuff.

The biggest football wind-up of all time involved Stevie Nicol. We went to Israel for an end-of-season tour. Every night we would go to a local bar. One evening Kenny Dalglish decided to stay in and Stevie asked where he was as we sat outside having a few beers. Alan Hansen said: "What do you mean?

Don't you know?" He said: "Know what?" and the lads said: "Come on, you do know. Kenny's found out that he has got an incurable illness." Stevie replied: "You're taking the piss" and so Alan said: "Ask Graeme."

As he turned towards Souey, Alan winked to Graeme and said: "Tell him. Kenny's got leukaemia." Graeme said: "Yes, all the lads know." Stevie turned to me for confirmation and repeated: "What's wrong with Kenny?" I just said: "He's got leukaemia." Nico said: "I need to see him," and with that he picked himself up and left.

The lads immediately grabbed the phone on the bar and contacted Kenny, saying: "He's on his way to your room. You've got to ham it up." I decided to go back with Nico and caught him up halfway down the road. He was just shaking his head and saying: "I can't believe it." When we got back to the hotel, he said: "Phil, can you leave me. I want to speak to Kenny on my own." I said: "Yeah, no problem. Look, he told the lads, but he really wanted this to be kept private." Nico said: "When did it happen?" I said: "Remember the bang he got on his arm in the Tottenham game at the end of the season? The reaction started from there." He was just looking at me blankly, saying: "No!"

When he finally got in the room, Kenny was saying: "Sorry Nico, I thought you knew. I have been keeping it low key because I wanted to be with the lads on this trip." Later Kenny would reveal how the conversation went. Nico said: "You have been a wonderful ambassador for the game and for this club. You are one of my idols. I can't believe what has happened."

I was standing at the door listening to all of this. Suddenly Stevie added a rider to his tribute to Kenny. He said: "I thought something was wrong with you because you have been playing so badly." Kenny's face changed at this point and he said: "I think it's best if you get off." He said later: "I didn't know whether to choke him or burst out laughing."

I returned with Nico to meet up again with the rest of the lads. He poured out his conversation. It was now about two hours since we started this wind-up and I said to Big Al: "We will have to break the news to him. He's really cut up."

I got hold of Nico and said: "Stevie, we've been winding you up." He said: "No, you don't know." I said: "Listen, it's just a wind-up." He was having none of it and replied: "I don't believe you." I had to get all the other lads to hammer home that he'd just been done by the longest wind-up in the history of the club.

I know it was wrong to use a serious illness like leukaemia as a joke, but it was just the first word that came out. It wasn't meant to offend anybody.

Anyway, people sometimes say that you have to be there and this was certainly one of the famous stories about Stevie Nicol. Kenny never let him forget those final words: "I knew something was wrong because you have been playing so badly."

Nico stories abound throughout our spell together. Another one was during my spell as reserve-team trainer. The first team were away over Christmas. Nico was out of the team and Kenny wanted him to have treatment so that he would be ready for the next game. I went in to meet him at Anfield at 9.30am and he was the only one in for treatment. I had the machines at the ready.

Who was to stagger in – and I mean stagger – but Stevie. He had been out at a family party and had turned up with one of his mates in tow. I summoned Nico to climb up on the treatment table, pulled his trousers round his ankles, which wasn't a pleasant sight, and started to administer the ultrasound on his groin. His head went back on the backrest and he fell asleep, snoring loudly.

This left me with his mate who was as inebriated as Nico was. He sat on the other treatment bed, extremely pleased to be in this inner sanctum. He started asking about all things football. Suddenly he said: "Do you scout much? Do you watch many players and many games?"

I said: "We are always pro-active and looking for players who might fit the bill." To this he said: "I've seen a player." My ears pricked up. He added: "This boy can do everything. He's a midfield player. He's hard as nails. He can head a ball. He scores goals and he's a great defender." I'm thinking: "Sounds quite a star." I said: "Who does he play for?" thinking that we could get this lad watched. In all seriousness, Nico's mate said: "The Bow and Arrow Pub." Having the ultrasound on Stevie's nuts at this time, I nearly took his wedding tackle off. He woke with a start as I said: "Oh, great!" At that point, I couldn't wait to get rid of them both so I could spray something to get shut of the fumes. What made it equally worse, was I forgot to ask which one of them was driving.

Returning to the start of Nico's career, he was to play a couple of games that season after we got back from Israel, but he would soon become a big influence on the pitch. He could play equally well in midfield or defence and became a real Anfield stalwart. I'm not surprised. With his size 13 boots he could actually play in two positions at once.

Once again, I started the 1982/83 season wearing my familiar number four shirt and things were going well for me. In the November I was to play in one of the most famous derby matches of all time. As a kid Evertonians would laugh and joke about beating Liverpool 4-0 at Anfield to humiliate us. Every time we played them after that I wanted us to exact revenge.

It therefore gave me the greatest pleasure on November 6, 1982, to be part of the side that crushed the old enemy 5-0 at Goodison Park. This was the occasion when the famous '1-2, 1-2-3, 1-2-3-4, 5-0' chant was born and a day when Ian Rush destroyed the opposition with four strikes of his own.

Howard Kendall had returned to Goodison as manager the season before and just brought in centre-back Glenn Keeley on loan from his previous club Blackburn. It would prove a nightmare afternoon for Keeley and Everton. Rushie showed his intent with the opening goal after 11 minutes. Then Kenny Dalglish broke clear, only to be dragged back by Keeley who was sent off.

We had been flying from the start, but now we played some majestic football against Everton's ten men and really battered them. Lawro scored somewhere in the middle of Rushie's one-man demolition job. There were joyous scenes in the visitors' section and it was a derby I will always cherish.

As soon as the final whistle went my mind went back to my boyhood and that 4-0 defeat. It had been well and truly avenged and Rushie would become a thorn in the side of Everton from that point, not least his Welsh international teammates Kevin Ratcliffe and Neville Southall.

I played in the opening 18 games that season and was enjoying my football when a match loomed at Anfield in mid-December against one of the new generation of clubs – Watford. Graham Taylor was their boss and he had surprised a few opponents with a direct long-ball game that missed out the midfield and relied on his strikers holding the ball up until support arrived. Of course, one of his up and coming players was a skilful young man by the name of John Barnes. Watford could be a handful because of their style, but we put them in their place at Anfield by securing a 3-0 interval lead.

As the game wore on in the second half I tackled their powerful striker Luther Blissett and came away from him midway inside our half towards the Anfield Road. He clipped me from behind and I suddenly felt this excruciating pain in my ankle. Ronnie Moran came on and thinking back to the nasty injury I sustained against Barnsley, I said: "I think I've been cut."

I did not wear shin pads and Ronnie pulled down my sock and said: "There's nothing there." I told him it was as if something had snapped. I tried to get up, but could only hobble. It did not feel right. I was on the touchline and Bob Paisley shouted: "Are you going to be able to play on? Are you going to be alright? Craig has a bad back out there." Bob was worried he might sub me and then lose Craig Johnston. I turned to Ronnie and said: "Just strap me up."

To save time he just put the bandage round my ankle and round my boot. I limped back into the fray, but was soon in trouble again. I leapt for this long high ball and as I came down and planted my foot on the ground it buckled under me. Ronnie came on with Roy Evans and they gave me a fireman's lift off the pitch. I looked like a horse with a bandage round its fetlock. I left the ground on crutches and was told to attend Walton Hospital on the Monday for an X-ray. It revealed that the whole of my ankle ligament had snapped off. The specialist said: "It's nasty. This injury can be worse than a break."

After having so many injury problems, I could not believe this latest setback. I was in my testimonial year and had wanted to do everything right, on-and-off the pitch. This knocked me back. What made it worse was the doctor's words: "We must put you in plaster." I had this gauze applied from ankle to knee and then the plaster that was like a rock. I thought ligament damage was fairly easy to get over, but realised straight away that with my ankle in a pot it would be extra difficult. The joint sets solid after so many weeks and it becomes harder to regain the movement.

It was frustrating to be on the sidelines as the lads drove on towards another title. I managed to make a couple more appearances up to the point when the Championship was won with five games still remaining. Ironically, we claimed our crown without kicking a ball that day. Everton, of all teams, beat Manchester United and that meant no one could eclipse our points tally.

Watford were in second place, but our dominance is highlighted by the fact that they had lost 13 games at that point while we had only lost four. It is no surprise that we won the league so early. I had played in a couple of comeback games, against Manchester United and Brighton, but I damaged my ankle again at the Goldstone Ground. I had felt something stretch and snap, but thankfully the doctor said that it was just the adhesions in my ankle breaking down and that I should look on this as good news, not bad.

I came back for the final four matches and it was great to be back in action again. We were champions again and this was my seventh title. I was hoping that there would be more to come, but this book could easily be about Walton Hospital instead of Anfield Road!

I would play close on 500 games, which was incredible when you look at the problems I had to deal with. It was hard. My old mucker Terry McDermott had only managed a couple of sub appearances during that '82/83 campaign and his days were numbered after a tremendous Liverpool career. The season finished at Watford on May 14, but not before I held my testimonial game at Anfield. It was a special night because it was on the first birthday of my son

Philip on May 10.

Bobby Robson brought a strong England XI to play Liverpool and about 18,000 fans turned up for the occasion. England won 2-0 and so that shows it was quite a keenly-fought affair. It was an emotional night and we had a great time. I think Bob Paisley probably had a different view of testimonials because it meant a busy and sometimes difficult year. However, I had to be totally committed because of the work that was being put in on my behalf. We had a great testimonial celebration involving all of the Liverpool and England players and partied late into the night.

Looking back, season '82/83 was one of swinging emotions for me. I've spoken about our league triumph, the injury that restricted me to 24 top-flight games and my testimonial game. We went out early in the FA Cup, ironically to a Brighton side inspired by Jimmy Case. I was to miss out on the club's third straight Milk Cup win because of injury although I was at Wembley to cheer on the lads in their 2-1 victory over Manchester United.

We made the third round of the European Cup after victories against Dundalk and JK Helsinki, only to stumble at the next hurdle against Widzew Lodz. I watched from the sidelines as we lost 2-0 in Poland. In the return leg I made a brief substitute's appearance for Ronnie Whelan in centre midfield. We won 3-2, but lost 4-3 on aggregate. That was a big disappointment to us, but it showed how difficult the season had been. We only managed to win TWO trophies!

In the summer of '83 we went on a trip to Hong Kong and Bangkok. I remember that a couple of the younger lads, Robbie Savage (no, not that one!) and Steve Foley, came along to gain experience.

We didn't realise it, but the sponsors Seiko had put up a $50,000 prize for the winning team. Even though it was still the close season and we were revelling in the break with a few drinks, we were all determined to play in the game against a Seiko XI. They had a couple of people making guest appearances, including Pat Jennings and Alan Sunderland.

It was hilarious when a commentator announced the names of the players before the kick-off. Everyone was applauded, but the crowd really started cheering when the name Sammy Lee came over the tannoy. I'm not sure if they thought he was the son of Bruce Lee or descended from one of the Lee family from Hong Kong, but the noise was deafening.

We won 2-0 and Robbie Savage hit this shot that flew into the top corner. What a day for him. After the game Graeme Souness, as captain, received the cheque for $50,000. Graeme got changed quickly, found a bank and cashed the cheque immediately, giving every player an equal share. The two younger lads were thrilled. Then Bob Paisley came onto the scene and said: "Where's the cheque. That's the club's money."

Graeme wasn't going to be pressured. He went to the Seiko representative and asked who the cash was for. The answer was: "The team." That was all he wanted to hear. It meant everybody had a few bob to get the presents for going home. It was an incredible thing and something I've never witnessed before or since. Bob was not happy. In fact, he went berserk because he would normally control those things.

On the field another team was taking shape. Jimmy Case and Ray Kennedy had gone the year before. That was always a matter of time after their famous skirmish with some hotel staff that led to a brush with the law. Of course, they were fantastic friends and remain so to this day.

Ray Clemence had gone. Lawro and Stevie Nicol had come in. Sammy Lee, Ian Rush and David Hodgson were all amongst the new brigade. The club did not shirk when it came to replacing people, regardless of whether they had become household names. It was harsh, but you always knew you could be chopped at any stage.

It was strange that I was having thoughts about my own future in as much as I had been involved with England that season. The European Championship qualifiers were to start in September, 1982. Bobby Robson was now the international manager following Ron Greenwood's decision to quit after the World Cup. I didn't figure in Bobby's first game against Denmark, a 2-2 draw. His second match was a friendly against West Germany in the October and England lost 2-1 at Wembley. In the middle of November when things were going well for me at Liverpool, Bobby called me up for the squad.

He said he wanted a triangle of players on the right who knew each other's game. This would involve Phil Neal at right-back, Sammy Lee in right midfield and myself at centre-back. The match in question was against Greece and was England's second Euro qualifier. Little did I know that this would be my last senior appearance for my country. The match was played in an angry atmosphere in Salonica where people were throwing bricks at the team coach.

The weather was horrendous. They switched the game from the Olympic Stadium in Athens to produce a more hostile environment in one of their provincial towns. The Greeks never admitted it, but this is what the FA thought. The home fans made their intentions known from the kick-off, but England produced a fantastic display to win the game 3-0. Sammy Lee scored the third goal with a free-kick so we were really happy. Everything had worked out well for the three Liverpool lads and the game was also significant for the fact that Bryan Robson assumed the captaincy for the first time. As a Liverpudlian I got fed up later seeing all of those 'Captain Marvel' headlines, but he was a very good player.

Looking back, I'm delighted that my England career went out on such a high. I was never picked again, mainly because of the injuries that would dog me. I finished with 42 caps, six as captain. I scored one goal, against Italy, but it was a good one!

I played in the World Cup Finals and the European Championship Finals and I felt that I distinguished myself and did Kirkby and Liverpool proud. Maybe with fewer injuries I would have overtaken Emlyn's achievement of 60 caps, but I am still extremely proud to have had a very good career with the England team.

I have to say that season 1983/84 was not how I dreamed my Anfield playing career might begin to wind down. Joe Fagan had taken over from Bob Paisley and he made his intentions clear when he left me out from the word go. It was a bombshell when I was omitted for the first part of the pre-season tour. Then he brought me back into the fold for the last part of the pre-season action in Spain and Morocco.

When we beat Morocco 3-0 I thought things were looking up. I then played in the Charity Shield at Wembley against Manchester United, only for Joe to shock me again. We were losing 1-0 when United won a corner. Suddenly the manager signalled for me to come off with substitute Craig Johnston waiting on the touchline. I couldn't understand why he took off a defender at that moment in time. United scored from the kick to make it 2-0. I think it was a learning process for Joe that day.

I was then not to take part in the whole of that season, which was extremely disappointing. I was even offered out on loan. Former Liverpool player Gordon Milne was running Leicester at that time and he asked me to go to Filbert Street. I said no because I wanted to stay and fight for my place. It was difficult playing in the reserves, but I was determined to be ready should a recall come. In the meantime I tried to help some of the younger lads in the side. Chris Lawler was running the reserves at this point. We got on well, but I must admit that it was a difficult season for me as I watched the first-team lads storm to another title success with 32 incredible goals from Ian Rush.

Joe had brought in Michael Robinson from Brighton and John Wark from Ipswich. He was looking to shape his own team and the side was picking itself. Only 15 players were used all season as the team won the

Championship, the Milk Cup and the European Cup. I was disappointed to miss out on the Milk Cup because it culminated in the first all-Merseyside final. The occasion was superb with Liverpudlians and Evertonians side-by-side at Wembley. It was a unique occasion and it seemed fitting that the match was drawn. Of course, Graeme Souness scored the only goal in the replay held at Maine Road.

I was even omitted from most of the European stuff although I remember getting a call-up to play Dinamo Bucharest in the semi-final, second leg. We had won the first game at Anfield 1-0 with a goal from Sammy Lee. The match exploded when Souey broke the jaw of one of the Romanian players as they came out of a challenge on the edge of the box. It was a short right hook that did the damage and it was clear that they would be looking for Graeme in the second leg.

Joe gave him the option of sitting it out, but that was never going to happen. They were spitting at us at the airport and it was a hate-filled stadium. All eyes were on Graeme Souness. Of course, I was pointing out where he was! He was lapping it up and loved every minute of it. He played in the game and while they tried to knee-cap him, he was a wily character. He knew when to jump out of the way, but he never shirked a tackle when it had to be made. They didn't lay a stud on him.

I didn't get off the bench, but I was thrilled when an Ian Rush double clinched the tie to take us to our fourth European Cup Final. Having held this famous trophy above my head as skipper, I desperately wanted to be involved against AS Roma in Rome, the scene of that legendary 1977 triumph. However, Joe Fagan did something that rocked me to my boots.

David Hodgson had said that he was suffering from groin, knee and ankle injuries, but he was saying that he would not duck out if he was made a sub. Only 17 players went to Rome and with 16 in the squad someone was always going to suffer a heart-breaker. I was delighted to be involved after the season I had endured. I was experienced and ready for action, although I was well aware that sentiment would not play a part in Joe's decision.

In the final training session Hodgy was rooted to the spot. I was convinced Joe could not pick him, but when the squad was announced I was the odd man out. I was gutted. I didn't mention Hodgy to the staff, but worse was to come.

When we came out of the hotel to go to the Olympic Stadium three coaches were parked up. There was one for the players and staff, one for the wives and girlfriends and one for the VIPs. I was determined to remain upbeat for the lads as they prepared for a difficult game. I walked out with the other players and began to climb onto the bus when Joe Fagan said: "You can't come on here Phil." It cut me to death. I looked at him in disbelief and he repeated: "You can't come on the bus." I said: "You're joking," but he replied: "There is only room for the 16 and the staff."

I knew that wasn't right and I was gutted. I had to step off and walk back past the players, who were looking out of the coach as shocked as I was. I had to get on the bus with the wives and girlfriends and found a seat in the middle section. Paul Walsh had just signed and there was a place alongside him. He said: "What happened?" I had a lump in my throat the size of a rugby ball. I could not speak. My wife was shouting: "Phil, what happened?" I was so embarrassed and my head was swimming. When we got to the stadium I watched the lads head into the dressing room and made my way into the stand to sit with the wives and VIPs. These included Joe Fagan's wife.

I sat down and thought back to 1977 and the final in the same stadium. Tosh and myself were not playing, but were both on the bench and made to feel involved. We even had the BBC's Stuart Hall on the bench and a couple of the chefs who the club had taken with us. Why was this so different? I learned later that we were allowed to have five subs and five staff on the bench. In those days we only had three main staff members in Joe, Ronnie Moran and Roy Evans. Roy was the physio/trainer who ran on to administer treatment.

What the boss did was bang out of order, no doubt about that. I know Chris Lawler, the reserve coach, was on the bench. I don't know who the other one was. I don't even think it was the doctor. That incident destroyed me and I know that many of the lads were furious in the dressing room at the way I had been treated. I was the club's longest-serving player. I like to think that I was a good lad and that I had never caused any problems. I wasn't asking for any favours. If I had been told in advance what was in Joe's mind, I would not have put myself in that humiliating situation on the steps of the bus.

I didn't let my disappointment show in the game, screaming my support for the lads and standing on the seats when we eventually won on penalties. Of course, I missed all the celebrations on the pitch and in the dressing room. When I eventually met the players at the reception they were sympathetic, but I was still hurting inside during the party that followed.

When I woke up the next morning, I began to consider the consequences. Was this Joe's way of telling me he wanted me out? Did he want a reaction? We came home for the tour of the city and were then due to head out for a trip to Swaziland the next day. When we got off the plane from Rome I was still very angry and I'd had a few drinks. That lump had still not gone from my throat. I went up to Joe Fagan and said: "You can shove your trip to Swaziland. You have to understand me. I don't want to go."

He said: "I knew you would be disappointed, but I didn't understand how much. My wife said you were still incredible in the stands, supporting the team." I shrugged my shoulders, but didn't want him to think I was just accepting the situation. I was still gutted. The lads were receiving £1,000 each to go to Swaziland, but the money was irrelevant. I was kept involved in 1977, even if I only sat on the bench, and Bob Paisley made sure I got a medal for playing earlier in the competition. I played in my own right in the 1978 European Cup Final and had been captain in '81. I felt that with Hodgy injured my experience could have been invaluable to the younger ones in the dressing room in Rome. I could have been utilised in a positive way and that would have meant my fourth medal. I had to make my point and didn't see anyone until the start of the following season.

I knew that 1984/85 was going to be a crunch season for me. I was now playing in the reserves and not even at centre-back. I was operating in central midfield, my old position, and found it quite enjoyable. My situation gave me the chance to help the younger lads who were looking to break through.

Chris Lawler was in charge and I had a great time, but always with a desire to get back in the first team. Of course, I was continually wondering what the future might have in store for me. That summer Graeme Souness had left Liverpool for an Italian challenge with Sampdoria. I wondered if an opportunity might arise for me, either in defence or midfield. I was finishing my career where it had started, in a defensive midfield role.

A couple of clubs were sniffing around to see if I might go on loan. Southampton and Leicester were mentioned, but I was not interested. Then, at the start of the season, I got a phone call from Swindon Town who said they would like to talk to me about the manager's job. I was still only 30 and wondered if the time was right. Joe said: "Go down and think about it. If you are looking to go into management, it's an opportunity. Just look on it as a chat at this stage." The papers had been talking about Lou Macari and myself as the main candidates for Swindon. I spoke to their chairman and he said: "Just come and look round."

I drove down with Marg and thought the journey was never going to end. That was playing on my mind, but it was a nice place and a decent little stadium. Swindon had a good fanbase and after looking round for three quarters of an hour the chairman took me into the offices. I saw this sign that said 'Boardroom' and was shocked when we walked in to see about 16 people sitting round a table. Marg had to wait outside.

I sat down and suddenly they were all firing questions at me. What could I bring to Swindon? What players would I try to sign? I wasn't expecting this and wondered whether I should mention my previous managerial success with Falcon? I thought: "Nah, it won't look too good on my c.v."

They might have been impressed by the five or six pints we put away after every game, but I just looked at this sea of faces and said: "I've got great experience in the game and I've also had the benefit of having seen a lot of reserve players who might fit the bill." I couldn't talk about First Division stars. My nose would have been even longer.

At the same time I was thinking: "What am I doing here? This group interview is not in the script." The questions lasted about 45 minutes and then I had lunch with the chairman.

I said: "I didn't think this was going to happen." He said: "I didn't want to tell you." Maybe this was my first spin from a chairman.

If I'd realised I was going to be meeting such a large group it might have frightened me off. We had a further chat and then I spoke to Marg. I felt I had a couple of years left in me as a player. I wasn't sure about a player manager's role although it was a great opportunity. The chairman left it with me. He said he would have a chat with his board and get back to me.

It was a long journey home. Marg and I chatted long and hard. I'd heard stories of how difficult it could be as a player manager, and thought: "I will speak to Joe Fagan." We had only been in the house for around 30 minutes when the phone rang. It was the chairman of Swindon saying: "Hi Phil, get home safely? Your interview went well today. We would like to offer you the job." For the first time in my life I sounded like Bob Paisley. I mumbled something about needing time to speak to Joe Fagan, and the Swindon chief said: "Not a problem."

When I finally got in front of Joe I was expecting him to tell me to go for it. I was probably one of Liverpool's highest earners at that time, bringing home even more than someone like Kenny Dalglish. I said to Joe: "They want me to take the job and that has frightened the living daylights out of me. I'm not sure I'm ready for the hassle or responsibility of management just yet. There doesn't seem to be a lot of help down there."

Joe listened carefully and said: "You are not sure. Being a manager is tough enough. Being a player manager is even tougher and you are not ready. You are not taking it." I thought that was very honest and open of him, especially after what had happened the previous year at the European Cup Final. I thanked Swindon for their offer, but said I was not ready for it. Inside 48 hours they had installed Lou Macari as manager.

Soon after that Joe called me and said: "You can go on a free." Some people thought that was a slap in the face, but I would have been amazed if they had asked for a fee. As it stood, it increased my options. I was still determined to fight for my place and took note when the first team conceded three in the opening game at Norwich.

Joe had signed another midfielder in Jan Molby and I would build up a really good relationship with the Great Dane. He had so much ability, but off the field he had this easy-going lifestyle. Jan was more skilful than most of the players I had ever seen and while he was right-footed, he could pass the ball accurately with both feet. I'd watch in awe as he pinged the ball 40 yards with the outside of his foot, using what was allegedly his weaker foot.

He did have a problem in the weight department, but he ruled the roost in centre midfield and was one of the best passers of the ball I have ever seen. Jan was one of the first foreigners the club had ever signed, but he developed this amazing Scouse accent. He had a difficult time settling in to the demands of the First Division, and that is where I thought my chance might come.

We went off to play Lech Poznan of Poland in the European Cup and I was called up to the squad. Jan was ineligible and I thought: "This is my chance." Joe was giving all the right vibes to the Press. He was suggesting this was a great opportunity for me, and I felt ready because I had been playing well for the reserves.

However, when it came to the game I was sub. Joe moved Sammy Lee into centre midfield from the right and while Sammy was perfectly capable in there, I felt I was more experienced. We won 1-0, but that didn't help me by any means.

I continued to believe I could get back in the Liverpool first team, but Joe's decision to overlook me again for that Poznan game was probably the final straw. Yes, I'd turned down Swindon, but I was increasingly beginning to think that if anything worthwhile came up then I would really think about it.

In the October, Lawrie McMenemy came on again to see if I would go to The Dell on loan. I warmed to him straight away. I felt he was a guy I could work with and he said: "Once you have been to Hampshire, you will never want to leave." I was impressed with his words. Here was somebody who wanted me and these positive vibes were brilliant. I asked to play for Liverpool reserves on the Thursday and said I would travel to Southampton on the Friday. Lawrie agreed.

It's incredible how things can happen. In that reserve match I was playing alongside Gary Gillespie. He went up for a ball with our keeper Bob Bolder, who missed his punch and smashed Gary's nose all over his face. Straight away I knew Gary faced a lay-off and that this could have implications for the first team. I asked Chris Lawler to remind Joe I was heading to Southampton to start my loan spell the next day.

Of course, Joe's reaction on hearing about Gary was to say that he could not release me. It didn't hurt me. I had another Liverpool chance and Lawrie was fine with it. The final straw for me came when Mark Lawrenson got injured and I was not called on. That was the lowest I had felt for a long time and I knew the leaving of Liverpool was now not far away. One afternoon I was shocked when Sheffield United manager Ian Porterfield and his assistant John McSeverny turned up at Anfield. Joe asked me to meet them. Ian must have felt that the best way of getting somebody was face to face.

I had been really fed up prior to Christmas 1984, but Porterfield impressed me. I had memories of his greatest moment as a player when he scored a famous goal for Sunderland against Leeds in an FA Cup Final. He asked me to help Sheffield United. I didn't even know where they were in the table when I agreed to go on loan for a month.

Later that day I found out that they were second from bottom in the old Second Division. However, the Sheffield people were very nice and made Marg and myself feel welcome. It had been agreed that I would only travel over there on Mondays, Wednesdays and Fridays and that I would continue to train with Liverpool on the other days.

I travelled across to Sheffield on the Friday night ahead of my first game and stayed in a local hotel. I then turned up at the ground for a pre-match meal and team meeting. At 1pm I was called down to the office by Ian Porterfield. He said: "I've got something to tell you Phil. You are not playing." I thought it was a wind-up of Stevie Nicol proportions, but he said: "Your papers did not go through. I don't know whether it went wrong at the Liverpool end, the Football League end or our end."

I thought: "This is not meant to happen." I had built myself up because when I was hyped I played even better. The Blades drew the game with Brighton 1-1 as I watched from the stands. I had to wait until the following week and a game against Cardiff for my debut. From that point we started to climb out of the relegation zone. Ian brought in one of my old Kirkby mates Dennis Mortimer from Aston Villa, and Mel Eaves also arrived from Wolves. This gave added strength in defence, midfield and attack.

We beat Cardiff 3-1 and I was delighted to get man-of-the-match plaudits. Things went swimmingly during the month and I felt content enough to extend my loan for another four weeks. It went into a third month and we were playing a derby game against Barnsley at home. With 15 minutes to go I turned into this short, stocky midfielder and we collided. They talk about having the wind knocked out of you. That's exactly how I felt.

I was dizzy and woozy and didn't know what had hit me. I got up, but was clearly in trouble and had to come off the pitch. I wondered if I had fractured something in my chest and was taken to the Sheffield Infirmary. They did X-rays, but could not find any breaks. Throughout the following week it was difficult to train. I was constantly short of wind and just couldn't get my breathing right.

We met on the Friday to travel to Wimbledon. I took my car to 'Watford Gap' where I was to be picked up by the team coach. I was in pain even before we kicked off and it didn't help when the game started and the Dons started launching those high balls forward for which they were famous. I thought I was going to collapse. At half-time I said: "I'm really struggling."

They gave me a couple of Panadol, but I could not carry on. Their doc came in and he sat me down on a chair to check me over. He was tapping on my back with his fingers and telling me to cough. Then he said: "I don't want to frighten you, but you might have a problem with one of your lungs. When you get back to Liverpool you need to check it out." The team ended up losing 5-0 and they dropped me off at Watford Gap, where our goalkeeper John Burridge asked for a lift up the M6. I dropped him off at the Thistle Hotel in Haydock and continued home.

Marg was shocked when I said I needed to go to hospital for a check on my lungs. She phoned her mum to mind Philip and we went to Walton Hospital which was now familiar territory. You can imagine what it was like on a Saturday night. It was packed, but they took me into a side room and I managed to get seen a bit quicker.

The doc asked me questions about what had gone on. I went for an x-ray and then waited in the cubicle where I heard a commotion outside. Another doctor came in and said: "Tell me what you have done and where you have been today."

I said: "I trained all week, drove to Watford Gap and then played in a football match against Wimbledon. Then I drove home again from Watford Gap." He was shocked and said: "You've got a collapsed lung, one side is down" and went on to explain that even though I had been X-rayed the previous week, it can be like a slow puncture. The lung had been deflating slowly and the doc declared: "We will have to sort this out now." I saw that wry smile on the face of my wife as she left with the doc saying: "Lay down on the bed."

They put a blanket over my head as the doc revealed that they would have to insert a tube into my lung. "I will just make a small insertion into the top of your chest to get it down," he said. My next words were predictable. "You are going to give me a needle, aren't you?"

I lay back as he put this green cloth with a large hole in it over my chest. He then put a needle in the chest area before opening up an inch long gash. A rubber tube was produced which he started to insert into the hole. I was in agony and it didn't help when he said: "I can't get it in."

I was so tense. He said: "You have got big strong chest muscles" to which I naturally replied: "Chest muscles? Me?" I looked at his nose to see if it was growing! He said: "Relax" and at that moment I felt the tube slide down inside my chest wall. It was an amazing feeling of relief. This tube went into a bung in a big jar that contained liquid. It was about two feet high and you could see the bubbles in the liquid. I was told I would be in for four or five days and they wheeled me out onto one of the wards.

I was feeling down, but Ian Porterfield came to see me and offered me a contract to stay at Sheffield United. I had quite enjoyed it and he conjured up these forms that I signed while propped up in my hospital bed. It proved they had faith in me. That was the leaving of my beloved Liverpool. The great thing was that they allowed me to continue training part of the week at Melwood. I helped United stave off the threat of relegation and I felt wanted again.

At the end of that season I played in three games in the States. We were based in Texas and it was here that I made my comeback from injury. The heat was tremendous, but I was just delighted to be back in action. It was during that trip that Liverpool met Juventus in the European Cup Final in Brussels. I was sitting in my American hotel room, flicking through the channels to try and find someone who was showing the game. I finally hit on a Mexican channel showing live pictures, although I was surprised that the match itself had not started.

The camera was panning around the crowd and I was trying to work out what was going on. I was seeing all of these skirmishes and thinking to myself: "This is not right." Obviously the commentary was in Spanish and I could not understand it, but they flashed up a news header across the bottom of the screen like SKY do now that didn't need any translation. It indicated that there had been 15 deaths, mostly Italian. I began to panic. I was shocked that anyone had died at a football match, but I was also panicking because my brothers Owen and Ian were in the stadium.

I was on the phone for hours. The chairman of Sheffield United, Reg Brierley, was a fantastic guy and he told me not to worry about the phone bill. He just wanted me to find out if my brothers were safe. Of course, 39 Juve fans died in the final reckoning and that made the football match that followed totally meaningless. I never thought for one moment that Liverpool would win. I knew what would be going through the minds of our lads and I really felt for Joe Fagan and for captain Phil Neal.

The European Cup Final should provide you with one of the greatest days of your life and in this instance Liverpool had the opportunity to make it five remarkable triumphs. It was never going to happen that night and we were all horrified by the death toll. The pain of that night was still being felt 20 years later and when Liverpool and Juve met for the first time in two decades towards the end of the 2004/05 campaign, now in the renamed Champions League, the Reds did everything in their power to hold out the hand of friendship and pay respect to the 39 who died.

The irony is that we, more than any other club in the world, can understand the depth of Juve feeling. We would have our own tragedy to deal with and when you are faced with these things it puts everything into perspective about what is important in life.

My time at Sheffield United had some ups and some downs, certainly on the playing side. Things could have been better, but I also had some great times there. One of them was in October 1985 when my second son Daniel was born. This was to give me great joy. I had always known it was going to be a boy. Everybody used to ask me what sex I thought the baby might be. Although we didn't know I would always say: "It's another boy." He was to grow up and look the most like me, tall, skinny and athletic, a chip off the old block, but we won't mention noses, although there is a similarity!

Also, I got the opportunity at this time to go into business. Every player likes to think about this. Going to run a pub was not my style although it suited many players. Friends of Marg's, who she had known for many years and grown up with, were now building a business in Kirkby called Pine DIY. Paul Rice and Steve Silker were behind this venture. Paul's sister Jackie had been Marg's best friend and we had often gone out as a foursome with Jackie, her husband Peter and Marg and myself. In a roundabout way I knew a bit about the lads, the business and its potential.

They were looking to develop and wanted to import Brazilian mahogany doors by the container load. To do it needed a cash injection and they asked if I wanted to join the business. We met and I talked to my solicitor and accountant and we thought it was a decent proposition. It was good to know that when I finished with football I would have something to fall back on. Every professional footballer is worried about what he might do towards the end of his career.

Kenny Dalglish calls me home, but Hillsborough rocks our whole world

Joe Fagan never recovered from the Heysel Stadium tragedy, although his subsequent decision to quit was still a shock to all concerned. It launched Kenny Dalglish into the spotlight as the club's first player manager. The appointment would prove to be another masterstroke by the club, although it must have come as a bit of a shock to Ronnie Moran, who had been caretaker boss without being offered the big one at that time.

Joe and Ronnie had been extremely close down the years, but Joe never gave any inclination to his old sparring partner that he was planning to retire. This was to be the start of a new era. I went to see Kenny, who had been a great teammate. I wanted to know if I could continue to train at Melwood twice a week and he said straight away that it would not be a problem.

My own season started well at Sheffield United. Dennis Mortimer had gone from our midfield, but we replaced one former Aston Villa player with two more. Scouser Peter Withe came in up front while Ken McNaught joined me in the heart of defence. Peter, of course had scored Villa's winning goal in the 1982 European Cup against Bayern Munich. Ken also played in that final. He was an experienced defender who had been at Everton for a while.

With a strengthened team we made a great start, winning 3-1 at Stoke and we were top of the league after ten games. Porterfield had chosen to operate with three centre-backs, Ken, Paul Stancliffe and myself. Everything was going well until we suffered our first setback, a 2-0 defeat against Charlton who were sharing the Crystal Palace ground at that stage.

On the Monday morning it was as though we had been crap all season. The success in the first ten games was thrown out of the window just because of one defeat. We had this self-belief at Liverpool that meant we did not panic if one result suddenly went against us. It was what we had been doing before that was most important.

Porterfield immediately changed the training with a lot of cross-country runs at Graves Park in Sheffield. All the players were low and from that moment it was backs to the wall. It ended with Ian Porterfield getting the sack. Billy McEwan took over and one of the first things he did was take me out of the side. He was the manager and I had to get on with it, but I was interested to see what would happen. In the meantime I carried on training twice a week at Liverpool. Kenny Dalglish was a little more open than Joe had been and we would sit and chat.

Of course, Kenny was now playing in the famous Melwood staff games on 'Little Wembley' with the kids. Because I was technically an outsider, I did not get involved with the first team or even the reserves. I would also play in these staff games and tried to help, encourage and coach the kids.

I don't know if something struck a chord with Kenny, but he came up to me one day just before his regular Anfield press conference. He took me into his office and I thought something was wrong. Was he going to put an end to my training stints at Melwood? He said: "I believe things are not going too well at Sheffield United and that you are not in the team. If anything goes wrong then I would like you to come back here as a coach."

It was right out of the blue and I was taken aback. Was he offering me a job? A couple of weeks went by and I thought: "I'll have to take a second look at this." I went in to see Kenny and said: "A couple of weeks ago you mentioned a possible coaching post. Are you still serious about it?" He said: "Yes, I'm just waiting to hear from you. If you finish at Sheffield United I would like you here."

I still had a year to run on my contract, but I went to see Billy McEwan. I said: "I'm not in the team. It doesn't look as if I will get a starting position again. If you don't need me, let's be men about it and forget it. If we can come to an agreement over my contract, I will look after myself." Within 24 hours he came back and said: "On the footballing side we can call it a day. The chairman will come to some arrangement over your contract." I went to see chief executive Derek Dooley, who was amiable about sorting things out.

The amazing thing was that as things had gone on that season, I had heard some whispers suggesting that the only reason I had gone to Bramall Lane was to be manager and that I wanted Ian Porterfield out. The talk was that Peter Withe and myself were somehow conspiring to get Porterfield the sack. I had the greatest respect for Ian. There was no way I wanted to be the manager there, yet I had heard these whispers on more than one occasion. It was even the subject of a letter in the local paper.

It all came to a head one day. I had no idea which players were instigating these rumours. We had lost at home and quite a few fans were in the car park. I was not going to hide and confronted them. I was having a chat with these supporters, who were letting out their frustrations. They were saying: "We know why you came here. You have come to be the manager." I said: "How can you say that?" One of them replied: "We drink in the same pubs as Keith Edwards. He told us that all you are after is to be the manager."

Edwards was United's star striker at the time although I didn't rate him as a professional. I was furious and kept running these words through my mind as I drove home. On the Monday morning I came in for training. My mind had been in turmoil all over the weekend. I just pinned Edwards against the wall and said: "You bastard. You've been shit-stirring behind my back."

I told him what those fans had said and he immediately denied it. In all my years in the game I'd never had this situation with a teammate before apart from the spat with Souness over the captaincy issue. I knew that was the end for me at Sheffield United and that is when I made up my mind to discuss Kenny's offer. I was quite pleased to get out.

Of course, the one thing I still did not know was my exact role at Liverpool. I asked him and he said: "Reserve player/coach." That appealed to me because I was 31 and looking to expand my coaching skills, but it also meant I could still play a bit, which was lovely. My next question was an obvious one. "What about Chris?" He just replied: "Look Phil, I am offering you a job. What happens to Chris Lawler has got nothing to do with you."

It was too good an opportunity for me to turn down. I thought Chris would step down to work with the junior teams, but before the start of the season we were all brought together before the players were in. Chris was told the club no longer required his services. I had struck up a great relationship with him while playing in the reserves during my last season with the Reds. It was a tough situation, but that is what happens in football. There had been an overlap for a couple of weeks with Chris still there until Kenny finally made his announcement. It was a little bit difficult during that time and Chris hardly spoke to me. He thought I had something to do with it.

I said to him: "I know what you are thinking, but Kenny asked me, not the other way round. It was such a good opportunity that I could not turn it down. I thought you would be doing the youth side." I really was gutted for Chris, but Kenny clearly wanted to change things and in these situations managers have to make big decisions. These things go in circles and years later Sammy Lee would take my role when Graeme Souness sacked me. Sammy was humble about it at the time, but I had no problems with him. He also had to take the opportunity when it was put in front of him.

This was to be the start of my coaching career. I was on a steep learning curve and I remember an incident early on involving Ronnie Moran. I liked to plan a morning session for the lads who were at my disposal. Each day the senior staff would decide who they wanted in their squad and in turn I would take a couple from Steve Heighway's youth set-up to make up my numbers.

I would write down the details of the session and how long it would take. The first team would get on with their eight-a-sides or whatever, but I felt the younger ones needed more drills and work on different aspects of their game. I said to the other coaches: "Right, I'm getting off to set up my session on the 'B' team pitch." Ronnie immediately piped up: "You are not the manager yet, you know. You will wait until we have picked our squad."

I thought: "Uh oh, young Phil Thompson has just been put in his place by the experienced Ronnie Moran." I had to have a re-think and began to sit back until I knew the players I had at my disposal. It was an early rude-awakening with Ronnie regarding seniority, but these were great times for me.

I was delighted to be part of the famous Boot Room and I would look at Ronnie Moran, who had what seemed to be the biggest bunch of keys in the world that must have opened every single door at Melwood and Anfield. As a coach, I also had my own bunch of keys. Ronnie kept his on his belt. I was more of a tracksuit person and kept mine in my pocket, although the bulge must have made it look as if I was quite endowed in the marital department.

I was able to start writing in the famous training ground books that were updated meticulously every day, putting down everything from injuries to weather conditions and the state of the pitches. These were the books that would be consulted if anything went wrong and the staff needed to find out if we had changed anything that might have contributed to a particular situation.

I would even be Doctor Phil at times, giving treatments out until Kenny brought in part-time physio Paul Chadwick, who was great at what he did. It was brilliant being in the Boot Room and I used to love taking people in there to show them what this famous inner sanctum was all about. The other staff used to call it 'Thompson Tours'. I would take people round the trophy room and the dressing room, and would always have a great pride in pointing out the 'This Is Anfield' sign on the way out to the pitch.

I remember taking the Falcon lads round one day, people I'd known for years from our Sunday League team. They turned up in vans at Anfield with all the kids. The groundsman never used to let anybody go on the pitch. We walked down the tunnel and I was pointing out the sign. The next thing the lads are all on the pitch running towards the Kop.

Suddenly a ball came out from nowhere and they were all playing 'heading in', just like we used to do at Windy Arbor in Kirkby before a Sunday game. The crosses were coming in and the lads were all trying to score in the Kop end. Meanwhile, all the kids were sitting on the grass watching their dads. If the groundsman had seen this he would have hit the roof!

The whole day was really funny. We would be in the trophy room and the kids would be pulling at their dads' trousers, asking: "Where are we going now?" The dads would be saying: "Just a minute son, just another pose in front of this trophy." It was hard to work out who were the kids and who were the adults, but it showed the tremendous pride all supporters have in our famous football club.

I'd been famous for Thompson Tours as a player and here I was, carrying on the tradition as a staff member. Of course, the real job was to look after the reserves and it was an interesting bunch. I had known many of the lads for a long time. Some of my old mates from my playing days were now having to battle away with the second string. I had the young lads hoping to make their way in the game and various first-team stars who were recovering from injury.

I worked hard on my sessions and I like to think that the younger ones quite looked forward to them. Of course, I would soon become famous on matchdays for my legendary shouting and screaming. I wanted us to win at all costs. As player/coach, I would be letting them have it on and off the pitch.

Of course, this arrangement didn't last too long. Again, it was a word from Ronnie that put me straight. He said: "The reserve team is not about you any more. It's about the kids who are coming through." Even if I pulled on a shirt for a couple of games, that was too many for Ronnie. Now I would only play when we were really short to give a helping hand. I knew Ronnie was right. In fact, I only played in four reserve games in total.

He also put his foot down in another way, saying: "Now that you are on the coaching side, you will have to pack in running your Falcon Sunday side." I asked if I could finish the season off and it was agreed that would be okay. The staff always went in on Sundays to help with the treatment and they were not going to make an exception for me.

It made sense to step away from Sunday football because of the potential for trouble. I remember having a bit of a set-to with a Sunday League referee when Bob Paisley was Liverpool manager. I gave the ref a right bollocking and he said: "You will hear about this."

Two weeks later I was called into Bob's office. He told me that the FA had made a call and pointed out my row with the official. Apparently he had reported me to the County FA. They in turn had escalated it to the FA. Bob said: "I can understand your passion, but you can't be verbally abusing officials. You have to be careful."

Now that I was in a more responsible position, I knew my Sunday League days were numbered and I had to tell the Falcon lads that they would need a new manager at the end of the season. I suppose it was a bit bizarre anyway, a coach with one of the world's most famous clubs also running a Sunday team. However, my days with the Falcon had given me tremendous pleasure and it certainly helped to keep your feet on the ground. It all had to end some time.

I put all of my energy into the Liverpool reserves set-up and the Anfield stewards used to laugh. They suggested selling season tickets so that people could stand outside the dressing room door to listen to me ranting and raving after games. They said they would all stand at the top of the steps leading from the pitch from where they could hear me letting fly. I'm sure some of the first-team players who found themselves in the reserves got their bit of stick as well.

The day after reserve games, Ronnie and Roy used to come to me and say: "Not too bad last night, Phil. There were only 15 swear words in your summing up." Here's me thinking it was all private inside the dressing room, not realising that I had an audience of stewards outside! I just wanted the lads to play the game in the right manner. Every game, in my book, was like a European Cup Final.

I treated everyone the same, whether they were young lads making their way in the game or established seniors coming back from injury. The most difficult people to deal with were the disgruntled ones who might have lost their place. I tried to understand their feelings, but demanded that they gave everything because that is the only way you can get back into the first team. I always remembered the words that Joe and Ronnie had said to me when I was in the reserves. "Always make sure you are ready."

I don't know how many times I said that to unhappy pros who were distraught at having dropped down. I could see them looking at me and thinking exactly what I always thought in their situation. "This is all a bit of toffee to get me working hard." The fact of the matter is that Joe and Ronnie were always right, and as a coach I now fully understood the logic.

Big Jan Molby was amongst those I loved to hate at this time. It was hard to get him to run round in the first team, let alone the reserves. That wasn't his game. He had brilliant skills and a special ability to shield the ball. I can't count the number of times I gave him a bollocking after a game. The stewards would be outside listening. Jan was just so laid back. He would say: "Phil, don't panic."

Jan always used to come to me. We were great friends. He would say: "Don't worry Phil, against Everton and Manchester United I will be your star player and turn it on." He was always true to his word. He would dominate the games and be the match-winner and it proved that the bigger the game, the better the player, even in the reserves.

Of course, he was a good lad and a great player. Another one who could get a lashing from me was Paul Walsh, another first teamer who found himself in my company. I remember preparing for a mini derby at Goodison. I arranged for the players to meet at Anfield at noon prior to taking the coach to Everton. There was no sign of Walshy. I couldn't contact him and just about had enough players to deal with the situation.

When we reached Goodison I finally got a phone call from him. He said: "Phil, it's me. I've broken down and I'm stuck in Chester." I said: "Chester? How long has it taken you to get hold of a phone? I know where you are and what you are up to. Just leave it. We'll get by without you."

Years later I found out from Jan that he had been with Walshy earlier. They had both had a couple of bevvies, but Jan had made it to the game. It was not the first time this had happened. It was just the devilment that went on. Walshy played a number of games for me, but he would get a bad ankle injury. In any case, it was not about the established ones, but more about the younger ones coming through, people like Robbie Fowler. I had seen him training with Steve Heighway and was impressed. When Ronnie Moran used to take people off me for the first-team sessions, I would pick the likes of Robbie and Steve McManaman from the youth set-up.

McManaman was another who was laid-back, but he had this tremendous ability and it really shone in those early days in the reserves. I can remember a game at Crewe in which Alan Hansen was trying to come back from a knee injury. This was one of Steve McManaman's first games. He was just 16, but he was unbelievable. He loved taking people on and he astonished some older pros in the Crewe set-up that day.

Steve Staunton was another who impressed as a kid. He was such an honest lad. I remember the great Tom Saunders being with us one day when 'Stan' Staunton played his first game for us at Stafford Rangers. He was only 17, but he knew what to do. I spoke to Tom after the game and he said: "That lad can be a player." We signed him straight away.

I can remember other boys making an impression like Gary Ablett, Mike Marsh and Nick Tanner. All of them got the chance to play in the first team. I had a young Jamie Redknapp and can also remember Don Hutchison. He was one you loved to hate. Don had ability, but there was a horrible side to him. I've seen many like him, people who can play but who can also let themselves down at times.

He was another who got into the first team, but who had some right skirmishes off the field. One day we were having a six-a-side game and the ball fell between us. I was not going to hold back, but came off worse. I had a six-inch gash going down the front of my shin that was covered in mud. I had to turn to coach John Bennison and say: "Benno, take care of the lads while I try to clean this up." I ended up having seven stitches inserted in the wound. Then it got infected and so I had every reason to remember Don Hutchison.

The years that I spent with the reserves were always incredible after the games. Joe Fagan, who had retired by then, would always come and sit in the Boot Room. We would have one drink with the coaching staff from the opposition and then they would get off. Joe would stay and have Scotch while I had a beer. He would help me and talk me through things with some sound advice. He would do this after nearly every home game.

It was nice and I appreciated it, but I would look at him and wonder why he would sit with me for over an hour. I looked into his eyes and wondered: "Was it because of that night in Rome in 1984 when he barred me from getting on the team bus before the European Cup Final?" Was he trying to put right all the wrongs of that night by helping me, or was this just my insecurities coming through?

At this time Marg and I suffered a shock with our son Daniel, who was just two then. We had gone away for a couple of nights to the Last Drop Village in Bolton. It was a weekend break. When we arrived back home on the Sunday morning, Marg's sister Denise was at our house. She said Dan was not feeling well. We drove him to Alder Hey Hospital, ignoring red lights. I was in a panic. He was put on a drip in a special room to help with his dehydration. That frightened us. He had a string of tests and in the end the doctor said he was certain the problem was his appendix.

He told us not to worry, but said it would be best to operate straight away. We put him in the hands of the doctors and within a few hours he was prepared and ready. It was one of the worst moments of my life. We were brave when we were with him, but in bits when we kissed him and he went down to the theatre. They said the procedure would take an hour. Two hours later they finally came out. Every extra minute was like a day. The doctor said: "I'm glad we got him when we did. When we opened him up, the appendix burst everywhere. It was near to perforation. It would have been a huge problem if that had happened while it was inside him."

Everything turned out fine and the staff were magnificent. It was a moment to savour when we were able to see Dan. That experience certainly helped me to put things in perspective.

I've spoken about how a personal situation can threaten to turn your life upside down. Something happened to Liverpool Football Club on April 15, 1989 that rocked a whole city and brought an incredible response from the family of football. I'm talking, of course, about the Hillsborough Disaster that claimed the lives of 96 loyal Liverpudlians.

Just prior to coming back to the club as coach in the summer of 1986, Merseyside had witnessed the first-ever all-Merseyside FA Cup Final. It was a truly historic day. I was not involved with the club at that time, having moved on as a player, and so I was in my role as passionate fan. I celebrated along with the rest of the red army as we completed an historic FA Cup and League Double.

Three years later another all-Merseyside FA Cup Final affair was on the cards when Liverpool and Everton were kept apart in the semi-finals. The Blues, under Colin Harvey, were drawn to play Norwich City at Villa Park. The Reds faced a clash with Brian Clough's Nottingham Forest at Sheffield Wednesday's Hillsborough Stadium. Obviously I was now part of the Anfield backroom team and as reserve-team coach I was sitting on the bench that day.

Because I remained a fan at heart I was always interested in the supporters and everything that surrounded them on big match days. I always knew how they would be feeling. I enjoyed listening to the songs and chants and always looked at the banners to try to spot new ones.

I remember coming out of the Hillsborough dressing room a few minutes early so that I could take in the pageant and colour that I expected to see at the Leppings Lane End where I knew our fans would be gathered in their thousands. I came out of the tunnel and looked towards that goal end. My first thought was: "It seems like the middle section is jam-packed." The sections either side were not as full. My second thought was: "I wish I was amongst the fans and revelling in the game as a supporter" as I had been at Wembley three years earlier for the final itself.

Then I began to focus on the challenge against Forest, aware that victory could set up the possibility of another Wembley date against Everton. My gaze went from the fans to the pitch and in those opening minutes I wasn't aware of the chaos that was unfolding to my left.

Then I saw a fan climbing up on the fence at the Leppings Lane End. He was trying to get out, but a policeman pushed him back in. I nudged Ian Rush, who was sitting by me and said: "Look at that." We trained our eyes on the fans as the referee signalled a suspension to the proceedings with just six minutes on the clock.

It was incredible as a nightmare began to unfold in front of our eyes. The players came off the pitch and we all went down into the dressing room. Kenny Dalglish said to me: "Go and find out what's happening." I stepped out of the dressing room and looked down the tunnel. I couldn't believe the commotion that was going on out on the pitch. I knew it was serious, but I didn't realise the real magnitude of the problem at that time. I went back in to see Kenny and said: "It looks really serious." Immediately I went back out, to be confronted by someone who said: "People are dying out there."

I heard a policeman saying: "Liverpool fans broke a gate down." They were already accusing us before any investigation had taken place. I found that quite weird. That policeman was nowhere near the scene and so obviously information, or misinformation, was being passed around. It sounded as if people were already getting their stories together.

What was absolutely clear was that chaos was unfolding outside. I dashed back into the dressing room and spoke privately to Kenny: I said: "They are saying people are dying out there." The players were lying on the floor and on the benches, stretching and trying to stay loose. In those seconds, they were unaware of the tragedy that was unfolding. Kenny went out to check for himself, but I knew the game would not be going ahead. We were told to stay in the dressing room. Kenny came back and announced that some fans had been killed in a crush at the Leppings Lane End. The room was totally silent. Everyone was in shock.

We were all devastated. It was a real feeling of helplessness and I was desperately worried because I knew many fans who had bought tickets for that end of the ground. I also knew there would be fear and panic back home as family and fans tried to get to grips with what had happened. We were still unaware of how many people had died as we boarded the coach to drive back to Merseyside.

Clearly the drama was still unfolding. Everybody was stunned. We had the radio on, desperate for more news. As I looked out of the window of the coach, people in cars all around were doing exactly the same. It was revealed that several people had died. Then the figure rose to 20, then 30. A chill went down the back of my neck. These were not just our fans. They were our friends. They had gone to Sheffield to enjoy a football match, happy and excited.

Now we were going home in mourning. We all made plans to come back into Anfield first thing the following day. Already, a special service had been arranged at one of the cathedrals. When we arrived at Anfield we were taken pitchside and then onto the Kop. People were already arriving in their droves and leaving mementos on the terrace. Scarves were being tied to the crush barriers and the fencing. Fans were beginning to place flowers in the Kop goalmouth where a Salvation Army Band was playing. It was an incredibly moving sight.

I remember having to walk away into a quiet corner. I was welling up and starting to cry. I was by one of the pylons in the top right-hand corner of the Kop as you look at it from the pitch. That was where the old boys' pen was when I was a kid. Someone put his arm round me. I was saying: "Why us? Why has this happened to our football club?"

I wondered if Heysel had come back to haunt us. We were all feeling totally distraught and stood there motionless for a while. I saw many grown men crying openly, unable to comprehend what had taken place. The Salvation Army Band played on, their members ready to offer help and support. It had been a wonderful gesture. Unannounced, they had instinctively come to the Shankly Gates that morning. Chief executive Peter Robinson saw them and asked them to come into the stadium itself.

Obviously, the death toll had risen dramatically overnight and it would eventually reach 96. The pain for the families and friends of the victims would go on for months. Indeed, I suspect it will never go away because of the sheer scale of the disaster. There were many incredible stories of ordinary people trying to help the injured and the dying.

We made plans to go across to Sheffield the next morning to see the fans in hospital. On the way we stopped at Anfield and raided the souvenir shop, grabbing as many items as possible to sign and take with us.

One thing will live with me forever. A dedicated fan by the name of Lee Nicol was in a coma. Nothing could be done for him, but his mum was so brave. She had waited and kept his life support machine going until the players arrived. We were in bits as we went round the wards. I marvelled at the courage of ladies like Mrs Nicol and all of the families who must have been going through hell.

Of course, the papers were carrying page after page about the disaster. The Liverpool Echo produced a special Sunday edition and would later stand up powerfully for our city as the accusations began to fly.

More than one national paper picked up on the stories suggesting that drunken Liverpudlians had been responsible for breaking down the gate at the Leppings Lane End, leading to the crush. The Sun went right over the top with a series of sickening accusations that disgusted the whole of Merseyside. Under the giant headline 'THE TRUTH', they repeated these claims of drunkenness, but went even further. They claimed that Merseyside fans had urinated on the dead and stolen from the bodies. These claims were all unsubstantiated.

It seems unbelievable how they made the front page. Of course, mud sticks, and for years many people outside of Liverpool were still repeating these stories, even though the respected Lord Justice Taylor, in his subsequent Hillsborough Report, completely vindicated the Liverpool fans.

I don't know what was going through the minds of the families of the dead and injured at that time. I have nothing but the highest respect for the way they handled themselves. We spent hours at the hospital and came back with incredible stories of compassion. One of the big things was the way fans of other clubs came to Merseyside to pay their respects, often leaving their own scarves and little messages of support. The Kop probably had scarves and banners from clubs all over the country as supporters stood as one with rivalries forgotten.

Liverpool's biggest rivals have always been Everton and Manchester United, but their fans were prominent with their messages of condolence. I recall that a 'Chain of Hope' was organised stretching between Everton's Goodison Park and Anfield. Fans were asked to come and tie scarves together and ultimately that line stretched right across Stanley Park, linking the two famous grounds in an incredible show of unity.

Meanwhile, the sea of flowers at Anfield grew bigger and bigger, stretching out across the pitch. After training I used to go and sit in the Directors' Box. I'd watch people placing single roses or full bunches of flowers and cards. They would walk along the side of the pitch and then go up into the Kop, which had become a shrine. The club opened the lounges up for people who had lost sons, daughters, fathers and mothers. They would stream in, often to be greeted by the wives of the players and the staff.

I have to pay a special salute to Kenny Dalglish and his wife Marina, who played a huge part in trying to help people come to terms with what had happened. They worked incredible hours to be close to the fans. We all did, but Kenny and Marina gave everything of themselves at that time, more than anyone could envisage. Kenny was a legend anyway. Now his stature would increase, if that was possible, in the eyes of the fans for the quality time he gave everybody.

Life always has to go on, but it was hard trying to think about playing football again. At that time we didn't know if the semi-final against Forest would be played. Kenny was adamant that this decision should come from the families and this was exactly right.

Then came the funerals. My old mate Terry Mac came back to help people. He accompanied me to eight or nine funerals. All the players and staff were split up so that we could cover all of the funerals. I remember that each and every one of them finished with 'You'll Never Walk Alone'. It used to be a battle cry. Now it was a hymn that united us. Whenever I hear it being played I get a lump in my throat because of those Hillsborough memories.

Somewhere down the line you know that the decision will be taken to play again. That first game for Liverpool turned out to be a friendly against Celtic in Glasgow that raised money for the Hillsborough Fund. This was a highly moving occasion.

As for the issue of safety at football grounds, there is no doubt in my mind that the disaster changed the face of football forever. Before Hillsborough the attitude was: "Herd them in and then herd them out again." Obviously the fences had to come down. We moved into the era of all-seater stadia. The end product is that some fantastic new grounds have been built all over the country and these stand as a tribute to the 96 who died.

After consultation with the families, it was decided that the Forest game should be replayed, this time at Old Trafford. The victory had no other meaning than to act as a salute to the fans who had died in Sheffield. In some respects it was fitting that we would meet our city neighbours Everton at Wembley, but the fierce rivalry of the historic 1986 affair had now been replaced by something that rose above football. There had to be a winner on the day and we claimed the cup, but it was more about paying tribute to the people we had lost. It couldn't be a fervent football triumph in any sense other than to salute the 96. We will never forget them.

For all of us it was about trying to get on with life. The highlight of my coaching honours at this point had been a Sunday League title with Falcon! It was time to move things along and I would now coach the Liverpool reserves to a title success with lads in the side like Charlie Boyd, Mike Marsh, John

McGregor and Mark Seagraves.

Then there was a young lad called Wayne Harrison who had won all of these headlines as the new teen sensation of Anfield when he was signed from Oldham. Wayne had been given the big build-up, but he had gone through an extremely difficult time. He had originally impressed against the Reds in a youth game. In fairness to the player himself, the other lads didn't take to him straight away and that must have been a problem.

He was in and out of his car going back to Oldham and came across as being a bit arrogant and big-headed. Wayne took a long time to settle, but the headlines persisted that he was going to be the next big thing. Liverpool signed him on a four-year contract, but he didn't do anything early on. I tried a number of things. I put my arm around him and offered encouragement. I tried the rollickings. Nothing seemed to work.

He was extremely unlucky with injuries and the Reds could easily have let him go at the end of his final year, but they gave him another 12 months which was a great gesture. The lad himself suddenly responded. It was if he had grown up. During that Championship year for the reserves he scored goals galore. He was confident, a team player and, just as important, one of the lads. Things were finally looking good for him.

However, on the day we won the title this big goalkeeper fell on Wayne right on the goalline and snapped his cruciate ligament. It put him out for the whole of the following season. He was never the same player after that, but as a person he had become a really good lad and I became very good friends with him. It hurt me that he had finally won everybody over, only to pick up this knee injury that would later require 12 operations.

We used to go to the south coast for some pre-season reserve action in Devon. We started our own mini tournament involving the likes of Manchester United and Tottenham. These were arranged through our supporters clubs down there. It built up and became quite enjoyable, although one particular year sticks in my mind for reasons other than the football. We had played in a game and I allowed the lads to have a few drinks in a lovely hotel in Honiton. They were having a really good time and I was happy for them to relax because we were going home the next day.

As the evening wore on I left them to their own devices in the hotel bar. They didn't want the reserve manager hanging around and I was happy that everything would be fine. How wrong can you be? At 2am there was a banging on my bedroom door and someone said: "Phil, you better come downstairs. We have a problem."

I quickly pulled on my tracksuit and went down, by which time the paramedics had arrived. I could see the flashing lights outside. I rushed into this little room by the bar and there was Wayne, completely out of it. It had nothing to do with alcohol. He was clearly in shock. The paramedics had a compression bandage on his arm. I said: "What happened? This is serious and I need to know."

I got a couple of the lads out of bed. I was wondering if there had been a fight or something. They were all very much on the defensive and the back foot. Mr Corkish, one of the directors, was with us. I thought: "I've got some explaining to do here." I watched the ambulance disappear and continued my questioning of the other players. It turned out that a little bit of fun had turned into high jinx. They had started the type of game you normally play in a swimming pool. One lad would get on the shoulders of another. They would then face their opponents, trying to knock each other off. There is no danger when you crash down into the water. However, Wayne had come off and gone straight through a glass door.

I contacted Mr Corkish and explained what had happened. Clearly, the priority was to go to the hospital to see if Wayne was alright. When we got there the doctors were talking about possible skin grafts. Wayne had this huge 10-inch gash across his arm. He had been stitched up, but had lost a lot of blood. They said he needed a transfusion and that the injury was too severe for him to travel home with us. We had to leave him there, but arranged for a car to take him home. One of the lads stayed with him.

I knew people back at the club would be asking questions and rightly so. As it turned out, our chairman Sir John Smith called me to a meeting. I was expecting a grilling, even though I had not been directly involved.

However, I wasn't expecting to have the finger pointed at me. Somehow they got it all mixed up and accused me of being in the bar when the accident happened. Naturally I stood my ground and said that I had explained to Mr Corkish exactly what had happened. If I had been there the incident would not have materialised. In effect I was being given a bollocking and I was really upset, but I was more interested in Wayne's condition. I felt really sorry for him because he was just coming out of his difficult period. This knocked him back, which was a blow because we had a fantastic bunch of lads at that time and his development would have continued.

At this time I had a shock problem of my own. I found I couldn't fasten my boots across the front because of a severe pain in my foot. Even when I was having a meal, I had to slip my shoe off because it was so uncomfortable, not pleasant if we were in a restaurant!

I had to go to the hospital and they actually amputated the top two digits of the toe next to my little toe on my left foot. They said this was the only way they could relieve the pain.

I had it done pre-season, but it still felt uncomfortable when I went back to work. I didn't think much about it until physio Paul Chadwick came in one day and said they had received the biopsy back from the operation. He said it had been a tumour, but that I wasn't to worry because it was benign.

I asked a few questions and he said: "It's not malignant. It's not that sort of cancer." As soon as he mentioned the word 'cancer' I was shocked. I never even thought that the little lump on the side of my toe could have had such serious implications. After you finish playing you think your injury problems are over. The worst thing about it was the pain across my foot remained for years, even though I was told I was okay. They said they had taken everything out that could be a problem and that possibly it was a phantom pain. It felt pretty real to me.

I concentrated on my coaching challenge. Of course, I'd always been told that results did not matter and that it was more about bringing people through. I've already mentioned how Ronnie Moran emphasised that to me when I considered playing the odd game myself. He was more interested in seeing the younger ones getting a chance, regardless of whether we might win or lose.

Then we got a trouncing at Manchester City. I had a number of young lads playing against a very experienced City side. We'd never had a drubbing like it and lost 5-0. I still thought nothing of it, happy that the reversal was all part of our younger ones growing up and learning from seasoned pros. I was leaving Anfield one day and met chairman Sir John Smith in the car park. He gave me the biggest dressing down of my coaching career. He said: "Don't you know the importance of these reserve games to Liverpool FC. It doesn't matter what team you put out, we should not lose 5-0." I started to explain about the education of the up and coming stars, but he just cut me dead and said: "I don't care."

What do you do in this situation? You can't over-react with the chairman of the club. It was really frustrating. Let's just say that with the lessons from Ronnie, the episode with Wayne and the chairman's rebuff, I had been through my baptism of fire in the world of coaching.

While my clash with the chairman was a stunner, nothing could prepare me for what happened next. I can distinctly remember walking through the door at Anfield one morning to meet Ronnie and Roy Evans. I walked into the Boot

Room where Ronnie was making out all kinds of lists. Roy said: "You are going to have to tell Phil now before anyone else finds out?" I didn't have a clue what he was talking about. Ronnie just said: "Kenny has gone."

I just stood there, waiting for the end of the sentence. Gone where? Gone training? Gone on a scouting trip? Ronnie saw the look on my face and said: "He's gone. Kenny has packed it in." I thought they were winding me up, but Ronnie quickly added: "He feels as if some screws are being tightened either side of his head."

That was all he said. I just sat down shaking my head. It was an incredible situation and I was shocked. Of course, we had to tell the players what was happening. The first team had been involved in two epic games with Everton in the fifth round of the FA Cup. The first match was drawn 0-0 at Anfield on a day when the Evertonians were left fuming. Referee Neil Midgley denied them a penalty after Gary Ablett brought down Pat Nevin in the box. Possibly it fired them up for what turned out to be an incredible replay on February 20, 1991. The tie finished 4-4 with the Reds losing the lead four times.

Everton just wouldn't lie down and while we scored some fantastic goals at Goodison, we could not kill them off. Clearly the pressures on Kenny must have been enormous at this time although we were not really aware that anything was wrong.

Possibly it all started for him after the Hillsborough Disaster. We all played our part, but Kenny and his wife Marina put a tremendous amount of effort into attending the funerals and comforting those who had lost family and friends. Kenny took a huge amount on himself and spent hours at Anfield as well as at people's homes offering his support. He was emotionally drained.

He carried on and at the time of the Everton cup confrontation the team was still good enough to be leading the top flight. However, it was an ageing team and while he had many very good players he must have known that he would have to make significant changes moving forward. I don't know whether this added to the pressure, but his decision to quit caused a sensation throughout football. Ronnie Moran took over in a caretaker capacity as the lads faced a third game against Everton, one they would lose by a single Dave Watson goal at Goodison Park.

Everyone was trying to analyse the Dalglish situation. Kenny could be ruthless, but it is never easy when you have to consider replacing people who have been friends and teammates. He tried different things in terms of tactics and possibly, for the first time in his life, one or two people were starting to question certain decisions. This must have been hard because he had given everything for the Reds as a player and a manager. He was King of the Kop and nothing can alter the fact that he had done a tremendous job, initially as player manager in 1986 when Liverpool won an historic League and FA Cup Double. He also won the title in 1988 and 1990 and collected a second FA Cup in 1989. His record was outstanding, but they don't call it the Anfield hotseat for nothing. It was a truly astonishing time.

I hoped that Kenny might be able to take a sabbatical and come back refreshed. With hindsight that might have been the best solution because when he eventually returned with unfashionable Blackburn Rovers he won yet another title. Obviously he still had something to offer and might have come back stronger after a break.

In times of stress, humour often comes to the fore to ease the tension. This is exactly what happened as we all waited to hear the outcome of Kenny's decision to quit. It all seemed quite simple really. Let's wind Stevie Nicol up. Big Al said: "I will say that I'm the new manager and that I'm going to make Nico the new captain. I'll tell him that things are going to have to change because these are important times for him and that he can't be the class clown any more". It was all done between the staff and Big Al. Of course, when the word got round that a special announcement was about to be made all the apprentices were milling around outside the closed dressing room door, trying to hear what was going on.

Big Al had come in and declared to the other lads that Kenny had packed in and he was to be the new manager. He said he was really pleased and proud. Having got everybody's attention he declared that he was making his first appointment with Stevie Nicol named as the new captain. He said: "Nico, this is a great opportunity for you. You must understand that you will have to change your ways and be more thoughtful about what you are doing"

You could hear this noise outside the dressing room door as all the young Irish lads suddenly rushed off to tell their dads to get some money on Alan Hansen as the new manager. Twenty minutes later, when the joke was revealed, these kids were thinking: "How much has this just cost my parents?" It was an absolute scream and I would like to think that even Kenny saw the funny side when he was told about it later. He was always game for a laugh, not least where Nico was concerned.

However, behind this show of team spirit and humour was the cold fact of life that the manager was leaving with all the implications that come with that. Everyone starts to think: "What is going to happen now? Who is going to take over?" The obvious person to do that was Ronnie Moran.

He was the caretaker manager and it seemed the ideal time for him to take the next step. He had all of this experience that stretched right back to Bob Paisley and Shanks. Ronnie was a good coach. He could communicate and he was a driving force. Yes, he was a professional moaner as well, but he knew the game. He was my mentor and I believed in everything he did. He could suss things out before they happened which was the sign of a good coach. I thought that the time was finally right for him, even though he was one of those people who was happy to be in the background. Ronnie was truly a fascinating character.

Even if the lads had won 5-0, he would still come in and find something to moan about, some issue that he felt we could improve. Sometimes you would feel like saying: "Get a life, Ronnie," but later you would realise that every club needs people like him. You could never rest on your laurels with him. I just felt it was time for Ronnie to step forward, but he was saying: "I can't handle the Press. I don't want it."

It was suggested I should go with the first team for matches and help out on the coaching side with Roy administering the treatment on the pitch. I would get more responsibility helping Ronnie because Roy had other things to do. We walloped Derby County 7-0 and the fans were in party mode. Every move was greeted by the Kop with a loud 'Ole!' They were chanting for Ronnie, chanting for Roy and as they moved along the bench they were chanting for me. It felt really good being down there and part of the first-team scene in a different way. If Ronnie had taken the job and Roy had stepped up as his assistant, I would have stepped up a notch as well.

As things moved on and Ronnie realised that he could actually handle the press as well as all of the other things that come with the manager's role, it was clear that his attitude towards the job was changing. He actually went to Peter Robinson and said: "If you want me, I will take the job." Peter said: "Oh, if only you had made that clear earlier. We have appointed a new manager. We have asked Graeme Souness to come back."

Although we all felt disappointed for Ronnie, we were aware that Graeme knew how the club was run. He had also done a very good job at Glasgow Rangers where he had been brave enough to make big changes. He had reversed the transfer scene north of the border, taking good players from England to Scotland whereas the market had always worked the other way. He had shown his strength of character by signing Rangers' first Catholic player. He was clearly delighted to be coming back to Liverpool, but we were naturally wondering what would happen on the coaching side. Phil Boersma had been with Graeme at Ibrox. In what capacity would he come in? It seemed my days with the first team were numbered.

When Boersma arrived, his role was to administer the treatment and deal with the rehabilitation of injured players along with Paul Chadwick, who was a good physio. We had never had anyone like Paul before and this was one of the positive steps that Graeme took at that time.

I settled back into running the reserves. Of course, there had been a problem between Graeme and myself when I lost the captaincy to him in 1981, but I spent three years with him after that and it was water under the bridge. In fact, we were very friendly. It had always been Kenny, Graeme, Terry Mac and myself and we were close. I must admit, I thought it was a great coup to have him back as manager. He seemed the ideal person, he knew the football club and he was thrilled to be back. He was also extremely passionate about his football and did not suffer fools lightly. The players were going to have to do things his way and he did have some good ideas. Clearly he wanted to change things and move the club on.

Graeme had been in Italy with Sampdoria and he had learned some different methods over there. He had transformed Scottish football by taking the likes of Ray Wilkins, Terry Butcher, Graham Roberts and Mark Hateley to Rangers. He was ready to court controversy and some of the older players in the Liverpool squad knew their time had come.

Graeme was like a whirlwind. He was clear no one would be taking money under false pretences at Anfield. He would weed out those who were not good enough or past their best. As I said, Graeme had good ideas, but he possibly did things too quickly for his own good. Possibly this would be one of his big regrets, but these were early days and as things began to unfold, I was more than pleased that Graeme was there.

Souness says I can be his young Ronnie Moran but I end up sacked

In those days it was common practice to go straight to Peter Robinson if you had an issue over something like your wages. I felt I was getting a pittance in my coaching role and believed I had done enough for it to be reviewed. I went to see Peter, only for Graeme to pull me to one side the next day. He said: "I believe you have been to see Peter Robinson about a rise? I don't want you doing this. In future I will deal with any of those decisions. I am dealing with everything."

I said: "I'm sorry, but what I did was standard practice. We've always gone to the chief executive over things like this." He said: "That ends now. I am dealing with it. I will see what can be done." I immediately took the opportunity to ask how I fitted into his plans. I said: "I know you have brought in Phil Boersma, but where do you see me fitting in?" Graeme said: "I see you as my young Ronnie Moran. I want you with me." I thought: "Fair enough. He seems to have confidence in my coaching ability and what I might offer." I felt it was a step in the right direction and settled back into my job.

The one big problem that confronted us at that time was a rush of injuries. We had five players with their left Achilles tendon in plaster. I thought we were going to start selling red and white crutches in the souvenir shop because they were so popular, and so many were knocking about in the dressing room. We had started training by running on hard ground.

The players found it difficult dealing with some of the new ideas. The sound of these crutches was evident for weeks on end. Obviously you assess it. Five with exactly the same injury?

With these players out obviously their places needed filling. That is where our younger reserve lads came to the fore and they did well. It was nice for them and a boost for me. It's always pleasing to help bring players through and those lads saved Graeme from any more criticism.

Graeme was now well into his role and continuing to evolve his ideas when news suddenly broke that he needed a heart by-pass operation. This came as a real shock to everyone. His popularity had waned over the way that season was going, but the FA Cup continued to offer possibilities for him. We were doing extremely well in that. Graeme would have his operation, but he then made a fundamental mistake. He gave his first big interview to The Sun newspaper that had been reviled by Liverpudlians ever since their disgusting allegations about our fans after Hillsborough. When people on Merseyside realised Graeme had co-operated with The Sun they were shocked and disgusted. Being one of his coaches, people would ask me why he did that. They would slaughter him for it.

I knew he had made a mistake and Graeme probably knew it as well. Whenever people asked me about it, I would try and explain that he did not understand the depth of feeling about The Sun because he had been in Scotland when all of the controversy unfolded. He was my boss and my instinct was to try and be protective towards him. That was my stance.

As he continued on the recovery path there were naturally stories about who might run things in the short term. My name would crop up now and again. I can remember my mum saying: "People were talking in the bingo last night and I heard them saying that Phil Thompson should get a chance." I pointed my finger at my mum and said: "Talk like that could get me the sack. If people say things like that, don't respond."

There was a little bit of an undercurrent, but life at Liverpool went on with Ronnie, Roy and Phil Boersma running the first team while I continued with the reserves. Graeme was recovering in hospital in Manchester. I said: "I'm going in to see him," but Roy reacted by saying: "Don't do that. We will go in and see Graeme together."

I then found out that Roy had been in without mentioning it to me. I thought: 'Why?' By now, Graeme had come out of hospital and because I had been holding back for Roy, I had not been in to see him. My wife said: "He might be annoyed with you over that." I was angry that Roy had told me to leave it and then gone in to see Graeme without mentioning it to me.

I can remember Graeme returning just before the FA Cup Final. We were in the dressing room and he showed us his operation scars. Clearly it had been a difficult time and I think he had a relapse in hospital because of his battle to be fit for Wembley. He was a fighter and he really wanted to be at the final. From my side, I just felt that something was not right. I even mentioned it to my wife and brought it up in conversation with Ronnie and Roy. I felt things were afoot. We were coming back to Merseyside the day after the final and I recall a conversation between Tom Saunders, Ronnie, Roy and myself. We were all talking about what was going to happen.

Ronnie said: "I am not feeling safe." I said: "I have a distinct feeling that something is happening behind my back. I could be looking for a new job in the summer."

Tom was a very astute man who would have known what was going on behind the scenes. He asked me an interesting question. "What would you do Phil if you did leave the club?" I just said: "I don't know."

Later I thought long and hard about his question. Tom had been very close to Kenny. He was also close to Graeme. He was respected by everyone and handed out advice at the right time. He would have had an understanding of the situation as it was developing. The team had beaten Sunderland 2-0 to win the FA Cup. We had the tour of the city and were beginning the process of preparing for the following season.

One of my jobs was to number all the kit up for the new season. I had gone into Anfield and Roy and Ronnie were there. I said: "Have you had your bonus?" As a coach you got an end-of-season reward that was better if a trophy had been won. Of course, the club had claimed the FA Cup. They said: "Yes, we have had ours." It was a bit of a shock and I wondered if I should see Peter Robinson. Maybe something had happened. In fact, I was convinced of it. I said: "I'll tell you something. I'm out of here. I'm a gonner."

I felt that they knew something was going on. My head was spinning. I came across Peter on the balcony at the top of the stairs in the Anfield main entrance and took the opportunity to ask the obvious question. "Ronnie and Roy have had their bonus," I said. "Is there a problem?" He choked on my words and said: "You will need to see the manager."

I went downstairs and said: "I'm finished here." For the next couple of hours I rang Graeme's house, his mobile and other numbers on which I thought I might get him. It was a very difficult time.

My thoughts went immediately to my family. Max had been born the year before in 1991 and so we still had a young baby. We wanted to complete our family and had set our sights on having a child fairly quickly after Max because there had been a five-year gap between him and Dan. Philip was growing up. I thought: "I've got three kids here." Although life had been good to me in a family sense, it appeared that my career was in jeopardy.

Even though nothing had been confirmed I said to Marg: "I'm finished at Liverpool." She was in the garden and I remember her looking through the patio doors, clearly concerned. I continued to ring and ring and finally got hold of Graeme. I said: "Peter Robinson has said that I'm not getting a bonus." He replied: "Come in and see me on Monday and we will discuss it."

It was only Thursday and I said: "There is no way I can leave it like this all over the weekend. I've got a terrible feeling about this. My mind has been in turmoil and I have a wife and young family to consider. If you have bad news for me I need you to tell me now. I'm not coming off this phone until you tell me what is going on."

He said: "Okay, you are out." I said: "Finished? Why?" and the response was: "I'll tell you on Monday," but I pressed him further. Finally he said: "You have been rollicking the young lads in the reserves too much."

I couldn't accept this. Yes, they got the verbals at times, but I had a great relationship with them. I felt they needed to know how to take criticism and still be positive. If they were ever to progress into the first team with Ronnie, they would know what a tongue-lashing was. He could also be relentless.

I said: "I am not having that," but the reply was emphatic. "That's the way it is," said Graeme. I just said it was a load of crap and that I would be in on the Monday to see him. I can remember Marg looking through the window again and her head dropped. She knew by my face what had happened. I was in tears.

Of course, I started thinking what I could do. This was not right. In fact, it was a nightmare. I'd gone from being the next young Ronnie Moran, to use Graeme's words, to being out on my arse inside 12 months. I thought I would speak to new chairman David Moores. He had been a good friend of mine. He said: "Phil, I know that is what he wants to do. Leave it with me. I will try and have a word with him to arrange a meeting."

I had always had a fantastic relationship with David. He would come to reserve games when he was a director and we used to sit and chat. Of course, over the weekend I was continually thinking about what might happen. He had told me not to meet Graeme on the Monday, but leave it until he had been in touch. That gave me a bit of hope.

It was an extremely hard few days and it was funny. Sammy Lee had been released by Bolton the week before. He was a good friend of mine and I knew he wanted to get into coaching. Sammy had rung me to ask if there might be any openings for him at Liverpool. I had said: "Leave it with me. I will mention it to Ronnie and Roy."

I had heard that John Bennison might be packing it in. He was a great guy who had really helped me with the reserves. I would certainly not be suggesting that Sammy should replace John. It was more a case of seeing if Sammy could be at the top of the list if anything came up.

Sammy had rung me again to see if I had heard anything for him. Of course, this was before my own bombshell news. I told him that Graeme was up at Anfield signing a player and suggested that he should pop up there to speak directly to the manager. This would be the best way of him finding out if any jobs were coming up. Of course, I didn't think for a moment that the first vacancy might actually be mine!

I said to Sammy: "Get in the car and get up there now. If John does decide to retire you will be in there." The strange thing is, I did not hear back from Sammy. Then everything blew up on the Thursday.

The papers arrived on Sunday morning and a number of them were revealing that some shock news was about to break at Anfield. Sources were saying that I was going to be sacked from my job as reserve-team coach and that Sammy Lee was going to replace me.

Who were these sources? I thought: 'Clever! Before I can get anything done through the chairman it has been leaked to the press that I'm out. Things have been turned on their head and now that it's in the public arena there is no way back.' I rang the chairman almost immediately. He was annoyed that it had leaked out and said: "Don't come in tomorrow. We are going to have a meeting at Anfield on Tuesday."

I sat down and thought about it. Was the reason why the story made the Sunday papers a clever move to make the whole thing cut and dried, regardless of the chairman's view? Was it now just a forlorn hope on my part that I could somehow turn things round? Was it significant that I had not heard back from Sammy?

It must have been difficult for him. Sammy had asked me about a job and ended up getting mine! He was probably embarrassed, but it was a fantastic appointment for him. I came in similar circumstances when Chris Lawler went. I finally spoke to Sammy and said: "Look, no problem at all. It's a great opportunity for you and one you can only accept. Don't worry about it. I will never think badly of you."

I had more immediate things to concentrate on, like the meeting at Anfield. Kevin Dooley was my solicitor. I had been talking to him. He was a good friend of the family and was related to Roy Evans through marriage. However, I was the one who had introduced Kevin to a number of people at Anfield like Terry Mac, Kenny Dalglish and even Graeme Souness. The thing with Kevin was that he acted for Graeme and the football club on a number of issues, even though he was not the official club solicitor. He was also acting for me and so there was a bit of a conflict there.

He would say some strange things to me, like: "Don't ring me on my private line any more, Phil. You never know who might be listening." I thought: "That is very strange. After all these years of me ringing him on his private line as a player and a coach, he was now telling me not to. Was it because of the fact that I was on a potential collision course with the club over what was happening?"

Anyway, Kevin and myself went to the meeting on the Tuesday. I saw Graeme there, but we didn't speak. The chairman and vice-chairman Syd Moss were already in the boardroom. Syd was a wonderful old guy. Then there was Tom Saunders, who was a highly respected director. Tony Ensor was their financial guy and chief executive Peter Robinson completed the group. They were all in the boardroom, including Graeme, and Peter asked me to give them a few minutes.

I waited outside in the directors' lounge with Kevin. While they were in discussion I put my ear to the door. Syd Moss was saying to Graeme Souness: "You have enough problems at this club. You cannot do this to the lad. This will cause murder if you do this. You will have to re-think." Graeme said: "I want him out. I want him to leave and I want you to back me." Kevin Dooley said: "Thommo, get away from that door." I moved away and ten minutes later Peter Robinson came out to call me in.

The chairman was sitting at the head of the table with Graeme Souness next to him. He said: "Phil, we have had a discussion and chatted about the situation. We are all in full agreement that we have to back the manager's decision over this."

I said: "Fair enough, but what is the reason for my dismissal?" They said: "We will give it to you in writing." I immediately said that the reason the manager had given me for my sacking was that I was shouting too much at the younger lads.

I added that I was not accepting that as the real reason for being sacked. I said: "You know and I know that this is personal. It is something wider than this and you are not going to tell me."

I added: "I would like to thank you for all the help you have given me at this football club. I have had a wonderful time as a player and a coach. I'd like to think that I have never been any trouble. I've done things with dignity and always done my job as well as I can." The chairman said: "You have done your bit. Thank you for your efforts."

Tony Ensor said: "We need to discuss your settlement." This surprised me and I said: "Now? Here? You are joking. You want me to discuss my terms of settlement in front of Graeme Souness, who has just sacked me?" The chairman said: "Graeme is allowed to sit in on everything we do." I was not having it and said: "Sorry. I'm not discussing terms now. I need to do this another time."

Tony Ensor said that he would give me the number of ACAS in case I needed any help. I know these were all technicalities they had to observe, but it was developing into a union meeting. He gave me a card with the number on. I thanked everyone again. Graeme Souness did not look up as I went out of the room.

I can remember meeting new goalkeeper David James downstairs, who was just signing from Watford. I said: "Welcome to the football club David, but keep your back to the wall. Make sure there is no one with a knife to stab you." I was distraught.

Twelve months later I would speak to Alan Kennedy and David Johnson and tell them that I could not accept the reason I was given for my departure. I said: "I still can't find out the real reason." I was surprised when they said: "We can tell you."

Apparently, when the team beat Manchester United 2-0 at Anfield when Graeme Souness was ill, I am supposed to have said something to their coach Brian Kidd in the Boot Room about Graeme changing things too much at the club. I am alleged to have said: "This club is not the same. There is not the same closeness."

Whether I had said those words about Graeme changing things too much, I don't know. However, Brian is said to have told Alex Ferguson. He then told Everton coach Archie Knox, who told manager Walter Smith.

Walter, of course, had been with Graeme at Rangers. The suggestion was that this was the route by which Graeme picked up on my supposed words. Whether they were misconstrued, I don't know, but Alan and David relayed this chain of events to me. I went back and told Marg. She said: "If this is the case, how could he have done this to you without asking for your version?"

I had never had a falling out with him, putting the captaincy issue to one side all of those years earlier. I was always behind him and supportive of him while I was a coach. Even if I did say those words, surely a rollicking would have been enough. Why did he have to give me the sack? To this day I don't know. What I do know is that it caused me tremendous personal grief and affected all of my family, not least my sons.

I always think back to the Monday after being told by Graeme that he wanted me out. I had to tell my two older boys what had happened before they found out from somebody else.

We had this dining room area, I called Philip, 11, and Dan, 7, into the room and sat them down. I said: "You know we have had a good time at Liverpool. I have to tell you that your dad has been sacked."

The older one said 'why?' and I said: "I don't know." He said: "Does that mean you won't be going back and coaching the players?" I said: "No, that is the end of it" and the two of them started crying. They were real Liverpool fans, even at that age. The two of them were hugging each other and sobbing and I vowed at that moment never to talk to Graeme Souness ever again.

Even now my wife Marg says: "Why can't you come together? You were good teammates.

"Why can't you sit down with him and ask if he got it wrong?" I just have these pictures in my mind of my boys being so broken-hearted and the answer is: "No, never again."

That was a sad end to my second spell at the club. I'm still uptight all these years on that he never gave me the chance to explain those 'alleged' words to Brian Kidd in the Boot Room about "changing things too quickly."

Even in the months immediately after ending my third spell at Liverpool with Gerard Houllier, the subject came up in a conversation with one of the guys down at SKY. He asked about my relationship with Graeme and I repeated my view that it was over a petty decision about my so-called conversation with Brian Kidd. He said: "Graeme had told me that you were after his job."

After all of those years, this was the first time I had heard this comment. Was this the real reason why he sacked me? The simple fact is that I could never have done his job at that time. I was never ready at that point to manage Liverpool. If he was questioning my loyalty, why didn't he ask me about it? People in Liverpool know me well. I have been all over the place in pubs and clubs meeting people and making presentations. People who understand my character know I am not disloyal.

The same chairman who officiated over my sacking, David Moores, would eventually give me the opportunity to come back under Gerard Houllier. I was invited back to Anfield for my loyalty, my ability and my honesty. I feel this says everything about who was right and who was wrong in the Graeme Souness affair.

I was out on my ear and having to think about life without football. At this moment in time I didn't know what I was going to do with myself. Of course, I had my wonderful family to support me. I could give more time to our older boys, Philip and Dan, and one-year-old Max was a bundle of joy. This was a hat-trick that I could really treasure. My wife Marg was a rock, especially as I was feeling so sorry for myself.

Obviously we had to be positive and look to the future for the sake of our lovely family. After Max was born in 1991, Marg and I had decided that we didn't want such a big gap between him and our next child. We decided to try and complete our family sooner rather than later. Then we had Josh. He was born on New Year's Eve, 1993. In a sporting sense the date was significant. Let me explain.

All of our kids had been competitive swimmers. In fact, they all swam for Everton Swimming Club whose colours, dare I say it, were blue and white. We would go to places like Sheffield for a big gala and all of the other parents would be trying to pin these Everton rosettes on me. During the races I would find myself shouting: "Come on Everton!" It was all very strange, but back to our new baby Josh.

December 31 is the worst birthday you can have if you are a youngster wanting to make your way in any sport. The age range runs from January 1 to December 31 and so if you are born on a New Year's Eve, like Josh, you will always compete against kids who are considerably older. Not that I was complaining when he was born. Like all of the kids, he was beautiful.

We had gone to the hospital for an appointment with gynaecologist Peter Bousefield, a friend who had been present for the birth of all the boys. However, he could not be there and we saw a midwife who started pushing and prodding Marg's very large lump. The midwife said the baby still wasn't ready and so we actually went to Asda to do some shopping. Lo and behold, Marg suddenly felt the first labour pains in the supermarket. She knew that she was starting and went into hospital on the night of December 30.

Marg had Josh at 3am on the morning of December 31 and I could not believe it. The midwife got all the blame for making the baby's future sporting career a tough one! We now had our complete family and I have to say that there was a bonus. Now we have a big party for family and friends on New Year's Eve when we also celebrate Josh's birthday at the same time. Of course, it didn't help with the swimming. People asked me to tell lies and say he was born on January 1 to deal with the age-range problem, but my nose is long enough!

Anyway, he was a good swimmer but not as fanatical about it as the other boys. Josh likes his tennis, but his birthday still comes back to haunt him. In competitions he is regularly playing against lads almost 12 months his senior. Fortunately he is good at most sports. He spent two years at the Liverpool FC Academy and likes his football, but he prefers his tennis. As you might gather, I immersed myself in my kids and their sporting pastimes.

I tried to put the Souness affair behind me, but it was hard. I could still not get my head round what had happened. That was the really hard thing, not knowing initially the real reason for my departure. Of course, having to break the news to my family and friends was hard and the support I got was tremendous. They could not take my dismissal lightly and said: "It's payback time, Phil." People wanted to let their feelings be known.

The local radio phone-ins were hot to say the least. It seemed that everyone supported me. This was the can of worms Graeme Souness did not need at that time with things not going too well for him and the team.

I tried to be positive for myself and this is where having the business to fall back into, Pine DIY, was a godsend. I would sit in the office and chat about football to the lads. I say football – they are Evertonians and so that was the only downside! They were incredibly supportive and began to teach me about the business in more detail. I had invested in the company, but had been more of a sleeping partner. Now I could really learn how things were run.

One of the big things the lads decided was to change the name to Phil Thompson Pine DIY. My name on Merseyside was still good for a few sales, I think. One day I went to the counter because one of the sales staff was missing. This old couple came and asked for some help. I thought: "I can serve. It must be easy." They wanted to buy a door and so I picked up the invoice book. I was explaining about all of the different types of glass. The man kept staring at me. He said: "Don't I know you?" I said: "I don't know."

He said: "I know your face from somewhere" and his wife, as if to back him up, added: "If my husband says he knows you, he has certainly met you at some time." Suddenly the husband declared: "I know you. You used to work in Huyton Post Office!" The bill went up instantly from £90 to £150. Here's me thinking I'm Mr Popular and I'm cut to the raw.

The guys on the counter have all got this typical Scouse wit. A woman would come in and say: "I need one of those things you get at the bottom of the door." The lads would immediately go into this Morecambe and Wise-type script. "You mean a bottle of milk?" The woman would say: "No."

The lads would say: "Oh, you mean a letter?" The reply would come back: "No." "Oh, you mean a doormat," the lads would say, revelling in her inability to describe that what she really wanted. "A bolt on the door?" Of course, they would know that she simply wanted a weather board, but we would always go round the houses to get there.

Someone would buy quite a few items. The customer would say: "How much?" and the salesman would immediately say: "£5.99 all together." The other three salesmen would immediately chime up in unison "5.99." I would be sitting there giggling. Of course, the customers loved it. I didn't think going to buy something like that could be so much fun. At times I might have even enjoyed it more than the football.

SKY Sports started in 1992. I would be sitting in the back of the office, holding court about football, and the lads would say: "You should be on this SKY Sports Channel. You know the game inside out." They drifted away and the next thing the phone rings and the shop secretary says to me: "Phil, I have a phone call for you. He says it's a Mr Richard Keys from SKY Television." I'm thinking: "Nice one, it's the lads winding me up." I shouted: "Tell them to behave," but she said: "No, it's a genuine call."

I still wasn't convinced, but picked up the receiver. "Who is it?" I said, expecting to hear a fit of the giggles on the other end of the line. "It's Richard," said a familiar voice. "Is that you Keysie?" I said, seeking double confirmation. Of course, he had no idea why I was being so cagey. He just said: "We are doing this programme called the 'Footballers' Football Show.' We have two panels discussing issues about the game. This show is about Liverpool and why things have gone wrong. Can it go in the right direction?"

I explained that I might be involved in an industrial tribunal about my sacking and that it might be wrong for me to do something like that. Richard said: "Phil, I would not ask you anything that you could not answer. There will be no tricky questions. It will be good for you to go on and get your feelings across." He said that on the Liverpool side would be Brian Hall, Syd Moss and Mark Lawrenson. On the other side with me would be Tommy Smith and journalist Colin Wood. Richard said: "Come on, it will be good for you." I relented on the understanding that there would be no dodgy questions.

On the day of the programme we were getting ready to go on air. Richard did a bit of a promo ten minutes before things started, as much to test out the equipment as anything. He said: "We have former player Brian Hall with us, who these days runs Liverpool's public relations. We also have the club's vice-chairman Syd Moss." At this point Syd immediately began to read from a prepared script, believing the show had started. He said: "We all fully appreciate Phil's time at the club, but we all support the manager."

Mr Moss was a lovely man, but he must have been panicking and keen to get the right words out. He jumped the gun and thought the programme had started. At least I knew where we were going. When we finally went on air, I was asked the first question. This time Brian Hall jumped in and said: "Phil, you have a case against the club. You should be careful in what you say." I said: "Don't you ever tell me what I can and can't say. I am not daft. I would never embarrass the club. Never tell me how to act."

I saw the eyes light up of the SKY staff. I don't know whether this helped me at that time, but I began to be asked back regularly by SKY. I never said anything bad about Liverpool in the full hour of the show. However, I had been forceful and proved that when something needed to be said I would not be found wanting.

I hoped I handled myself with dignity while giving my point of view. When it was all over Syd Moss threw his arms round me and said: "Phil, I hope one day we will be back together again." My mind flashed back to listening at the boardroom door and hearing Mr Moss supporting me. Brian Hall was also very good. He was just fulfilling his role and trying to protect the football club, but he had no reason to worry about me.

This was the start of my journalistic career. I got more and more calls from SKY to do matches and programmes. SKY itself was getting bigger. It was only with the help and support of my business partners that I could do all of this. I must admit, I was enjoying it. Jeff Shreeves, who does all of the interviews, was a great guy. He would ring me and say: "Bognor, can you come and help us out." I would say: "Bognor?" and Jeff would reply: "Yes, the last resort." I would say: "You bastard!"

The programmes were serious stuff, but we could have a real laugh. These were the days of the colourful woollen jackets – purple, orange, blue and red. We would ring each other up and say: "What colour jacket are you wearing tomorrow?" Looking back, they were horrendous.

SKY asked George Best, Ray Clemence, Frank McLintock and myself to take the Footballers' Football Show on the road. We would go to clubs like Norwich and Newcastle. It was good to be out and about and listening to opinions right across the board, but bad when fans started attacking their local chairman. At Newcastle George was a bit worse-for-wear. In the hotel I asked him if he was okay. He said he had fallen out with his girlfriend. He opened his jacket and pulled out wads of twenty-pound notes. He said: "This is my little stash. I hide them in the pots and pans for when I might go on a session after an argument." This was one of those moments and he got off straight after the show. He was a remarkable character.

When Soccer Saturday started I had this love/hate relationship with my good friend Rodney Marsh. We would argue for argument's sake, but we built up a great relationship. I would be on holiday and people would be saying: "Give it to that Rodney Marsh. He is an arrogant bastard." Obviously it made for good TV because everyone was talking about it. That was the great thing about the programme. We all had our own ideas and opinions, but we got on really well. Rodney was one of the first to congratulate me when I got the Liverpool assistant manager's job.

It was strange, but the week before I got the call to go back to Liverpool with Gerard Houllier, SKY offered good contracts to Rodney, Frank, Clive Allen and myself. George was paid per show because there might be occasions when they would not see him. I was mulling over that offer when I got the call from Anfield.

Things were going really well for me at this time. I was writing a column for the Liverpool Echo and the Kop Magazine. I was doing co-commentaries on Radio City with the likes of Kev Keatings. I was seeing how the other half lived and building my own little journalistic empire that I enjoyed greatly. Off the back of all of this the business was getting some great publicity.

I remember speaking to my big mate Tommy Smith at a function. He was saying: "You should go into the after dinner speaking business." I thought: "I can't handle anything like that," but I did one and it escalated from there. I was not like Smithy, who did quite a few of these shows all over the place. I always wanted to be able to drive home.

My first booking came when I got a call from this event organiser called Kevin Pilkington. He said: "We have a function tomorrow and Alan Kennedy has double-booked. We have no one to do it."

I immediately thought: "Bognor." Kevin added: "We are in a mess. Could you just do a question and answer session?" It was reasonably near in Southport and he offered me some money, which helped. It turned out I would be working with former Everton captain Brian Labone. I listened to Labby, who made it look quite easy. I wrote down a few notes about Shanks and Bob and was introduced.

I said: "When Kevin rang me yesterday and asked me to come along, he explained it was because Alan Kennedy had let him down and was not able to do the function. When I put the phone down I thought: 'Here I am, ten years after I've finished playing and I'm still covering for Alan Kennedy'."

They all laughed and I cracked a few more jokes, telling them about my experiences with Shanks and Bob. I told a couple of one-liners about Shanks and how he used to say that I must have told some terrible lies as a boy because of the size of my nose. It was just ten minutes and then questions and answers, but I found it very enjoyable. I started to get offered quite a few functions with agents in the showbiz industry regularly offering me work.

However, as a family we suddenly had to come to terms at this time with the death of Marg's mum who had been suffering from Alzheimer's. Agnes was a wonderful lady and a very caring woman who had worked at Walton Hospital as a nurse. During her illness we tried to give Marg's dad Jimmy a break whenever we could. A good group of friends would visit Agnes and sit with her. It was still difficult to come to terms with the Alzheimer's, a debilitating disease in which you gradually lose your memory.

Agnes had been great with our kids. The two mums used to baby-sit, but it was natural for Marg's mum to have them more. It was a massive shock when Agnes died. If Alzheimer's wasn't enough, she had also developed cancer. This was a difficult time for Marg because she was very close to her mum.

In our early courting days it was slightly difficult because I was five or six years older. I met Marg when she was 16. She was very young while I was a 22-year-old footballer and lad about town. I had known Marg's parents for many years. Both families used to go to the Liberal Club together in Kirkby and they lived just 200 yards apart. They also went to St Laurence's Club together. Agnes knew me and was worried for her daughter when we started going out.

It was amazing. I actually approached Marg for the first time when she was playing a mean game of darts in the Liberal Club. This was the week after the famous ladies football match that I refereed in which she played and clearly made an impression on me. I asked if I could walk her home and we went into her house. Agnes was a bit wary, but Jimmy and me sat in the back kitchen sharing a drink and chatting about Liverpool. He was a big fan and often took Marg into the Anfield Road End. He was recalling how he would take her as a young teenager and say: "See that fella there wearing the number four. He lives just round the corner from us." We went on to talk about all of the games. Jimmy was a great fella.

Over the years Agnes began to trust me a bit more. When Marg and myself finally got engaged and then married she believed in me 100 per cent. She was a great woman. At times I would stay in their house, having wined and dined Marg on fish and chips after coming out of the pub.

Agnes would always have this big roast dinner available. How I was always so skinny is astonishing to me. She took care of me. It would be bacon sandwiches in bed. That was the honoured life of a guest. As I said, when she passed away it was such a sad time because she had made an impact on so many people.

Jimmy would die 16 months later of leukaemia. He had a few problems, but just got on with it. He was one of the old school. He just knuckled down. In his early days he had been a good footballer and had the option of going pro with Port Vale or Stoke. Because he had started his family he opted for the more secure job of full-time welder. It showed how down-to-earth he was. It was sad that he died so soon after Agnes.

We had to get on with life and one of the strangest things I did at this time was to chair the Vernons 'Spot The Ball' panel. I got a call from a guy called Ken Hamilton. He said they were breaking away from Zetters and Littlewoods and needed to create a three-strong panel to judge where the ball might be on a photograph. He asked if I would like to be chairman. I was invited down to his office. Ken was an easy guy to talk to and he encouraged me to believe this would be good.

In choosing the remainder of the panel, he said he would prefer a former Everton and Liverpool player. I said that David Johnson used to play for Everton as well as the Reds and that Alan Kennedy would be good for the Liverpool representative. I told the lads the deal and they were both up for it.

We would meet at 8am every Saturday morning at the Vernons headquarters in Liverpool. We would each have an identical coupon in front of us and then proceed to decide where the crosses would go. I would have the deciding vote. Of course, as a defender Alan always felt that when the ball was in the air the full-back or centre-back would be winning it and heading away. Johnno would want the attacker flicking the ball on. I would adjudicate between them. Of course, most of the time Johnno's thoughts would be thrown out as the defenders' club worked together!

This process would actually take about five minutes. By 8.05am we would be finished, having decided where the 'X' was going to be. Someone would then come along and process it. It would come down to a microdot right in the middle of the X. You might think you had hit the spot, but it had to be exact and there was this equipment that electronically judged the entries.

We had a fanfare launch in Brighton with television presenter Keith Chegwin involved. The prize for the launch day was £150,000. We had this routine of meeting at Vernons every Saturday morning for a couple of years. I would leave by 8.30am to catch a plane so that I was in the SKY studios by noon. At Vernons we always had the best breakfast in the world while enjoying ourselves and talking about all the old times.

This is how the Christmas get-togethers came about with the former players. There would be Kenny Dalglish, Alan Hansen, Alan Kennedy, David Johnson, myself and a few others like Gary Gillespie, John Aldridge and John Barnes. Yes, you're right. No Souness!

In the early days we would invite about a dozen and only four or five of us would turn up. It became a bit of a legendary night out. Of course, the official Former Players' Association bridging all of the decades would soon be born and what a tremendous organisation it is. But we like to think our little gatherings showed the way.

I had put the agony of being sacked behind me, although I always carried the pain and the anger deep down inside. During these years I really enjoyed myself with my media work and all of the other things that made up what had become Phil Thompson Football Ltd. I got asked to go on some fantastic tours. A guy in Southampton wanted me to do some corporate work. I never wanted to be too far from home because of the children's education and the like and so I put Alan Kennedy in touch. I think he ended up going to somewhere like the Cayman Islands. One ex-player's loss was another's gain.

The business was going well. We started to branch out and opened another store near the Tranmere Rovers ground in Birkenhead. We stopped selling the doors and moved into fireplaces, something that was taking over most of our business. We were now called Phil Thompson's Home Improvements. We also opened a fantastic new store opposite Aintree Racecourse. This was now to be our main offices and main branch. It was everything that Stevie, Paul and myself had dreamed of doing and a really top-class fireplace showroom that we were all extremely proud of.

The Vernons routine ended because the new Lottery was taking up people's spare money. Unfortunately it meant some redundancies at Vernons and this was hard for the people concerned. It had been really enjoyable while it lasted. The lads still drool over the memories of the crispy bacon and the wonderful sausages we had for breakfast.

Throughout my time away from the game, things were getting stickier for Graeme Souness at Anfield. It was no surprise when the club ended things after a FA Cup tie against Bristol City at Anfield that didn't go well.

I have to admit, I did not shed too many tears. It was right that Roy Evans was then given a shot. I did harbour thoughts for the first time in ages that I might be able to resurrect my coaching career. It would have been the ideal opportunity to go back to Liverpool. Roy had let it be known that he was going to bring in a right-hand man to work with him with support from Ronnie Moran. A lot of people were asking me if I was that man.

To say I was shocked when I heard that Doug Livermore had been appointed was an understatement to say the least. My mind went back to that episode when Graeme Souness was on his sickbed and Roy asked me to hold back on a visit so that we could go together. Then he went himself without telling me. Of course, it was his right to appoint who he liked, but I have already mentioned that when I was made Gerard's assistant and Roy and Doug were leaving Anfield, Roy had said that it was a fantastic decision by the football club to bring me back. Again, I thought: "My goodness. If it was such a good decision, why couldn't you see it?"

Life comes full circle and I'm invited back to help revive the glory days

This brings me full circle to where we came in with this book. By reading it, you have been with me on a remarkable football journey. I hope it has given you an insight into life at a world-famous football club, the ups and downs with no punches pulled.

I was now moving into one of the most exciting phases of my football life, asked to work closely with Gerard Houllier to resurrect the fortunes of the club I had loved all my life.

It was November, 1998. By the amazing standards of the past, thing had not been too good for Liverpool for a number of years. Graeme won the FA Cup in 1992. Roy won the Coca-Cola Cup in 1995. Now I was being asked to try and help revive the glory days. We wanted to bring trophies back to Anfield, but most of all we wanted to win the Premier League.

Having been out of the game for six years I felt that I understood the passion of the fans even more. There had been all of that Spice Boys stuff, the White Suit Final. Most of those boys were young lads. Most were single and they enjoyed themselves. During my playing career we always had the peer factor to help us. There were unwritten rules and the older ones would keep us in our place.

These lads had developed into big stars without that steadying influence and there were not enough people to point them in the right direction. It's all about knowing when to party. I sometimes thought there was unfair criticism of the players, at that time, but in the years when I was out they had made themselves into superstars. We had all heard the stories about £20 notes being burned on the coach. Fans criticised them for their lack of passion and commitment.

I knew one of the things I could do to help Gerard was to tighten things up on the discipline side. That might make me Mr Nasty to some, but I didn't want to shirk the responsibility. I remember Tommy Smith writing in his Echo column that the crew had been running the ship and that this had to change. I knew this was one of the reasons why Gerard had brought me in.

He was now his own man after spending a couple of months trying to make it work with Roy, a joint managerial partnership that was never going to work. That first season, 1998/1999, was exceptionally hard. I think Gerard must have wondered in those early days what he had let himself in for when he saw me on the touchline, shouting and screaming. He must have looked at me and thought: "I can help this lad to progress as a coach." This is what he did.

Of course, my first thought was always why Liverpool had asked me back. The standing of Liverpool FC had never diminished in my mind, but I had heard all of the stories and the rumours about indiscipline in the ranks. Gerard had made sure I knew the truth about what had gone on.

In my mind, certain people needed to be taken to task. When Roy left there had obviously been an opportunity for Patrice Bergues to step up as Gerard's right hand man. He was a great coach, but he didn't want to be assistant manager. He had said to Gerard: "You need someone who is English and who understands the history of the club."

Gerard's respect for Patrice was total and he might have wanted his French countryman as his assistant, but Patrice saw it as being more of a burden to the manager. When I arrived, Gerard and myself sat down with the staff and the players to lay down a clear set of rules. Apparently when Liverpool had gone to Paris St Germain for a European game in France many people said that they had seen our players sitting on the grass before the game talking on their mobile phones for ten to 15 minutes. What kind of focus was this before any match?

I'd heard that many of the foreign players were sitting outside at the back of Melwood, talking incessantly on their mobiles to the people at home. We only wanted one focus at the training ground and that was football. We decided to invoke a ban on mobile phones from the moment anyone came through the gates of Melwood.

Gerard also decided that the universal language of the training ground had to be English. He had always made a big thing of that. He wanted the players to mix more. He didn't want the English, French, Norwegians and Czechs sitting at different tables in the dining room.

The mobile phone ban set the standard for everything. People were going to have to communicate more. Players were going into the toilet cubicles and talking on their phones before training. It was all stopped and not because we wanted to be pedantic. It was to change the atmosphere of Melwood and bring everybody together. How can you communicate with someone when he has constantly got a mobile up to his ear?

Of course, not everyone took too kindly to the new rule. I can remember on the very day that Gerard was announcing his new plans. David James' mobile phone went off to interrupt the manager. It couldn't have been a more timely phone call because it summed up everything about the culture that had developed

Gerard said that the most important meeting you have is always the first one. It all started there and we started to work on the discipline with a clear set of guidelines. Discipline was the big thing at this time. We made it absolutely clear to the players that things would have to change. It wasn't for the benefit of the staff. It was for the good of the club and to improve the quality of life of the players.

Eyebrows continued to be raised in certain quarters, specifically at the phone ban. We all know that the mobile is an extension of a youngster's life these days, but there is a time and place for everything.

Of course, Graeme Souness had tried to change things. He had ideas to upgrade the club. Things had gone into a bit of limbo and the time was now right to get things running again, like no alcohol in the players' lounge at Anfield after games. That was a big statement.

We put the notion to them. It was actually the second year when they took the decision, but it demonstrated how far we had gone. We were trying to get inside the players' minds. I can remember our first game in that 1998/99 season. It was against Leeds and was quite amazing. I had more butterflies in my stomach than I had ever had as a player. To travel to Anfield as the club's Assistant Manager after everything that had gone on in the previous years was a bit of a dream.

My mind when back to 1972/73 and another home game against Leeds as I closed in on my first Championship success. I've already stated how I sang 'You'll Never Walk Alone' in my mind as the coach approached Anfield. That had been the biggest game of my life up to that time. This was just as big for me in a different way. The car park at Anfield was chockablock. I had a lump in my throat and all I wanted was for us to win this first game.

David O'Leary was manager of Leeds at that time and his assistant was Eddie Gray who was a big friend of mine. Like me, he had also come back from a difficult situation and we had this mutual respect. The game got underway and Karlheinz Riedle won us a penalty that was converted by

Robbie Fowler. Leeds brought on a young kid by the name of Alan Smith and he would help to ruin my day. Leeds scored three goals in the last 15 minutes and Smith got two of them. That was a difficult 'debut' for me as assistant manager.

Of course, I was on the touchline and as passionate as ever. People had this perception of me as this ranting and raving lunatic, like a fan on the touchline. They did not give me the credit for the fact that I had been a coach for six years and knew the game. My whole career had been about understanding and reading the game. This is central to being a good coach. Ronnie Moran always said that a good coach knows what is going to happen before it happens. Yes, I was vocal, but I passed on good knowledge, particularly to the defensive unit.

I liked to organise the defensive section. I don't think I got any real credit for that until I became caretaker manager. After the Leeds game I could not speak. My voice was hoarse. Clearly, my vocal chords were out of practice, but I would soon put that right. The following week we got our first victory, beating Aston Villa 4-2 with a Robbie Fowler hat-trick.

It was a long week. After the Leeds defeat we were trying to lay down the new training routine with Gerard Houllier now in sole charge. Patrice, Sammy, Gerard and myself had planned some new sessions. It was difficult at first to get these new ideas across. We would do ten minutes here, six minutes there, five minutes on something else. The sessions were completely structured and the field was all set out before the players came out. It was difficult for some of them.

There were not as many five-a-sides as they were accustomed to. Some of the players often said: "When you were a player, all that you apparently did was five-a-sides all the time."

My retort to that was: "Yes, but we were winning everything in sight in my day. That's the major difference. This team needs more organised and disciplined sessions to get to where we want to be."

Younger minds need stimulating more. I thought the coaching sessions were fantastic because they were so varied. Even Sammy Lee's warm-ups were funny but highly effective. There were different sessions every day.

Back in the old days the routine never varied under people like Reuben Bennett who was a wonderful man. His attitude, learnt from Shanks, was 'if it's not broken don't fix it'. Now, with the lack of success at the club, there was a need for fresh ideas. Why change the manager and the coaching staff if nothing else is going to change?

Gerard and myself would have regular meetings with Chief Executive Peter Robinson. Gerard's thinking was to have two players for every position. We'd sit in Peter's office with this chart, showing little boxes in a 4-4-2 formation. We'd write in the players we had for every position. We'd also write in the players we would like to target and highlight the names of the ones we did not think were good enough. We would go through this routine on a regular basis in the first few months.

I can remember flying in and out of Holland watching players, sometimes three times in ten days. I'd set off after training and always be back the next day before the players arrived. I was physically shattered. I can remember lying in bed at night and thinking: "Is the manager testing me? Is he checking out my willingness and my loyalty?" I even wondered if he was trying to get me out of the way, but I realised that it had to be done. Gerard would say: "We need a central defender." I would say: "No, we need two."

This had been a big problem for the team. We needed to show the fans that we had a complete grasp of the priorities. Most of the potential targets I looked at during this period were centre-backs. That first ten days was like a whirlwind. I had a very good look at Sparta Rotterdam star Peter Wijzer. I also went to see Ajax and it just so happened that I saw Sander Westerveld playing for Vitesse Arnhem that day.

I went back a second time to see Wijzer, but it was a Europe-wide quest for talent. I saw Nikos Dabizas playing for Greece. On the home front I watched Dean Richards playing for Wolves on quite a few occasions.

Merseyside fans will be fascinated by one particular high powered scouting mission north of the border to see a promising Hearts defender who had been recommended to us. His name was David Weir, later to become captain of Everton. We'd heard good reports about him and treated it seriously enough to take a scouting delegation to Edinburgh that included Gerard Houllier, Peter Robinson, Ron Yeats, Norman Gard and myself. We were all in Gerard's car.

We drove and we drove and it seemed like the journey that was never going to end. It took nearly five hours and by the time we eventually found the ground the match had kicked off at 7.45pm. We eventually got into our seats, but not the ones that were originally reserved for us because these had been given away. It meant we were in different rows. Gerard was two in front of me and Peter was to our left. We eventually settled at 7.52. At 8pm Weir was sent off. A ball came over his head and he was done for pace. He pulled the guy back and got a red card. We knew he wasn't the quickest, but he had good defensive qualities.

Gerard turned round and mouthed to me: "Should we go?" I don't think Weir had touched the ball. We giggled and indicated that we would give it to half time. We went down into the guest room at the interval and they made us very welcome. As everyone started drifting out for the second half, we were enjoying these lovely pies and cups of tea. We said: "Just another cup." Then we picked ourselves up and slipped out for a five-hour journey in reverse back home. Of course, we discussed whether we should look at David again. Did anyone fancy another marathon? We all looked at each other and agreed his pace was a problem and that we should leave it there.

After seeing his consistent performances over many years at Goodison, you wonder if we dismissed him too quickly. He had his limitations, but he was strong and his positional play was good. Then I think about all those road signs that said "Edinburgh, still miles away!" Seriously, if David reads this he might say that we got it wrong. I would respond with Hyypia and Henchoz.

There would be a punchline to the Weir episode years later. I was to have more contact, but in a different way. After one of our derby successes against Everton at Goodison I went onto the pitch to walk towards our fans in the corner of the Bullens Road. I was speaking out loud to myself saying: "We deserved that. We were easily the better side. We deserved the three points." It was a bit louder than that and possibly more on the sarcastic side.

David didn't take kindly to it. As he walked off he launched a large plastic Lucozade bottle in my direction that caught me on the shoulder. I must admit, I had a giggle because I was in a good mood. I didn't want to take it any further because I like the kind of passion someone like David shows. The next day a couple of the Press guys picked up on it and tried to get me to say something, but I wasn't having any of it. After all, if things had been different he might have been wearing Red that day!

After closing the book on Weir, we'd heard about Stephane Henchoz being unhappy at Blackburn. We felt he would be a genuine target if the price was in our area.

We had been told that we only had £12m to spend and that we would have to cut our cloth accordingly. We were not going to take a rash decision. Stephane had injury problems at this time. Rovers had brought him back early and we watched him against Manchester United. He was fantastic. It was a good game to measure him because United were going to be a dominant force in the match. It can be a problem watching defenders at home because the men in front of them inevitably have more of the ball. You want to see them when they are being tested. He was playing against Andy Cole and Dwight Yorke in

Paris '81 and my greatest personal football triumph. Captain of the Mighty Reds and holding aloft the European Cup

Waving the Red flag. It's Wembley 1978 and I celebrate winning a European Cup Final medal in my own right after our victory over Bruges. I picked up a medal in '77 but didn't play in the final

One of my few goals (above) but one to relish, a great volley against Peter Shilton in his Stoke City days. Close range action (below), scoring against Stromsgodset in the European Cup Winners' Cup. Believe it or not, I got two on the night, but it was an 11-0 win

The world's press can wait! Some pictures from the European Cup's famous visit to the Falcon pub in Kirkby after our 1981 victory over Real Madrid. I'm pictured with a young fan

The glorious Falcon FC. We won the treble, a feat that had never been done before in the history of the Kirkby Newtown League which made me a very proud manager

Up and down those Kop steps coming back from injury

Tug of war with Terry Mac for that prized No.4 shirt

Another treasured picture of my mum and dad, together on a night out

Next to Tosh and the great Shanks prior to the '74 FA Cup Final. Below, at an Anfield Wall of Fame

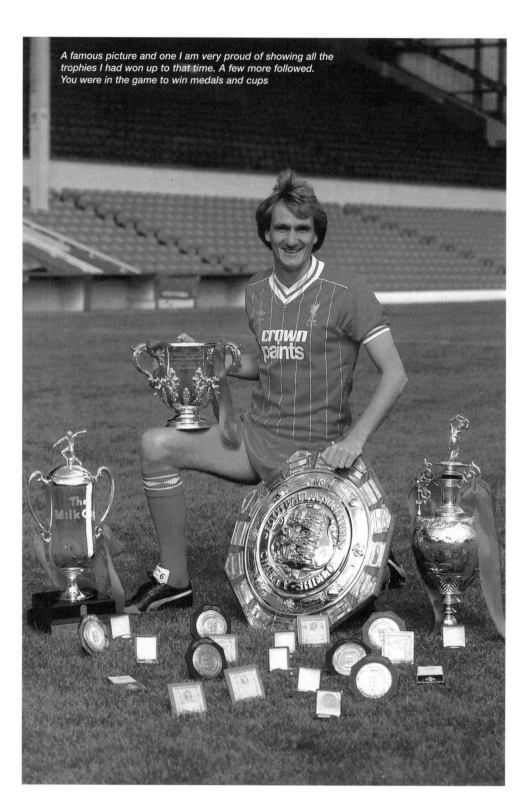

A famous picture and one I am very proud of showing all the trophies I had won up to that time. A few more followed. You were in the game to win medals and cups

this game and he was fantastic, tackling like a demon and also showing good positional play in and around the box which is what I like from my defenders.

Peter Robinson started the ball rolling. He had also met an agent who said this giant was playing for Finland who was also a very good player. His name was Sami Hyypia. Peter found out that he was playing in Holland and got a tape that he gave to me. I hated watching players on video. People could put a video together showing me scoring the 13 goals I managed in my career. With careful editing I would look like a tall, skinny striker with the deadly accuracy of a Michael Owen. I liked to see a player in a real situation so that I could assess how he handled himself. A tape follows the ball. I want to know what they are doing off the ball. What are their ball-watching instincts?

I arranged to go and see Sami playing for Finland against Germany in Nuremberg. I knew that would be a real test. I met the agent who was going to take me to the game. Sami was marking the world-class Oliver Bierhoff, one of the best centre-forwards in Europe. Bierhoff was particularly good in the air so it would be a major test for the defender. He came through with flying colours and showed a great appetite for the game. He didn't have to show great pace. Most of his defending was in the defensive third where his positional play was good. We needed a character like him in the heart of our defence. I came back and made a positive report, but said that the Germans didn't ask too much of him. The conclusion was that he deserved another look.

Gerard made plans to see Sami himself. He came back and reported that he did not see too much aerial contact in that match, but that Sami was great on the ball. I said: "If you saw him like that then this is a boy we need." It was one of our shrewdest deals and we paid just £2.6m for someone who would become Anfield's new Colossus, a nickname that Bill Shankly had proudly given to Ron Yeats in the Sixties. Fittingly, Ronnie was now our chief scout. Gerard and myself were keen to get deals for the summer tied up before the end of the season. It was all done in the right manner as befits Liverpool FC. That is what we tried to do.

The Stephane and Sami deals were put to bed. When I look back at that period we were watching this game and that game. It was a busy time because we would also meet with Peter Robinson to review Gerard's charts with his lovely boxes in which he would write in the names of players we had, those we might want and those we did not want. Gerard had been there from the start of the season. I only came in the November. The first thing Gerard said to me was: "Go away and write your list of all the players we have on the staff. List all those you would like to stay and those we should let go and for what price.

I will do my own list and we will then compare notes."

Our lists turned out to be very similar. Some of the prices were within £100k of each other. It showed we were on the same wavelength. The idea was not to act immediately, but make things happen between the November and the beginning of May. We kept our pieces of paper throughout that time and the plan was to take shape as we went along.

Centre-back was a priority for both of us. We also felt we needed a goalkeeper. That was Joe Corrigan's department and he was all over the place looking at players. We eventually identified Sander Westerveld as our number one target. I knew David James and Brad Friedel would not be too happy, but I felt some of the players had a lack of confidence in them and so did the fans. We had to do something about it.

One of our first signings was Rigobert Song. We just thought that we needed to freshen things up. He only cost £1.5m, but he was a lovely character. He was lacking in a few skills, but he was a real competitor who could play full-back or centre-back. He was not tall, but he leapt really well and put his foot in.

The other players liked him. He was a bundle of fun and energy. You could not help but like him. The fans took to him and reminded us why they are so special with the famous "We've only got one Song!" Subtle, but excellent.

One of the biggest things to deal with in that first season was Paul Ince. He was going to be a problem. We knew that from day one. He was all-powerful in the dressing room. Everyone knew about the 'Guv'nor' hype. He was a strong character.

If we were to move on, he needed to move on. He was still a vital member of the team at that time, but he clearly didn't like the new training routines. Patrice Bergues had put on a session on this six-minute running track we had put in. You would do six minutes flat out and be timed. Ince had been injured. Patrice asked him to do the run so that his aerobic capacity could be checked. Ince said: "I don't do running."

Patrice, who was a great guy, said: "Pardon?" Ince repeated: "I don't do running. Don't you know who I am?" Patrice said: "I don't care who you are. You do the run." Patrice put it in a good way because that's what he was like. Ince completed the six-minute run at his pace, showing his reluctance. If you asked if I had difficult times with him then I would say: "Yes."

I felt he was not putting enough into some of the sessions. There were no direct arguments. I knew he disliked me and the fact that training had become harder. We were determined to do things better. Let's just say there was a mutual mistrust. I remember an FA Cup game against Manchester United on 24 January, 1999. We played with three centre-backs that day in Steve Harkness, Dominic Matteo and Jamie Carragher. We knew we were up against it and we had not beaten United for a while. This was the fourth round of the cup.

We were winning 1-0. Vegard Heggem had crossed for Michael Owen to score with a flying header. Everything was going great, but Manchester United never stop. Our three centre-backs worked like Trojans. With 20 minutes to go Paul Ince started to make signs to us. He indicated to the players that he had a problem with his calf. A few minutes later he starts giving us a sign that he needed to be substituted. He was our captain and he trooped off to a standing ovation from the Liverpool fans who were delighted with our lead, while boos rained down from the United fans. We were looking at him thinking: "What's going on here?"

We conceded two goals in injury time and finished up losing 2-1. Everyone was totally gutted. This was on the Sunday. A calf injury can be tricky. The players had Monday off and on the Tuesday Ince trained without a problem. The following Saturday we played at Coventry and who should be fit and ready to lead the side? Paul Ince.

He was one of those characters who had great self-belief, often thinking about himself. When Gerard pulled him in during the summer to say he was no longer in our plans, he could not accept it. When he eventually left for Wolves he went to the Press and slighted Gerard and myself, saying we were the worst things to happen to Liverpool and that we would drag the club down. Later we declared: "Paul Ince was absolutely correct in his assessment. We dragged the team down to the Carling Cup Final in Cardiff and dragged the team down to the FA Cup Final at the same venue." His words were only what we expected.

When a club makes a managerial change in the November, as Liverpool did when letting Roy go and putting Gerard in sole charge, it is always going to be difficult early on. We were putting things in place to make a difference in our first full year. I always believe a manager should be given two years grace. Until he has his own team together with eight of his own players making a difference, it is wrong to judge. In the December we gave a certain young Steven Gerrard his debut at Spurs. We knew he would have to play in Europe against Celta Vigo. Steven was to play alongside Paul Ince. We felt he could ultimately replace Ince, but at that time he was still growing and we were not sure if he was ready for the burden. Even when Ince had gone we remained unsure if he was ready. Fans will remember the "growing pains" that made his life difficult early on, but what a magnificent talent.

In February 1999, we met West Ham at home. I was on the touchline as usual, but I was conscious that something kept hitting me on the back. I kept thinking: "What's going on here?" I kept turning round and looking at the bench. Then it would happen again. I thought: "I'm imagining it."

That night a friend of mine, Alan Whalley, rang me. He sits in the Paddock with his family about five seats from the dugout. He said: "Do you know what was going on during the game?" I replied: "What do you mean?"

He said: "Ian Wright was throwing chewing gum and paper at you. He was turning away and giggling every time you turned round. It was awful."

Wright wasn't playing. He was sub. Paul Ince was on our bench. Him and Incey are big mates. Wright has hamming it up. Alan told me: "We were all watching him doing it. All of our subs were laughing. I must admit, the likes of Riedle and Friedel were not laughing. The rest found it dead funny. Every time you turned back to the pitch, Wright was putting his hand to his nose and pulling it away to say 'Big Nose'. He was also giving the wanker sign."

I couldn't believe what I was hearing. Alan had actually taken Ian Wright's book to the ground to try and get it signed, but he said they ended up shouting at Wright, saying: "You're out of order." Alan said: "He just put his middle finger up to us. It was disgraceful."

I went into the training ground on the Sunday morning and got all of our subs into my office, including Paul Ince. I started quite calmly, believe it or not. I said to Ince: "What was going on with your mate Wrighty?" He said: "What do you mean?"

I said: "He was throwing things at my back and making insulting signs." He said: "You know what he's like."

I said that I deserved more respect. If any of our lads had done that to the West Ham assistant manager, they would have been down in the dressing room. I said: "What about the laughing?"

The response was: "What do you want us to do?" My voice was beginning to rise. I said: "Don't encourage him."

I was getting riled and started screaming blue murder about what was expected from the players. Gerard Houllier was passing. His office was opposite mine. Later he said: "Thommo, what happened in there?" When I told him he said: "That is disgraceful."

I actually rang Harry Redknapp, saying: "This is a bit difficult, but there was a bit of a thing with Ian Wright yesterday." I told him what had happened.

Harry said: "Phil, I can tell you now he did it, I will ask him, but he will say: 'Me? Doing what? I didn't do anything at all.' That is the way he is." Harry rang back and said: "I pulled him up and he said he had not done anything of the sort."

I just thought it showed a total lack of respect. It shows him in a different light to the friendly, chirpy face we see on TV. He thinks he's a funny, good guy but he lacks something in my book.

Okay, he might argue that because I was shouting on the touchline that I deserved it, but one professional shouldn't show a lack of respect to another.

There were more important things than Ian Wright to focus on as the season progressed. Because the club had failed to progress in the two domestic Cups, it was decided that we would go to Le Touquet in France where Gerard had played his football for Boulogne. We flew on a scheduled flight to Paris on Tuesday, March 16, only to find that Manchester Airport was full of United fans heading out to Italy for their Champions League quarter-final against Juve. We were going for a three-day break in Northern France against a side who were on a par with a Third Division team in England. I can remember walking through the airport and being slaughtered by this United fan. He was in my face saying: "You're a load of crap. You will never be as good as us."

I said: "Listen son. If you've got a couple of hours to spare come to my house and look at my trophy collection, particularly the three European Cup winners' medals. Now piss off."

Gerard laughed at my audacity. I gave it to this fellow double-barrelled and walked on with Gerard giggling. We still talk about it now. We had three great days training and working hard while allowing the lads to play golf and enjoy themselves. Patrice invited some friends over to watch the game against Boulogne. I said: "I hate these games because these little teams always raise their game against us." The match was sold out, even though the attendance was only about 4,000. Patrice said: "We will beat them seven or eight," but I replied that football never works like that. We got beat 2-1 and he was devastated. We were winning 1-0, but our players took it too easy while their players were fired up. They scored a last minute winner. It was a real lesson.

To make it worse, after the game we went into the clubhouse where the Juve v United game was being shown live on TV. Of course, United came back to win that game 3-2 and it felt as though somebody was kicking us between the legs. This had been my lowest point since returning to the club and I didn't want to experience anything like that again.

April 1999 brought along the second derby of the season. Gerard had still been joint manager with Roy when the first game took place. The Goodison game produced a goalless draw, but it would be much more eventful at Anfield. Everton had a little bit of an Indian sign over the Reds at this time. I couldn't wait for the challenge, although I wasn't so sure when Olivier Dacourt lashed home an opener after just 40 seconds. I was amazed to find that this was only the fourth fastest goal in derby history. We would come storming back to win 3-2 and this was the day when Robbie Fowler went down on his hands and knees sniffing the white line in the penalty area, his own personal protest at the verbal abuse he had been taking from the Evertonians at a time when there were totally unfounded rumours across the city that he was taking drugs. Can you begin to imagine how hard this was for a local boy to face up to? Eventually Robbie would be forced to go into the media and make a powerful denial about those rumours, but it should never have come to that.

The day had started with great expectations on both sides. Walter Smith had captured Kevin Campbell and Scot Gemmill on transfer deadline day and both were handed their debuts. We had to concentrate hard after Dacourt's lightning strike, but we were soon back on terms when Robbie despatched a penalty after Paul Ince was fouled. Robbie's unorthodox celebrations infuriated the Evertonians and the atmosphere was intense. I must admit, I didn't think too much about the implications at the time. I was just thrilled we were level and I was also concentrating on our back four.

Robbie gave us the lead with a great header from a corner and Patrik Berger made it 3-1 early in the second half. I was annoyed that we allowed Francis Jeffers to reduce the arrears, but we were all ecstatic to have beaten the old enemy in this 160th derby.

Gerard often asked for some thoughts before he dealt with the Press although he was an excellent talker in his own right who was never short of an opinion. However, this day he was completely unprepared for the questions that would be fired his way about Robbie's celebration. Thinking on his feet he replied: "I think you've got it wrong. That was an African celebration that Rigobert Song taught the lads."

This was Gerard instinctively protecting one of his players. Of course, it backfired and proved embarrassing, but he was just trying to take the sting out of things for Robbie whose only crime had been to hit back in anger. Let's not mix this up with those drug-taking allegations. These were malicious rumours and I'm not surprised that Robbie was furious about them.

Mid-April saw the start of Michael Owen's hamstring problems. He was sprinting away to the Kop end at Leeds when he pulled up like a sprinter in the Olympics. It was as if he had been shot. This injury would dog him over the next few years. We had these outstanding young strikers and everybody wanted to see them together.

Robbie was a god to the fans. Michael had stormed onto the scene. The two of them were very good goalscorers, but some asked if it really was our dream ticket. Could they play together? We had Karlheinz Riedle as a third striker at the time and this season was his swansong in a way. We actually felt we needed four strikers and said so, something that brought some ridiculous criticism in the press at the time. It was if they were blind to the reality of the situation. Robbie's injuries were piling up. He had operations on his knees as well as ankle problems.

It was always a difficult one as to which of them would dominate. Would it be the up and coming Michael Owen or would Robbie come back strongly from his injuries and revisit his past glories?

We'd played Derby County away and this is where my angry head got me into an amusing tangle. We lost 3-2 and I was fuming during the game. There is a long distance at Derby between the dugout and the pitch because of a track and a large area of grass. They stand the advertising hoardings between the two. I had been to the touchline to give some instructions to the players. I was shouting and screaming. As I made my way back we lost another goal. I kicked the advertising hoarding, not realising it was plastic. My boot went straight through and I ended up flat on my back with my leg sticking out of this hoarding.

Of course, the fans were roaring with laughter and when I turned round all our subs were hysterical. I knew they were thinking: "You deserved that." I took my leg out and it was clear that I had scraped the back of my calf. The hoarding had splintered everywhere and I was feeling so embarrassed. I tried to pass it off, saying: "Did you see that?"

Gerard was saying: "What?" He had been concentrating on the game and had not witnessed this pantomime.

On the Monday I rang Derby County and asked to be put through to the marketing department. I said: "Have you had any complaints about a broken advertising hoarding? I think you will find there is a large hole in the one nearest the dugout. I put my foot through it on Saturday."

When they realised who it was there was this hysterical laughter at the other end of the phone. I apologised and asked them to send me the bill. I had to send a cheque off for £150.

That '98/99 season was to end on a sour note. One of the last games was at Sheffield Wednesday where we lost 1-0. We were better than that, even at this poor time. I was in the dressing room. Gerard had gone up to do the Press. Sammy and Patrice were in the shower and seven or eight of the lads were still there. I set off on one, saying: "It's not good enough. We are better than this. We are Liverpool Football Club and we've been beaten by a team who shouldn't be fit to lace our boots."

The remaining lads continued to get changed, but goalkeeper Brad Friedel piped up: "I don't know what's up with you. All you ever do is shout, scream and moan. You never give us any encouragement. You don't think we care."

I took it, but said: "Let me tell you something – and the rest of you. I think you do care and want to win every game. It's just that you don't care enough. That is the difference and there is a difference. You have to believe me. That is where we need to go."

Not a word was said. Yes, they wanted to win and play well, but when things went wrong they did not dig deep enough. It was passed over too much. The giggling on the back of the bus was too evident when we had lost. This rant of mine ended that first half season as Gerard's assistant.

We were still building and learning about the team and finished seventh. It was not good, but better than the twelfth position when Gerard and myself came together. You could have speculated about what would have happened if the change had not been made at the top. Things could have gone the other way. I believe that seventh was a positive sign of improvement and quite a feat in a difficult year.

We now prepared for the 1999/2000, my first full season as Gerard Houllier's assistant. What I admired about Gerard was that he was not one of those who had clearly had enough at the end of a long and stressful campaign. He wanted to get all of his transfer dealings done in the first week of the summer at a time when most other managers had gone on holiday.

We already had our targets. We had this great guy Norman Gard who was there to look after the players, particularly the new ones. He would meet them at the airport and must have put thousands of miles in driving them round the city so they could get their bearings. He would show them the best places to live, organise cars and do anything and everything, even paying gas and electric bills.

Norman would view a house with a new star and handle all of the problems so the player could concentrate on his football. He was a great character with contacts everywhere. Norman was a tremendous help to Gerard and myself, not to mention the players who knew they could always rely on him. He first came to the club when Liverpool bought Patrik Berger. Norman had good language and personal skills, but he would have his work cut out this particular summer.

We brought in six players – Sami Hyypia, Stephane Henchoz, Vladimir Smicer, Sander Westerveld, Titi Camara and Erik Meijer. We realised it was not ideal to bring in so many, but felt it was a necessity at the time. Certainly, the central defensive pairing of Sami and Stephane was crucial to our progress. We were looking for players who were bigger, taller and more athletic. We needed to be more physically imposing.

Even when we started the pre-season work we were still unsure as to whether we had it right. Peter Robinson had said £12m was the spending limit, but we knew there was probably £15m and that we could tweak things if necessary.

We were still asking questions. For instance, could a young Steven Gerrard come through and stand up to the rigours of the top flight? He was still growing. We knew he was a sensational prospect. Paul Ince had gone and David James had gone. One or two others were to follow. We needed an anchor in centre midfield.

Again, Gerard had his charts out in Peter Robinson's office with all of those boxes. The new players were put in their positions. We were looking to Michael, Robbie, Titi and Erik to give us the options up front. Erik gave us something that was a little different with his height and muscle. He didn't have great pace, but he was good at holding the ball up. Titi was a free spirit. Love him or hate him, he did well for us, but if he was not scoring goals then he was something of a luxury that we could not afford. As it happened, he did well when Michael was struggling with his hamstring problem in the early part of the season.

Vlad Smicer would literally get off on the wrong foot. He damaged his ankle playing tennis and was always playing catch-up, something that was been symbolic of his Anfield career. We still had those questions about centre midfield. We had lists of people who could possibly do the business. We continued to wrestle with this through most of the pre-season. Someone said: "What about the big fella Didi Hamann at Newcastle?"

We'd heard he wasn't very happy. It was an interesting thought. He certainly fitted the profile. He was 6ft 2ins, a good passer of the ball and gave protection to the back four. All of this was being discussed in Peter Robinson's office. Of course, Peter would make contact with Newcastle. We also needed to know who the agent was. We set the ball rolling with phone calls flying all over the place. In the end we paid £8m which was a big lay-out, but we were determined to change and improve the squad.

Incredibly, during the first game of the season against Sheffield Wednesday, Didi was to take a terrible tackle that did his ankle ligaments. What made it worse was that he tried to carry on for five or ten minutes and that did not help. However, we made a dream start with Robbie and Titi scoring in a 2-1 win. Titi was in the team because Michael had re-injured his hamstring at our training camp.

Prior to Hamann coming we played a pre-season game at Wolves. Steven Gerrard had taken the holding midfield role that day and played particularly well. I remember tapping Gerard on the knee and saying: "He's getting there." Gerard said: "We still need a midfield player." I said: "I don't disagree, but the lad is going to be a great player."

Gerard was right in his assessment that Steven was too young to be playing in that particular team at that time. To come into a team that is in its infancy can be tough. Young players are still growing and you have to be careful with them.

We were off to a flier and more than happy about that. It was important that the new signings hit it off, but Didi's injury knocked us back. It was my first knowledge that Didi had it in his contract that he could go back to Germany to have his treatment. Before we knew it, he had been operated on and was in plaster. He stayed in Germany for four weeks, something we didn't take kindly to. I had to learn that this was the way of the world with modern contracts.

We didn't think he needed an operation. We thought proper rehabilitation and rest would have sorted it out. His ankle was immobilised in plaster and that always makes it a bigger rehabilitation challenge.

The following week we had our first home game against Watford. We felt confident about victory and set off from Melwood to travel the short distance to the ground. En route we got stuck in traffic and got a call from the police saying that we would have to park up and wait because Watford were ahead of us and would get to the stadium first. The police needed to clear their coach before we could drive in. Gerard said: "Get the police to park them up instead. We are only minutes behind."

We came up by Sleepers Hill to drive up Anfield Road and there was the Watford coach, pulled over on the side of the road. As we passed we could see a furious Graham Taylor sitting at the front. He realised what had happened.

If we had been delayed, our out-rider would have received the same abuse. It obviously wound them up and they beat us 1-0. It made us think: "Maybe we got it wrong there."

From our wonderful start we were back down to earth. Just after that I went to Northern Ireland with Gerard to watch them play France. We were running the rule over Mikael Silvestre who was later to sign for Manchester United. Gerard spoke to him in the corridor before and after the game. He did not feel any warmth coming back, even though he had coached the player as a young kid. We wanted Silvestre to play left-back. He wanted to play centre-back. In the end he chose United who then promptly used him at left-back. Alex probably gave him all this 'toffee' about playing centre-half knowing that once he had signed he would play where he was told. Silvestre was a good player and that was one we missed out on.

Probably one of my best early times with Gerard was when we beat Arsenal towards the end of August that season. There was always a big pride thing between Gerard and Arsene Wenger, two great French managers, and we took great delight in beating the Gunners 2-0. Robbie Fowler and Liverpool had a hoodoo over them at this time. We could beat them for fun. Gerard was very proud. We had still not seen Stephane Henchoz at this point. He had a groin problem in the close season that developed into a double hernia. He was always playing catch-up and we had to wait a while for him.

Then we had a strange game against Everton at the end of September, 1999. I had been so proud after our victory over them the previous year. Now we entertained them again and Kevin Campbell scored the only goal of the game to give them victory. We lost the plot a bit. Steven Gerrard was sent-off and then Sander Westerveld and Franny Jeffers had their handbag fight on the edge of the box. They were also red-carded. We were really ill-disciplined in the game.

It was a big learning point for Gerard and myself. He used that game to say it would never happen again. One of my big motivational things before a game was controlled aggression. This came to light after this one. Everton kept their control and attacked us in a disciplined way. It could have been 3-0. It was something we used in a positive way for future derbies.

Another thing that sticks in my mind towards the end of that game was Steve Staunton stepping in as an emergency goalkeeper. He made one of the saves of the season, tipping a powerful half volley onto the crossbar and over the top. It was a fantastic save.

We could not get a consistent run together and we were looking to tighten up at the back and stop conceding goals. Gerard made a big decision that Stephane Henchoz would be needed for the game at Aston Villa. Gerard had to cajole him into playing. Stephane felt he needed more time. Gerard used all of his psychology to get him to play at Villa. He said we would take him off after an hour. We needed that solidity.

Stephane was brilliant. He always gave this impression that he was blowing for tugs. He used to blow out his cheeks, a bit like Kenny Dalglish. Stephane always looked shattered with these red cheeks, but that wasn't the case.

We wondered about taking him off in that game. Gerard said: "Just don't look at him. Don't talk to him. Don't tell him how long there is to go." It worked and he completed the 90 minutes as we secured a goalless draw. It was a tremendous boost for us because Sami and Stephane were to become the best centre-back pairing for years to come.

We were to go out of the League Cup to Southampton early on at the Dell. We played well, only to be hit by a sucker punch in the last minute. It summed up our season, up and down. In fairness, that cup defeat possibly helped us. We could concentrate and get everyone together to make a sustained Premier challenge.

We wanted Champions League football. That was one of the criteria we had set. We wanted European football, hopefully in the Champions League. At the end of October and beginning of November we had three games at home. If we could get maximum points it would put us into a really healthy position. We took all nine points.

One was quite an emotional night. Titi's father had died in the morning. Gerard asked him if he wanted to play. He said: "Yes, that's what my dad would have wanted."

There is this great photograph behind the Anfield Road goal of Titi offering a prayer for his father after scoring against West Ham. We then beat Bradford 3-1 with Titi on target again. Then we beat Derby County 2-0. Thankfully, none of their players took revenge on the advertising hoardings at Anfield. A victory over Sunderland made it four in a row and that really pushed us up the table. The fans started to believe that a Championship charge was possible.

However, like the previous season we went out early in the cups. Again, this probably helped us to prepare on the league front. We had time on our hands and were looking for a friendly challenge, as had been the case at Le Touquet. This time we were looking at Southern Spain or Portugal, but not somewhere that was going to cost the earth. During my first season with Gerard I had befriended some fans from the Maltese Supporters Club.

They were lovely people. They would come to Liverpool and we allowed them to visit Melwood. Their chairman was Matthew Pace who had invited Sammy Lee and myself to open their new Supporters Club. We were also invited to visit the neighbouring island of Gozo. When we got there it was as if it was a royal visit. There were hundreds to meet us at the airport. We were taken by helicopter to Gozo where the branch chairman was Charlie Farigula. He was this little guy, smaller than Sammy! The Supporters Club was an annexe to his house, entered through a smaller version of the Shankly Gates.

Charlie had this Liverpool flag that was half as big as his house. It was made from the sail of a schooner and had the LFC crest on it. This was the first time it was going to be flown.

The Maltese were wonderful. They had banners up across the street saying 'Welcome Mr and Mrs Thompson' and 'Welcome Mr and Mrs Lee.' It was very moving. Of course, we attended a number of dinners over there. There was another chap who befriended us called Charlie Scribas. We had three lovely, but exhausting days and at one of the dinners I made a statement that was to come back to haunt me.

I said: "Not if, but when we win a trophy, I will come back to Malta and bring it with me. I guarantee this will happen."

When we were looking for somewhere to take the players for this second break, I mentioned it to Matthew. Of course, he was saying: "Why don't you come here. We would love you to come."

I went to Gerard and he said: "Yes, I quite fancy that." We started to make the arrangements and our contacts got us great rates at the best hotels. The flights would be through Air Malta who did things in a sponsorship way to help the Maltese supporters clubs and us. I was ringing up Matthew saying: "What's the weather like?" He would reply: "Sunny and warm, 18 degrees." I would look at the weather charts and it would say 16 degrees.

They didn't want anything to deflect us from coming. They sorted out a training ground for us next to the national stadium. Then there were thunder-storms and the pitches were waterlogged, but it cleared and we were able to do some special training. Gerard called it "regeneration." Behind all of this the hospitality was amazing and they were all remarkable Liverpudlians.

The official function went down a storm, although they reminded me of my trophy promise. We returned to Merseyside at the back end of January and beat Leeds 3-1 at home. It was a great result because they had been flying.

Then we went to Arsenal and won 1-0 with a goal by Titi Camara who raced onto a Steven Gerrard through ball. We led at Manchester United through a fantastic Patrik Berger free-kick. They equalised when Sami Hyypia was off the pitch receiving stitches after a nasty tackle by Ole Gunner Solskjaer. I had been really pleased with Sami. He was cool, calm and collected and an excellent footballer with the ability of a midfield player. He was a dream in the heart of defence because of his temperament.

We drew against Sunderland and Villa and then beat Derby County. This was the kind of consistency we had been working towards where previously we were up and down. I wanted to see us going ten to twelve games undefeated. Jamie Redknapp won a game against Newcastle with a last-minute header. We cruised to three points at Coventry, beat Spurs at home and Wimbledon away. This was all off the back of Gerard's 'regeneration' in Malta. The run continued with a goalless derby draw against Everton before we finally lost 2-0 at Chelsea. The run had stretched to eleven games unbeaten.

In the middle of this activity we signed Emile Heskey on March 10, 2000. The deal was struck with Leicester before their Worthington Cup Final against Tranmere. If all went well for them and they were in a good position, Leicester said they would allow the deal to go through.

Emile arrived the week after winning at Wembley. He made his debut in a 1-1 draw against Sunderland. He actually started up front that day with Erik Meijer, with Michael Owen on the bench until the last 15 minutes. The Heskey-Owen partnership was to be excellent for years to come. Emile's first goal came in a 3-0 win at Coventry on April 1.

Robbie Fowler, because of his injuries, was to pay the price for being out as Michael and Emile forged a link.

The season would end with joyous celebrations for our opponents Bradford who avoided relegation, forcing us to settle for the UEFA Cup instead of the Champions League.

My first full season with Gerard was over and we had improved again to fourth place. I'm not sure if we were actually ready for the Champions League at that stage although we would have taken it. The important thing is that we had shown some real consistency and the fans recognised that there had been another improvement.

Some of the newly signed players had been a success, although not all of them. We would have to revisit the key areas and start the 'swap shop' again. Another tough summer lay ahead, but for now it was a time to reflect and look forward, although no one could have envisaged what was to happen next.

Treble glory sparks remarkable scenes as triumphant Reds return to big time

We started training on July 11, 2000, for a season that would become part of Anfield folklore. It would be a real roller coaster campaign. Gerard, having worked so hard after the previous season ended, was having a few extra days away.

I was to meet and greet all of the new players who were to arrive that summer. I've already said that signing six players is not ideal, but sometimes it's a necessity and we believed the changes were required to enable us to take the next step after improving from eleventh to seventh and then to fourth. Our international players were still away, but I was able to introduce the new boys to everyone else.

We had brought in Pegguy Arphexad as goalkeeping cover because Brad was looking to get away to find first-team football elsewhere. We brought in Bernard Diomede, who had won a World Cup winners medal as a substitute for France in 1998. He was not to make much of an impact in the team. We signed a real professional in Markus Babbel. There had been an interest in him years before. He lacked a bit of pace, but he was a fantastic footballer.

Then there was a controversial one in Nick Barmby who the previous season had been player of the year for our old rivals Everton. He had this knack of scoring vital goals from midfield, but his capture brought all kinds of problems because of the rivalry between our two great clubs. A lot of players had gone from Anfield to Goodison, including Peter Beardsley, but not many had gone in the opposite direction. The last time this happened in any high profile way was when Everton's idolised centre-forward Dave Hickson joined the Reds in the late Fifties. That was a strange one. The Evertonians said they would boycott Goodison if Hickson was allowed to leave. The Liverpudlians said they would boycott Anfield if he signed. Then Davie scored a hat-trick on his debut and he was a Kop hero. We would eventually sign another Blue, Abel Xavier, but this move would not inspire the same hype as the Barmby transfer.

Another incoming player that raised a few eyebrows was the signing of 35-year-old Gary McAllister from Coventry. I have to admit that I didn't know whether the move would be welcomed by the fans, simply because of his age. I wondered if his time had gone. In actual fact, his time had just come. His capture was to prove an absolute masterstroke by Gerard. He was another with a great goalscoring record from midfield. I will come back to Macca later.

Our pre-season campaign started in Switzerland. We then played in an Irish tournament against Glentoran. It proved an easy 4-0 victory, but Robbie Fowler picked up another injury to knacker his preparation and confidence. He had desperately wanted to make an impact, but an ankle injury put him out for months. It was a blow to the team and Robbie.

The new thing was a high profile friendly at Anfield, which was against Parma who had been making some big waves in Serie A in Italy. It was a big game for us. We played some scintillating football and won 5-0. This really whetted the appetite of the fans.

Our first Premiership clash was against Bradford. It's amazing how the computer pans these fixtures out. Of course, we had played them on the final day of the previous season when they had defied the odds to stay up. We were up for this one, but it was not the hiding I thought we were going to dish out. We won 1-0 thanks to Emile Heskey.

As things happen, live TV games throw things up and we were paired with Arsenal on the Monday night. This was to prove a bit different. We had two sent off and the Gunners had one. Didi Hamann went for a second booking that was ridiculous. We got that overturned. Gary Mac also went. Referee Graham Poll said he went over the top against Patrick Vieira. The replay showed that he took the ball. There was no malicious intent and we said we would fight it.

I was sent down to the commission hearing to try and get Gary off. The FA's Adam Crozier had led us to believe that there was nothing to worry about. He had viewed the tapes, although this new commission had been brought in made up of ex-players, media guys and ex-refs. Having been told that the video panel appeared positive for Gary after viewing the incident, the player did not go down. I was the club's sole representative.

I went in front of the three-man committee and its chairman said: "Welcome, Mr Thompson. I'd like to tell you that my two colleagues and I will be the ones making the decision, no one else. We will let you have our verdict before you leave today. It will be down to what we believe."

I thought: "Uh oh." This is not as cut and dried as we thought. I tried to keep composed and gave Gary's long-standing record of good behaviour in the game. I pointed out that Gary had made clear contact with the ball and I pointed out that there had been a lot of coverage of that. They seemed oblivious to the facts, saying: "He makes contact with the player." I had to hold back from saying: "Yes, but he makes contact with the ball first." I knew they were going to do us.

I left the room to allow them to deliberate, but I wasn't out for long. They had already made their minds up. Gary got a three-match ban and my Perry Mason exploits didn't help. It reminded me of the commission I had attended as a player with Bob Paisley. I thought Bob was going to get me a six-month jail sentence, but we only got a £300 fine. I could have done with Bob. Gerard and Rick Parry were furious when they heard the news. It had looked an open and shut case. This was true, but not in our favour.

We were still looking to strengthen the team. The opportunity came for us to sign Christian Ziege from Boro. He was a fine footballer, but I had my doubts as to whether he was a good defender. I believed that Christian's abilities were as a wing-back, but Gerard had spoken to people in Germany who had assured him he could defend. He was certainly good at free-kicks and getting the ball in from wide positions. He gave us more clout.

We were bringing things together and my mind would go to Gerard's charts and his little boxes. The plan was taking shape. We beat Bradford, lost to Arsenal and then drew 3-3 at Southampton. It's always a hard place to go to. We were 3-0 up and cruising with 17 minutes left, but then the Saints started to put us under pressure. I thought: "I don't like the look of this." As I fidgeted nervously in the dugout Pegguy Arphexad said: "Thommo, this is cut and dried." I said: "It's never cut and dried until it's finished." Then the ball flashed into our net and their 16,000 sounded like 60,000. It ended up 3-3 and we could have lost it.

After that game we had a team meeting, not about losing three goals, but about the subs. Gerard made a big thing of it. A lot of his substitutions had usually brought about a major impact. He was quite harsh with Steve Staunton as he illustrated how he could have made a better impact. Stan had two chances in the game. We had a great opportunity to score, but he chose to shoot from 30 yards when he had a clear run on goal. In other words, he went for a 'Hollywood' finish. Then he could have played Danny Murphy in for a great chance, but he chose to try and beat the last defender and lost the ball.

We were confronting issues and not hiding from them.

Our UEFA Cup campaign started in the less than auspicious surroundings of Rapid Bucharest. It was a hostile place, but Nick Barmby earned us a 1-0 win. He was to make quite an impact in this competition. However, the BBC decided to hammer us. They said we were not good enough. As it turned out, they followed us throughout a long journey. The criticism also followed us right through from certain panel members.

In the Premiership we had a fantastic 4-0 win at Derby County. Michael Owen was challenged when scoring one of the goals and somebody's knee split the back of his head open. Doc Waller and Dave Galley had gone on to administer treatment, but he was saying that he wanted to continue. All the way off the pitch on the stretcher he was repeating: "I want to go on." He was taken straight down to the dressing room and when he finally tried to get up the room just started whizzing round.

We were to see off Bucharest at home with a 0-0 draw. We then met Czech Republic side Slovan Liberec, winning 1-0 at home. Before the return leg we beat Everton 3-1 at Anfield to boost our confidence. Every fan in the stadium could have won a fortune that day on who would score the first goal. A certain Nick Barmby poached the opener to chants of 'Die, Nicky Die' from some Evertonians. Some people had questioned whether Nick should play because of the potential for trouble, but he was never going to step aside and had a very good game.

We also had a famous game against Leeds that ended 4-3 in their favour. David O'Leary only named four subs, which we found strange. He had a few other injury problems that day. I thought he was trying to be too clever and making a point about the size of his squad. He should have named a younger professional to give him experience, but we knew what he was trying to do.

We scored after two minutes. After six minutes O'Leary was calling for Jonathan Woodgate to come off. He was confirming to the world that he had injury problems and no cover. We scored again after 18 minutes, but I thought: "David O'Leary has put himself in a no-lose situation. If they lose, he can say they only had four on the bench and had to take Woodgate off. If they turned things round what a masterstroke it would have been."

At 2-0 this ball went into our left-back slot. Christian Ziege was ambling towards the ball. That was mistake one. He then went round the ball to get on his right foot. That was mistake two. This allowed a young and lively Alan Smith, as he always does, to close down rapidly from 30 yards. The striker was allowed to get in a block and Mark Viduka scored their first goal. You can imagine my reaction to this sloppy defending. That was midway through the half and it got the crowd going. When we came in for the interval, Gerard was ready to give his team talk. He was looking round for Christian Ziege. Gerard did not want to rollick him, but keep everyone together. He said: "Where's Christian?" Someone said: "He's down by the showers." I found him sitting on a skip with his head in his hands. He was told to get back in the dressing room and listen up.

Viduka equalised just after half-time but we went 3-2 ahead on the hour with a goal from Vladimir Smicer. Then Viduka got another two goals to put an unbelievable slant on things. You can imagine O'Leary's delight on the final whistle. We were on the wrong side of an incredible result.

As we were heading down the tunnel, who came running up the other way to get on the pitch but Leeds chairman Peter Ridsdale. He was going to bask in the limelight. I was to have a right pop at the Leeds chief. Can you ever imagine Liverpool chairman David Moores ever pulling a stunt like that? Of course not.

We had to go to Liberec after that. People were questioning if we could defend our 1-0 lead. We won 3-2 in the Czech Republic and Barmby was a scorer once again. When we arrived back at Liverpool Airport a director sidled up in a strange way and said: "What's up with Christian Ziege? Is he a defender or not because he's not shaping up like one?" He knew I was the defensive coach and I wasn't going to agree with him. I said: "He's got a lot to learn," although I knew his performances were not adequate. Gerard said: "It's none of his business" but he also knew that there were big question marks over Ziege's defensive qualities.

Our next opponents in the UEFA Cup were Olympiakos. This is where our stroke of luck began to appear. We were drawn at home first, but this would have meant Olympiakos clashing in the away leg with Athens rivals Panathinaikos, who were in the Champions League which took precedence. The fixtures were reversed and it suited us to have the away leg first.

It's strange how you grab hold of things as omens. When we had played Bucharest we had witnessed a crash while we were in the team coach. In Liberec we witnessed another crash. The same thing happened in Greece. It all seemed to be fitting into place although you could just say that we were proving a jinx to a few unfortunates.

The Olympic Stadium in Athens was something to behold. The running track reduced the crowd intimidation, but the atmosphere was still white hot. We were leading 2-1 in the game and then lost a goal in the last minute against the run of play. Vladi had two or three chances to finish it off, but the result was a blow to us.

Something was happening that would grab our focus for the rest of the season. We started losing a lot of goals – four at Leeds, two at Liberec, two at Spurs, two at Olympiakos. We were not tight enough and another two hit the back of our net at Newcastle to make it 13 in six games. We changed things that day by playing Jamie Carragher at left-back for the first time. It was Babbel, Hyypia, Henchoz and Carragher and this backline was to remain together more or less for the remainder of the season.

We then went to Stoke City in the League Cup and blasted them 8-0. It was a great result, but the clean sheet elated me more than the eight goals! I remember an incident after five minutes when their striker went round Pegguy Arphexad and rolled the ball towards the net. It hit the post and went back into the keeper's hands. I said to Gerard: "Maybe our luck is changing."

We were then to enjoy a nice couple of wins, beating Charlton 3-0 and Olympiakos 2-0. The defensive bonus encouraged me, but a couple of big games were looming at Manchester United and at home to Arsenal. We needed to make a statement that we were back and playing better. We had a couple of other games before the 'big two', losing at home to Ipswich and then knocking Fulham out of the League Cup 3-0.

People questioned whether we were tired and whether we were good enough. We had not beaten United for a long time. This was the night it all changed. Danny Murphy scored with a fantastic free-kick, bending it round the wall to give us a famous 1-0 win. Gerard was buzzing more than I had ever seen before. In the Old Trafford Boot Room I was talking about the game. We never revelled in a victory in front of opposing coaches. I was keeping it low key with Sammy Lee, Patrice Bergues and Joe Corrigan. Their guys were saying: "You played well." We were saying: "Yes, but we had a bit of luck." It stemmed from the Shankly days. You always tried to be humble because you never wanted to stir people up for the next one. Sir Alex Ferguson shook our hands and said: "Well done lads." Then he stood with his back to us watching the racing results. Sammy and myself kept calm and composed, even though we were bubbling inside.

Then Gerard comes bursting through the door like a whirlwind. Immediately he says: "Hello Alex. Well, we deserved that. We played really well. We dominated the game." Alex was staring at him. I was willing Gerard to take on the calm and composed approach, but Gerard was in full flow. "Fantastic free-kick by Danny Murphy. What a goal." He had a quick glass of red wine and then we were off. I'm sure as soon as we left, they would have been saying: "Those bastards. Rubbing our noses in it."

When you leave the Old Trafford main entrance there is always about 1,000 people there to cheer or jeer. We got on the coach to be greeted by a delighted David Moores and an ecstatic Rick Parry. We allowed the coach to drive clear of the fans and then we looked at each other and shouted: "YES!!" I got hold of Gerard's leg and said: "That was fucking great!" I told him about the Boot Room and his whirlwind entrance. We all smiled. You have to celebrate days like that. United would be no different.

After that we thumped Arsenal 4-0 at Anfield. Things were looking up going into Christmas, although a lone-goal defeat at Boro on Boxing Day kept our feet on the ground. The game produced one famous quote. Sander Westerveld should have saved their goal. It was a straightforward shot that skidded and bounced over his hand. Sander said: "There was too much ice on the ball." I don't know where he got that one from.

Into the New Year the FA Cup started. We entertained Rotherham at Anfield, who were managed by Scouser and former Tranmere player Ronnie Moore. It wasn't the easy game that we envisaged, especially when Igor Biscan was sent off to leave us with ten men and an uphill battle. Ronnie's Rotherham side was both physical and imposing. We had watched them and they always played with a back five. At set pieces and corners they were extremely dangerous. We eventually won the game 3-0, which was all credit to the players themselves. Some people would say: 'It's only Rotherham', but in all walks of life, particularly in the FA Cup, it's a challenge. We were fortunate that the game was at Anfield because the crowd helped the ten men through.

The 2000/2001 campaign continued to unfold. We lost 2-1 to Crystal Palace away in the first leg of the Worthington Cup semi-final. We were thankful for a late Vladimir Smicer goal that kept us in the tie. Liverpudlians will remember that their striker Clinton Morrison stupidly went to the Press and had a go at Michael Owen. Michael was a popular figure in our dressing room. He took Morrison's criticism personally and so did the rest of the players.

We used it to inspire a reaction and I would have put my house on us beating them convincingly in the return. They had a lively Latvian winger in Andrejs Rubins, who had caused us some trouble. In the return we played Igor in centre-midfield and put Steven Gerrard at right-back to deal with the wide threat. I remember Stevie putting in this tackle early on that took me back to the old days of Tommy Smith when players could take the ball and the man and put them in the stands.

Stevie's sliding tackle carried all of his bodyweight behind it and this boy ended up on the track. He wasn't much of a threat after that. We had shown our intent and won 5-0. Dear old Clinton Morrison had missed a sitter late on to howls of delight from the baying Kop. I'm sure he learned a painful lesson that day. This win would take us into our first final and start the club's love affair with 'Anfield South', or the Millennium Stadium as it is better known in Cardiff.

The Worthington Cup was not the be-all-and-end-all but it was a start. And our confidence was high, not least when we gained revenge over Leeds with a fourth round FA Cup win at Elland Road, secured thanks to late goals from substitutes Nick Barmby and Emile Heskey.

The UEFA Cup started again. After our easy win over Olympiakos we now faced our old foes Roma, arriving in the Eternal City where we had enjoyed so many fantastic times in the European Cup. A strange thing was to happen. Roma had dropped out of the Champions League into the UEFA Cup. Lazio, their city rivals, were still in the Champions League and so once again our home and away legs were switched, which was another stroke of luck with the away game first.

Gerard Houllier was fantastic. In our staff meetings he gave us the chance to air our views on selection. He never felt he was always right and at times he would change things based on the input of the staff. However, at one such meeting before the Roma game he suddenly said: "I'm going to shock everyone. I've got a plan to beat them. I will tell you tomorrow on the day of the game." When we discussed the team the next day, Gerard took our opinions as normal. Then he repeated his words by saying: "I'm going to shock you all now. I'm going to play with three strikers."

We had signed Jari Litmanen and he had scored his first goal at Sunderland, a late pen in a 1-1 draw prior to the Roma game. It had given another option, but we all thought Rome was not the place to be adventurous. We needed solidity because they were one of the top teams in Europe with Cafu on the right and Vincent Candela on the left. We thought: "Gerard has not seen this right. They will murder us down the flanks."

We offered our reservations, but Gerard had his plan and he went to his room. We continued to chat about it and someone said: "This is incredible. It's only the first leg. Why do we have to attack?" We had never questioned Gerard before once a decision had been taken, but I went to his room and explained the feelings of the staff about us being too adventurous. I gave him our tactical views and he listened and took it all in. He then changed the formation and the team and I took my hat off to him.

A manager has to be single-minded at times, but he also has to take on board the views of those around him. It showed the bond of respect and togetherness amongst the staff and we appreciated it. It told us that he trusted in what we said while also being strong enough to make his own decisions. As it turned out we had a great night and won 2-0 with a fine Michael Owen double. It was one of our great victories.

Encouraged, we then beat Manchester City 4-2 at Anfield in the FA Cup although Joe Royle claimed they were the better team. I don't think Joe could ever admit that he lost a game to Liverpool fair and square. It was the Evertonian in him.

We were now bubbling along towards the Roma return. It had been fantastic just taking in the fixtures. We had played Roma (UEFA Cup) and Manchester City (FA Cup), and now we faced the Roma return and Birmingham (Worthington Cup Final). Roma were really fired up at Anfield and the last 20 minutes proved stomach wrenching. We couldn't get the ball and then Gianni Guigou scored a tremendous goal from the edge of the box to make it 2-1 on aggregate in our favour. It was getting out of control as they stepped things up. No matter what the players or the subs did, we could not stem the flow.

Then Roma chipped a ball into the box and it struck the back of Markus Babbel's elbow. The ref pointed to the spot and we all jumped up saying: "Oh my God." Incredibly, the official's arm kept moving and now, instead of pointing to the spot, he was pointing for a corner. Batistuta had sprinted to get the ball when it went out, presumably because he thought it was a corner and he wanted it taken quickly. He must have been the only one in the ground with that viewpoint. Clearly his body language influenced the referee who must have thought: "I've got this wrong." He refused to change his mind, even though the Italians started to protest. The whole Kop breathed a huge sigh of relief. After that the Italian anger bubbled to the surface and Damiano Tommasi was sent off. We thought this might give us a breather, but Roma kept coming. It was an incredible game, but we managed to hang on to reach the quarter-final.

The excitement didn't stop and it was then straight on to Cardiff for the Birmingham game. Liverpool fans were down there in their droves. It was our first final for five years and a big decision had to be made up front. Robbie and Emile or Michael and Emile? Robbie was playing slightly better at the time, but if Michael was to miss the final it would be difficult for him. Robbie was to prove his worth, crashing home a dipping volley following a Heskey flick-on. We were cruising in the 90 minutes and should have won 3-0, but they got a last-gasp penalty that Darren Purse converted.

It was incredible and we knew they would be up for it in extra time. When you listen to people from Birmingham recalling that day, including Trevor Francis who was their manager at the time, it's as if they murdered us from start-to-finish. That is ridiculous. The result should have been out of sight. As it was, the result was settled by penalties with the three players we put on as subs playing a major part.

Gary Mac, Christian Ziege and Nick Barmby all scored from the spot. Didi Hamann missed his, but Robbie Fowler scored. That just left Jamie Carragher. I was going: "Oh no, it's not down to Carra!" I could hardly bare to look. Then he struck it home and I thought: "Never doubted you son."

When Andrew Johnson's kick was saved by Sander Westerveld the red army erupted and the scenes in the stadium were amazing. The fans had changed the words of Baha Men's 'Who Let The Dogs Out?' to 'Hou Let The Reds Out, Hou, Hou.' It rung around the stadium and we were so proud to have our first trophy in the bag. We had a fantastic night in the Vale of Glamorgan Hotel, more than happy in the knowledge that we were still fighting on three other fronts – the UEFA Cup, the FA Cup and the Premier League with a view to securing Champions League status.

There was no time to catch breath. It was Porto after that in the quarter-final of the UEFA Cup. It sounds a bit disrespectful, but it was a doddle in the away leg that was goalless. Porto, like Roma, had started in the Champions League, but fell out into the UEFA Cup. These were good teams and we were more than a match for them.

John Aldridge, an old Liverpool mate, would then entertain us at Tranmere in the quarter-final of the FA Cup. Aldo had developed this knack of upsetting big teams and we decided we had to do something different to combat them. We picked eight British players that day because we knew it would be a blood and thunder English cup tie and that we had to be up for it. We had to compete for every ball.

This made it a fascinating game, a great English cup tie and Aldo's boys gave it their all, but we managed to overcome them 4-2. It shows that they still gave us a fright because they had every right to fight for a semi-final spot as much as ourselves.

That semi-final pairing would be confirmed even quicker than I thought. We had only just shook hands with Aldo and his staff and got back to the top of the tunnel right outside our dressing room door when somebody shouted: "You've got Wycombe in the semi-final," knowing that they had competed and won the previous day.

As you can imagine, I thought the person was winding us up because I didn't think the draw had been made. Equally, it would be like our wildest dreams coming true. It would be confirmed minutes later by Ian Cotton, our press officer, and chief executive Rick Parry. Why the draw was made so soon after our game finishing, only the FA will ever know, although it's one thing I can thank them for.

The matches were coming thick and fast now. We despatched Porto 2-0 at Anfield with goals from Danny Murphy and Michael Owen to claim a place in the semi-final of the UEFA Cup where we would face the mighty Barcelona. We then had the chance to nail a famous Premier double over Manchester United. We knew it would be a real feather in our caps if we could win this Anfield clash. The match would be famous for a sensational shot from Steven Gerrard that whizzed past Fabien Barthez. Robbie Fowler also lashed one home from the edge of the box for a memorable 2-0 victory.

The UEFA Cup semi would spark some controversy when a world football legend, Johan Cruyff, criticised our style of play. He said it was disrespectful to football. Maybe he was trying to get us to attack Barcelona at the Nou Camp and be reckless. That never happened and while the goalless draw might not have suited Cruyff, it certainly had our supporters partying down the famous Ramblas in the Spanish city.

The opportunities were opening up for us, not least when we faced Wycombe Wanderers in the semi-final of the FA Cup. They worked very hard against us as we knew they would. We finally opened the scoring thanks to sub Emile Heskey with a fantastic header from a Stevie Gerrard cross. Gerard Houllier had sent Emile on with the words: "Go on, give us a goal." Our big striker responded

It still wasn't over, but a chance came when we got a free-kick on the edge of the box. We had been working on free-kicks in training and we knew who we wanted to take them, but they were brushed aside by a bristling Robbie Fowler. I was shouting: "What is he doing? I can't believe it. Doesn't our work in training count? GREAT GOAL ROBBIE!"

The subs were killing themselves laughing. Then I thought about the Jamie Carragher pen in the Carling Cup Final and I smiled to myself. I said the decent thing to Carra that day and did the same with Robbie. I told them how I got it wrong. Never doubt the Scousers in the side! The Wycombe win now meant a second trip to Cardiff. Our fans picked up on the famous song: 'Tell me ma, me ma, to put the champagne on ice, we're going to Cardiff twice, tell me ma, me ma.'

Because of our success, games were backing up for us. We now had a game looming at Ipswich with just two days to recover. We went to London to try and get the fixture switched, but in the end Ipswich would not co-operate because they said it coincided with something they were doing. One of the excuses was that the pies had already been ordered. It was outrageous. Their manager George Burley was looking to take advantage of our tiredness after the FA Cup semi-final. We had to make changes to the team, but took the lead within 45 seconds of the restart. Ipswich came back and we drew the game 1-1. Whether that was mission accomplished for them, I'm not sure.

Leeds had been a thorn and they knocked us out of our momentum with a 2-1 win at Anfield. Now it was do or die for a Champions League spot. We could not afford to lose at Everton on the Easter Monday. Dear old Jeff Winter was in charge. We played really well, but he gave them a ridiculous penalty. Winter said Sami Hyypia was climbing all over Duncan Ferguson. Can you feel sorry for big Dunc in these situations? He gives it and he takes it. It enabled Everton to pull back to 2-2 and we were really disappointed.

We thought the game was drifting away, but we had players who would keep going. Gary Mac had been inspirational on and off the pitch. He is a good reader of the game and wanted to win as many matches as he could, and we watched him as a free-kick was won over 40 yards out. The first thing he did was work the ball forward five or six yards. Then he starts to wave to the players with his right hand to position themselves for the free-kick.

We could see goalkeeper Paul Gerrard moving as if directed by Gary. Then our midfielder whipped the ball in the opposite corner, right in injury time with about ten seconds to go. I remember seeing Sammy Lee in the goalmouth celebrating with the lads. It was one of the most amazing derby games I had witnessed for sheer emotion and it provided the three precious points we needed. Gary achieved legendary status that day and he was now on a personal crusade.

We played Barca a few days later. After the taunts that we were not good enough, we played exceptionally well once more. The tie was settled when Patrick Kluivert inexplicably handled the ball. I did exactly the same thing once against Manchester United and you don't know why you put your hand there. We were not complaining and that man McAllister confidently put the penalty away. This took us through to the UEFA Cup Final against Spanish side Alaves in Dortmund.

We still had our sights on Champions League qualification and needed to crack on. We beat Spurs 3-1 and Macca scored again. We won 2-0 at his old club Coventry and Macca scored again. We won at Bradford and Macca scored again. He'd netted in five games on the trot and was building up a cult status at the club. Now the mantle would be passed to Michael Owen who also scored in that Bradford game. We were finishing like a train and no one was surprised when we thumped Newcastle 3-0 with a Michael hat-trick. Chelsea held us 2-2 at Anfield, but an Owen double was a good omen and as this was the last home game the crowd gave the lads a sensational send-off as they looked forward to the FA and UEFA Cup Finals.

There were now just three games to go. The FA Cup Final against Arsenal, the UEFA challenge against Alaves and our final Premier game at Charlton where we could claim that Champions League spot. Now it was off to Cardiff with real hope in our hearts. Naturally it was billed as the showdown between two talented and intelligent French managers who respected each other, but who were also great rivals. We stayed in our favourite Vale of Glamorgan Hotel. It was amazing going into the game. When we left Liverpool to go to Cardiff I was in the treatment room where Michael had hold of these new Umbro boots. I looked at him with a wry grin and said: "What are you doing with those new boots?"

He said: "These are my new Umbros." I said: "You are surely not thinking of wearing them at Cardiff are you? Those old ones are hot. You must be crazy to think about a change. You've just scored six goals in three games and you're thinking about changing your boots."

He just looked admiringly at his new ones as if he didn't have any superstitions at all. I went into Gerard's office and told him the story. Gerard was horrified and he saw Michael, who realised we were right and relented. It was a roasting hot day in the Millennium Stadium. Macca was on the bench, which was a big surprise to him because he had been inspirational. A big decision was made, but he would play a vital part in the match. Arsenal were the better team. They missed loads of chances. We even changed goalkeepers in as much as Stephane Henchoz handled on the line and got away with it.

They took the lead through Freddie Ljungberg, but couldn't build on their advantage. You will always get a chance, especially with someone like Markus Babbel charging down the flank like a right winger. Gary Mac was now on the pitch and from a free-kick on the left he bent a great ball into the box. Markus made a challenge on Tony Adams and the ball dropped to Michael Owen, who whipped a volley beyond David Seaman for the equaliser.

Macca had made an impact. Michael had made an impact. My third thought was how we might react in extra time. I thought: "It could be the hardest game of our lives." Then Patrik Berger played a long ball from defence to Michael. He was to squeeze the ball beyond the left arm of Seaman and into the net. It was an astonishing finish. The joy and disbelief at what the fans had just seen was incredible. We held on for the most unlikely of 2-1 wins and there were remarkable scenes of jubilation on the pitch.

The Kop end at the Millennium Stadium was booming as our fans sang You'll Never Walk Alone. It was nice to see Jamie Redknapp, Robbie Fowler and Sami Hyypia all getting their hands on the trophy, three players who had skippered the side. It was really nice for Jamie, who missed out with a knee problem. The lads did not forget him. Again they played those songs over the tannoy that reminded us of the Worthington Final, but this was the FA Cup and it was extra special.

On the way back to the hotel some of the lads said: "Ask the boss if we can party and have a drink?" I asked Gerard and thought he would relent, but he was the supreme professional and said: "No. We will all have a glass of champagne, but we have Alaves on Wednesday and Charlton next Saturday." He went to the back of the bus to explain, saying: "Trust me. We will celebrate after we beat Charlton. If we party now it won't help our preparation for Alaves. It will be the same after the Alaves game, but you have to trust me on that." The lads were great. We had a couple of glasses of champagne, then Coca-Cola and orange juice and went to bed. It showed they were good professionals. No, they didn't raid the mini bars. We always ensured they were locked up!

My thoughts at this time were not totally focused on our trophy challenge. One of my good friends, Tony Upham, was in hospital with cancer. I had made a little promise to myself that if we won the FA Cup I would take the trophy into the Aintree and Fazakerley Hospital to show him. Tony, who lived in Knowsley Village, was a lovely man and a massive Liverpool fan. I obtained permission from the club to borrow the cup and rang Tony's wife Janice to tell her I was on my way. She knew he would be absolutely thrilled.

He was extremely frail, but the sight of the FA Cup coming through the door of the ward immediately gave him a lift. We took some special photographs and all of the nurses and staff came over to touch or hold the trophy. I said to Tony: "Just wait until we win the UEFA Cup on Wednesday. I will bring that in as well." Sadly, I never got the chance. In the early hours of the morning

Tony died. It was an extremely sad occasion and it certainly puts all your own troubles and worries into perspective.

It was on to Dortmund and the clash with Alaves. I knew Tony would be with us in spirit for the Reds had been a big part of his life. Johan Cruyff's negative words about Liverpool were still an irritant in our ears. It was especially ridiculous because his son Jordi was playing for our opponents. Cruyff Snr suggested we would make it the worst final ever. He claimed it would be boring. Those words were rammed down his throat. How boring is 5-4 in any European final? We went two up inside 16 minutes through Markus and Stevie. We thought it was going to be a doddle, but the big Spanish teams are never a pushover. They made a tactical change and took off Dan Eggen, their tall Norwegian centre-half. They had started with five at the back.

Now striker Alonso came on in a 4-4-2 and it changed things instantly. The Uruguayan climbed above Babbel at the far post to head home Contra's cross to make it 2-1. We increased our advantage to 3-1 when Macca slotted home a pen after Michael was fouled. We really needed to concentrate, but suffered an early second-half blow when Javi Moreno pulled it back to 3-2. The same player would then beat us with a free-kick from the edge of the box. Having been in control, it was now 3-3. Thankfully for us the dangerous Moreno was subbed after 64 minutes while Robbie came on for Emile. These were both significant changes.

Within nine minutes Robbie had put us in front by shooting low into the corner after good play by Macca. Boring game? I don't know what Johan was thinking in the stands. Surely this would settle it for us at 4-3. Incredibly, Jordi Cruyff levelled matters as normal time drew to a close. I can't confirm it but someone allegedly heard his dad Johan shouting: "What a great game!"

It was now extra time and I had mentioned in the dressing room that this could be settled by a golden goal. Some listened. Some didn't in the heat of the moment. We started the extra period and at that point I had already compiled my list of penalty takers should the scores remain level.

Alaves, as tired as us, had lost some of their discipline and they actually had two players sent off in this period. Then Patrik Berger was chopped as he went down the left-hand side. I'm looking at my pad as Gary Mac began to set up the ball. I'm saying: "They had two sent off. We potentially need nine penalty takers. What about Didi?" I put a circle round his name as Gary took the kick. I saw it flick off someone's head, defender Geli as it turned out, although I didn't care at that moment in time. The ball looped into the back of the net.

We all ran onto the pitch, aware that it was a golden goal winner. Patrice Bergues stayed relatively calm and didn't move. Later he told us that he wondered where we were going. He thought our celebrating was a bit over-the-top. He had not realised the golden goal applied.

We just stood and watched in awe as 40,000 Liverpudlians started to celebrate. It was an astonishing sight. As Alaves went up to get their medals we got in the biggest huddle we had ever had in the centre circle with everybody involved. Then the lads went forward to get their medals, including Gerard whose planning and dedication had paid off big style. The crowd started to sing You'll Never Walk Alone and I got everybody to put their arms around the next person's shoulders. We all joined in and it was a most moving experience.

I thought: "Eat your heart out Johan Cruyff." Everyone had just witnessed one of the most fantastic European finals ever, as eventful as the Real Madrid v Eintracht Frankfurt European Cup Final, won 7-3 by the legendary Spaniards in the Fifties. I'll mention Istanbul later.

We did not get back to the hotel until 1am. We had something to eat and Gerard once again told the players: "No drinking." As it was, everyone was so tired we just had a couple of glasses of champagne and went to bed, ready to make the journey home the next day. We were cruising, but had to bring the lads down to earth for the final Premier game at Charlton. If we won this we would have Champions League football as well.

People asked me about those three massive games – FA Cup Final, UEFA Cup Final and Charlton with its potential Champions League prize. If we had to give one or two up to get the other, which would it be? The simple fact is that we were focused on every challenge as it reared up in front of us. We had three trophies in the bag and we wanted to finish the job.

Of course, you can get your feet back on the ground, but the sheer mental and physical energy that it takes to start again can be tough. It's fair to say that Charlton murdered us in the first half of that final match of this amazing 2000/2001 season. Sander Westerveld made three or four outstanding saves. The gods were with us and we were able to regroup at the interval to ensure that a season of effort on the league front had a major end product. We talked to the lads and Gerard reminded them of the prize. We went out transformed and could have won by eight, although we happily settled for 4-0. Maybe they thought we would be easy meat in the second half. We were the opposite. Now, at last, we could celebrate. We had three cups and a Champions League place in the bag.

This is what we had worked so hard for. I remember our five-man backroom team – Gerard, Sammy, Patrice, Joe and myself – hugging each other on the halfway line. It had been a long, hard season, but what a campaign. Gerard lived up to his word. We already had a couple of cases of champagne in the boot of the team coach and set off for home from London with our party already in full swing.

We then pulled into this giant car park at either an Asda or Tesco's and sent someone in to empty the shelves of beer and wine. It was an incredible sight and they piled this stuff on the bus. Gerard had forced the lads to be patient and supremely professional. Now they could let their hair down. I'm glad it was a long journey. We insisted that the first thing the lads did was ring home to ensure they were being picked up.

The scene was set on the Sunday for our homecoming parade with the Worthington Cup, FA Cup and UEFA Cup. We received the most fantastic welcome. It was extra special for lads like Gary Mac, who had given us so much while understanding that it was probably his swansong. What a signing that turned out to be. The streets were packed with Liverpudlians and we all celebrated late into the night, the players having a special party at Heathcotes.

We had decided that all of the staff should go away together to celebrate. We had organised this trip to Marbella in a hotel with a golf course. It proved to be a timely thing. The sad thing was that Patrice had told us he was going to leave, which was a massive blow. He was a great guy and a fantastic coach. His departure would be a big loss to us all, not least Gerard who had known him for a long time. Patrice had great humility. He had worked well with Sammy, but had decided he should take on a new challenge at Lens which was his home town. For him, it was the equivalent of me returning to Liverpool.

I now wondered what the summer had in store. I knew that one thing was for certain. I would soon be getting those phone calls from our friends in Malta, reminding me of my pledge. The phone rang within days of our homecoming tour. "Hi Phil, many congratulations. How are things in Liverpool?" I just replied: "I know what you are saying. When can I bring the cups over?"

I sought permission from Rick Parry who said: "No problem." Sammy Lee could not make it this time and so I decided to take along a couple of friends, Alan and Jill Whalley, who are great Liverpudlians. It would be a journey and a half with three famous trophies and we needed some help and support. They could not believe they were travelling with this famous silverware.

The people in Malta made all of the arrangements. It was wonderful to see their faces when we arrived. Manchester United had taken the European Cup over there in 1999. This was now a big statement for the Maltese Liverpudlians because we had THREE trophies. We had our hotel rooms and the trophies had their own 'bed' with three security guards staying with them day and night. Of course, we found out later that these guys had their friends and relatives round to have their pictures taken with the cups. You can imagine the scenes of joy.

When we took them to functions and events there was an armed guard to take care of the trophies so that everyone could see them. We had VIP Mercedes cars to transport us around and Alan and Jill could not believe it. Of course, we had to do the trip to the nearby island of Gozo and travelled by helicopter between the small islands. It was an incredible few days. I was just delighted that I had kept my promise. Of course, I had spoken about a trophy. No one in their wildest dreams could have predicted it would be three. The fans were asking if they were the real ones. There had been rumours that United had taken a replica European Cup. I'm not sure if that's true, but ours were very much the real thing. The Maltese Liverpudlians really appreciated it. I could have been the next Prime Minister of Malta after that trip.

My Robbie row and super five before the boss stares death in the face

The season started with our now customary pre-season camp in Switzerland. It was all to come crashing down one day when Gerard and Rick Parry came to me and said that Tom Saunders had died. Tom had undergone a heart bypass operation, only to die on the operating table.

I know it was a huge blow to everyone at the training camp – players, staff and Rick Parry – but I had extremely personal things to thank Tom for, going back as far as the FA Youth Cup Final side in 1972. He had been a great friend throughout the years, but none more so than that day when he advised the board that Phil Thompson should come back as assistant to Gerard Houllier.

He had helped me realise a dream to help the club win more major honours. Tom was a fantastic guy, so knowledgeable and a man who was full of humility. Tom and his wife Anne had become great friends of Marg and our family. I have two pictures of him in the house. One is a very thoughtful image in which he is looking at a football match, a lot younger and thinking of the game all the time. The other is our celebratory night showing Gerard, Tom and myself with the three trophies we had won. He was at the dinner we had organised at Heathcotes after our tour round the city. This is a picture of Tom looking extremely ill when I look at it now.

We were to move on from our Swiss camp, taking our three trophies with us for a tour of the Far East to Bangkok and Singapore amid absolutely incredible scenes. The trip had been planned months in advance long before we had even won our League Cup so it could not have worked out better. It showed how much LFC had moved on. These wonderful, humble fans were absolutely ecstatic to see their heroes close up and with the three beautiful silver trophies. The fans camped out all day and night in the hotel foyers just to catch a glimpse of their heroes.

I'd been to Bangkok many years earlier and although we had big support then, it was nothing like we witnessed with incredible sights wherever we went and with 20,000 people at training sessions. To quote the great man, Bill Shankly, we certainly made the people happy on that trip.

The 2001/2002 season naturally started with expectations soaring that we could now win our first Championship in 12 years. It seems incredible to think that after winning a record 18 titles, Liverpool had gone so long without claiming English football's most important prize.

The fans were right to be full of confidence. We had gone from seventh to fourth and now to third and we wanted to show our supporters that the Premier League was now in our grasp. It was going to be another big season. The Champions League qualifying games started and we also had to face Bayern Munich in the European Super Cup.

The Champions League campaign began with a relatively easy challenge against FC Haka from Finland, who had only qualified because an Israeli team had been kicked out after playing an ineligible player. Haka stepped in and it was nice for Sami Hyypia and Jari Litmanen. Both would play in the game against their Finnish countrymen, Jari operating as one of three attackers. Yes, we could be more attack-minded this time, but Gerard wasn't going to get another knock on the door. This was nothing like the Roma challenge and we won 5-0 although it took us some time to get into our stride with the Finns utilising a frustrating tactical system. When we did break it down Michael got a hat-trick, Emile hit the first and Sami celebrated with a fitting goal.

Four days later we were back in Cardiff again to play champions Manchester United in the Charity Shield. Although we knew it was about fitness, we also accepted that any Liverpool v United clash is also about the result. We had hit on this formula to play them which involved four at the back, a protector just in front, three tight in midfield and two up front. It seems illogical when you first look at it. They had two outstanding wide men at the time in David Beckham and Ryan Giggs. Why leave gaps wide and give them space to break into? The idea was to use the width in the final third, but give them the ball in the middle third. We allowed United to go wide up to the halfway line and then we would shuffle back. We had learned that this strategic formation could prove fruitful against them.

We went into the game with the same formation and won 2-1, but with one significant absentee – Robbie Fowler. It doesn't give me any great delight to re-live this story, but it has become part of Mersey folklore and people always ask about it. One of my pet hates on the training ground was lads kicking balls about in an indisciplined way. They'd get a bag of balls and launch them from one end of the pitch to the other as if they were firing a scatter gun. This would mean that the players would have to go round collecting them later or more likely one of the staff.

Another thing that really annoyed me was people who just lashed balls about in the penalty area with no thought for the other players in that vicinity. Someone might be standing between the posts looking the other way before things had started and a ball would rocket into them, or narrowly miss them. It wasn't as if we hadn't spoken about the dangers.

It just happened that I was right next to one of the goalposts this day, ready to get a session going. It was a couple of days before we were down in Cardiff. The next thing this ball whistled between my head and the post, missing me by inches. How it didn't hit my nose I'll never know! I felt the wind as it sped past. If it had hit me full in the face it could have done some real damage. I immediately turned round and said: "Who did that?" Everyone looked at me, including Robbie Fowler. To be fair, he didn't try to hide the fact. He said: "It was me." I said: "That was so stupid. How many times have I told you about that." He said something like: "Fuck off, big nose."

I just blew and said: "You what? We've got rid of people for doing things like that." Maybe this was a difficult thing to say. I was referring to the ill-discipline that had dogged the club before Gerard and myself teamed up. We were heading towards each other and the lads jumped in to keep us apart and ensure there would be no fisticuffs. Gerard came over and asked what had happened. I explained and he immediately asked the other players and other members of staff what had gone on.

After training we spoke as a staff and Gerard said: "Obviously we will give Robbie the chance to see if he will come up and apologise." Nothing happened. This was on the Friday morning before the Charity Shield. Saturday morning arrived and nothing happened. Gerard said: "If he doesn't come back and apologise he won't play in the Charity Shield." The manager was adamant about that. I said: "Look Gerard, I will go and square it off with Robbie."

Gerard was having none of it. He said: "No, it's not about that Phil. He did something wrong. If he had apologised straight away there would not be a problem." I explained that this was all I wanted. I was ready to put it behind me. If I had taken it further that would have been my problem, but there was no remorse from Robbie. When the team selection was made he was not in our line-up. Gerard had pulled him and he had said: "I'm not apologising."

He still came down with the squad to Cardiff. Naturally he was very disappointed. The following week he trained as normal. We gave each other a wide berth. In the end I went to Gerard and said: "The season is starting next week against West Ham. I think it's time that I squared this off with Robbie." This was my second offer to do this. Gerard said: "No! This is a wider issue now. It is a club thing. We can't be seen to be backing down. If Robbie had apologised that would have been the end of it. All of the work we have done over the past couple of years to tighten up the discipline could go out of the window if we are weak on this." There is no doubt we had come a long way on that score from the days when the crew were running the ship. I backed down to Gerard's greater experience.

In his recently published book, Robbie gives his side of the story. He suggests that he was punished just because he was having some shooting practice. If this was the case and I was behind the net as he suggests, there would have been no case to answer and his teammates would have backed him up. In fact, I would have been the one in the dock. He knew what the drill was and was aware we hadn't started the session at that time.

He was right to observe in his book that Gerard Houllier wasn't there, but wrong to suggest we treated him unfairly. If Gerard had one special quality it was that he was absolutely meticulous in how he dealt with things. You can rest assured that he sought advice from everybody who was present and that was a lot of people, players and staff. He wanted to be certain that he was taking the right action. If Robbie still harbours any doubts or worries, he should ask some of his teammates who backed up what I said.

It is also alleged that Jamie Redknapp later laughed and said Robbie was caught up in a sting by being photographed on the training ground with Gerard and myself, as if we were all making up. A 'sting' suggests we were party to a photographer snatching a picture over the wall at Melwood. In fact, Gerard was paranoid about such unofficial pictures being taken and had actually spoken to the press about one particular individual who kept doing it. It was this guy, Chris Neill, who took that image and sold it to the media. It would be a total lack of respect on anyone's part to suggest that we somehow tried to manipulate that situation to make it look as if Robbie had made some kind of public apology. Can you imagine Gerard Houllier being party to something like that with a pirate photographer? It defies belief.

The whole episode was sad because Robbie missed the opening 2-1 league win over West Ham. To wrap it all up, when he did finally apologise in the office there was no smug smile on my face to suggest I had won. I was just happy that this unhappy period was behind us. We actually gave each other a hug. You must remember that I originally had him in my reserve set-up. No one was ever more delighted than me to see Liverpool lads doing well.

This was a big issue for me. I not only liked Robbie, I loved the club. He'd struggled with injuries and he was fighting back. Now he was competing for a place with Michael, Emile and Jari. It was a relief for me that things were finally sorted out. All kinds of things were being said and the rumour mill was in overdrive. People were saying that I disliked him. It was no such thing. We had an incident and both of us were stubborn in not coming to our senses quicker. The longer it went the more difficult it became. Gerard had informed chairman David Moores and chief executive Rick Parry, who understood the implications as explained. I was more than pleased when this was eventually put to bed although later in the season Robbie would leave the club.

On the Friday after the first league game of the season, we were off to play Bayern Munich in the Super Cup. I had played in this competition when it wasn't as significant as it is now. We played the Champions League winners in Monaco, which was a beautiful setting. It was a big one for our German players Hamann and Babbel. It brought back plenty of memories and we were up for it. We raced into a 3-0 lead just after half-time. Of course, we were thinking: "Where is all of this going to end?"

We'd won three major trophies. We'd won the Charity Shield. Now we seemed on course to overshadow the Champions League winners to claim the Super Cup. I had to give myself a slap to make sure I wasn't dreaming. A sense of reality returned when Bayern grabbed two late goals and this made it a nervous ending. However, the trophy would be ours on a warm night in Monaco when it seemed that everything was right with the world. It was a great victory and Robbie came on for Michael to play his part. It was all looking rosy again.

That afternoon Gerard and myself had been invited by Elton John's office to go to his luxury villa for lunch. Liverpudlian John Hargreaves, who runs the giant Matalan empire, also invited us to lunch. He had his yacht in the famous harbour. Sadly, we were not there for a jolly and had to say no on both counts, but these were heady days.

I should add quickly that there was one very significant element of the Super Cup victory that was extremely troubling. We noticed that Markus Babbel was sweating profusely at half-time, but he did not want to come off. He pushed himself to the limit and finished up physically shattered. The Doc tested him and was not happy with his condition, but he couldn't pin it down.

Being the top pro he was, Markus wanted to play in the following game against Bolton on the Monday. Again, he came off physically shattered at half-time, but it had gone a step further.

Doc Waller was always in control, but we knew from the sound of his voice that Markus needed to be checked out quickly by a specialist. Maybe it was glandular fever. John Arne Riise replaced him as the Doc's worries grew. Markus didn't play again that season because all of the tests diagnosed Guillain-Barre Syndrome. It affected his walking. He lost weight. It was an extremely difficult time for Markus.

We had to remain positive for the club because these were crucial days for us. The Super Cup had taken place on August 24, 2001 and we had now won five trophies in six months. It would make for a great team photo. Gerard organised it so that the players and staff would have a fantastic memory of this remarkable spell. It was unfortunate that one or two had left and couldn't be on the picture. These included Patrice, which was a shame.

John Arne Riise, having joined us from Monaco, scored against Bayern. It was especially nice for him because he was back at his former club in Monaco and meeting many of his old friends. The one drawback of this excursion was that it broke up the rhythm of the league. Our season had started positively enough. We had put five past Haka with a Michael Owen hat-trick. We had beaten United and Michael had scored again. We then opened our league campaign with a win over West Ham and beat Haka 4-1 in our Champions League return.

This had been a great spell for Michael Owen. He had scored three against Haka, one against United, two against West Ham and one against Bayern. I was wondering if he still had his old shooting boots, but I'm not sure. Probably his new ones were serving him just as well.

Now we would be brought down to earth with a bang at Bolton where we lost 2-1. Gary Mac played well in the game as did Didi Hamann, but we could not score. We were one down and brought on Emile for Robbie. He made it 1-1 at the end of a 15-man move. However, Dean Holdsworth struck from 25 yards to frustrate us. I can remember Sander Westerveld going down and lying on the floor as the ball bounced over his body. He had gone down too early and it gave Bolton an unexpected victory.

I think that was the beginning of our search for a new keeper. Sander had done well for us, but this capped a few costly mistakes and we needed something better. It was the start of a busy week. International games were looming and I was sent out to Warsaw where we were giving a medical to Jerzy Dudek, who had also been linked with Arsenal. We had wanted to sign Chris Kirkland, but Coventry had proved stubborn. It was decided that we would switch our attentions to Jerzy, who had been watched by Joe Corrigan and given some good reports. He was preparing for an international game and I made all of the arrangements to progress the formalities.

Then the phone rang and it was Rick Parry. He said: "Phil, we have agreed a deal with Coventry for Kirkland." I said: "What?" Rick explained that Coventry had come back and accepted our offer, presumably aware that we were about to sign the Polish star. I said: "I'm just going to a meeting with Dudek and his agent in ten minutes. You need to tell me what to do." It was agreed that Rick would contact Gerard to gauge his thoughts. I met up with Jerzy and his agent in the hotel.

It was tricky because there were camera crews everywhere, expecting Poland's international keeper to be putting pen-to-paper on a Liverpool deal. This was clearly big news in Poland. I spoke to Gerard and said: "What about us signing both Chris and Jerzy? Have we got enough money? We are in the Champions League." It was an interesting thought and Gerard said he would speak to Rick. Straight away Rick came on and said: "Let's do it."

It was a relief for me. I had been walking round this hotel trying to keep away from the agent. Suddenly we were signing the best young keeper in Europe and one of the top goalkeepers in Europe, someone Arsene Wenger had courted. It was a fantastic double boost. After the international weekend we entertained Aston Villa. It was Jerzy's first game. Steven Gerrard was sent off and we would lose 3-1. On the back of the Bolton defeat, this was a massive blow.

We moved back into Europe with a game against Boavista. It was a famous date for reasons that you will immediately recognise when I say September 11, 2001. We were all looking forward to being back in the Champions League proper against the Portuguese champions. They were a lively team, Latin and volatile. However, only one thing was on everyone's minds that afternoon. We had watched the horrifying events unfolding in New York as the hijacked planes flew into the Twin Towers. The players were resting in their hotel rooms before the game. They were glued to their TV screens. It was a day when you simply could not take your eyes off the screen as you tried to take in the enormity of the catastrophe.

I don't know how we played the game after witnessing those scenes. That's the amazing thing about TV these days. You can watch something unfolding live thousands of miles away and feel as if you are in the centre of it. The evening started badly when Boavista scored after three minutes. Michael equalised to continue his run and that is how it finished. After our great start we had now gone three games without a win with two major challenges looming – Everton at Goodison in the derby and Dortmund in the Champions League. The Everton players were pinning their hopes on an upset, but we were fired up and after Kevin Campbell's early opener, levelled the scoring when Steven Gerrard shot across the keeper. We were up and running. Michael got a penalty and John Arne Riise capped off a 3-1 victory.

The games were now coming thick and fast. Dortmund were talked about as the favourites to win our Champions League group, which also included Dynamo Kiev and Boavista. We secured a credible 0-0 draw in Germany where Michael had two clear pens turned down. We did not get the rub of the green at times.

Back on the Premier front we beat Spurs 1-0 before our home game with Kiev. We knew they were not the best of travellers and felt our home form could see us through in this group. Of course, we then had that setback against Boavista and it made the Kiev game even more crucial. We beat them 1-0 on a night when Jari Litmanen got his second goal in four days.

We then saw off Newcastle, but our inconsistency cost us dearly as we began our defence of the Worthington Cup. Grimsby Town proved to be giantkillers at Anfield where former Everton player Phil Jevons scored in the last minute of extra time. Maybe it was a blessing in disguise with more significant action unfolding in the Champions League, but we were still disappointed because that competition had given us the springboard to glory the previous year. What happened next, however, put everything in its correct perspective.

There is no doubt that October 13, 2001, will remain etched in my mind forever. It was one of the most incredible days of my whole football career. After a fantastic year, this game against Leeds United at Anfield would take on a significance that no one had thought possible. This Saturday match was live on TV and therefore kicked off early, but that was the only thing that made it different from any other Saturday in terms of build up and preparation. It was a special day for Gerard and myself because this was the fixture that had first marked our partnership. We had also had some eventful games against Leeds, like the 4-3 defeat.

David O'Leary's men were winning this game 1-0 at half-time, which was a real blow to us. You have to try and picture the scene in our dressing room during the interval. Two massage benches sit in the middle of the floor. The players sit around these on three sides. Gerard always stood behind one of these benches to give his interval talk, although he always gave the players three or four minutes to get their drinks and have any minor bits and pieces of treatment for cuts and bruises.

At this point he would come into his own. He would deliver quite a bit of tactical stuff, but keep it to about two minutes. This is how it unfolded. I was on his left-hand shoulder, but then he walked into the corner, came back and immediately went out. I said to Joe Corrigan: "Go and see what is wrong."

I then gave my little talk to the players before allowing them to have the final couple of minutes to themselves when Sammy would have one or two individual chats. As the players were getting ready to go out, Joe came back in. The Doc had followed Gerard out and so I knew something wasn't right. It turned out he had nodded to Doc Waller that he needed to see him. Joe said to me: "Gerard has a problem with his chest. He is lying down in the treatment room."

We didn't give any negative vibes to the players. I encouraged them that they could go out and do the business. They all trooped down the tunnel for the second half, but I went to the treatment room. On one bed was Emile Heskey who had been injured in the first half. On the other was Gerard looking pale and worried. I held his hand and said: "Stay here. We will take care of the players and get you a win." I knew that despite his condition, he would still be thinking about the team. He squeezed my hand. I looked across at Emile who looked terrified as he surveyed the boss who had an oxygen mask over his face.

I ran to the dugout and sat down. It suddenly dawned on me that I was now in charge. I would have to make the substitutions and tactical decisions. I was trying to concentrate while worrying about Gerard. I was telling myself that possibly it was just a bit of fatigue. These were tense and hectic times for the club with those expectations still sky high after our trophy haul.

It was amazing how things happen. It was a live TV game which had kicked-off at midday. Naturally the cameras were focusing on the bench with people wondering where Gerard was. You could see people whispering and straining their necks to try and double check if they could see the boss. When they realised Gerard was not there they started nudging each other while speculating about what had happened. Even the directors did not know what had gone on.

We didn't get the win for Gerard. Robbie Fowler chipped the keeper and hit the bar and Danny Murphy followed up for the equaliser. To be honest, there were more pressing worries as the game came to an end. The only thing on my mind was Gerard's health. You realise later just how fortunate he was that things happened at half-time. There were no crowds outside. The ambulance could get through. He was able to be whisked to the Royal Liverpool Hospital.

I went in to see the players. I had to sit them down and tell them what was going on. I explained that we didn't know what it was, but that we would keep them informed. I gave out the itineraries for our impending trip to Kiev. We were leaving the following morning, Sunday, because the game was to be played on Tuesday.

Again, this is where fate played a part. Gerard could have been in a plane at 25,000 feet when he took ill. That would have been dangerous enough. Then we would have landed in Kiev where they almost certainly don't have the same specialist facilities and expertise that we have.

I had to do the press conference, which was difficult. I used all of the experience I had gained and kept myself composed. I needed to keep myself together for Gerard, the players and the club. I'd done a lot of TV stuff during my time out of the game and this helped. I gave the media the only information we had to hand, which was very little. I then got changed quickly and saw the Leeds staff before setting off to the Royal Liverpool.

I arrived there, only to find that Gerard was just about to leave in an ambulance to be taken to the specialist heart unit at Broadgreen. His wife Isobel had remained at the Royal, waiting for Norman Gard to bring their car to follow the ambulance. I consoled Isobel before getting into my own car to make my way up to the hospital to be with them.

I couldn't believe, as Gerard was leaving, that cameramen were trying to snatch pictures of him on his stretcher in the back of the ambulance. I thought that was disgusting. In fact, it was gruesome. As I was waiting with Isobel, Doc Waller and Norman at Broadgreen, Dr. Rod Staples came out and explained they had received a diagnosis from the Royal Liverpool. He said this had helped to focus them on a specific thing and that the diagnosis was on the right lines. He said: "We believe Gerard has a problem with his aorta." He did a little diagram of where the problem probably was and showed Isobel and Doc Waller. Then he stunned us all by saying: "We will operate, but it's 70-30."

This was incredible. I know they give it to you straight in these situations because there is no time to dwell on things, but we were all taken aback. Isobel is a wonderful, dignified lady and she held herself together. Clearly, they needed to operate immediately. Dr. Staples said: "We are preparing him now. He will be through here in a few moments."

Isobel went to see Gerard and I waited just outside. After a while Gerard came past on his bed going to theatre. He had drips everywhere and he was sitting up slightly. Isobel was with him. I went over and got hold of his hand and said: "Don't worry, you are going to be alright. You are in good hands." I know football is the last thing you want to think about at moments like this, but I knew what Gerard was like. The club had become his life. I said: "I will take care of everything. You can rely on the staff and me. Just make sure you are alright."

I was so emotional it was untrue. I still had those "70-30" words ringing in my ears. We stayed a short while and chatted. We knew it was going to be a long evening and even longer night. They had predicted an operation lasting up to five hours. Isobel went home and I also set-off. Doc Waller said he would stay and that he would give us a call if there was any information. This was at 6.30pm. I went home expecting a phone call, certainly before midnight.

In the end I had to ring Doc Waller. He said: "Gerard is still down there." This was incredible. I didn't know what to do. In the middle of the night Marg and myself just lay awake. The Doc promised to ring me as soon as the boss was out of surgery. I dropped off and woke up with a start in the morning. No calls had been made and I rang the Doc again.

We had to set off at 11am to go to Kiev. Even at that time we had still not clarified how Gerard's health was. I knew it had been a massive operation. We were in a difficult position. The press were clamouring for information and chasing around. More importantly, we wanted to focus the players while keeping them informed. Now we faced a four-hour journey during which there would be no further news.

I settled down on the plane. During every flight, Gerard and myself always sat together in three seats with two bags of wine gums occupying the middle seat between us. I always sat by the window. He had the aisle seat. I just kept looking at the empty aisle seat and hoping and praying he was alright. I put the wine gums in their usual place and was sitting there chewing them with my mind in turmoil. I was thinking: "You should be with us."

We finally landed and Doc Waller made contact with Broadgreen by mobile. He was told that everything had been done. Gerard had come through it, but it had been a difficult one. They said he was good, but was in intensive care. That seemed to be a contradiction, but I knew what they meant. I said to Doc Waller: "We are having a meal this evening. I will get everyone together and then call you up to give an update on what has happened. The players need to be kept informed."

At this moment in time my thoughts were all with Gerard, but I had another worry. It was giving the team talk. I had never had a problem giving chats and talks. I'd been on telly and stood up at functions to speak to hundreds of people. But Gerard was top notch with his team talks. He had two separate flip charts with diagrams and headings. I was thinking: "What have you done to me?"

My heart was with Gerard. My mind was getting round this most difficult of team talks. I had 24 hours to sort myself out. That evening the Doc explained that Gerard had undergone a dissection of the aorta, the main artery that carries blood from the heart to all the branch arteries except the lungs.

Obviously we tried to give the players regular updates as to the boss's situation. I was giving press conferences and liaising with press officer Ian Cotton more than ever to ensure exactly the right message was coming across. The press wanted updates by the minute and we had to work out exactly what we could reveal, always taking account of the wishes of Gerard's family.

These were difficult times but I had to try and focus on the team and what Gerard would have wanted me to do. We had spoken days before the Leeds game about the Kiev challenge and how we would approach it, injuries permitting. I already had in my mind what the team selection would be although I consulted with the rest of the staff as normal.

I had a meeting with coach Sammy Lee and informed him that he would have to take over more of my mantle. I wanted him on the touchline encouraging the players and giving them a rollicking if necessary. I was not going to change completely, but I knew I would have to take a step backwards to enable me to take crucial decisions about substitutions and the like. I was going to need Sammy's help and I knew I could trust him completely. He had been great in my time back at the club. I knew I could rely on Sammy and the rest of the staff. In some ways it was good to be away at that time. We could try and focus on the game. We knew that the newspapers at home would be full of Gerard's illness, his operation and what the future might hold.

It was important to keep the players' spirits up. They had been very close to the boss, not least because of the success we had enjoyed the previous season. We had gone early to Kiev, but the time wore on and it was dawning on me that this pre-match team talk was looming. It was rankling with me. I was working on ideas, how I would approach it and what I might say.

I took two flip charts to my room and prepared as much as I could, as Gerard would have done. I had something up my sleeve that I thought I might use to capture the hearts and minds of the players and spur them on. That Tuesday evening, before leaving for the game, I nervously started my first-team talk. I said a few words before giving out the team.

Gerard and myself had spoken about playing one up front which meant there would be a key role for Emile Heskey. The team talk went as well as could be expected. I got my thoughts across and made some tactical points. I also thought that, motivationally, I got it right. As it ended I flipped over the very last sheet on the chart on which I had written in big capital letters: LET'S DO IT FOR THE BOSS.

That was the big thing I wanted to drive home. I told the players how much the boss loved his European football. It was not IF he would come back but WHEN and I declared that I wanted us to still be in the Champions League when that time came. In my mind was something Gerard had raised the previous season when he asked the players which cup they liked the best.

All of the English lads pointed to the FA Cup. All the foreign players opted for the UEFA Cup. Gerard said to me: "Which one do you like best?" and I said the FA Cup. He said: "As much as I like it, when I look at the FA Cup and UEFA Cup together it is the UEFA Cup that gives me more joy."

I knew how much he valued his Euro exploits. Being in the Champions League was extremely important to him although we had not made a great start in the competition. It emphasised why this Kiev game was so important. We were to win 2-1 while not playing brilliantly. One thing that did lift the players was the fact that we were the first British team to win in Kiev. Without doubt, the victory helped me to get over one of the most nerve-wracking 90 minutes of my coaching career.

There were so many little things to worry about. I had to be aware of all of the photographers who were pointing their lenses at the dugout, looking for a reaction. As a staff, we had to show that we were in control. It didn't help that there was a rumpus as we came off the pitch. I was aware of an altercation between some of their players and Emile. He had played like a gladiator up front and gave their back four a torrid time. One of the centre-backs had spat at Emile and slapped him across the face. We had to deal with it quickly and pulled him away into the dressing room.

I had a quick word with press officer Ian Cotton. I said: "Before I do the press conference I want to make a formal complaint to the referee about what happened to Emile." I went to the ref's room and explained what had gone on. One of the assistant referees immediately opened up and said: "I saw exactly what happened." He confirmed my version of events. That made my job a lot easier. I was not trying to stir up trouble, but we couldn't let them get away with that. Later the Kiev defender was given a four-match ban. He had even tried to put the blame onto Emile, claiming that he was the instigator.

I went into the post-match press conference and dedicated the victory to Gerard in his intensive care room. I knew he would not be awake, but I made it clear that the lads and the staff had won it for the boss. That was to get me through this press conference but I knew there would be more hazardous tests to come.

We flew back the following day and as we landed at the airport I was amazed when Rick Parry said to me: "Phil, I know it's early days, but we have a board meeting on Thursday. You will have to attend." I said: "What?" I thought he was winding me up. He saw my concern, and said: "Don't worry. It will be easy. I will speak to you before then."

Even the chairman said: "See you on Thursday." He knew it was a daunting prospect for me and also offered some encouragement. We arrived at Melwood to pick up our cars and I went straight to Broadgreen to see Gerard with Norman Gard and Doc Waller. I knew it was going to be difficult to see him in intensive care, but I was still shocked when I went into the dimly-lit unit. It was packed full of equipment with flashing lights. Gerard had a drip in the side of his neck and one coming out of his nose. It was frightening to say the least.

We were told it was important not to stay too long. Even minutes might be too much. I didn't want to burden him with what had gone on. He opened his eyes and I asked if he had seen anything or knew the result. He said: "Yes, I saw the game. The boys did well." His voice was shallow and we had to remind ourselves that this was only the Wednesday after his marathon operation on Saturday night and Sunday morning.

We were assured that Gerard was on his way to recovery and we knew he was in good hands. We quickly told the boss that we would continue to take care of things for him and that the players sent their best wishes. Then we left. It was a journey that I was to make on a regular basis in the weeks to come.

My own thoughts began to turn to the impending board meeting. The days were hectic as I focused on training while dealing with the press. This involved seeing the Liverpool Echo's correspondent Chris Bascombe on a daily basis. We only saw the national press the day before a game.

It was important to keep the fans informed and we tried to help all of the media channels, including Radio City and Radio Merseyside. On the Thursday I spoke with Rick and he reassured me that the board meeting would not be as daunting as I was thinking. He said: "Update the directors on fixtures that are coming up and any injury problems. Just reassure them about the situation."

Chapter 15

Pinocchio sits down, the boss returns and mighty Roma are tamed

At this time many people were doubting my ability and the staff's ability to hold the fort during Gerard's long absence. Some people were throwing in the names of people who might be brought in on a short-term basis. I knew that this was not what Gerard would want. He was going to make a full recovery and he would be back. I had a complete grasp of his love for the club and his passion for football.

If we brought in a third party, what would happen at the end of it? We'd had a situation in which Gerard had operated in a dual role with Roy Evans. I was annoyed because this speculation was a sleight on my ability and what I had learned under Gerard. As it turned out, the board meeting only lasted 20 minutes. Chairman David Moores was good. He said: "It's a difficult time, but we are all pulling together."

I spoke about Gerard's health, how results had gone and then reassured the board that I was capable of taking care of the team in the boss's absence. I said I had the confidence of the staff and the players to carry on with the job. I said that the club could rely on me 100 per cent.

I tried to be as confident as possible to make them understand that I was in total charge of the team. I had learned enough to put Gerard's practices into action on the training ground. It really helped that the likes of Sammy Lee, Jacques Crevoisier, Joe Corrigan and all the medical staff were right behind me.

I didn't get too many calls from other people. Some clearly thought I should be left to my own devices. Others thought I should be allowed to fall on my own sword. I was not going to allow that to happen. Of course, many of my friends amongst the former players were behind me. The people who did call in the main were coaches from outside of Liverpool who were checking out if there might be any coaching opportunities. I just said: "No, we've got great staff here who are getting on with it."

We now went on to Leicester for our first test after Kiev. People had been quite shocked that Robbie Fowler had been left on the bench for the Euro game as we played with one up front. Robbie had been in the team on that ill-fated day when Gerard took ill during the Leeds game.

However, we had already made the decision to go with one up front in Kiev and now was the time for Robbie to come back in at Filbert Street where it was now down to me to have the final say. I did as Gerard would have wanted and listened to the staff, but I also felt it was the right stage for Robbie and also for Emile who was in action against his former team.

We were to win 4-1 with a majestic performance. Guess who scored three? A certain Robbie Fowler. It was funny, but after all of the problems between us at the start of the season, here we were with so much to smile about. Robbie had his hat-trick and I had my first Premier win as caretaker boss. It's an amazing game. I had given my team talk and once again finished off with another little comment at the back of the flip chart about Gerard. I kept this going throughout my time in charge, sending the lads out with this rallying cry that also kept the boss in our thoughts.

It was always just a simple few lines. I tried to make it different each time, but the fundamental message was the same.

Now we were off to Boavista to continue our Champions League challenge. We knew they would be lively and temperamental. We also knew about their diving antics, having witnessed all of that in the 1-1 draw at Anfield on September 11. We would have to be ready for them and put in a good performance in another 1-1 draw, but not everything went to plan. After six minutes Sami Hyypia signalled that he had a hamstring problem and needed to come off.

I switched Jamie Carragher into a centre-back position and put Stephen Wright at right-back. Carra operated on the left of Stephane Henchoz and it all worked well. Danny Murphy struck a great free-kick to give us the lead, but their equaliser meant we still had it all to do to progress,

Our league programme then took us to Charlton where we had finished the previous season with that great 4-0 success. This time it was only 2-0, but I felt it was a better all-round 90 minutes than the outstanding 45 minutes of the previous campaign. I brought Jamie Redknapp back after his long absence and played a 4-1-3-2 formation. This encouraged Jamie to get forward more and he scored the opening goal. The only blow was that Stephen Wright was dismissed for two yellow cards.

I was suddenly starting to believe that this managerial thing was quite a doddle after three victories and a draw. I was actually beginning to enjoy myself and settling into the challenge. Our European odyssey was about to continue with Borussia Dortmund heading for Anfield. I kept talking to Gerard who was keeping track of our matches, either on the telly or by listening to the radio. It was uncanny, but the boss would say to me: "I knew what changes you would make. It was exactly what I would have done."

It demonstrated that we were very much on the same wavelength. Michael Owen was now back from injury but I felt it was important to handle him carefully with limited minutes on the pitch, although that often didn't go down too well with the player who wanted to play in every phase of every game.

I felt it was all fitting into place and it made me feel better when Gerard supported my decisions. As the Borussia clash loomed, I began to think that if we could make it through this stage, the European winter break would give Gerard more recuperation time.

It was crucially important to beat the Germans. It was a huge game for us and I was delighted when Vladimir Smicer put us ahead. Young Stephen Wright also scored and had a fantastic game at full-back. Things were going well, even with Sami Hyypia out. Carra was holding the fort in the middle alongside Stephane and the 2-0 final result was just what we needed.

This took us on to a massive Premier game at home to Manchester United on November 4, 2001. I thought: "Now it's your big test, Thommo lad." Could we follow up the Dortmund result with something just as special for the fans? We pulled off a fantastic 3-1 win. David Beckham made life tricky for us and scored a goal for United, but Michael Owen struck twice for us. The day will be remembered for a sensational free-kick from John Arne Riise who was to earn superstar status that day and his very own song: 'John Arne Riise, Ooh Aah, I want to know-o-oh-oh, how you scored that goal.'

When we moved on to play Blackburn at Ewood Park, all eyes were on what might happen between Graeme Souness and myself. Everyone knew there was no love lost between us and the reasons have already been well documented in this book. How would he react now that I was in charge of Liverpool, albeit in a caretaker capacity?

The fact of the matter was that the game was between Blackburn and Liverpool, not Souness and Thompson. He did the honourable thing and came to our dugout to shake hands before the kick-off. We would draw 1-1 and so it was probably right in the circumstances. The one thing that did stir me up a bit had nothing to do with Souness. I've said that we were still trying to nurse

Michael Owen through games and protect him after his injury problems. We wanted to ease his fitness levels back up and I substituted him with around 20 minutes to go.

We had Barcelona at Anfield on the Tuesday and I wanted to save Michael for that game. As he was coming off, it was being picked up on a big screen in the corner of the ground where the Liverpool fans were encamped. The camera zoomed in on Michael's head and shoulders. He was shaking his head and making it clear he was unhappy with my decision, but I was looking at the bigger picture.

I've said that Michael wanted to play in every minute of every game, but I felt I had to speak to him. We had a warm-down session on the Sunday and I called him into my office and asked why he did it.

He said: "I was disappointed and felt I had a bit more. Surely you want me to be upset when I'm brought off."

I agreed with that, but asked him to think about the wider situation. I wanted him fit and fresh for Barca. The substitution was not a sleight on his game or form. This type of conversation was something Gerard would always do. I would be Mr Angry. We had this good cop, bad cop thing, but now I was in the role in which I had to think about the welfare of the players, always thinking one step ahead.

I said to Michael: "Your point is right about showing disappointment at being subbed, but it can sometimes show a lack of respect for the person coming on. He must feel confident." Gerard always demanded that players coming off should shake hands with the lad going on and wish him well. That is what I wanted Michael to think about and I know he understood.

Now that I was in the front line, my profile increased dramatically and all of a sudden it inspired something on the terraces that was to take on a little bit of folklore. Someone started this song that would go to the top of the charts with football supporters all over the country. When we travelled away, the home fans would roar: 'Sit Down Pinocchio!' When we played at home, it was constantly ringing out from the Anfield Road End visitors' section. What could they be singing about?

Of course, it was Bill Shankly who had predicted that my nose would get me into trouble. I decided that the best way to deal with these chants was to ham it up.

I'd go to the touchline. The visiting fans would kick off. I'd go to sit down, touching my nose to acknowledge their words. Then I'd stand straight back up and they would go mad again.

It had struck me when United visited Anfield that many of their fans were not even watching the match. They were too busy roaring 'Sit Down Pinocchio' in my direction. It's not too bad when it's restricted to 3,000 visitors. When we travelled away and 40,000 home fans struck up the chorus it was quite something to behold.

The song became a bit of a soap opera. Away I would raise my hands as if I was leading an orchestra. I thought that the easiest thing to do was to laugh at myself. Fans hate people who take themselves too seriously.

I hope they appreciated my humour. By reacting in a light-hearted way I was signalling that I appreciated theirs. Not too many fans came up with anything different. Although the Manchester City supporters came up with: 'Your nose is on the pitch!'

That was good although they should know. One of their legends was Sixties star Mike Summerbee and I'd have to say that in the 'Nose Hall of Fame' he was one of the kings. Mike was another who had a great sense of humour and played up to the chants of rival fans. Someone told me that he once went out at Everton wearing a false nose to give everyone a laugh. Don't know if it's true or folklore, but it's great.

What is correct is that The Mirror newspaper produced a list of the 'Ten Things Sung Most At Football Grounds.' What was number one? 'Sit Down Pinocchio!' Even when I went back to my assistant manager's role the words reverberated around every stadium. When I was thinking of a title for this book, it seemed an obvious thing to reverse it round and declare 'Stand Up Pinocchio!' It's just my way of saying that you can't keep a good man down. I've had some glorious moments in the game. I've also had moments of personal pain and frustration.

I've always bounced back and I remain committed to the sport that has been my life in every way – fan, player, coach, assistant manager, caretaker manager and media pundit. I love it and I always will.

My story continues in that 2001/2002 season with the visit to Anfield of Barcelona in the Champions League, a night when Michael Owen was in the starting line-up and scoring again. However, it was also an occasion when we ended up getting a real football lesson in a punishing 3-1 defeat.

Maybe our victory over them in the semi-final of the UEFA Cup still rankled. Whatever the case, they played really well that night although I dispute the claims that it was one of the greatest performances seen at Anfield. I have forced myself to watch it time and again on video. The reality is that things were quite even until the last 20 minutes. I have to admit that at that point they gave possibly the best display of keep ball I have ever seen from a team. It was as if they were in a training session. They absolutely murdered us.

It was so emphatic in that late spell that people remember it as if the whole game was like that. They finished in majestic style and their third goal came at the end of a 30-pass move that saw us well and truly buried. My unbeaten run of eight games had come to an end and I wanted an immediate response.

Thankfully I got it when we beat Sunderland at Anfield and while the 1-0 victory was not as emphatic as some of the others, it was a welcome win thanks to a goal from Emile Heskey. The downer was that Didi Hamann was sent off.

We were now moving into December and it was reaching the time when Gerard was looking to come out of hospital. He was going to need a long rehabilitation. My journeys to Broadgreen had stopped. I was now visiting the boss's home to keep him involved although it was agreed with the docs that we would not burden him with too much football.

In our conversations I tried to keep football to a minimum, trying to drip-feed him information rather than swamp him with it. However, it was difficult with Gerard. Even though he was still weak he was keen to know everything about the lads. He would talk to me about the teams I had picked. I would say: "Don't worry yourself," but he still had this remarkable appetite for all things Liverpool, even though he had been through a near death experience. Training was continuing on his lines and I would say: "Just get your strength and health back." However, each time I would give him a little more info and let him give more input. These were interesting times leading up to Christmas 2001.

It was at this time that we had another arrival a little earlier than we had anticipated. A deal had been done to bring Czech international Milan Baros to Anfield. It had been agreed that he would join us at the end of the season, but because he was so young and with all the hype surrounding his impending move, we felt it would be right for him to come early. When we saw him he was clearly overweight and we knew he would have to shed some of that before he could show his real potential.

Milan was lightning-quick and could score goals, but he looked poor in the reserves. That could be put down to his lack of fitness, but more was to come later from this determined young man.

We were preparing to move from the old Melwood complex into the new world-class facility on the other side of the field that Gerard, myself and the staff had put so much thought into along with Rick Parry and Anfield stadium manager Ged Poynton. They had listened to us about how we would like everything to be structured at the complex and they studied the best angles at other facilities.

We had seen it grow from the foundations and now was the time to move across and leave the ghosts of the greats like Shankly, Paisley and Fagan to play their five-a-sides on their old 'Wembley' pitch. We knew it would take a week to move everything across and put a plan in action for the medical staff, groundstaff and office staff to start the migration with the players following behind. It would make Melwood the best training ground in the country and we were all pleased and proud with the end product.

These were really exciting times. I know Gerard was particularly pleased that Melwood was taking a mighty leap forward. He had said: "This facility will be a wonderful legacy to leave behind."

Not that we had any thoughts about leaving at that stage. The boss was getting stronger with every passing day and our Liverpool ambitions were soaring higher than ever. We beat Derby County 1-0 and around that time there was constant speculation that Leeds United were in for Robbie Fowler. This made us feel uncomfortable because the stories happened too often. You don't know what's happening behind the scenes.

It would be a huge decision for Robbie to leave. He knew he would not be playing regularly with the likes of Owen and Heskey already forming a good partnership and with Jari Litmanen in contention. It was hard for Robbie to take. Clearly, he looked at it and decided the time was right to move on. Of course, people put two and two together and came up with five because I was in charge. In his own book Robbie claims we tried to get him out.

The truth is that Robbie could see Leeds buying a lot of big players at that time. They seemed to be on the up. Their interest in Robbie was the worst kept secret in football and we later heard that a national football journalist had acted as a third party in negotiations. Let's be clear, Robbie was still a hero with our fans. Gerard was still not back in harness, but he was involved in the discussions about our stance. It certainly wasn't just down to me. It couldn't happen that way.

The £12m we received was a good deal for the club. It was the right time to do it for all concerned and the decision proved to be correct. Robbie had been one of the greatest goalscorers the club had ever had. He was a local lad who led our goal charts for many years and that was something all Liverpudlians could relate to. He would always be a hero in their minds, but people had seen other striking legends move on like Hunt, St John, Keegan and Rush.

Of course, people were looking at our team to see if I could handle all of this. When Michael Owen subsequently scored the winner against Derby, it emphasised that we had moved on.

We continued our European journey with a trip to Rome which is always a thrilling thing because of its special place in the hearts of all Liverpudlians. We knew Roma would be up for beating us, but we secured a hard-earned goalless draw in the Olympic Stadium.

Back in the league, we overcame Boro 2-0 with Michael continuing his scoring exploits. Then it was a goalless home draw with Fulham, a result that set a few nerves jangling. However, it was our fifth consecutive clean sheet and that gave everyone hope. When you are tight at the back it gives the attackers more freedom to do their stuff in the knowledge that things are rock-solid behind.

We had now gone 14 games with just one defeat, against Barca, and everybody was saying how well we had done. The plaudits were raining in and some people took the opportunity to apologise about earlier statements they might have made about whether I was up to the caretaker role. For my part, I knew I just had to keep my head down and keep going. Football has a habit of bringing you back down to earth.

Stamford Bridge had been something of a hoodoo venue for Liverpool and so it proved again. The records show that we lost 4-0, but we actually played really well. Gary Mac missed a pen which was unlike him. The score was 1-0 at that stage. Chelsea goalkeeper Carlo Cudicini had an outstanding game. On the final whistle their players jumped all over him. There would be a picture used in the papers showing me with my hands on my head in disbelief at the result. Then an announcement came over the tannoy about the man-of -the-match. It was Cudicini and that said it all about our performance.

I couldn't give the lads a bollocking, even though the score seemed to suggest we had been on the end of a drubbing, but did the Press make anything of how well we played? No!

I certainly praised the players in the dressing room. It was just one of those days and the message had to be to keep our heads up. It was doubly important because another of the London giants, Arsenal, were up next. This game was just two days before Christmas, but we were not able to give our fans an early present. We were beaten 2-1 and it was a crushing blow. At 2-0 Jari Litmanen got us back in the match with a header, but it was not enough and it set some alarm bells ringing with questions being asked. We needed a victory quickly to turn things round and got it at Villa on the Boxing Day.

A player who strengthened our squad at that time was former Arsenal star Nicolas Anelka who we took on loan from Paris St Germain. We realised that we needed some more attacking depth, having sold Robbie, and while he couldn't play in the Champions League he would give us options in the Premiership. I remember Gerard calling me up and saying: "Phil, we need to add to our attacking strength. Would you take Anelka on loan?"

Of course, I knew all about his problems at Arsenal and Real Madrid, but I said yes straight away. It was a boost for the players and the fans and there was the opportunity of taking him full time at the end of the season. I knew Nicolas would pull out all the stops with a permanent move in the offing. We remained realistic because of the problems that had occurred with the player and his brothers who were his advisers. Nicolas was on the bench for the Villa game and I gave him his first taste back in the Premiership when he came on as a sub for Jari.

It was another striker who was celebrating when we moved on to Upton Park to face West Ham. Michael Owen got his 100th Liverpool goal in a 1-1 draw against the Hammers as New Year dawned. He had previously gone four games without scoring, with the fans and the Press waiting and waiting for him to complete the magical ton. In fact, he was only a sub at Upton Park, but finally got that precious strike.

I started with Nicolas and Emile in that game. We desperately needed something from the match and I brought on Michael for Danny Murphy to give us a three-pronged attack. Jari also came on and so we had four mainline attackers on the pitch. We were pushing and pushing and it was fitting that Michael did the business with a typical effort from inside the box.

As we began to board the coach after the game, I spotted a big friend and famous Liverpudlian – Joe the Redman. Lots of fans will know who I mean. Joe has supported the club through thick and thin and is always positive. He said: "Phil, I have a cake for Michael to mark his 100th goal. Can you wait while one of my friends gets it from the car?"

Aware that Michael's ton had been some time in coming, I said: "How long have you had it?" Joe said: "I know, I've carried it home and away for five games." I didn't know if the cake was off, but it was the symbolism that mattered. We let Joe onto the coach to make his presentation. I didn't ask for a slice as it happened!

Our statistics were beginning to come under scrutiny. After beating Boro at Anfield on December 8, we had played six league games and managed just one win, against Villa. This was the focus of attention as we prepared for an

FA Cup clash with Birmingham on January 5, 2002, the team we had beaten in the previous year's Worthington Cup Final. Everyone was talking about how unlucky they were in that final and how they had improved since then. It was being built up as a big game and a potential shock, but we would win convincingly 3-0.

It was the first time Michael and Nicolas had played up front together. Michael grabbed a double and his new partner claimed his first goal for the club. You begin to think that everything is going to be alright and that winning results will begin to flow, but we immediately lost 2-0 at Southampton which was a real blow. I can remember a ball coming off the head of John Arne Riise and looping over Jerzy Dudek. That is when you know that things are really starting to turn against you. It was a bitter blow for everybody.

You start to question everything. A 1-1 draw at Arsenal should be a good result at any time, but there were just too many draws at this time and another followed at home to Southampton and this made it just one win in nine Premier games. It stacked up as five draws, three defeats and that one victory, at Villa.

Naturally, I was under the spotlight. The media were beginning to say that the club had got it all wrong in appointing me. I remember Des Kelly, then at The Mirror, having a right go. He said things were not good, I was being found out and that the club should have made a change. At times like this you need real support.

After the Southampton game Sammy Lee had spoken up in front of the players on my behalf. You try and keep things in perspective, even when people are having a go. I tried to show a bit of humility, aware that the players needed my support more than ever. I tried to be positive with the Press, but Sammy clearly felt it was time to say something. He stood up and said: "You lot need to get your fingers out. This fella has taken all the flak and never criticised any of you in public. He has taken all the stick and the criticism, but has always been there to back you."

I knew that came from deep down inside and I appreciated Sammy's support, but these were still challenging dates. You certainly find out who your friends are. Sammy clearly understood the pressure I was under and one day he said: "I'm going to get a few of the ex-players. We will go out for a bite to eat and a drink."

As it turned out and because it was hastily arranged it was just Sammy, Kenny Dalglish, David Johnson and myself who turned up at the Tapas Bar in Queens Square. We spoke about what had gone on, talked about the old times and very soon we were laughing and giggling as about 15 bottles of wine piled up on the table. It was a great night in town with people I knew and trusted and it was just what I needed. I can remember falling out of there and all of us getting into different taxis to head home. It was the most I had drunk for a very long time and I felt better for having let my hair down. It helped me to get things in perspective.

One thing was clear in my mind and again it related to that Southampton game. Danny Murphy had a nightmare, but he was a big, brave lad out on a football pitch. He never hid and always wanted the ball, even when things were going wrong. I substituted him and it reminded me of years earlier when Sammy was in a similar situation after being brought off. The crowd cheered the decision and booed all in the same breath. It should never happen to one of our own players, especially one with his heart steeped in the club.

Danny was cheered sarcastically and then booed off. The team was having a hard time. Danny was having a hard time. Who should we be playing the following week but Manchester United at Old Trafford. People were saying we would get nothing out of the game. It was all about how many goals they would beat us by. Our own fans were going up there with fear, but one of the first names on my team sheet that day was...DANNY MURPHY.

He was a strong character. It was also a psychological thing on my part. I spoke to him and highlighted that the substitution nightmare he had endured had once also happened to Sammy. I said that he would have to rise above it. The other players knew Danny's qualities and appreciated the vote of confidence. We went to United with our tried and trusted 4-1-3-2 formation and against all of the predictions we had a fantastic day. It was the first time we had more possession than United at Old Trafford.

I remember Steven Gerrard dissecting their backline with an exquisite ball. Danny made a perfect run and while he was close to goalkeeper Fabien Barthez, he somehow managed to get the ball up and over him. It was a fantastic piece of skill. I can remember his face as he wheeled away to our fans, not to make a personal point, but just to celebrate a wonderful personal moment. He was just thrilled that he had scored at Old Trafford again.

I even put Nicolas Anelka on for Michael Owen and he gave a cameo display of his skills and came close to scoring himself. There was another substitution that I made for a specific purpose. I took Danny off again near the end. This time I knew that when he moved towards the touchline he would get a standing ovation from our fans and that is exactly what happened. I was thrilled for him and delighted with the 1-0 win that cheered everybody up.

We didn't have much time to draw breath because the next game that loomed was Arsenal at Highbury in the third round of the FA Cup. We knew that despite the United victory we would be up against it. As it happened we would go out 1-0, but what made it worse was the famous coin-throwing incident involving Jamie Carragher. How one coin could bounce around and hit so many people was astonishing. I'm not under-playing what happened in any way. It was wrong and Jamie knew it, but we couldn't believe how many people were coming to the fore.

It was lobbed rather than launched into the crowd. Carra was devastated and we knew it would be high profile with the FA because the previous week bottles had been thrown in London and coin incidents had happened elsewhere. I had played Nicolas in this game against his old club, hoping he would come up trumps, but it was all too much for him and he had a quiet game. I subbed him for Jari Litmanen and then the Carra uproar happened. On the way home we were listening to the radio phone-ins and all of these people were pontificating about how bad it was. We knew we had to act quickly.

I got together with Rick Parry and press officer Ian Cotton and we said: "We must stifle this now." We got Carra down to the front of the bus on our return back to Merseyside and said: "You need to apologise straight away through the Press." In a nutshell, we needed to get our apologies in first before they hit us.

Ian produced a statement with Carra who apologised while pointing out that it wasn't one coin that was thrown at him, but several. He said he tossed one back under severe provocation, but he was genuine in his words to the Arsenal fans. He had no intention of hurting anybody. His words helped to stem the torrent of criticism and I felt we had acted in a professional manner in dealing with the situation.

This was all a learning curve for me. The main thing was to try and help Carra through this situation, but it was soon back to the drawing board. I was still confident in the players who were still upbeat. We had Leicester in the midweek and a 1-0 victory helped us to get the Arsenal setback and the controversy out of our system. We then went to Leeds who had Robbie Fowler in their team.

Even our fans were taking bets that he would score against us. Sometimes these things appear to be in the stars. However, we were majestic and won 4-0. In the last 15 minutes Robbie had a couple of gilt-edged chances to reduce the arrears. One shot went straight at Jerzy Dudek and another was tipped over the bar. Naturally he was disappointed because he had clearly wanted to do well against us.

On the whistle he still gave our fans a great wave and they responded. They were in raptures and I went across to give Robbie a big hug. There was no animosity. We had both moved on, but the performance was a great statement by our team.

Someone else came in the team at that time who you simply could not miss in a crowd. If I said the 'Big Smurf', 'Santa Claus' or a 'Pint of Guinness' you would immediately know I was talking about Abel Xavier. We felt some cover was needed at the back. We had heard reports about sickness and injuries at Everton, but felt he could do a job for us. I gave him his first start at Ipswich, a club that had not been helpful to us when we were playing all of those games the previous year and they refused to move a fixture.

It gave us great delight to blitz them 6-0 at Portman Road. Who should score a goal after 16 minutes but Abel. He had never managed to score for Everton and so that was a bonus. Emile and Michael both got doubles that day and Sami Hyypia was another on the scoresheet. We'd scored ten goals in two games without reply to turn things round for our fans.

One thing stuck in my mind. Jerzy Dudek was injured against Ipswich and so Pegguy Arphexad came on late in the game. Even in the short time he was on the pitch he did not look as convincing as we would have liked. Thankfully we now went into an international break and I was wondering if we might have Chris Kirkland available for our home clash against Galatasaray on February 20, 2002 as the Champions League resumed after the winter break.

We had a derby match, of all things, sandwiched between the return against the Turks. Chris was available for this game at Anfield and he was not at fault when Everton took the lead. The Blues held their advantage until the last 20 minutes when Nicolas Anelka came up trumps to grab a draw. We would have preferred a win against the old enemy, but now we were interpreting the stats in a different way with just one defeat in nine games.

We were not exactly in heaven when we went to hell, if you know what I mean, but Istanbul now beckoned and we were confident. Of course, they had greeted Leeds fans with those 'Welcome To Hell' banners on an occasion when a Leeds fan was stabbed to death. After taking advice we urged our fans not to travel. We travelled with some trepidation, but from the moment we got off the plane they could not have treated us better.

They were desperate to show a different face after being castigated by fans all over the world following that Leeds incident. They handed us bunches of flowers as we arrived in the airport. The 'Hell' banners had clearly been banned and they took us to a wonderful hotel in the centre of Istanbul.

This did not make us feel any less disgusted in what had happened to our English compatriots. We still had to be on our guard and it was significant how many police and army vans were surrounding the hotel. The Turkish fans were not allowed anywhere near us.

I should say that the stadium was quite intimidating. There was no question of them holding back their emotions there. It was packed an hour before kick-off and they were chanting loudly, but it was not as bad as we had thought and I played on this with our players.

I continued to finish my team talk with the now familiar focus on Gerard, urging the players to keep doing it for the boss. I said he was with us in spirit in every way. Of course, he could not travel, but before we went he was having an input with bits in training and team selection. On the day it was still down to me.

Chris gave a majestic performance in a 1-1 draw. It was everything we had hoped for from him. He didn't have much to do, but he was solid when he was needed. It confirmed that he could become a top-class keeper if he could get his injuries sorted out. It was a fantastic experience to go to Galatasaray and come away unscathed, but it was another draw. It meant the situation in the group was very tight between Barca, Roma, Galatasaray and ourselves. We had three draws in four games.

We were beginning to motor now and we beat Fulham away 2-0. I specifically remember the goal from Jari Litmanen. Goalkeeper Edwin Van der Sar made this Bruce Grobbelaar-style run outside of his box when he was never going to get to the ball 25 yards out towards the touchline. Jari got there first and headed the ball over the keeper's head. From an acute angle he then played this ball into the net that seemed to take forever to get there with the defenders racing back.

We beat Newcastle 3-0 at home on a night when the lights went out. It was a live SKY match and everything had to be delayed, but didn't affect the mood of our lads who eventually went out to completely dominate the game.

Then it was off to Barcelona with our fans now able to book cheap flights via easyJet which was a bonus. They already knew about all of the famous bars in the Ramblas and everything was prepared for a great trip. We were up for it and decided to play a real attacking game with Jari and Emile up front. I remember Steven Gerrard missing a fantastic opportunity, flashing the ball across the Barca goal. Emile also missed a header at the far post and I wondered if these misses might come back to haunt us.

Our Dutch friends at Barca had once again been sniping at us, saying how defensive we were and that we were not good enough to grace the Champions League. The match finished 0-0, but the onus was always on the Spanish side to take the initiative. In the press conference I said that it was a shame their Dutch people could not just concentrate on their own international futures. If they had thought more about those international games instead of having a go at us they would be going to the World Cup in Japan and South Korea instead of holidaying in Disney and meeting Mickey Mouse. It got a few laughs in the press room. Back home we won 2-1 at Boro and we were now putting pressure on to finish as high in the league as we possibly could.

Our Champions League challenge was still there and it led to possibly the most emotional night I have ever been involved in at Anfield, with Roma the opposition. The game was played on March 19, 2002. Gerard had said many weeks before that if he felt we needed something in the last game of our Champions League group then he would consider making his comeback that night. It was just between the both of us at that time and we continued to monitor the situation.

Gerard was visiting Melwood to give team talks and to gee up the players, but he was still not going to games. He would speak to the players on a Friday if we were away or on a Saturday morning if we were at home. This Roma game was on a Wednesday night and on the Monday he said: "What do you think, Phil?" I said: "Gerard, if you feel up for it, great. It would make a massive impact on the club, supporters and most of all the players, but you have to feel right."

The boss was still not 100 per cent. It had to be his decision. He said: "I feel I can do it." I told him that I would be right behind him. Of course, we had to plan how it would happen. We didn't want anyone to get wind of it. On the Tuesday, Gerard said: "I will give my team talk to the players tomorrow before they go to rest in the hotel in the afternoon. I will actually come back to the hotel at 6pm to give a final team talk, but when I speak to the players earlier at Melwood I will just wish them good luck. They will not know anything."

Only two people knew about Gerard's plans to make a shock return to the Anfield stage at this moment – him and me. The idea was to make it a major surprise to give everyone a boost right before kick-off. I realised that we had to inform press officer Ian Cotton, Rick Parry and David Moores. I knew it would be a media scrum when people realised Gerard was at Anfield.

Ian needed to be ready without giving anything away. We were looking for a massive impact and I knew Gerard's presence against Roma would have the desired effect. At that moment in time I would have put my house on us ultimately getting the right result against the Italians. I knew we would win the game.

We told Ian on the Tuesday and so he was able to get prepared. Gerard, as planned, gave his team talk to the players at 11.45am on the Wednesday. He said it would be a huge night and wished the players well. They thought that was the last they would see of him for the day.

For my part, I had built up the game in the Press as being a modern St Etienne and the biggest game we had ever witnessed at Anfield. I was quite relieved that Gerard had now reclaimed the flip charts and had taken them home. I set off with the team to the hotel with the likes of Sammy Lee, Joe Corrigan and Jacques Crevoisier all still oblivious to what was happening. This was all playing on my mind. Gerard went to his house from Melwood to prepare his secret team talk.

Norman Gard was instructed to pick him up in time to be at the hotel for the 5.45pm team talk. The players all started to come down. We opened the back fire escape doors where Gerard was waiting with Norman to come in and arrange his now completed flip charts for the Roma game. When Sammy, Joe and Jacques came down, Gerard was in the room. It was a massive boost for them. Then the players started to walk in and the look on their faces was incredible. First it was shock. Then it was sheer delight that the boss was going to be with us for this major challenge.

Possibly they were thinking that it was just a double-header team talk ahead of the game and that he would be going home. Whatever the case, they were really pleased to see him and he gave a fantastic rallying team talk, even though he was probably only 80 per cent fit. I looked at the lads. They were really fired up. They immediately headed out to get on the coach at the back of the hotel. Then Gerard came out and started to climb up the steps to take his seat. You could hear all the whispers. "The boss is on the bus and with us."

As we travelled to Anfield in the dark, I was building up inside. We got to the ground where this old guy on the Shankly Gates always used to look in the bus and give the thumbs up to Gerard. The boss would respond with a thumbs-up of his own. When the steward saw Gerard he had to rub his eyes to believe what he was seeing. The coach edged through the gauntlet of fans packing the Main Stand car park by the players' entrance. As we pulled up, the look on people's faces was incredible.

The cheer Gerard got was unbelievable, just from that small section. Of course, the TV cameras were there and they got pictures of the boss heading for the dressing room. News began to sweep around the stadium via the bush telegraph that Gerard Houllier was back. In the dressing room everyone was on such a high. We were flying and couldn't wait to get out.

It was fitting that there was a big Kop mosaic for Gerard that night, obviously trying to boost the club, the fans and the players. My St Etienne battle cry in the Press had made an impression and the atmosphere was already electric. The players went out and we got ready. Gerard and myself always went out last.

He went into the corner of the room and got out his little book. I don't know whether he said a little prayer, but he had this private moment with himself. I said: "Get that red scarf around your neck," and he said: "Do I look okay?" I just had one word. "FANTASTIC!" I gave him a hug and he said: "Let's do it."

As we walked down the steps from the dressing room I had the biggest lump in my throat ever. I was willing him to look up, but didn't need to worry. He touched the famous 'This Is Anfield' sign. The boss, having been through so much with that life or death surgery, was back where he belonged.

As he walked out, the flash of cameras all over the stadium was blinding. It was like the first night at a film premier. Everyone remembers how Roma boss Fabio Capello came across and gave him a big hug and embrace. It was a real show of friendship and comradeship amongst managers. As Anfield exploded and the Kop raised their banners higher than ever, I'm sure the Italian boss knew that they could not win this game.

I moved to the side. It really was time for Pinocchio to sit down. I knew Gerard still wasn't right yet, but I knew he had an iron will to get there and my time as caretaker manager was effectively over. I was proud to see the boss standing there, soaking up the acclaim. It was a moment we all wanted for him and his courage meant that he deserved all the plaudits. Once again he had put the club before his own situation because he knew how important the Roma game was.

As I sat there, I began to think back to October 13 of the previous year and that fateful day against Leeds when the boss left the ground on a stretcher. The whispers had gone right round the stadium that day when he did not come out for the second half. Now it was a wall of sound reverberating around the ground with people chanting his name.

The game was secondary, to be honest. That may sound strange having built up the importance of it, but to have Gerard back in the fold was the bigger thing. In the end the game was won 2-0. We went ahead with a first half Jari Litmanen penalty after Danny Murphy had his leg taken away as he shaped to shoot. Emile Heskey finished Roma off after the break with a header that took us into the quarter-finals.

It was a fantastic night, as good as anything I have witnessed. There were incredible scenes of joy in the dressing room and it was tremendous knowing that we had not only taken a further step in the Champions League, but fulfilled our pledge to ensure we were still involved when Gerard returned.

Fans still talk to me about the Roma experience, but what many people don't know is that I had a little problem of my own before and during that game linked with a problem tooth. I had a cap that had come loose the day before the big game. Clearly, this was not the time to be going to the dentist. I just kept pushing it back in, hoping that I would get by. Fans will recall that I would stand on the touchline and whistle to gain the attention of the players. With the Roma game at its height, I tried to whistle loudly over the noise of the crowd and my tooth flew out and landed on the pitch. I was down on my knees on the line, moving the turf in front of me to try and find it.

Gerard was calling to me, saying: "Phil, what are you doing? Come back here." I found my cap, turned round and pulled down my bottom lip to show this big gap where the tooth should have been. There was a great shot of me on TV pointing this out to Gerard and the staff who were all killing themselves laughing. When I later watched a video of the match, the commentator says: "They can certainly enjoy themselves on the Liverpool bench, as big a game as it is." I smiled when I heard those words.

The big challenge now was to get our teeth back in while keeping our feet back on the ground and prepare for a big home game with Chelsea. This would be settled by a late Vladimir Smicer goal that kept our run going while improving our chances of finishing as high as possible. We saw off Charlton to keep our spirits up and four days later we faced a Champions League quarter-final clash against Germans Bayer Leverkusen. The one disappointing thing was that the first leg was at home, which players don't like.

We knew at this point that if we could see off Leverkusen and Manchester United could beat their opponents, a semi-final between two of Britain's biggest rivals would be a reality. We all know what a sensational atmosphere ensued when Liverpool faced Chelsea at Anfield in the Champions League semi-final of 2005. Can you imagine what it would have been like against our arch-rivals from the other end of the East Lancashire Road? What a potential prize that would have been, a Champions League Final slot at the expense of Sir Alex Ferguson and Co. Of course, we had to focus first on Leverkusen and the first leg went according to plan with a 1-0 win and the clean sheet that is

Bob Paisley and England's Bobby Robson at my testimonial game

Taking the plaudits from fans and teammates after that England game on a memorable testimonial night

Thrown in at the deep end – but learning to swim as caretaker manager with an important Champions League victory over Dynamo Kiev inspired by the message: 'Do it for Gerard'

While Gerard was still recovering from his surgery, Danny Murphy claimed Player of the Month and I proudly took Manager of the Month as caretaker boss

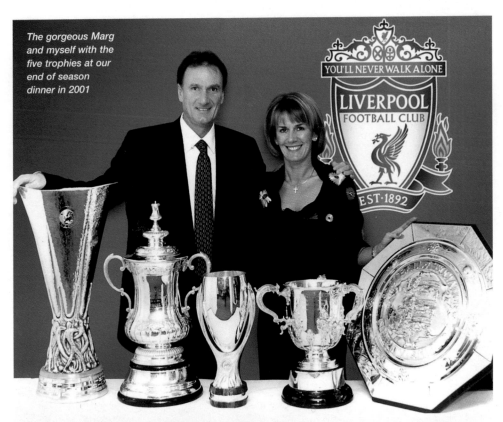

The gorgeous Marg and myself with the five trophies at our end of season dinner in 2001

The famous five – Gerard's team behind the team – Joe Corrigan, Sammy Lee, Patrice Bergues and yours truly

Me and my Scouse mate Sammy after our
FA Cup victory in 2001 over Arsenal

*They say LFC is only about winning trophies, something the chairman always told us.
This picture says it all with Gerard, David Moores and Rick Parry – a proud and happy group*

*The way we are – the lads back together again at Anfield for the Tsunami game.
Note the Thompson tan. Too much time on my hands these days*

At home with my lovely family (from left to right): Marg, Josh, Max, Philip and Daniel

My last appearance at Anfield in the Tsunami game – same legs, similar physique, but less hair!

so crucial. Maybe we needed another goal to settle us for the return, but we were reasonably happy and felt confident.

We didn't have a game on the Saturday before the return leg and that was a bonus. In Germany Leverkusen scored first to make it 1-1 on aggregate, but Abel Xavier restored our advantage and we thought we were home and dry. However, it was a topsy-turvy encounter and they came back again twice to lead. Finally, Jari came on for Emile and he scored the key goal that looked set to take us to the semis at 3-3 on aggregate and with the away goals to our advantage. However, they would not lie down and Lucio conjured up what proved to be their winner to knock us out.

The amazing thing was that Michael Owen had three one-on-ones with their keeper. I can picture one in particular. He did his normal dink, but because he was in the inside-right position it was always drifting away. We could just see it going beyond the left-hand post. To go out at that stage was a bitter blow.

This was the game in which Didi Hamann was replaced by Vladimir Smicer. Gerard didn't think the midfield was getting close enough to the likes of Michael Ballack. You make these decisions. At that time your name is on the trophy or it's not as we witnessed years later on a famous night in Istanbul.

Maybe it just wasn't to be. It was not down to the Didi decision in my opinion although many people thought that the change disrupted the team. It's always easy to look back with hindsight. What is certain is that the result was a massive disappointment when you consider that we were just six minutes away from a Champions League semi-final. Manchester United got through to add to the pain and they were more than happy to be playing Leverkusen rather than Liverpool. Possibly it also meant that they lowered their guard a little because they suffered a shock reversal against the Germans, who went on to meet Real Madrid in the final.

We had to pick ourselves up because we still had a chance to finish in second spot. We had to go to Sunderland. That is always a difficult test. Their fans are up for it whether they are at the top or the bottom. We won with a superb effort from Michael, a lift over the keeper. Maybe it was his way of showing that he had not lost his touch. He followed up with two even better goals against Derby County and the force was with us again.

With not having any Champions League games we could concentrate on that second-spot challenge. We not only wanted to ensure qualification for the following year's Champions League, we also wanted to keep United out of the top two again.

The Championship itself was not completely beyond us, but when we lost

1-0 to Spurs at one of our hoodoo grounds, White Hart Lane, it closed that particular door. We had just two games left, at home to Blackburn and Ipswich, and it had to be WIN, WIN.

We couldn't afford a slip-up and in a fantastic midweek clash at Anfield we beat Blackburn 4-3 in a match that ebbed and flowed. At 3-3 Emile Heskey took a ball on the edge of the box. In these situations we always encouraged him to use his body strength to shrug people off. He turned his marker and rattled a ball into the bottom corner to give us victory. It wasn't good for the defensive coach to see three goals hitting the back of our net, but the end result was all that mattered.

This took us to the last game of that eventful 2001/02 season and it was perhaps fitting that our visitors were our old friends from Ipswich Town. We were still smarting from the fact that Gerard had been overlooked for Manager of the Year 12 months earlier when the accolade went to Ipswich boss George Burley. They'd had a good season by their standards, but I still found that decision astonishing. It gave us great delight to beat them 5-0 at Anfield in a party atmosphere.

It sealed second spot and once again we had improved on the Premier front. In successive seasons we'd finished 7th, 4th, 3rd, and 2nd and the expectation level for season 2002/03 was now soaring amongst our fans. Equally, Nicolas Anelka had scored in that last game and people were wondering what the future would hold for him. That was soon to unfold.

Anelka released, Bowyer dithers and Diouf's antics cause a stir

There was now only one thing for it as season 2002/03 loomed. Our steady Premier improvement into the runners-up slot meant that there was only one way to go as we took our summer break. We needed to take that final giant step to the top of the pile.

Obviously we had made a rod for our own backs, but this was all part of our plan to take Liverpool back to the summit of English football. We had won the UEFA Cup, the FA Cup and the League Cup, but one statistic still haunted everyone at the club. The Reds had not won a league title since 1989/90 and that also meant we had never claimed a Premier League crown.

We knew it would be a massive task to win domestic football's 'Holy Grail', but we could look back and reflect on what we had achieved to date with real pride, not least because of the challenge we had faced because of Gerard Houllier's heart problem that had shocked everyone to the core. To come back from such a major operation was all credit to the man whose pride in his role as Liverpool manager was there for all to see. I felt it was disgraceful that some people doubted him while claiming he should not return. That was always uppermost in my mind during my time as caretaker boss.

In every press conference I always pushed the same line. I wanted Gerard to come back and lead us as soon as he felt the time was right. As much as I enjoyed my time in charge I was ready to slip back into my old role. I never thought about being the manager of the football club.

That would have been discourteous and disloyal to Gerard. My association with him, the togetherness that we had and the team spirit that we worked so hard on was everything to me.

It doesn't mean that I didn't have a real pride in being caretaker during the period of Gerard's illness. I hope I showed the people that there was a different side to Phil Thompson. They had this in-your-face image of me on the touchline. I wanted to demonstrate that I had the knowledge and character to run the club. I wanted to prove that I could do it at the highest level with dignity and that I could also show a sense of calm in times of adversity. You also need a sense of humour to defuse difficult situations at times.

All in all, I was determined that the fans and the media would see me in a different light. People had this image of me, acting like a raving lunatic while screaming instructions and advice to the players from the edge of the pitch. That had always been about motivating players.

As caretaker manager I had to take a step back. It was more about reading the game and organising the players in a wider sense. I had to act in a way that would reflect the standing of Liverpool FC in the game. I took that on from my very first board meeting, stating clearly that I would do things in the right manner without letting the club down.

It was nice to read the press analysis when I finally handed the reins back to Gerard. Even Des Kelly, still working for the The Mirror at that time, held his hands up after being critical of my caretaker appointment, admitting that he had made a mistake. Des said: "When you get it wrong you have to admit it. I have apologised to Phil Thompson." I appreciated his words.

It had not just been Des who doubted me. I remember looking at the back of one of the Liverpool fanzines. They had a picture of me on the touchline under the heading: 'Man Of The Season.' I was touched by that.

Gerard and myself both received awards from the League Managers Association. I had won two Manager of the Month awards as caretaker boss. Now the LMA gave me a beautiful glass bowl inscribed: 'For services to football in difficult circumstances.'

Gerard had also received a bowl and a tribute although I felt they had previously failed to recognise him in the right light. I think they realised they had got it wrong in that momentous season in 2001.

Our thoughts were focused on the new campaign, but we both knew that the pressure would be on from the start after finishing second. I said to myself: "We must get out of the blocks quickly." Our fans were banking on us going one better to lift the title and this is what that whole spell was about. Jamie Carragher had been forced to have an operation on his knee in the summer. He had been playing through the pain barrier and was overlooked in the England squad named for the World Cup.

There was also a big question mark about Steven Gerrard. There had been issues with his back, groin and calf and we were trying to get to the root of these problems. It was decided that he would have a groin operation. It was a big decision. He would also miss the World Cup, but Stevie realised that his long-term situation was the priority and that he would have to sacrifice his short-term international ambitions.

He ended up having what was just a 20-minute operation either side of the groin to relieve the pressure. It was to make a remarkable difference to the number of games he could play. He hated it when the Press suggested he was injury prone. He wanted it sorted and this surgery did the trick. It changed him from someone who could only play a maximum of 25 league games a season to someone who could play all season.

We made some signings in a bid to further boost the squad in Bruno Cheyrou, Salif Diao and El-Hadji Diouf. None of these were well known in the English game.

It had been decided to let Nicolas Anelka go, which was a big decision. He had done well at times and less well on other occasions. There was no doubting his goalscoring qualities, but he had come with underlying problems. We also found out that there had been an attempt to sell him back to Arsenal while he was still at Anfield and this upset us greatly. He had been playing well at that time and there was a move to capitalise on that.

It told us a lot about the advice he was getting. It had caused issues at other clubs and we didn't want to take any chances. We had a great squad and good camaraderie. It was a big call to let Nicolas go, but Gerard took that decision.

The boss was friendly with the people at Paris St Germain, but didn't want to take the chance on Anelka. I believe he was right and that was proved by the subsequent problems the lad had with Manchester City. He scored some good goals for them, but the problems behind the scenes were well known.

We needed another striker. One day Gerard mentioned Diouf. I was unaware of him. Gerard said: "He plays for Lens in France." Of course, our old friend Patrice Bergues was the Lens manager. It was decided Diouf was the player we needed, a forward who could dribble and beat people. I had still never seen him play. Gerard felt he could fill the void.

The first time I saw him he was playing for Senegal against France in the opening game of the World Cup. He gave an outstanding performance and I was straight on the phone to Gerard. Senegal had claimed a shock 1-0 victory and Diouf was the name on everyone's lips. I said to Gerard: "You must sign him straight away." The boss said: "Don't worry, he signed forms this morning before the France game."

Dioufy was an incredible character. He was full of life and bounce, but he had a short fuse. You also sensed that you could not always believe him, something he brought on himself as I will explain shortly.

One player we did not get that summer was Lee Bowyer. We knew our move for him would cause some controversy amongst our fans because of the off-the-field headlines he had been involved in. Bowyer had been accused of taking part in an assault on a young Asian, Sarfraz Najeib, in Leeds city centre. He was cleared of the charge.

We knew our bid would cause a stir, but we thought it was a risk worth taking for the development of the team. Gerard offered Leeds £8m which was a lot of money and Bowyer came over to Merseyside to talk to us. He arrived with a mate and his agent. I had to take care of him in the players' lounge at Melwood where Bowyer and his pal played umpteen games of pool while the agent discussed terms with Gerard and Rick Parry.

When that meeting broke up I asked how things had gone. The response surprised me. "We are still far apart," said Gerard. We thought Lee Bowyer would be keen to move on his career with a club like Liverpool and I thought the deal would be struck fairly quickly.

Rick said: "We are still miles apart on the salary." Bowyer left and a series of phone calls followed between the club and his agent. It finally appeared that we were close to agreeing a deal. We went as far as having his new kit numbered up in anticipation as we prepared to leave for our pre-season training camp in Switzerland.

Some people were saying that we should not take Bowyer under any circumstances. Others said that he would be a good acquisition and would strengthen the team. As things moved on I rang the player and said: "Get yourself ready. Once the deal is done and dusted we will fly you out to Switzerland."

He was saying: "Yeah, okay," but there was no emotion from him to suggest that a decision was imminent. Rick and Gerard had another meeting with the agent, but they still failed to agree terms. I spoke to Bowyer again, once again asking him to be ready to travel should everything be sorted. His response was: "I don't know where my passport is," and added: "I'm not in Leeds, I'm in London." He was there with Rio Ferdinand.

By now the vibes were coming through loud and clear that he was just not sold on the club. We got to Switzerland where we were based in a beautiful hotel. We felt it was finally time to nail the Bowyer business one way or the other.

Rick and Gerard came into my room. Gerard rang up the player and started to say: "Lee, how are you doing? We must be near to a deal now. We are offering you a good salary and it will be an important move for your career." Bowyer replied that he would not bend on what he was asking for. Gerard was saying: "What we are offering you is the same as one of the top players at our club."

It turned out that Bowyer was still in London, having made no attempt to get his stuff together should he be required to fly out. Rick had a quick word with him. He came off the phone and said: "It's clear that he just doesn't want to do the deal." I said: "The boy's response has made it clear that he doesn't want to play for this club. It's as if he's pricing himself out of it."

I likened it to a tradesman who had tons of work on. He's happy to talk to potential customers, but pitches the price sky high. If that work comes through he is happy to do it. If not, he just sits back. I said: "This is all wrong. It's clear he is not committed to us and this must be getting through to our fans. To me, we need to pull it before Lee Bowyer and his agent come back and say the move is not right for them."

Rick and Gerard decided that we should tell the Press that night. I couldn't believe that Lee Bowyer had not jumped at the chance to play for Liverpool FC. Better players than him would have walked all the way to Anfield. We had made a big commitment on our side, but it had all been one way.

His career went down the pan after that. He was at West Ham for a while and was lucky, in my opinion, to revive his career at Newcastle. Everyone then witnessed what happened there and when Birmingham tried to buy him the move collapsed because of fierce opposition from Blues' fans who organised a petition urging the club to drop their interest in the 28-year-old. In the end it was the right decision for us to move forward without Bowyer.

One major boost that summer was that Markus Babbel was back in the fold and that was a boost to everyone. During his illness Sammy Lee and myself had made a surprise visit to see him at his rehabilitation clinic in Germany. We knew we would only have a couple of hours, but jumped on a flight to give Markus a boost. We had a chat, a bit of lunch and then flew straight back. I know it meant a lot to him.

He had lost a lot of weight, but he was thrilled to see us and it was an important statement from the club that he still figured in our plans, despite the tremendous setback he had suffered trying to deal with the debilitating Guillain-Barre Syndrome.

Markus had played a big part in our success of 2001 and now it was nice for him to be back at Melwood and going to Cardiff where we met Arsenal in the Community Shield that preceded this crucial 2002/03 season. As it turned out, one of their new signings, Gilberto Silva, scored the only goal of the game.

Expectations were still high as we opened our Premier campaign at Villa where John Arne Riise gave us a lone-goal victory. Diouf then introduced himself to our fans with a double in a 3-0 home win over Southampton. The chant 'Diouf, Diouf, Diouf's On Fire' immediately came out of the Kop, but it was one I would quickly find myself disagreeing with. We played well in a 2-2 draw at Blackburn, but one of the people who did not perform was Dioufy.

We had travelled to Ewood Park on the morning of the game because of its close proximity. We didn't leave Melwood until 11am. Gerard found out that Diouf had actually flown to Paris the day before straight after training. He spent the night in the French capital and flew back the following morning. We'd heard whispers, but we were not too sure. Gerard had good contacts at Air France and so it would not be too difficult to find out if he took that route. There was also the easyJet alternative. As it turned out, it was confirmed that he made the trip and Gerard was extremely unhappy.

The player was confronted about it and initially came up with a denial until he was told we had proof. He was warned as to his future conduct. It was the start of the learning process about Diouf. He was left out for the following game, a 2-2 home draw against Newcastle who equalised with a last minute Alan Shearer goal. Frustratingly, we then repeated the same scoreline for the third game running when Birmingham came to Anfield. It was annoying not just because of the result, but also for the fact that a certain Clinton Morrison scored both of their goals and it clearly delighted him after his earlier humiliating cup experience at Anfield with Crystal Palace.

It meant that after two straight league wins, we had now drawn three and this was not the sprint start we had hoped for. We were simply conceding too many goals. At the same time Michael Owen was having a difficult time at the other end of the pitch. A slimmer Milan Baros was improving and when we travelled to Bolton, determined to turn things round, it was decided that it was time to play him. He scored two great efforts, only for us to throw away the lead in frustrating fashion. Thankfully for us, Emile Heskey conjured up a tremendous winner to get us back on track.

This was the first league spell over before we began our Champions League campaign with a trip to Valencia. We were unbeaten in six games, but the three draws were costly and the report at this stage was: "Must do better."

We knew the pressure would be just as intense on a Euro stage because Valencia had been tipped by many people to go all the way. We actually had a decent start in the game. Emile had a great chance from an acute angle. The ball hit the inside of the far post and ran along the goalline. They went on to murder us although the final score was just 2-0. We had played Salif Diao at centre-back and it never really worked. He was dragged all over the place and the Spaniards capped a great performance with goals from Aimar and Baraja. The irony that night was that Rafa Benitez was in the dugout, having taken on the Valencia challenge.

We needed to get back to winning ways and to do that we had to tighten up at the back. We worked hard on the training ground. We also looked closely at the videos to show the players how and why things had gone wrong with ten goals conceded in five games. A 2-0 home win over West Brom, courtesy of Baros and Riise, was a boost. We had Michael up front with Milan in that game, but he was still looking for his shooting boots.

Then we played what was supposed to be our easiest challenge in the Champions League when FC Basel came to Anfield in late September. The stats show that we had 25 attempts on goal. The result shows a 1-1 draw and we still had what appeared on paper to be a real challenge against Spartak. We needed to beat Basel at home to set ourselves up, but it wasn't to be.

Back in the Premier League the big topic of discussion remained Michael Owen with everyone questioning him. We were heading to Manchester City and I remember manager Kevin Keegan saying: "I wish everyone would stop going on about it. Sooner or later Michael will hit top form."

Those were prophetic words because he bagged a hat-trick in a 3-0 win at Maine Road. It gave everyone a boost and I was not surprised when we then took Spartak apart, winning 5-0 to get back on track in the Champions League. Michael's revival continued with a lone goal winner over Chelsea at Anfield, but controversy would follow at Leeds.

The Elland Road game was a noon kick-off and it was live on TV. We decided to give Salif a run in his favourite centre-midfield role. He popped up with a winner that was created by his mate El-Hadji Diouf. They went to celebrate in the bottom corner, jumping for joy. Later we got a report that he had spat at the Leeds fans. We received quite a few letters, but nothing was carried through.

Then it was off to Moscow on October 22 for the return against Spartak. They shocked us by scoring first, but another Michael Owen hat-trick proved he was back in a big way. It put us in a decent position in our Champions League group. We had two wins, one draw and one defeat.

We beat Spurs in the league to boost our confidence ahead of the return against Valencia at Anfield. Once again they confirmed their reputation as one of the big favourites by beating us 1-0. It was a bitter blow, but we were still extremely well placed in the Premier League.

Indeed, we were top after beating West Ham and Southampton and this was our number one priority. We had remained unbeaten in 12 league games since the start of the season. Everything was going really well and I was beginning to think: "This is the time."

Then came a result that, looking back, was the start of a roller coaster period that would ultimately take our title charge right off the rails.

We lost 1-0 at Middlesbrough. They only had one shot in the opening 80 minutes, but then we pressed the self-destruct button. I remember they played a simple ball into the box. Jerzy Dudek came for it in two minds, not knowing whether to catch or punch. He put his two hands out and the ball hit his gloves and dropped to the floor for Gareth Southgate to prod home. We couldn't believe it.

Jerzy's indecision would begin to nag away at me. I thought: "He's making too many mistakes." That might sound harsh when we had previously gone 12 games undefeated in the league, but we had conceded too many goals and he looked shaky at times. In our Bunker, the new Boot Room, Gerard always gave us the opportunity to express our thoughts. We were now preparing for the Basel return and I said: "I'm going to make a big statement. We should leave Jerzy out."

Gerard looked at me in shock, as did goalkeeping coach Joe Corrigan. Gerard said: "Yes, he is not at his best, but I think he is alright."

He asked Joe for an opinion and he said that while he was not performing well, it was the wrong time to leave him out.

I repeated that I felt it was time to take him out of the firing line. We went to Basel needing to win to go forward to the next stage. We knew we could beat them, but they had a togetherness that would always make them tough and two good strikers. They roared into a 3-0 lead with Jerzy making two more mistakes. One he just palmed out when he could have easily caught it.

At half-time Gerard made a massive decision. He took Steven Gerrard off, who couldn't get his game together at this time. We scored three goals to level, but the all-important winner eluded us and so we were out of the Champions League at the first stage, having done so well the previous year.

Because of the potential financial rewards it was a major blow to the club and would definitely affect the transfer funds for the following season. The Boro setback, followed by this Euro blow, meant that the wheels had come off good style and things were to get even worse. We couldn't beat Sunderland at home, having to settle for a goalless draw. We lost to Fulham 3-2 with an abysmal performance. The only joy that day was a scorching Dietmar Hamann free-kick that nearly took the net out.

We had now been demoted to the UEFA Cup and travelled to Vitesse Arnhem at the end of November. They had a stand with a retractable roof and so it was cold outside, yet humid inside. Michael Owen gave us a much-needed 1-0 win, but the natives were restless and Manchester United were next up at Anfield.

We had turned it round before and I thought we had a great chance to beat an injury-hit United who had Diego Forlan up front. I can still see Jamie Carragher knocking the ball back to Jerzy, only for it to slip through his hands for an easy Forlan tap-in to the empty net. Even the next goal scored by Forlan went to the side of Jerzy. His confidence was shot at this time. Although Sami Hyypia pulled one back, it was not enough for us to turn things round and our fans were not happy. We had a fourth round Worthington Cup game against Ipswich and fielded a weaker side than normal. It was 1-1 after extra time and we came through 5-4 on pens.

We decided to play Jerzy in the Worthington Cup, using Chris Kirkland in the league. Chris had shown his capabilities in an earlier round against Southampton when he made four or five excellent saves. He was ready, but it didn't change anything. We lost 2-0 at Charlton and it was getting worse and worse in the league. A 1-0 success over Vitesse Arnhem failed to cover over the cracks and we lost at Sunderland in the league – another kick in the teeth.

The Worthington Cup had been the only real bonus although I wondered if we were jinxed when our next tie, at Aston Villa, was delayed for an hour in freezing conditions because of a floodlight failure. Our fans had turned up in huge numbers and we were grateful for that. They saw us win 4-3 with Steven Gerrard back in business and giving one of his best performances of the season. He scored, along with Danny Murphy (2) and Milan Baros.

Every time we hoped for an upturn in fortunes in the league it never happened. Our arch-rivals Everton had grabbed a goalless draw at Anfield and Blackburn held us 1-1. These draws were costing us dear and we were slipping down the league. From going 12 Premier games unbeaten we had now gone eight games without a win and the Press were starting to tally this all up. Only three points out of a possible 24 contributed to the agonising claim that this was Liverpool's worst start in 20 years, according to the stats. You can't argue with the figures and who was up next but Arsenal at Highbury.

We should have won that day, going in front with a Danny Murphy pen after

Milan Baros was brought down. The linesman was well-placed to give it.

Then Franny Jeffers went down at the other end late in the game as if he had been shot. The referee, Jeff Winter pointed to the spot. We leapt up, screaming our frustration at Winter. What can you do? Another draw!

It was one step forward, two steps back and nothing was going right. Salif Diao was dismissed at Newcastle for two yellow cards. They got a free-kick and Milan Baros jumped out of the way to give Laurent Robert a route to goal. It was a shocking four points from 30. Could it get any worse?

The FA Cup started to give us a break from what was going on and we claimed a third-round win over Manchester City. We had to change things, bringing in Neil Mellor up front who had been doing well and scoring all kinds of goals in the reserves. Michael Owen was injured and while we had Emile and Milan as options, we felt it was right to give Neil his chance.

We just needed someone in there with a bit of go in them at that time. The Mellor selection shocked a few people, but he did quite well operating as a lone striker. He had his rough edges, shooting from an angle 35 yards out, but you couldn't knock his enthusiasm and confidence. A Danny Murphy pen clinched us safe passage to round four.

In the midweek we had the semi-final of the Worthington Cup at Sheffield United. Neil Mellor had scored with a glancing header to give us a 1-0 interval lead. It was my old club and I knew all the little nooks and crannies in the stand. We'd heard they could listen to the opposition team talks at half-time. There was a door like a fire exit in the away dressing room that led out to where all our medical supplies were.

At half-time we put our masseur, Stewart Welsh, outside this fire door to keep watch. I said: "Climb over the bench and stand outside during the team talk."

After three or four minutes Neil Warnock and his assistant Kevin Blackwell appeared, but I accept that this was just a coincidence.

Some of the antics on the touchline in the second half were diabolical. I can lose myself in the game, but Sheffield United had some who put me to shame. One guy on their bench, a fitness coach, kept giving me dog's abuse. He was telling me to shut up and sit down. I said: "Who do you think you are?" He had no right to be getting involved, let alone hurling abuse at me.

Neil Warnock will always put out uncompromising teams and you have to expect a tough time at Bramall Lane. Michael Tonge got a couple of goals for them to wipe out Neil's opener and we went down 2-1 in this first leg. Let's just say the handshakes at the end were not very cordial. Gerard was perturbed by it all, not least a challenge by Michael Brown who came through with studs raised on Chris Kirkland. Chris was caught in the midriff and I felt Brown should have been sent off. Whenever a foul or decision went the other way, all of their players harassed the ref. It was just their way of playing and getting the upper hand. It reflected Warnock's own abrasive style. They were never going to let us settle and we knew it would be a heated return.

I don't know what the odds were on us drawing our next home league game, but it was a pretty good bet. Villa came and shared the spoils 1-1. Now it was five points out of 33 and the stats being thrown at us were going back donkey's years. The simple one was 11 league games without a win. We went to Southampton and the pressure was intense. We even brought in a psychologist to talk to the players. Every possible angle was covered as we tried to turn things round and it wasn't just the players we were looking at. We were assessing ourselves, and reviewing the coaching methods to find a formula that would get us back on the straight and narrow.

This game was at the new St Mary's Stadium. People talk about a pressure-cooker atmosphere. I sensed it that day, but we gave a great performance and won with an Emile Heskey header from a set piece we had worked on. That gave us real satisfaction and set us up for the Sheffield United return game.

It was important we scored quickly to wipe out their 2-1 aggregate lead and we were soon level. The Blades were as determined as we knew they would be and it went to extra time where Michael Owen finally sewed it up. I stood on the edge of the pitch as the players began to troop off. I remember being surprised at the anger in the face of Stephane Henchoz. Nothing usually riled him. He was a genuinely good guy. He was raging as he walked towards the dugout and Neil Warnock. He spat on the floor and Warnock, quite rightly, did not take too kindly to it. Later Stephane said: "It's not the Sheffield people that I dislike, but that man."

Stephane never spoke badly about anybody. He had spat on the ground with his eyes on Warnock, but he was nowhere near the visiting manager. As I said, I would never condone any action that showed a lack of respect for an opponent, but Neil had annoyed us all that day. We wouldn't be the first and we won't be the last.

The good news was that we were back at Anfield South. The bad news was that our inconsistency raised its head again when Crystal Palace held us 0-0 at Selhurst Park in the FA Cup. They were clearly up for it, possibly because we had beaten them in the 2001 Worthington Cup.

An extra blow was that Chris Kirkland was to pick up another injury. It was a nasty one in the lower part of his leg and the diagnosis showed cruciate ligament damage. This would put him out for the season. I really felt for the lad as we turned again to Jerzy Dudek.

At the end of January we then witnessed a performance from a team that was majestic, to say the least. Arsenal twice took the lead at Anfield with one of the most complete performances I have ever seen. It took a tremendous effort to twice hit back, but John Arne Riise gave us hope and then Emile Heskey equalised with a bullet header into the bottom corner in the closing seconds from a Salif Diao long cross. We pinched the draw, but I wasn't complaining. I'm realistic enough to know that if we had lost it would have all gone off. In the end it was a point won rather than two points lost.

More significantly, it put a spring in the step of players who had been in desperate need of a lift and the lads went on to crush West Ham 3-0 at Upton Park. This took us to our FA Cup replay at home to Palace on February 5, 2003. Every fan will remember that Emile Heskey went on a run almost the length of the pitch with Michael Owen in support. Emile took it on himself to try and chip the keeper rather than finding Michael in space. The Palace man made a comfortable save. When moments like this happen in the FA Cup you think: "Uh, oh!" Palace had Dougie Freeman sent off, but they were still able to beat us 2-0.

After everything we had achieved in the previous years, winning a famous treble while steadily improving our league position until we were within touching distance of the Championship, this season was supposed to be the defining moment of the Gerard Houllier reign.

There had been so much expectation and rightly so. Expectation comes from success, but we had set ourselves up for a fall. You can look at our signings at the start of 2002/03 and argue that maybe we should have bought one real superstar to help us take that final step instead of three comparative unknowns. You can pore over it and point to many things. The top and bottom of it is that we had a good squad of players and many things combined together to completely undermine our dreams.

I thought about it a lot as we prepared to entertain Boro on February 8. Three months earlier we had lost 1-0 in frustrating fashion at the Riverside. Little did we know that this was the marker for an agonising spell and it was probably quite appropriate that we failed to see off Boro at home, drawing 1-1. It symbolised the fact that between November and February we had found it virtually impossible to kill teams off. Too many draws, particularly at home, completely undermined us. We were in double figures on that score and this was just not good enough for a side with any aspirations, let alone title dreams.

The Worthington Cup had been a shaft of light and now we won at Auxerre in the UEFA Cup. Going back to France was always great for Gerard. There was a lot of speculation linking us with Auxerre's Djibril Cisse, but he was injured and didn't play in this game.

You are allowed to train on the pitch, even before these games, but Auxerre had decided to relay the surface. When we arrived there, they were only just getting the pitch down. It hadn't even been rolled. We had to train on an awful bone-hard pitch to the side of the stand. We asked if they could roll a bit of the stadium surface to let us have a five-a-side and they agreed. However, the turf just ripped up at the joins and we worried what might happen when the big game got underway.

As it turned out, there wasn't a problem and we gave a great display in winning 1-0. Sami Hyypia stayed up after an attack, cushioned the ball with his right foot, swivelled round and slotted home into the bottom corner. It gave Gerard great delight.

Dare I say it, our poor Premier form continued at Birmingham where we lost 2-1. It was Jekyll and Hyde and our campaign was a disaster area. In the UEFA Cup Cisse did play in the Auxerre return to give Liverpudlians a glimpse of what was to come. Thankfully he did not score and we went through 2-0. That was on the Thursday night.

Now we could think about another Cardiff final with everyone tipping our opponents Manchester United to win. Sometimes you look at these things and enjoy the role of underdog. Our fans were anything but downbeat. They had banners throughout the Liverpool sections and we painted the place in our red and white. There were very few flags in comparison in the United areas. The Liverpudlians knew they would have to lift us against Manchester United and once again they proved to be inspirational. Their support was deafening and we knew that we were becoming a bit of a jinx for Alex Ferguson's men.

The fans were up for it. The players were up for it and we were in our lucky dressing room. Nothing could be more perfect, especially when Steven Gerrard latched onto a ball and struck it against David Beckham. It looped over Fabien Barthez and we knew it was going to be our day.

They put us under pressure and I thought about an interesting comment the boss had made. Jerzy Dudek had blundered against them at Anfield, but Gerard said: "He will be our saviour today." He was to be absolutely right and our Polish goalkeeper won the man-of-the-match award. You don't want your keeper being nominated as star man, but I was happy for him because he had been under immense pressure.

Late in the game Michael Owen rampaged from one end of the pitch to the other after Dietmar Hamann harassed a defender into a mistake on the halfway line. Michael ran clear to drill past Barthez. I don't know what was in the keeper's mind, but he gave Michael half of the goal to aim at. We certainly weren't complaining.

The scenes on the final whistle were brilliant. Someone sent me a copy of the Manchester Evening News after the game in which Alex (Ferguson) was suggesting this cup wasn't top of their agenda. Maybe not, but when Liverpool and United meet, both clubs desperately want the right result. We got it and it was oh so sweet.

We now had to try and build on this and it helped when we beat Bolton 2-0. It set us up for a great UEFA Cup challenge at Celtic where there was a fantastic atmosphere at Parkhead. The singing of You'll Never Walk Alone by both sets of fans was superb. Their star striker Henrik Larsson had been out injured. There was talk that he would make a comeback. He actually scored within the first three minutes.

Celtic boss Martin O'Neill was being touted at this time as a possible successor to Gerard Houllier. Gerard said: "The only way Martin O'Neill will be coming to Liverpool is when he brings his side to Anfield for the second leg." We gave a majestic team performance at Parkhead in a 1-1 draw, as good as I have seen away from home, but it backfired on us. Some of the players were saying: "The ground was not as intimidating as we thought it would be." Others were saying: "Celtic were not as good as we anticipated. The game was quite easy." I thought: "Wrong!" It suggested that we were already complacent about the return.

An incident happened during the match that would have serious consequences. Things were going as planned in the second half when I looked to my right. Diouf had gone into the crowd on that side. There was clearly a commotion. Some fans were upset and some people had come pitchside.

I thought: "What's going on?" Every time he touched the ball after that he was booed. Word spread about what had happened. We came off more than pleased with our performance when press officer Ian Cotton came in to say: "Phil, I've got a problem. Diouf was caught spitting at the fans."

I told Gerard and he couldn't believe it. I said: "I'm only telling you what Ian said." We went to Diouf and asked a simple question. Did you spit at the fans? Diouf said: "No." Gerard was relieved because the player was adamant he didn't do it. Then Rick Parry came down and said: "I've just seen him do it with my own eyes on television." Gerard was furious. A lynch mob had gathered outside the ground to rightly express their anger at the player. We had to get him on the bus without incident. Again, Diouf had not told the whole truth. It was the way he was.

The irony was that he had given a great performance on the right of midfield and was beginning to win over our fans. We had a decision to make about his selection for the return. Between the two Euro games we faced a trip to Tottenham and broke our White Hart Lane jinx, winning 3-2. I remember that Mauricio Taricco was trying to get Diouf to respond. He took some heavy tackles, but didn't react. He was able to put his problems behind him for the time being.

It was a good display, but Jerzy Dudek was guilty of a howler for one of their goals to give them a sniff of a chance although we left him in when Celtic came to Anfield. I had a few words with the players about those comments that Celtic were not as good as we thought. We tried to get them focused on the game and it should not have been a problem because of the fantastic atmosphere in the ground. Our fans obviously decided to show them how to sing You'll Never Walk Alone and it was a night of high emotion from the word go. As it turned out Celtic beat us 2-0 to knock us out of the cup. It was a massive blow. Some time later Diouf, who we left out for the return, was fined £5,000 for his actions at Parkhead.

There were now just eight games left, including big games against Manchester United, Everton and Chelsea. We couldn't afford to let our heads drop. Problems on and off the pitch were piling up, but we beat Leeds 3-1 at Anfield. This took us towards a tough test at Old Trafford where we knew Manchester United would be up for it after losing to us in the Worthington Cup Final. I should add that we were also up for the fight, only to lose Sami Hyypia, who was sent off in the opening minutes.

We were just a goal down at half-time, Ruud van Nistelrooy opening their account. I remember Steven Gerrard and Jamie Carragher both whipping the lads up, saying to them: "We can get something here." But it was a warm day and our ten men tired. Mike Riley gave another pen against Igor Biscan and there was no way back. We lost 4-0.

We were bitterly disappointed, but still tuned in to SKY TV on the coach journey home. Who should be on, but Ian St John who had been critical of us for some time, not least on the Radio City phone-ins. It seemed as if he never gave Gerard any credit. There was all that stuff about him referring to the boss as "the Frenchman" as if he could not even say his name. He would later argue that it wasn't constant criticism and that he was only responding to the fans' views on the radio, but he hammered us after that United defeat and I thought: "Enough's enough."

I knew any criticism of a former Liverpool legend might open a can of worms, but I was determined to respond on Gerard's behalf. I had a go back at the Saint in the Liverpool Echo and said I felt his comments were becoming too personal. I felt he had it in for Gerard. Some people would say that Ian St John had every right to express his opinions as an ex-player and that I should have known better than to respond in the way I did, not least because of my own powerful connections with the media. Ian had developed a highly successful media career with his former Saint & Greavsie programme and his long-standing links with Radio City in Liverpool and a paper in Scotland. I just felt his criticism went too far.

It was hard for me to do that retaliatory piece because, as a kid, Ian was my idol and second only to the great Roger Hunt at that time in my list of Liverpool heroes. When I started out in the Liverpool reserve side he was coming to the end of his Anfield career and it was a great honour for me to get the chance to play alongside him.

Liverpool, more than most, have had a host of former players working within the media. As I said, I have been one of them. Prior to returning to the club as assistant manager I had been there and done it with Radio City. I'd also written columns for the Football Echo and The Kop Magazine and I'd begun a relationship with SKY Sports. I was constructively critical when I had to be, but I tried to find a balance based on my links with the club as a fan, player and captain.

Liverpool had no qualms in asking me to return as Gerard Houllier's assistant and that suggests I got the balance right with my media work. The Saint claimed that it wasn't all negative and that he got the balance right in his own way. I couldn't see it and I let fly in that Echo article. I still can't bring myself to talk to Ian to this day. I revealed he was one of my all-time playing heroes, so that will tell you how strongly I feel about what happened.

We had to put the United result behind us and things began to look up for us over the next few games with the season now very much in the home straight. There were six games left and we knew we had to win them all if we were to secure another season of Champions League action. We had dropped from the dizzy heights of leading the Premier League to a situation in which we were trying to secure a Champions League place through the back door.

We started our final push positively enough with a 2-0 home win over Fulham. We then travelled to Goodison Park without Sami Hyypia, whose suspension had started following his dismissal at Old Trafford. In fact, we had two comparatively inexperienced centre-backs in the heart of our defence that day, Igor Biscan and Djimi Traore. Within eight minutes Igor started complaining about a bang he had taken on the hip. We had to take a big decision and bring him off.

Carra was moved to centre-back alongside Traore with Salif Diao at right-back. The one thing about him was his physical attributes which you needed against Everton. We needed aerial strength in those fixtures and everyone had to stand up and be counted. The Blues would have Gary Naysmith and David Weir sent off. We didn't allow ourselves to get caught up in any of that, holding our own discipline to win the game 2-1. We had learned a big lesson when Steven Gerrard and Sander Westerveld were sent off in a previous derby. We lost the plot that day and subsequently came up with a solution based around composed aggression and a focus on our football skills. It paid off.

We then beat Charlton at Anfield with a late Steven Gerrard goal. Stevie was dragging us through at this time. I remember him twisting and turning at the Kop end and hitting a winner that Charlton keeper Dean Kiely allowed to go under him. It kept us on track to compete with Chelsea for fourth place.

We were to enjoy a fantastic afternoon at West Brom where four goals from Michael Owen and two from Milan Baros gave us a 6-0 win. It was nice to see our fans in party mood. I remember the boss laughing at me. We were 4-0 up and coasting and I was still on the line screaming. He said: "I can't understand you. You are screaming and getting excited over a throw-in. We are winning 4-0." I just giggled.

Now we had just two games left and the first, Manchester City at Anfield, was something of a disaster. We controlled the game, but lost 2-1 and who should score their goals but Nicolas Anelka. Robbie Fowler was also in opposition that day. It showed our total lack of consistency, especially at home. I was gutted. I put my arms around Robbie on the final whistle and he said: "You murdered us. How did we beat you?"

That was the game that killed us. It was do or die at Chelsea where it was winner-takes-all for Champions League football. It was hyped up as make-or-break. We actually made a great start when Sami Hyypia glanced home a Danny Murphy free-kick. Then Marcel Desailly equalised with a header from 12 yards into the bottom corner. I instinctively felt Jerzy should have done better. Jesper Gronkjaer settled matters and they claimed the Champions League opportunity while we had to settle for a UEFA Cup place.

It was easy to sum up our season...CRAP! It was doubly frustrating after making such a wonderful start. Twelve games in we could not have realised what was in store. It was absolutely unbelievable. The three signings we had made, Diouf, Diao and Cheyrou, never really hit it off. There were other question marks, not least Jerzy Dudek. I had made my feelings known, but we had persevered with him until we eventually left him out for the Worthington Cup tie against Ipswich.

A season of great hope and anticipation had ended with Liverpool in fifth place. This would have been a reasonable achievement for some clubs, but not us. I can only liken it to members of an Everest expedition who battle to within touching distance of the world's highest and most treacherous summit, only to be forced back down by an unexpected storm. It's heartbreaking. Just to undertake such an expedition takes courage, organisation, professionalism and an incredible strength of character, but there are no plaudits for nearly climbing to the top.

Football is a ruthless sport and we knew that the 2003/04 campaign would now be make-or-break for us. It was time to regroup.

Shearer bid, Ronaldo surprise, bad breaks at Ewood and tension mounts

After the difficult and frustrating 2002/03 season we now had to make some major new signings to get ourselves back on track. We needed to do things in the correct manner to get the new campaign off to a good start.

We signed two outstanding youngsters from France who had been stars of the show at the World Under 20s international tournament – Florent Sinama-Pongolle and Anthony Le Tallec. We had been focused on them for two years, but had left them at Le Havre to develop. Le Tallec was named player of the tournament in that world event and Gerard felt that the time was now right to bring both lads into the Anfield fold.

We needed an immediate impact at the start of that 2003/04 season and one player who came to our attention was the opposite of our two young hopefuls. He was a tried and trusted superstar, one of the great players in the game and a man whose stature could give everyone a lift – on and off the pitch. His name was Alan Shearer. Of course, Alan was still a god at Newcastle, but he had not signed his new contract. Gerard came to me and said: "Do you fancy Alan Shearer?" I said: "Of course," although I felt there was little or no chance of securing his services because of his ties to the North East.

Gerard felt he could be another Gary McAllister for us, a great pro who could spark things with his approach, attitude and quality. It would also have revived the Alan Shearer/Michael Owen partnership that had been so successful for England in the past. The boss said that he had this feeling that Alan would come to Anfield. The seeds were sown, encouraged by the fact that the player's contractual situation with Newcastle was showing no signs of being sorted.

Contact was made although Newcastle were obviously not keen to let him go. We said we would like to be kept informed, aware that it would be a major coup to capture someone of Shearer's stature. We also knew that that it would be a massive negotiation, but early indications were that he would come. Nothing happened over a period of ten days and then all of a sudden the Geordie hero got the contract at St James' Park that he had wanted.

That had been my only fear, that his advisers might have used Liverpool's interest to force Newcastle's hand, but Alan Shearer is as honest and down to earth as they come and Gerard was convinced that his interest in joining us was genuine. The boss had been in talks with Bobby Robson about a possible deal and we know that Shearer didn't use us. In the end it was his sheer love of all things Geordie that kept him in the North East.

Of course, we had other irons in the fire and had been looking at the Harry Kewell situation at Leeds for some time. The player's agent kept saying that Harry was excited about the prospect of playing for Liverpool. When you chase a player it's often suggested that he was a boyhood fan or that he always admired the club, but in Harry's case those things were true on both counts.

Barcelona were interested in him along with Manchester United and Arsenal, but it was a fact that the player had been a Liverpool fan as a kid in Australia. We had seen pictures of him in Sydney wearing his Liverpool kit. His interest in the club stemmed from the success at Anfield of another Aussie – Craig Johnston. It obviously put us in pole position and the deal was done. We felt it was a real coup at just £5m.

Harry had caused us so many problems whenever we played Leeds United. When the PFA teams of the year were announced he always seemed to be included. Kewell had always been an aggressive individual, whether playing down the middle or on the left. People were saying that he was only leaving Leeds because he wanted a striking role. That was not true. He was so versatile that he was prepared to play right, left or centre.

After the problems we had encountered the previous year we felt that Harry might be the final piece in the jigsaw that would see us back in the title hunt. We also felt that he would provide the width that many critics had been moaning about, although that criticism only came when we got beat. We were not paranoid about it. More to the point, we were just delighted that we had captured a player who everybody felt could make a difference.

One star who got away in surprising fashion was Cristiano Ronaldo who shocked us when he signed for Manchester United in August 2003, for an astonishing £12m. I say astonishing because we had been offered the player for £4m. A number of people still pull me up and ask why we didn't sign the young star. It's well known that I watched him. I would like to tell the real story behind it.

Yes, he was good. Portugal had two starlets, Quaresma and Ronaldo, who played right and left wing for the Under 21s. I saw them play and both were very good. It was a toss up as to who was the best.

I was then invited to watch Sporting Lisbon play Porto in the last game of the season. Ronaldo was playing for Sporting. Tony Henry, the former Manchester City player and agent with Paul Stretford's Proactive Agency, was on the phone on a regular basis to see if we would take Ronaldo and asking if he could take us to watch him.

I met Tony at the airport and travelled to Porto. I met the player's Portuguese agent before watching the game. Ronaldo was quite good, but not as impressive as the first time I saw him. Tony was pushing the boy and saying he was a talent. He was saying: "He will only cost £4m." He added: "It can be paid over the course of his contract at £1m a year." He also said the player wanted £1m tax-free. I said: "The boy is only 18. That is a massive problem," but Tony suggested it was negotiable.

I returned back the following day impressed with what I had seen and mentioned it to Gerard. He said: "I will ask Rick." We didn't have a lot of money, but it could have been sorted by spreading things over the four years.

We had just signed Florent Sinama-Pongolle and Anthony Le Tallec, both on far less than Ronaldo's aspirations. They were also two talented boys. We would have had anarchy if the other players had found out how much we were considering paying for an 18-year-old kid in Ronaldo.

We looked for a compromise. Ten days later I was sitting in a lounge at Anfield having some lunch and looking at the big TV screen. Up came the news that Manchester United had signed Ronaldo from Lisbon for £12.2m. Gerard and myself nearly choked on our food.

Gerard said: "Contact Tony Henry," and I went straight out and rang him. I said: "What happened? More importantly, what happened with the price?" He said: "After you had been with me, I got a phone call the following week and was told to drop everything on the deal. Hand on heart, I really don't know what happened."

I went back and told Gerard the story. What happened God only knows. For the fee to jump from £4m to £12m, especially as they seemed so desperate, was surprising to say the least. You can imagine the shock on our side when the deal was done. There lies another story.

We were now looking forward to our planned pre-season trip to Hong Kong and China. However, everything was put in doubt because of an outbreak of the SARS virus. Rick Parry and myself had gone out to check the hotel and training facilities just when the SARS publicity began to raise its head. Obviously it was a deadly virus and not something we could treat lightly. The club kept track of what was happening and we saw the problem hit its peak in the Far East and then start to abate.

However, because China had not been as up front with its casualty statistics as other places, a late decision was made to cut out this element of the tour. We agreed to go to Hong Kong where they had done everything possible to deal with the epidemic. It was decided that we would also go to Bangkok again because we had enjoyed fantastic times in Thailand a few years earlier.

The hospitality in both places was always top class. In Hong Kong all of the players saw one of the most amazing sights in the world when we went for a train ride to the summit of the peak that overlooks Hong Kong. We went up there just before dark and it was truly breathtaking, both in daylight and when the lights of the city began to illuminate down below. It was good to be in Asia where we were so popular, but the main thing for us was to get back to winning ways.

However, no one could have accounted for what happened next. A Russian billionaire by the name of Roman Abramovich appeared from nowhere to buy Chelsea and overnight we suddenly had another major player competing for the big honours. Prior to that, Chelsea had many problems. At one stage it had looked as if they might lose an unhappy John Terry and we had assessed that situation before Abramovich came into town to scupper all of those thoughts.

It was ironic that our first Premier fixture that season happened to be against the men from Stamford Bridge who in the final game of the previous season had denied us a Champions League place when they beat us 2-1 in London. It looked as if dear old Claudio Ranieri had hit the jackpot, able to exploit the new owner's fortune. I really warmed to the Chelsea boss who was an intelligent man with a really friendly character and a good sense of humour. I had exchanged words with him early on, but I grew to like him.

Everyone was interested how Chelsea would fare. They grabbed an early goal at Anfield through Juan Sebastian Veron, but a twice-taken Michael Owen penalty levelled matters. I remember seeing Michael's first spot-kick effort roll hopelessly wide, only for the linesman to order a re-take. We were all up on our feet when he blasted his second effort into the roof of the net. Then Jimmy-Floyd Hasselbaink grabbed a winner with just three minutes left which was devastating because for an hour we had played them off the park.

I remember Claudio being very animated after the game. He said: "After an hour we should have been 3-0 down." Then he slapped his hands together and said: "We would have been out of it, but that's football."

He was right. Goalless draws then followed at Villa and at home to Spurs. I was particularly angry that the home draw hoodoo had come back to haunt us. Trying to be positive, we had played some great attacking football. I saw Glenn Hoddle on TV claiming that the Spurs defence had been brilliant. He should have borrowed my nose for the night!

We then went to Everton for the fourth game of the season and put everything right. Prior to the game the Blues' fans were full of confidence. The cry at the time was: 'Rooney's gonna get you!' When it was shouted at me I just put my hand to my mouth and yawned. I'd heard it all before.

On the morning of the derby we were staying at the Marriott Hotel in Liverpool's city centre. I had breakfast and got in the lift to go to my room. Who was in the lift but former Everton player Ian Snodin and his mate. Snodin had taken on the task of fielding Everton questions on the Radio City phone-in. I remembered what he had said on the radio the year before about the derby game.

He claimed I had been bang out of order for kissing the Liverpool crest on my badge when coming off the field. I said to Snodin: "It's not a problem when Duncan Ferguson is kissing his tattoo or David Unsworth is running round kissing his badge. When I do it, it's a problem. You were out of order to mention it."

He said: "Who are you talking to?" And I gave the obvious response: "You!" He said: "I'll knock you out in a minute." I thought that was deplorable, not least because he had his mate with him in the lift. I thought to myself: "I don't even want to get involved." His parting words were: "I'll see if you are smiling after the game at Goodison today."

After we beat them 3-0 I was on the pitch and looking for him at the Radio City point which I thought was by the dugout. I was ready to kiss my badge again, but he must have been up in the press box. I did complain to Radio City because I was fuming about that exchange of words and how he dealt with it. The win got us back on track in a big way.

We beat Graeme Souness's Blackburn 3-1 at Ewood Park. Of course, I took no joy in that! It was strange because Markus Babbel was playing for Rovers, having joined them on a season-long loan. He had gone through a difficult time at Liverpool after his debilitating illness. He had never looked the same player, but it was hard for him to accept because he had been a top player and a top guy before his long lay-off. We made a plea for him to stay, but he wanted to get some first-team football at Rovers.

The irony was that early in the game Markus slid in to tackle Milan Baros. It was a fair tackle, but Milan broke his ankle. That was bad enough, but it all became quite heated. Lucas Neill came in with a challenge as Jamie Carragher went to clear the ball. It was over the top and caught him in the middle of the leg. Carra actually tried to stand up, but he waved his arms and was clearly in trouble. We didn't know he had broken his leg until later.

Of course, there was extreme anger and words were exchanged between Graeme Souness and Gerard. I was glad that, for once, I was not involved. It was Gerard who really had his angry head on and it took a lot for him to get in that state. We had to come to terms with losing two players with bad breaks. I thought all the bad luck had been taken up the previous season, but it clearly wasn't the case. We just had to get on with it and make changes. If there was a plus at this time it was that Michael Owen and Harry Kewell were both amongst the goals, but if anything was to kill us it would be our home form although we beat Leicester 2-1.

As often happens, a different challenge comes along to focus your attention. We went to Olimpija Ljubljana in the UEFA Cup and grabbed a 1-1 draw with Michael on target again. He was flying at this time and things were starting to look up. We had beaten Everton, Blackburn and Leicester in successive league games and secured that decent UEFA Cup draw.

Michael and Vladimir Smicer then scored at Charlton, but we lost the game 3-2. Their hero was Kevin Lisbie who grabbed a hat-trick. He scored one from just in our half out on the wing and that was extremely disappointing.

Now we faced Arsenal at Anfield, aware that our home form had a habit of letting us down. It was similar to the Chelsea game. We played well for an hour, but lost 2-1. It was like being on a roller coaster because we then saw off Ljubljana 3-0 with Harry in prolific form.

One thing that always worries you is when you sell players to other clubs and then have to face them fairly quickly. Patrik Berger had gone to Portsmouth and it is always in the back of your mind when that fixture comes round. We played well, but who should score their winning goal? You've guessed it! Portsmouth would prove a bogey team to us during this season.

Our problems were not on the same scale as Leeds United where Peter Reid was desperately trying to turn things round at this time to prevent a famous club from slipping into real trouble. We had our own priorities and won 3-1.

This took us to a fixture that would inevitably inspire extra media attention. We were drawn at Blackburn in the third round of the Coca-Cola Cup where

Gerard and Graeme Souness had exchanged angry words in the league game. I felt we played really well in the game and it looked positive when Rovers went down to ten men. Lucas Neill, sent off following the challenge that broke Jamie Carragher's leg, was dismissed again. It would turn into a real battle that we would win 4-3, a result that gave us great delight to say the least.

John Arne Riise would be the focus of attention in the next game, a trip to Fulham. He had turned them down to sign for us and their fans always perceived that it was John's mother, his adviser, who made that decision. Their fans always taunted him with the chant: 'Mummy's Boy!' We left him out this time and grabbed a 2-1 win in a game in which substitute Sinama-Pongolle caused havoc. I remember him spinning on a ball and being brought down to allow Danny Murphy to strike home a cool penalty. They had Luis Boa Morte sent off for a high tackle on 'Flo'.

This was all at the start of November 2003. It was a sad time for me because my mum had been extremely ill for a number of years. She had suffered with emphysema, a condition that makes your breathing difficult. I was always worried about her because she was quite ill and had been admitted back into hospital around this time.

Liverpool had drawn Steaua Bucharest in the UEFA Cup and we were going to the same hotel in the city where we had stayed before playing Rapid Bucharest in 2001. Steaua had a good history, peaking when they won the European Cup many years earlier. I knew it would be a tough one for us.

As we prepared for the tie my mum's health deteriorated. It was decided that I would still travel, but on the day of the game, November 6, club secretary Bryce Morrison came to me as I was preparing myself during the afternoon. He said: "I've had a call from your wife. You need to ring her immediately."

I knew straight away that it was serious. When I spoke to Marg she said that I needed to get home quickly because of my mum's condition. I contacted John Cheadle, who organises Liverpool's travel arrangements through Lonsdale Travel. He said: "Leave it with me, I will sort things out."

The problem was, there were no direct flights back to Manchester. The solution was to fly to Frankfurt in Germany and then connect to Manchester. I put on my club suit to travel in and as I was leaving to go to the airport I came across the directors and their wives in the hotel foyer. They were surprised to see me heading out of the door and I had to quickly explain the emergency. Obviously, they wished me well. I thought the journey would never end as I sat there on the plane, alone with my thoughts. I was desperately hoping that mum could hold on so that I could see her and speak to her.

You go through all the emotions, the good times and the bad times. Mum was a star when we were younger, looking after the seven of us with dad away at sea. There was Lynda, (the eldest), Owen, me, Denise, Ian and then the twins May and June, named after mum and her twin sister May. I thought about our times as kids and what she had done for us.

When I started my football career she would get me the best boots that she could afford. We were not wealthy by any means, but she always did her best with dad away. She would support me the length and breadth of the country in the early days when I was playing for Kirkby Boys, be it Cardiff in South Wales or Newcastle in the North East. She was always there, up and out at six in the morning. She made sure that I always ate right and that my kit was clean and ready. She gave me so much support and it continued throughout my life.

She was a big Liverpudlian. Of course, I never had a bad game for the club in my mum's eyes. She was always supportive, while offering sound sense. She told me to always be nice to people on the way up, because those were the same people I would meet on the way down. I have lived my life taking account of those wise words.

It meant that I would take on countless presentations and the like throughout the city, often with mum in tow. She never let me walk past anyone who wanted an autograph, whether it was a senior fan or a three-year-old kid. This kind of outlook is where you get your humility from. As I sat in the plane, I also thought about dad and how he had looked after mum throughout her long illness. He also had emphysema, but he battled to fight it. As a former seaman, he was a man's man, but now he was doing all of the cooking, cleaning and washing. He did everything he could to help mum. He just wanted to take care of her. She generated that kind of love and respect from everyone. Of course, I thought about all of the lovely times we had enjoyed as a family. I also thought about my mum's pride when I came back to Anfield as assistant manager. She was such a lifelong Liverpool fan.

I did get home in time, but mum was out of it in a side ward at the Aintree and Fazakerley Hospital. I whispered into her ear and she looked up. I knew she had heard me. This was a real comfort. I stayed with my family and we drew support from each other. Over in Bucharest the team had drawn 1-1 with a goal from Djimi Traore. I was actually given the result by a Liverpool fan as I touched down in Manchester Airport. He had received a text and passed the information on, surprised that I was not in Romania.

Gerard Houllier had told me to concentrate on my family. The hours that followed were difficult for all of us to handle. My family said that it was important for me to get back with the team, something that mum would have wanted. The lads were now in Liverpool's city centre Marriott Hotel ahead of a big Sunday home match with Manchester United. I popped home to get my tracksuit and coat. I was just coming out of our house when the phone rang.

It was my family, saying that mum had just passed away. I told Marg and we raced back to the hospital inside ten minutes. This was around 5.15 on the Saturday evening. Everyone was distraught. Mum had been the backbone of our lives with dad away for so long. She had been extremely close to the girls. As everyone knows who has lost a loved one, within hours you are discussing the funeral and the arrangements.

Although we were a Protestant family, mum had been leaning for a number of years to the Roman Catholic Church. The place she related to was St Joseph's in Kirkby where Marg and myself were married. In the years since her illness had started, mum and dad had spoken about where they would like to have the service held should anything happen and mum had made it known that she would like St Joseph's. A good friend, Father Jimmy Collins, had conducted our wedding. He was known all over Merseyside for his work. Father Collins said he would take the funeral and we knew mum would really appreciate it.

Dad was extremely brave at this time, as the older generation always are. I felt for him greatly. He had been through some difficult years and had not been in the best of health himself. The family insisted that I join up with the team. I arrived at the Marriott at around 8.30pm after the players had eaten. Everyone was supportive and Gerard was fantastic. He knew my mum and dad, especially my dad because mum had struggled to get to watch her beloved Liverpool in those final years.

In the team meeting the next morning the boss gave one of his fantastic team talks, finishing by saying: "Let's do it for Phil and his mum." It brought a lump to my throat. As it turned out United beat us 2-1. The lads tried desperately hard in the game, but I don't think mum must have arrived in heaven at that time because she would not have allowed us to go down to United.

Fortunately an international break followed and so I was able to get myself together. It sounds strange, but the funeral was fantastic with everyone determined to do mum proud. My lads go to St Edward's School and the headmaster John Waszek, who had become a friend, offered me the school choir. He knew it would be fitting and special for all of us and we were very grateful for that.

I knew the family wanted me to speak at the service which was extremely hard. Everyone was upset, but I knew she would have wanted me to do it. I didn't want it to feel as if I was reading from a script. I had seen how Gerard did his notes for the big AGMs, just bullet points for guidance. Big words on a single piece of paper, just reminding me about mum's life.

I buckled slightly, and my voice wavered, but I hope I delivered a nice portrait of what she achieved and what she meant to her family, her friends and my dad who was her rock.

People turned up from the club, including captain Sami Hyypia. That would have pleased her. She got the kind of send-off that would have made her proud. In the end life has to go on.

After the international break we resumed on November 22, 2003 with a game at Boro where we gained a goalless draw. Then we had the return against Steaua Bucharest at Anfield. Their president had made a remarkable statement, saying that if Steaua got through he would build a new church in Bucharest. That was his motivator. I had heard some things said before games in my time, but this was extraordinary. They were already a good team and now this challenge had been thrown down to them.

It didn't work because Harry Kewell continued his run with the only goal of the game. He was on the scoresheet again three days later when we beat Birmingham 3-1 at Anfield, his eighth strike of the season.

Looking back, people often say that he had a poor season, but that wasn't the case. The first phase of the season was good for him and he made a useful contribution to the team. He then picked up an ankle injury in that Birmingham game that would keep him out for months. He tried to come back off the sub's bench, but it wasn't right and Harry was never to scale the heights again that season. His problems started from there.

We just couldn't get anything going. We went out of the Coca-Cola Cup to Bolton, a match in which Jay-Jay Okocha scored one glorious goal in a 3-2 victory. You try to take some comfort by saying that if you had to go out of any of the cups then this would be it, even though we were the holders. I can remember the Bolton fans singing: 'You've only come to see Okocha' and that was true because he was playing some great stuff at the time.

We drew at Newcastle and then suffered a shock home reversal to Southampton. This is when you know that the pressure is going to crank up. The frustration of the crowd was beginning to bubble over. We managed to get our revenge over Bolton by beating them 3-1 in the league on Boxing Day and finished the year with a 2-2 draw at Manchester City. The result does not reveal that we were given one of our biggest drubbings for a long time.

We had given a debut to young Jon Otsemobor who had played four games on the run. He had this great ability to attack, but the defensive side of his game was suspect. Whenever I looked at him I also thought about an incident that had happened the previous October.

During an enforced break, we would go to Marbella with my business partners Paul and Stevie and their wives. It was just a short opportunity to switch off. On this occasion we had just settled down for a nice lunch at 12.30 when the phone rang. I was sitting there in my shorts, enjoying a glass of wine and took the call. It was Ged Poynton, the Liverpool stadium manager. He said: "Phil, one of my police contacts has just been on to say one of our young players has been shot." I said: "What?"

Ged replied that it was Jon Otsemobor. He was okay, but that he had been shot in the backside. I immediately tried to reach Gerard who had gone to Mauritius for a break. I rang Ian Cotton, but he had not heard anything. Ian said that he would check with the police. Of course, I was also trying to get hold of Jon Otsemobor. I knew John Welsh was his mate and tried his house.

Meanwhile, Otsemobor limped into Melwood in the afternoon, making his way into the treatment room where Dave Galley asked: "What's the matter?" Jon would then utter those immortal words: "I've been shot in the arse." Apparently, everyone fell about laughing because it was so unexpected. Luckily it was just a flesh wound, as the cowboys used to say in the movies.

Here I was, on this short break and spending about five hours with Ian Cotton on the end of a phone trying to get a press release together. Jon was just in the wrong place at the wrong time.

He was then able to get this run together and I remember speaking to the Press just before the Manchester City game. I said: "He has done very well and deserves another shot in the team." They burst out laughing, having picked up on my rather inappropriate choice of phrase. Jon was to have a difficult game against City. They murdered us down his right-back flank. After 25 minutes we had to make a substitution. Sometimes you have to make big decisions. It was difficult for the boy, but they had identified a weak link and we had to do something about it.

It was only 1-0 at half-time, but it could easily have been five. Lads like Steve McManaman, Robbie Fowler and Nicolas Anelka were all on fire, all wanting to make an impression against us. Everything was sticking for Robbie up front and Nicolas was winning balls in the air against Sami Hyypia. Everything was going right for them in that first half and they battered us.

We played much better after the break and actually went in front following a fantastic Dietmar Hamann volley from the edge of the box. In injury time Robbie Fowler, of all people, stabbed the ball home to level matters with just about the last kick. I remember seeing the board with two minutes on it. Referee Mike Riley blew at 2 minutes, 20 seconds and when Robbie's goal went in there was hardly any time to kick-off again. I was ready to go onto the pitch, but Gerard grabbed me.

My mind had gone and he was shouting: "Phil, no!" Incredibly, the stories in the Press the following day were all about me supposedly arguing with the boss. This was just not true. I was glad for what Gerard did because I could have been in serious trouble. Riley had given two penalties against us in the United game and given another in this game and I was furious, not to mention the extra time. It's amazing how the media can perceive something.

Now the FA Cup started on January 4, 2004. It actually gave us a bit of a break from the pressures of the league. The lads were actually able to enjoy New Year's Eve because the FA didn't want league games to interfere with the sponsorship of the cup. We'd been drawn at Yeovil where the people were extremely hospitable. You could call them nice, but cocky because they had this confidence that they could pull off a shock. The pitch was not the best and they had this huge Portuguese defender in the middle who had just joined them. His name was Hugo Rodrigues and at 6ft 8ins he was possibly the tallest defender in the country.

Emile rattled home the opener with 20 minutes to go, and we made the game safe soon after. Harry Kewell was touched in the box and went down. He was accused of diving, but it was a silly tackle and Danny Murphy scored from the resulting spot-kick.

It took us to Chelsea for a midweek game that was live on TV. Stamford Bridge and White Hart Lane had been the only two grounds we had failed to win at. We had beaten Tottenham at the end of the previous season and now we wanted to end the Chelsea hoodoo although they were a decent team now, having developed under Claudio Ranieri. Big signings had been made by the Londoners while we had a few injury problems. We gave Bruno a chance to play just off Emile in this game.

Michael Owen had been injured after scoring against Charlton the previous September. He would not reappear properly, despite a couple of attempted comebacks, until the December and he was named sub at Chelsea. Michael had made a blistering start to the season and if he had been able to continue in that goalscoring form we would not have been in the position we were in.

We made a point of telling the lads that it was crucial to end the jinx at the

Bridge where we just couldn't get a result. Bruno scored a brilliant goal in the first half, after a pass from Emile split the defence. Bruno came sliding in to slam the ball into the net.

It was a great victory, especially after our stuttering start to the season. Our elation was also increased because we achieved the win despite an injury late in the game to Jerzy Dudek. Chris Kirkland was already out injured and it meant a 20-minute cameo performance for untried youngster Patrice Luzi. We then needed a big judgment for the following game with our two main keepers still injured. Could we trust Patrice to continue in the Premiership at such a crucial time?

We decided he was not experienced enough and turned to Paul Jones at Southampton. He had been a Liverpool fan all his life and wanted to play for us as a kid. Paul seized the loan opportunity with both hands, even though a permanent deal with Portsmouth was on the cards. That was a tremendous decision and we appreciated it. He went straight in for our home game against Aston Villa and kept a clean sheet in a 1-0 win, thanks to a Mark Delaney own goal. This completed a mini-run of five games unbeaten, but that came to an abrupt end at Spurs, despite breaking our duck there the previous year. We lost 2-1 and Paul Jones was bitterly disappointed.

When things are up and down you have to knuckle down and fight for every point. We went one-up at Wolves thanks to another Cheyrou goal and seemed to be cruising to an important away win until the last minute when Kenny Miller gave them a share of the spoils. Danny Murphy had two great chances to wrap things up at 1-0, but hit the bar and the post. That's the way it seems to go when you are desperate for a boost. It was frustrating for me because Pinocchio had just turned 50 and I had taken all the family out the previous night to 60 Hope Street in Liverpool where we had a great meal. I had been hoping to follow up with another special celebration at Wolves.

Newcastle then came to Anfield in the FA Cup fourth round and they were full of confidence. Bruno, enjoying a great time, put them in their place with two excellent goals to take us through. The Geordies' consolation goal, scored by Laurent Robert, flashed past Jerzy from 40 yards. I don't know what he saw of it, but you never like it when your keeper is beaten from that distance.

I've said that our home form always seemed to let us down at this time. So it happened again against our arch-rivals Everton who claimed a goalless draw at Anfield. We squandered a lead at Bolton in a 2-2 draw and this was all proving very costly. You become thankful for small mercies. Michael Owen had been back for half a dozen games and now he got his first goal in a 2-1 home win over Manchester City.

We hoped the FA Cup would keep our options open, but Portsmouth stood in our path and while they were not the biggest club in the country, they had proved a bit of a jinx team. We were leading 1-0 and it could have been three or four. We failed to give ourselves any breathing space and they grabbed a late equaliser. The replay came straight up the following weekend and Emile hit the post at Fratton Park after just two minutes. He got through again and lobbed over and wide. Michael then missed a penalty at the end where our fans were encamped. It was an easy save for Shaka Hislop and I looked across at Gerard. You get this uncanny feeling that it is not going to be your day and Portsmouth went on to claim what was a famous cup victory for them with more pressure heaped on us.

It was becoming difficult to read our form. We beat Levski Sofia 2-0 at a comparative canter in a UEFA Cup third round, first-leg clash at Anfield with Harry Kewell on target again. Harry then had a great game as we drew 2-2 at Leeds. He took this ball, beat a couple of men and bent his shot from the inside-right position into the far corner of the goal. I bet a few people had money on him to score the first goal at his old ground. Milan Baros got our second.

When we travelled over to Sofia for the second leg against Levski there had been a real snowfall. We would normally train on the pitch the night before the game, but we had to use a different facility. Believe it or not, they actually had undersoil heating and when it did come on it left the pitch absolutely perfect, one of the best we have ever played on. It looked like Astroturf and it suited our game. We won 4-2 to make it 6-2 on aggregate.

We now went straight into our next UEFA game against Marseille at Anfield without playing a league game, which is unusual. They were a big strong team. I had looked at their videos and this huge guy Didier Drogba had clearly made an impact in the Champions League. They had now dropped into the UEFA Cup where his threat remained. We did well to keep him quiet in the game and went ahead through Milan Baros. Despite our focus on the big man, Drogba remained a threat and he equalised to give them a decent scoreline. We knew it was going to be a difficult return in France.

Back on the league front we suffered a 2-0 reversal at Southampton where Paul Sturrock was in charge for the first time. We knew the Saints would be fired up to impress the incoming manager. Michael Owen was having a difficult time trying to find the net at this stage. He couldn't seem to do anything right, missing chance after chance. We had our moments in this clash, but the home side scored against the run of play with a goal that looked offside. That's the way it goes when you need results. I remember going up to Paul Sturrock after the game and saying: "If you continue to enjoy as much luck as you had today, you will do well at this football club." He just smiled.

Luckily we had our outstanding home league game against Portsmouth to re-arrange and I was keen that we played it as soon as possible. It came up just three days later and I knew the players felt they had something to prove after our FA Cup exit against Pompey. We started right and finished right, winning 3-0, although I sensed Portsmouth were not too bothered after claiming our scalp. We then beat Wolves 1-0, but we were still way off a Champions League spot. We had been competing with the likes of Newcastle, Aston Villa, Chelsea and Birmingham to try and grab fourth place. It looked a difficult challenge for us at this stage, but we were not going to give up and six points from two games had helped.

We now had to turn our attentions back to the UEFA Cup and a trip to Marseille where there was a great atmosphere. It's an incredible stadium and our fans were in one corner where they made a tremendous racket. However, every time we came out of the dugout their fans threw beer, water and plastic cups in our direction. No one said anything. I was out there more often than anyone and so I had to be on my guard. A great Emile Heskey goal put us one-up and it was looking good.

Then Drogba ran onto a long ball into the box and came into contact with Igor Biscan. The striker got in his shot and it sailed wide, but the referee suddenly pointed to the spot. More than that, he showed Igor the red card. Even in training our Croatian player had this habit of dragging people back. We were now up against it with ten men. The ref didn't give us a thing and we lost 2-1. That was the end as far as our UEFA Cup hopes were concerned. We trudged off, knowing that the only thing left for us was to give everything to claim that fourth Premiership spot.

Our fans were not convinced and their irritation showed in a goalless draw at Leicester, We turned things round with a convincing 4-0 home win over Blackburn with Michael finally showing his real quality. He scored two along with his partner Emile. It meant we travelled to Arsenal feeling confident and a Sami Hyypia header put us in front. The Gunners equalised, but a fine Steven Gerrard through ball enabled Michael to restore our advantage at half-time. We felt we could press on for a crucial victory, but that man Thierry Henry inspired Arsenal to an unbelievable 4-2 victory that left us absolutely gutted.

We needed to tighten up and took a decision to play Jamie Carragher at centre-back. We should have taken this option sooner. It was one of the few things I had disagreed with Gerard about. He had great faith in Igor as a centre-back. He was good in the air and good with his feet. I felt he made too many mistakes. When the pressure was on I felt that he lacked the mental toughness to compete against Premier strikers.

When Stephane had his injury problems, I was keen for Jamie to play at centre-back. Djimi Traore played reasonably well there with Sami. Gerard had it in the back of his mind that Carra made mistakes. He would say: "Remember Manchester United." That was in our first season together, when Jamie scored two own goals playing at centre-back. I felt he was now a more experienced professional.

Anyway, after Igor's errors we had to turn to Carra. We played him in the middle with Stephane at right-back. I immediately felt there was more solidity there with Carra. He had always been a good organiser and a good shouter. We tightened up and didn't drop as deep.

Things were looking extremely uncomfortable when we lost 1-0 at home to Charlton. There seemed to be no rhyme or reason to our form. The only bonus was that Newcastle and Aston Villa, behind us in the table, were dropping points as well although that was of little consolation to our fans. We needed points desperately, but could only manage one at home to Fulham. Our supporters were now baying for blood.

Our response could not have been more positive. We went to Old Trafford and beat Manchester United 1-0. Who should score but Danny Murphy from the spot after Steven Gerrard went round Gary Neville and sucked in the tackle. This victory gave everybody belief again. We knew that a Champions League place was still in our grasp, but we felt it might go right down to the line and the final home game against Newcastle.

It was all about focus and we despatched Boro 2-0 at Anfield as we went into May 2004 aiming to keep ourselves on track. We now had just two games left. If other results went our way, we could actually clinch our Champions League place at Birmingham. St Andrews is always a tough place to go because of the passion of the fans and the spirit of the team. You knew the likes of Robbie Savage would be rattling into you and discipline and control was needed. As it turned out we stormed home 3-0 with a supreme performance from Steven Gerrard, who scored our final goal.

It meant we had achieved our aim and that Liverpool would be playing in the Champions League in the 2004/05 season. When you think about it, what an absolutely crucial result that was for the club. You could argue that it was the first step on the road to Istanbul and all of the glory that was to follow, although sadly not for Gerard and myself who had been totally committed to this dream. Gerard had always said that we would win the European Cup, but we didn't know what was ahead.

What we did know was that we still had to play Newcastle at home and they needed to win that game to secure a UEFA Cup place. The pressure was off the Reds, but we still wanted to finish in the right way for our fans, who had gone through a torrid season because of our roller coaster form.

I remember looking at the Newcastle bench at the start of that game. Bobby Robson was panicking on the touchline. His job, as much as ours, was very much on the line. The match would finish 1-1 and when they equalised I said to Bobby: "You are going to be alright. Don't worry." By clinching our Champions League place we had finished on a good note and Gerard and myself waved goodbye to the fans, not realising at that time that this would be our last time together in front of the Red Army.

That is frustrating because we would have liked to have said our farewells in a different way, not least because we had been part of an eventful and successful era, putting aside the frustration of that final year. Gerard had also put his life on the line for the club, but we knew that decisions about a management change are not made to a fairy-tale timetable.

THOMMO

Chapter 18

End of a dream, but the SKY is now the limit and I become a fan again

When you look back on that 2003/04 season it is clear that our home form suffered. Who knows, if our Anfield form had been better we might have finished much higher and challenged in a very different way. Football is all about ifs and buts.

What was clear is that the fans were now in overdrive on the question of a possible managerial change and the letters column in the Liverpool Echo was interesting to say the least. The media frenzy was increasing by the day. After the Newcastle game we had all gone up to chairman David Moores' house in the Lake District. Of course, this had all been planned for weeks, but you can imagine how Gerard and myself felt with all of the speculation swirling about.

It was an exclusive group: Gerard, Rick Parry, David and myself, plus our wives. We went up on the Sunday, staying over until the Monday. We enjoyed a nice evening with a lovely meal, but I was wondering if there would be a sting in the tail the following day. The conversations were relaxed and low key on arrival, but I had something in the back of my mind. On the Sunday afternoon we went for a ride in the chairman's speedboat up Windermere.

Gerard and myself were on the back of the boat as we moved up the Lake. We were joking quietly to each other: "Do you think we are going to get pushed overboard when we get in deep water? Keep your eyes on Rick in case his arm swings out as we spin round."

You have to smile, even in adversity. I knew that if Liverpool had it in mind to make a change, they would do everything right. As it turned out, it was a lovely spin on a beautiful stretch of water and we stopped for tea at one of the hotels on the edge of the lake before heading back to David's home.

At the hotel we sat outside on the lawn having our refreshments. Marg walked off to a small shale-like beach area where ducks and ducklings had come ashore. A guy was feeding them. We saw Marg chatting to this guy. I said: "We better rescue this chap from Marg's conversation. He will probably be slashing his wrists by now."

When we got over there Marg said: "This chap is from Aintree, not far from where we used to live in Wango Lane." I shook his hand. He was making small talk and looking at me strangely. I had my sunglasses on and he said: "I think I know you." I shrugged my shoulders. He said: "Do us a favour, take off your sunglasses." I removed them shyly, only for the guy to say: "No I don't!" I burst out laughing and couldn't wait to get back to David and Gerard to tell the story. The not so famous Phil Thompson!

We had a nice casual dinner that evening and went to bed wondering what the next day might hold. Nothing was said and so we had breakfast and said our goodbyes. It was the ideal opportunity on the Monday morning for Gerard and myself to get together and consider what our immediate futures might hold. The papers were still in overdrive as if they had some inside information. To read those stories was as if the dirty deed had been done without us knowing, but again I knew the club would act correctly, whatever the decision.

I went into Melwood on the Tuesday and Gerard had finally received a call to go to Anfield. I thought: "This is it." Of course, I told the boss to ring me the second there was any news. He did not call me, but returned to Melwood a couple of hours later. I said: "What happened?" Gerard said: "Nothing. We spoke about America and the pre-season tour. We also discussed possible transfer targets."

We were still not totally convinced, especially as things got worse in the Press. When we were at the chairman's house he said that he had no plans to go to his home in Marbella for the time being. Then we found out that on the Wednesday David and Rick had attended a business meeting in Marbella which we found extremely strange at the time. The week went by and the Sunday papers had a field day. Later that day Gerard found out that it was all over. The rest of the world would be told within 24 hours on May 24, 2004. Gerard had attended a long meeting with Rick and it was decided that a press conference would be called on the Monday. It was an extremely difficult time for the boss. He gave a magnificent parting speech. There was no bitterness.

He spoke about everyone at the club. He made a big point of thanking me for my loyalty to him, especially through that spell when he had his heart problem. He paid tribute to many people within Anfield and then he came down to Melwood to say his goodbyes. We opened a couple of bottles of champagne to toast the happy memories, not the sad ones. Then we got everybody together, including the ground staff, and Gerard thanked them for all the help they had given him.

That was the thing about the boss. He never forgot anybody. At Christmas time he would invite everyone at Melwood in for dinner with the players, be they secretaries or the guys who forked the pitches and mowed the grass. He would mix them up amongst the players and then he would personally thank everybody. Even at our own Christmas party he would always make a lovely speech, saying little personal things about people, from the youngest lad on the groundstaff to the most senior coach. Some people might have thought he looked high and mighty, but Gerard Houllier had a humility that came across as soon as you met him. He emphasised the importance of this to the players because he wanted them to treat everybody with a real professionalism.

When it was all over we walked out of Melwood together. He hugged me and my wife Marg, who had come down to join us. It was an awful situation. We had enjoyed such a powerful partnership and I knew that I would miss him. Although we didn't live in each other's pockets, the respect was always mutual. Gerard had this pride about being Liverpool manager. When Melwood was developed he had this wonderful office. The walls were covered with pictures of all of our triumphs and the people he held close to him.

The office reminded me of the captain's bridge on a ship. The far end was all glass, leading out onto a balcony from where he could look out on the whole of Melwood. Gerard was so proud of it. To leave it and put all of his stuff away must have been so difficult. I remember the Sunday when he rang me to say it was all over. He had gone to Melwood and it was probably around 7pm. I said: "Stay there, I'm coming down."

Marg came with me and Norman Gard, Gerard's great friend, was also there. We just helped him clear a lot of the cupboards and many of the really personal things he wanted to put away immediately. We also helped him the next day. It must have been heartbreaking.

All of his trophies and mementos were taken out and put to one side. The thing about Gerard Houllier is that he made you believe. He had a belief in his players and his staff. He protected his players so much it was untrue. He wouldn't hear a bad word said about any of them. He was like Bill Shankly in that sense. We would discuss things about players and be critical, but it was all within the four walls of his office. He would say that what happens in the Bunker stays in the Bunker. Unlike the famous Boot Room, the 'Bunker' was wherever we were encamped at the time, be it the training ground or a hotel room. Wherever we were planning tactics at the time, that was his Bunker. No one should ever doubt the positive impact Gerard Houllier had on Liverpool

Football Club.

Of course, I now began to wonder what was to happen to me. I spoke to Rick and he said: "We don't want you to leave. We want the staff to remain, although Christian Damiano has decided to leave. We have to wait to see who the new manager is before everything can be finalised."

I was quite pleased. I was with Gerard, but my life was in Liverpool. If I could help whoever was coming in then that would be great. It wasn't showing any disloyalty and Gerard knew that. I said to Rick: "Just keep me in the loop and let me know what is going on." That must have been difficult for him because he must have identified the new manager and realised that he would have his own ideas.

I just had to wait and took the opportunity to grab a week in Dubai at the end of May. It was hard hanging on for a call. When I got back I went into Melwood each day to work in the gym. I was ready to look after the shop and talk to any players who might be around. I remember Jamie Carragher turning up one day. I said to him: "You really need to plan your career around being a centre-back. That is your position at this football club. It might damage your England chances because of the challenge from the likes of Campbell, Ferdinand and Terry, but you are good enough to pick up on the challenge. Whichever manager comes in, if I am not here you must emphasise that this is your best position." Carra had given us solidity in the middle and helped us to secure that crucial Champions League slot. Sami Hyypia and Stephane Henchoz sometimes drifted, but Carra was not like that. If you told him what you wanted he would listen and keep that gap tight.

Soon after I got the call that Rafael Benitez was to be the new manager. I went in and had a long conversation with him. He asked me how we planned for games and what tactics we used. We spoke about the players, I asked him about some of his targets. He talked for some time about his players at Valencia. He explained that they had a different tier of management in Spain. The manager was the coach. Other people did the transfers. He said he didn't have an assistant manager as such. He believed in his fitness coach, who acted in that capacity. I said: "It's not a problem. These have been a difficult few weeks for me. If I am not to be here I need to know today."

Because of the language problem, Rafa was stumbling over his words and apologised for his English, but he had a good grasp of the language and I understood when he said he was planning to bring in some of his own people. Again, that would have been no problem to me, but I wanted to know if I was part of his future plans. He was a really nice guy and introduced me to Pako

Ayesteran, his fitness coach and effectively his trusted assistant.

Rick was at Melwood and I asked to see him before he returned to Anfield. He spent some time with Rafa and then we had a chat. I said: "Let's not mess about. You have given me six great years that I didn't expect. Now I need to know. If Rafa wants his own people then that's not a problem." Rick said: "He has got this guy from Valencia who he trusts implicitly. He's not a coach, he's a fitness trainer, but Pako will be his right-hand man."

I knew that was it. I had a year of my contract to run and it was agreed that this would be paid up. I later read a piece that we had walked away with a collective pay-off of £10-12 million, but that was ridiculous. I got my year's salary and that was it. It was disrespectful to say we had received a king's ransom as if we had robbed the club. That was just not the case.

I had a lovely conversation with Rick and thanked him for giving me the chance to live my dreams for a further six years with Liverpool. We came back to win trophies and we did that. We also sorted out the discipline which had become a major issue and that achievement should not be under-estimated. We took the club from the front pages to the back pages and left a physical legacy in the shape of a wonderful training ground. Yes, we had 18 difficult months at the end, but I do not accept that we failed. You only have to look at the trophies we won – one UEFA Cup, one FA Cup, two League Cups, one Super Cup and one Charity Shield.

We nurtured the likes of Steven Gerrard, Michael Owen, Sami Hyypia and Jamie Carragher. We came through a nightmare spell when Gerard stared death in the face and survived. Yes, we made some bad signings at a key moment and you can't get away from that, but I will look back on my time as Liverpool's assistant manager with real pride. It goes without saying that I gave it everything and my passion for the club never dipped at any time.

My third spell at the club was over, but I felt that I had enhanced my reputation with everyone because of my time as caretaker boss. That had taken me to another level. Of course, it was difficult to leave people behind, not least my great friend Sammy Lee. As soon as my departure had been confirmed I recommended that Sammy be promoted to assistant manager. He had worked with England and was a great coach. He could speak excellent Spanish, having played over there. I felt he could be extremely useful to Rafa while maintaining the local link that every club needs.

Rick said: "I don't think it is going to happen. If we were going to have an English assistant manager then we would keep you." I argued that Sammy would be ideal. I could see that Rafa would possibly link me too much with

Gerard and that he would want to change things, but Sammy was respected on the international scene and had been a coach for 12 years. I felt he deserved the chance, but it wasn't to be.

Sammy realised that and he decided to go. It was a big decision for him because he loved the place as much as me. I looked on him as a great friend and colleague. We had some wonderful times together. He gave me fantastic support during my time in charge and our relationship went all the way back to the great Bill Shankly. We remain tremendous friends.

I also retain an excellent relationship with Rick Parry. I respect him immensely just as I did his predecessor Peter Robinson, who was described in his time as the greatest administrator in the game. Peter had been extremely good to Gerard and myself and was always ready to back us. He worked hard into the night to help bring the right players in and get the right players out. It then came to that time in Peter's life when a decision had to be made about his own future.

Rick had been brought in as 'Chief Executive Designate' in June 1997, with Peter's retirement on the horizon. Peter was still active and sharp as a tack. Possibly he felt as if he could go on a little longer, but he had instigated strict retirement criteria at the club and if you make the rules you have to live by them. Looking to the future, it had been Peter's idea to poach Rick from his position of power at the Premier League. Rick had been at Anfield for a couple of years, expecting Peter to relinquish his role. Clearly Peter found it difficult handing over the reins totally because he was steeped in the club.

You talk about people who had played a massive role in developing Liverpool into the force it is today, men like the immortal Bill Shankly and Bob Paisley and influential chairmen like T.V. Williams and John Smith. Peter carried the title 'secretary' for years, but it did not do justice to him. He took Liverpool from a slumbering Football League side to one of the top clubs in the world.

Whenever people in the game wanted top class advice, the first port of call was always Peter. He was held in such high esteem and I always had the greatest of respect for how he ran the club. I would say that Peter Robinson must take as much credit as giants like Shanks, Bob, Ron Yeats, Kevin Keegan and Kenny Dalglish for making the club great. He was a star in his own field.

It was then a tremendous coup for Liverpool to get someone of Rick Parry's expertise to fill the void. Rick was a fantastic choice, someone who could see the way the game was changing. He had his own ideas, like flying the team to league games to keep them fresh and organising top class pre-season training camps. He organised trips to the Far East and North America, marketing the club more than ever before.

Liverpool FC have been fortunate to have two chief executives of such a high calibre, backed by a first-class chairman in David Moores, someone who never sought publicity through his position like some of his Premiership counterparts. People should remember that David is a chairman who has put his money where his mouth is. He only wants what's best for LFC, never interfering in team matters, but always being supportive.

It was people of this quality that I was now leaving behind. Now I had to start all over again. For the first time in years I was able to organise my holidays without the problems of pre-season and taking the kids out of school. I was wondering which way my career would go. I had begun to build a bit of a career with the media, not least SKY television, but that had all ended when the call came to return to Anfield. Could I go down that media track again?

As it turned out, the first call was from my old mate Sammy Lee. His brother-in-law at Chester City, Stephen Vaughan, was asking if I wanted to be their manager. It was not right for me at that time. I was looking for a little more. That is no disrespect to Chester. I felt they needed someone with a greater knowledge of their division. It was not for me.

I was thrilled when my great friend Ian Rush took the job after that, although he would soon have problems over there and so possibly my call was the right one. I could never understand my former teammate Mark Lawrenson questioning Rushie's potential at that time. That was a sleight on Rushie who had worked hard for his coaching qualifications, especially as Lawro's first job was at Oxford.

A couple of decent Championship sides approached me. One still had a manager in position and the other was searching for a new boss. Nothing came of either approach. You wonder at times whether your lifelong association with one club has an affect. People possibly think you are not prepared to step away from your home city. The truth is that it's all about the right job.

I received a couple of phone calls from Jeff Stelling, the anchorman at SKY who does such a fantastic job with 'Soccer Saturday'. Jeff had built up something of a cult status and he was a great friend who I had known for a long time because of my previous life contributing to the programme.

Jeff said that the new producer would like me to do some work for them. I questioned whether it was right for me to be discussing players and other coaches so soon after coming out of football. Jeff said: "You've done it before and always in the right manner." He argued that my experience would help me cope with anything that was thrown my way and that most of the time I would be doing Liverpool games. Deep down I was keen because it is a fantastic show. You can be on for six hours, but it only seems like 30 minutes. Soccer Saturday had always been very informative and full of good humour. I used to be one of the younger ones. Now the likes of Charlie Nicholas and Matt Le Tissier had come onto the scene. It was nice to get back in the groove.

On the home front, I was able to take the kids to school, the St Edwards College in West Derby, although the run potentially took me past the gates of Melwood. I could take a longer route and avoid it but that took me into heavy traffic. It was very strange to pass those high walls in the morning and wonder what was happening on the other side. Was the pre-season activity being done in a different way? How were the players feeling? All of these thoughts went through my mind every time I drove past. I was glad when my business partner Paul did his stint on the school run because he also had kids at St Edwards.

These were emotional times. Rick Parry and David Moores made it clear that I would always be welcome at Anfield, but it was all too soon and I wished them luck for the opening games. I didn't feel it was right to go to either Melwood or Anfield while the new regime was settling in. Working with SKY was different, but I still wouldn't go in the directors' guest room or boardroom. It would not have been right at that time for Rafa to have the old guard around. He needed to get his feet under the carpet.

I also wondered how I would react watching at Anfield. I would inevitably be thinking about the dressing room and what might be going on to lift the players. As it turned out, I only did two games at the ground during the 2004/05 season, one as a co-commentator in the Champions League game against Monaco, the other as a studio guest for the Charlton game which was a 5.15pm kick-off. I must admit, everybody from the girls working in the offices and corridors to the stewards were all really nice to me. Stadium manager Ged Poynton also made me feel welcome. As I made my way round the ground it brought a lump to my throat.

I had to do an interview pitchside. These three guys walked towards me, all UEFA delegates. One said: "You don't remember me, do you? I was the referee in the 1981 European Cup Final in Paris when you were Liverpool captain." I felt like giving him a big hug rather than shaking his hand. He remembered me and inspired a wonderful memory which was very nice.

As the season went on I became more and more involved on the media side. I also began to help out at Liverpool University, speaking to students on the

Football Industry course. These are more mature students who are looking to get into areas like the media, football finance and marketing. I talk to them about specific aspects of the game. Rogan Taylor, a Liverpool fan who launched the Football Supporters Association after Heysel and later became a powerful voice for fans all over the country, helps run the course. I have continued to work with him to try and gain placements in football for students in their own specialist field.

Some of them come out with fantastic jobs in places like Hong Kong, Singapore and New York. Others have to work much harder to get into the game. When you think about it, many people fall into jobs without too much training. Courses like these ensure that people of the highest quality come through because football is a massive business these days and needs top quality. I enjoy watching the various seminars. One session involved a guy from Stockport County who had been marketing his club in China. It's not just the giants who seek to exploit every opportunity.

Rick Parry is a great friend of the university. So is Trevor Birch who worked with Chelsea, Leeds and Everton in a chief executive role. I'm proud to say that I have been given an Honorary Fellowship of Liverpool University for my work, something that fills me with pride. No one ever thought they would see the lad from Kirkby in a cap and gown.

My media opportunities gradually began to increase. I worked for Channel Five and Radio Five began to use me on a regular basis. I was pleased to have more than a few strings to my media bow. It took a long time to get over the leaving of Liverpool FC. I enjoyed having more time with my wife and family again, but in the end it was Marg who said that I needed to get out and about and focus myself on some new challenges.

My son Daniel and I went to the David Lloyd Fitness Centre in Kirkby where all the family are members. I started doing a couple of hours in the gym. I began to chat to people again about football and enjoyed it when my opinion was sought on a number of topics. Marg would also be at the gym doing one of her regular classes in the studio. She would say: "I've been watching how many people have been stopping to talk to you. It's good that you can relax and chat again." I should add that one particular friend, Billy Ratcliffe, who enjoys more of a spot of chatting than exercising, keeps me well entertained throughout my session.

I even started getting involved in the coffee mornings after the girls had finished which is a bit sad, but I enjoyed it. I was also able to spend time with the kids at their tennis and football sessions and other activities. I was back to being a 'taxi driver' again.

My SKY work flourished and I continued to enjoy it, particularly when Liverpool began to make progress in the 2004/05 Champions League. I was able to be constructive while also showing my passion for the Reds when the occasion demanded it. I remember Andy Gray when Liverpool met Greek side Olympiakos on what was one of the great Euro nights. We were six or seven minutes from going out when Stevie G let fly with that famous strike. Andy's subsequent comments became part of folklore, demonstrated on a banner in Istanbul which colourfully declared: 'YOU BEAUTY, YOU BEAUTY. ANDY GRAY IS A KOPITE.' It was a Liverpool fan's humorous way of referring to a famous Anfield moment.

Liverpool's route to the final had many high points, like the quarter-final against Juventus. One of my friends, Richard Green, is a solicitor at Hill Dickinson. He said: "Phil, we are going to win the European Cup. I had a £50 bet at 66-1 after Olympiakos. Our name is on the cup." I didn't disagree, but I didn't put money on it, even though we were in with a shout.

The Juve game was exceptional. It was a great performance at home, backed up by everything that went with it as the club acted superbly to mark the anniversary of Heysel in the right way. All the emotional ties came back. It was our first meeting with Juve since the European Cup Final in Brussels 20 years earlier, but it was crucial that we retained our focus on the football challenge. I thought the club came out of it with flying colours. They got the ceremonial side spot on, while ensuring the players were in the right frame of mind. All credit to Rick Parry and David Moores, the board, Rafa and even the ex-players who played their part in doing things the right way on what was potentially a tricky night at Anfield.

My old pal Phil Neal took some criticism in one paper with a suggestion that he had asked for money for an interview about Heysel, but that was tremendously unfair. No one has greater humility or dignity than Phil. His attitude and compassion is beyond question. He is a great guy who has always bent over backwards to help the media.

I've seen him do hundreds of interviews, always making himself available. To try and nail him on this was out of order. I know he made himself available to go to Turin to act as an ambassador for the club. He took part in a banner of friendship ceremony on the pitch before the Juve game at Anfield along with Ian Rush and Michel Platini. Here is a man who has more Liverpool honours than any another player. What a claim to fame that is. He remains a Liverpool legend and someone who will always go the extra mile to help the club. I've got nothing but admiration for Phil Neal.

After Juve it was Chelsea. It was great doing those games for SKY. I was with Ray Wilkins at Stamford Bridge where Liverpool put up a really great performance. Petr Cech made some great saves, particularly one from Milan Baros. John Arne Riise missed a great chance with his right foot. Enough said! It always comes back to big moments in games that tell you whether it is your day. When Frank Lampard dropped his shoulder six yards out and fired over the top, all the pointers said we were on our way.

After the game Jose Mourinho went on TV and said: "Ninety per cent of Liverpool supporters think they are through, but it's going to be different at Anfield." I did an interview for SKY Sports and wagged my finger, saying: "No, no Jose. Not ninety per cent. One hundred per cent of us believe we are going through!"

In the second leg I couldn't believe my eyes when the time board went up to show six extra minutes would be played. Was the ref trying to balance the fact that he was still uncertain as to whether the ball had crossed the line for Luis Garcia's early goal? Every Kopite knows that it was well in! Anyway, who cares? In 20 years time the stats will show a 1-0 scoreline in our favour and that's all that matters.

I now took the road to Istanbul with thousands of fellow Kopites. I was delighted when SKY asked me to be one of the studio guests in the Ataturk Stadium. Ahead of the match itself we did a show on the Tuesday looking at the tactics. It was amazing. We went through it and looked at the team selections and how they might shape up. Andy Gray asked me about it and I said: "Rafa will go with the same team although I'm not sure if it will be Cisse or Baros as the lone striker up front with Steven Gerrard just behind." I continued to give some further thoughts.

Andy said: "What would you say Phil if Rafa suddenly thought: 'Let's have a go at this ageing back four by playing Harry Kewell just behind Milan with Steven Gerrard and Xabi Alonso in centre midfield and no Didi Hamann'." I said: "I can understand what you are saying, but we will need some real strength in midfield."

The following night we were back in position and waiting on the official team news. About half an hour before kick-off Jeff Shreeves came through and said: "Harry Kewell plays." I immediately said to presenter Richard Keys: "You knew" and he said: "We had a tip-off." That was 24 hours before the kick-off.

We all know that Harry was forced to come off injured early on when we were 1-0 down with a torn groin. I must admit, I was surprised Didi did not come on straight away. No one will ever forget that moment in the 38th minute when Alessandro Nesta clearly handled inside his own area under pressure from Luis Garcia. I couldn't believe the ref never gave what should have been a cast iron penalty. Nesta dragged his arm into the ball and should have been sent off for the advantage he gained.

I was fuming and was getting quite agitated as we slumped to 3-0 down at half-time. Richard turned to me when we were off the air and said: "Phil, can you watch your language a bit. It's getting over the top." There's no doubt that my language had been choice at times, not least after the Nesta penalty incident, but we were not going out live in the studio. The match at this stage was in the commentators' hands, Andy Gray and Martin Tyler.

I was devastated during the interval as I reflected on the scoreline. Thankfully, Richard went first to Ray Wilkins and Gianluca Vialli to get the Milan viewpoint. It gave me time to reflect. They both said: "It looks as if the match is finished." I thought about Andy's comment when the third Italian goal went in. It was a simple: "Game over."

Richard finally came to me and said: "Phil, what do you think?" I just said: "Richard, you have to believe. If you don't believe you should pack in and go home now. That is the meaning of football."

Sometimes you curse yourself for saying things to camera, like when Alan Hansen analysed Manchester United after the first game of the 1995/96 Double-winning season (a 3-1 defeat at Aston Villa), by declaring: "You'll win nothing with kids." Sorry for reminding you Al. We all do it. My comment was more to do with what I might have been saying if I had been in the dressing room myself, desperately trying to lift the lads. Later on, Richard said: "Phil, you got it spot on." It was lovely.

Anyway, the second half commenced. Then our first goal went in, scored by Steven Gerrard. I was up on my feet celebrating and screaming encouragement as Stevie headed back to the halfway line, lifting his arms to get the fans going. I knew what he was thinking because the same thought was in my head. Let's go down fighting.

Incredibly, I was able to celebrate with my sons who by an absolute coincidence ended up sitting just outside of the SKY box in the stand. On the morning of the game I had rung Philip, Daniel and Max on my mobile. I said: "So that I know you are in the ground and safe, I will come out onto the balcony ten minutes after the kick-off and phone you." Fifteen minutes before the match started we went off air for a short break and I looked over my right shoulder to see what was happening in the stadium. Who should be sitting about ten feet in front of the window but my sons. I was thrilled. I had been worrying about them and here they were, within touching distance.

When Vladimir Smicer reduced the deficit still further with that great drive I scanned the faces of all of the players. Immediately I knew this game was turning and that things were happening. I was up on my feet and banging on the window of the box and punching the air as I looked at my sons. Thankfully it was toughened glass.

Then Xabi took his pen and I just exploded as the keeper saved it, only for our midfielder to turn in the rebound for a sensational equaliser. I hammered even louder on the window. Thankfully it held firm and I apologised to Gianluca Vialli and Ray Wilkins for a second time.

Extra time was a nightmare as we fought to hold on. Stevie went to right-wing back to try and stem the tide, but we clearly lost our impetus, having made such a massive effort to get back in the game. Serginho came on for Milan and they took the initiative, but I thought about the two misses from the normally lethal Shevchenko right at the death and knew it was Liverpool's cup. Jerzy Dudek deserves every praise for blocking the striker's header on the line and then somehow diverting the rebound over the bar.

However, I don't know how the referee allowed our Polish keeper to save AC's second pen from Pirlo. The official was clearly instructing the keepers to stay on their line, but Jerzy had moved three or four yards forward when he made the save. This time I wasn't going to react. Shevchenko completed a miserable personal night when he missed from the spot. It meant that the successful kicks of Hamann, Cisse and Smicer clinched us our fifth European Cup triumph.

I was leaping up and down, unaware that a camera had been trained on me throughout the game. I only realised when Richard said: "Let's see how Phil reacted to the victory?" They showed me, fist in the air, shouting and banging on the window of the SKY studio. I said: "You bastard, did you have the camera on me all the time?" Richard explained that this was the reason I had been asked to tone down my language. They never told me about the camera because my reactions would not have been the same.

We won that trophy in the most unbelievable of circumstances. It will never be repeated in a Champions League Final. There is only one club in the world with an incredible set of fans capable of inspiring such a fightback. I can't say what happened in the dressing room. I can say what happened on the terraces. At the start of the half-time break the Liverpudlians were just dumbstruck.

Then they regrouped. We then witnessed one of the most wonderful things I have ever seen in a football stadium.

The Reds fans began to sing You'll Never Walk Alone. It started quietly, like a hymn rather than a battle cry. We all knew the situation we were in, but here were the fans saying to the players: "We are with you." 'When you walk through a storm, hold your head up high.' Never give up on any challenge. Always believe.

The players later said they heard the singing in the dressing room. That must have been better than any team talk. All the words were relevant. Have hope in your heart. You'll Never Walk Alone. It was the right song at the right time and it made the hairs stand up on the back of my neck. It was something really special and maybe that was the turning point of an incredible night.

I was asked where this victory stood balanced against all of the other glories of the past. I had no hesitation in saying: "This was the greatest ever game." This team, to be fair, are not as great yet as the lads who made history in 1977, 1978, 1981 and 1984.

However, they went on an incredible roller coaster ride to win the Champions League and to come back from 3-0 down was a truly incredible feat. When we were ruling Europe we were expected to win the game's biggest honours. Stevie and the lads beat all the odds to secure an astonishing success.

You might ask if I am jealous of the Champions League glory that Gerard Houllier and myself aspired to and Rafa enjoyed. I would answer that in a simple way. I'm a fan and I was proud to be part of a magnificent day in Istanbul. There are legends that people talk about from the past. I would like to think that I am part of that Anfield folklore as a former European Cup-winning captain.

Now there are new legends, lads like Steven Gerrard and Jamie Carragher who are Liverpool through and through. They have become a part of this elite group and thoroughly deserve to be in the Anfield Hall of Fame. I have no jealousy, just a real pride that people I worked with finally achieved their dream. I did not make it back in time to witness the homecoming from Istanbul, but my heart and soul was with the players. As a player and assistant manager of Liverpool, I enjoyed famous tours of the city, but I instinctively knew this one would be special because of the way the game turned round.

In 2001 we did a tour after winning the League Cup, the FA Cup and the UEFA Cup. We played Charlton on the Saturday to gain third place and then had the tour on the Sunday. This one was memorable because the Champions League victory was so fresh in the memory, having happened just hours before. It was estimated that 750,000 people filled the streets and it made me really proud to be a Liverpudlian. Later that night I received text messages from Carra and Stevie inviting me to go to the Sir Thomas Hotel in Victoria Street where the players were gathered. I thanked them, but said I didn't think it would be right for me to be there. Philip and Daniel, my two eldest boys, went along to party the night away. I was there with all the lads in spirit.

As I set off from my Istanbul hotel for the airport I rang Rick Parry to offer my congratulations for a wonderful achievement. We had a good chat and then he put me on to chairman David Moores. It highlighted that my relationship with the club was still excellent and that really pleased me.

David then said: "I've got the captain here. Do you want to talk to him?" Stevie came on the phone and my first words to him were: "Feels good doesn't it." He said: "Not half. I watched you lift the European Cup many times on video and now I've done it myself." I felt a real bond with him at that moment, two local lads and Liverpool skippers with a wonderful link called the European Cup. Stevie said: "Lifting it was the best moment in my football life." I knew where he was coming from. It had been exactly the same for me.

My career was now progressing in different ways. I've mentioned my media work. One role I didn't expect was that of political activist. During my first year out of the game there was a General Election. I got a phone call asking if I could attend a Labour Party rally. Many years earlier I had actually supported the Conservative Party, but in the last ten years I had reverted to my roots and been very much a Labour man. I was a staunch supporter of Tony Blair and admired what he had achieved.

The caller said: "Can you come to the rally?" and I said: "When is it?" The answer was a bit of a surprise. "It's tonight at St George's Hall in Liverpool! Can you get down there for about 6.30?" Not much notice, but I agreed. The person on the phone said: "Alistair Campbell will ring you in a minute to organise things." He came on and said: "We are pleased you can support our rally." I said: "What do you want me to do?"

Alistair explained that he would like me to introduce a special video that was aimed at Conservative leader Michael Howard. He said he would organise car parking at St George's Hall. I asked if I could bring my son Daniel. I knew it would be an experience for him. I mentioned that Dan was a good friend of Tony's son Euan. He said: "Here is Tony now."

Here I was, standing in the kitchen at home and chatting to the Prime Minister. He said: "Euan often talks about your sons Daniel and Philip. He is a massive Liverpool fan." Euan loved coming up for the matches and Phil and

Dan would take him out. He stayed at our house after the Champions League second leg against Chelsea. The PM thanked us for taking care of Euan and getting him tickets for various games. After a couple of minutes I said: "Thanks 'To', see you later." Well, I probably said "Thanks Prime Minister" but you know what it's like when you have mates in the corridors of power!

When I arrived at St George's Hall I didn't see too many people although the police were everywhere. I got instructions to go to one end where about a hundred people were demonstrating. As I approached they all started shouting: "Alright Thommo." I said: "Alright lads." I thought to myself: "You won't be saying 'Hello' in a minute." I was right. When they saw me starting to walk into the Hall the boos rang out across Lime Street. They were shouting: "Don't do it Thommo!" I fully expected the next chant to be "Sit Down Pinocchio."

It was hilarious although I knew it was also serious. I'd gone from hero to villain inside a few seconds, but that's what football and politics can do to you. I was met by some officials and went through security. We were shown into a VIP room where Liverpudlian builder Craig Phillips, who won Channel 4's Big Brother, was pacing up and down with Jimmy McKenna who plays Jack Osbourne in Hollyoaks. They were nice guys and both had been asked to say a few words at the rally.

They were walking round, pen and paper in hand, writing things down and saying the words as if it was the rehearsal for a stage show. It suddenly dawned on me that I wasn't prepared in any way. I thought: "What am I going to say? What am I expected to do?"

Alistair Campbell had said that I was to introduce this video which was none too complimentary about Michael Howard, ironically a big Liverpool fan. Alistair suggested that I just say these words: "Do you remember what I remember?" It would immediately remind people of the infamous speech Howard made to the Conservative Party Conference in 2004 when he used the phrase "Do you remember?" over and over to attack Labour on a variety of issues. I just had those three little words written on a card, but Craig and Jimmy seemed to have loads of stuff written down as they fretted over their words in this VIP room.

This secretary guy came in and said: "Mr Thompson, can I have a word?" He said that Cherie would like to see me for a minute. Cherie? It had to be the PM's wife. He said she was in the next room. I went in and she was standing there on her own. We shook hands and she thanked me for the time we had given to Euan during his visits to Liverpool. She said: "He talks about you a lot and I appreciate what you've done." We then had a chat about Euan and my two boys.

I went back into the other VIP room where Craig and Jimmy were still going through their lines. Then we were taken into the magnificent St George's Hall where 500 people were waiting to hear the various speeches. Huge screens were in place and there was a real air of excitement amongst the delegates.

I sat down next to Craig with Liz Dawn from Coronation Street on the other side. All kinds of personalities had turned up to give their support, including my good friend Phil Redmond. Jimmy got up to introduce the proceedings. He was sweating cobs at the lectern. He introduced Craig who got into full flow to talk about some trade workshops he was involved in and how Labour had helped to set up the initiative.

Jimmy then introduced Jane Kennedy, the MP for Wavertree. Jane made a great speech and as she came to the end she smiled and turned to George Howarth, the MP for Knowsley. She said: "I know our next guest was brought up in your constituency, but he was born in Kensington which is my patch."

She gave me the big build-up. "I would like you to meet a man who, in his day, was one of the finest central defenders in the world." I immediately began to panic, thinking: "My few words are hardly going to be enough." I was changing tack almost as I began to take the stage. I looked out across the massive expanse of the Hall and said: "Thanks for the introduction. When you said 'one of the finest central defenders in the world' I was expecting Alan Hansen to step forward."

This broke the ice as everyone laughed. I said: "I don't want any jokes about Pinocchio until I sit down." There was another giggle and it gave me more confidence. I went on to talk about the city and how the development of Liverpool in recent years had been astonishing. I spoke about the Albert Dock and how cranes could be seen everywhere as things began to take off ahead of Capital of Culture status. I was able to highlight the booming housing market and said: "It's a fantastic place to live and work at present. I am proud of the city and it's because of Tony Blair and the Labour Party."

I was thinking: "Where are these words coming from? You sound like a city councillor." I caught a glimpse of my son Dan at the front. Apparently the guy next to him had said: "He's going to be the next Minister of Sport."

I don't know about that, but I was into my stride and raised my arm, pointing to the giant screen behind me before uttering the words: "Do you remember what I remember?" The whole place erupted as the video rolled. It was all about what Howard had promised and what hadn't come true, turning his own words against him.

It made me think about some negative football comments Howard had made about Gerard Houllier and myself not too long before. I sat down and Tony Blair got up to make a fantastic speech. At the end Cherie got up and asked all of the guests to join them on stage to acknowledge the audience. I couldn't believe that the humble Phil Thompson was taking some applause alongside the Prime Minister.

We returned to the VIP room and Alistair Campbell was there. He's a big Burnley fan and he said: "Here a minute Phil. That programme you do on SKY with Jeff Stelling is absolutely fantastic. Jeff is a brilliant presenter, top class. Let me tell you that when we were starting to build our election plans, the top brass in the Labour Party got together to decide on a strategy. We had to come up with a saying or highlight a person as a kind symbol of what the party should be about. I asked for ideas.

"Some mentioned the words of great political leaders. Others mentioned top sportsmen. Some pointed to famous movie stars. Then it came to me. I said 'Jeff Stelling.' They all said 'Who?' and I said 'He's a symbol of solidity, stability and knowledge.' It was all tongue-in-cheek, of course, but it was to make a serious point." I was saying: "Hang on a minute, I'll have to write this down. Jeff will love this." Alistair said: "I love the way he holds the programme together with his knowledge and sincerity. He was my 'symbol' of what the party should be about."

Before I left with Daniel, Tony Blair said: "Thanks for what you did tonight and thanks again for helping Euan." He also said how much he enjoyed the Soccer Saturday programme and always watched it when able to. The one thing he didn't mention was Jeff Stelling, so maybe my SKY mate was not that popular after all! It was certainly nice to know that the PM was tuned to our Saturday afternoon football discussions.

I drove home with my head full of the images of the previous few hours. This skinny Kirkby kid from Brookfield Comprehensive had ended up on stage with the Prime Minister of the United Kingdom. I was very proud.

The girl who helped me to 'Get A Life' and the families I love and cherish

I wouldn't want anything to change in my life. It all comes back to my mum's wise words about getting back what you put in. I've been dedicated, but I've been well rewarded. I think back to those early days in school and that all-red kit that she bought me and I treasured. I would play out and pretend I was Roger Hunt.

I think about the football journey I started as a boy, playing in all of those teams and progressing until I played in the greatest team of all. I was not the greatest player ever, but I knew it was more about having that burning desire to succeed. I was the Kirkby kid who rose to become the captain of my beloved Liverpool. At this point my great mentor Tom Saunders called me the Mayor of Knowsley.

I've always been proud of my background. I think that is crucially important. From day one it was never a bind to meet people or make a presentation. I've probably been inside every social club and pub in Liverpool on official business, often with my mum in tow encouraging me to sign every single autograph.

I have this incredible memory of meeting the football messiah that was Bill Shankly and then listening and learning from my peers who also happened to be my heroes, the likes of Smith, Cally and Chris Lawler. I would hang on to their every word and also hang on carefully to every drink I was sent to fetch for them. They would fire out their instructions: "Get me this and get me that," and I would be loving every minute of it because these were the legends I was brought up with.

Then I became a star in my own right and it was all about coming to terms with the direction my life would take. I would continue living on the edge between the social and professional side. You have to go through these times to get your head right or, as they say in Liverpool: 'Get a life!'

I got mine the day I met Marg. I had been one of the boys, always ready to have a laugh and a drink. I began to realise that my body couldn't take it any more. I needed to slow down to meet my football goals and to sort out my future. The only way I was to achieve that was in partnership with Marg. That didn't mean I was not enjoying myself. In fact, life was better.

It became a bit of a joke at the time with the other lads. I was always on the phone to Marg because we had become so close. My career began to take off because I was now focused and getting my priorities right. I became captain of Liverpool. I became captain of England. I lost my perm! I married Marg and she helped me take everything to a different plane. The whole direction of my life changed.

I got to the top of the tree on the night when I skippered Liverpool to a famous European Cup victory in Paris. I won seven League Championships and claimed 42 England caps. I played in a World Cup and the dream went on.

Then we started our family and Philip, Daniel, Max and Josh came along to really make our lives complete. I like to think I kept my feet on the ground, helped by my decision to run a Sunday League team while I was involved with Liverpool. These were two absolute extremes, but it was all part of never losing sight of my roots.

I can remember playing for England and picking up bits and pieces of gear thrown on the floor by the lads, eventually having enough to kit out the Falcon lads in international colours! Who knows, the FA could still send me a bill. Sorry Brian Barwick, the cheque is in the post.

I always think about my mum and dad and my upbringing. It means a lot to me. I look at pictures of myself walking the hills in Kirkby and I'm fiercely proud of where I was brought up. I've championed the cause of the area and will continue to do so. Kirkby has had its problems and could be a difficult town, but it's a great place with great people. I'm more than happy to be one of them.

I met many people during my football life. You'd be hard pressed to find anyone saying I was a big head. I hope people think of me as a good lad – one of us. I try to talk to people. I've never been one of those footballers who would not give you the time of day.

I've been very lucky to have three bites of the football cherry with the greatest club in the world. I've been a player, coach and assistant manager. I've had some fantastic times and fulfilled more expectations than I could ever have hoped for. Hopefully I made my mum and dad proud. As I've described, I ended up shaking hands with the Prime Minister while speaking up for my city. I've achieved a lot in my life and by reading this story you have taken that incredible journey with me. I hope you enjoyed it.

I would like to dedicate this book to my two families. The first consists of my mum and dad and my brothers and sisters. The eldest sister Lynda is the leader of the family. Then there is Owen and Ian, who gave me great moral support down the years. This brings me to our Denise or Dee as she is affectionately known. Finally the twins May and June. Those names keep alive the memory of my mum June and her twin Aunty May. It was sad that Aunty May died last year, so soon after mum.

The twins went on to make a great life for themselves in Australia on the Gold Coast. They have done very well for themselves. They have their kids who are all proud of Liverpool and the two teams. Believe it or not, some are even Evertonians!

To all of them a very big thank you. We had some difficult times in Kirkby, but they were still great times. We didn't have a lot, but we all pulled together to take a trip to Southport, Blackpool or Chester Zoo on the old charabancs. Mum brought us up in exactly the right way, especially when dad was away at sea.

Later, when I was playing for Liverpool, we all came together as a family for the big finals. These produced wonderful memories. I can picture my mum and dad in the players' lounge after games, proud of their son. In reverse, I was fiercely proud of them for what they did for me.

My dad was probably more popular than me, knowing so many people through his job in the Merchant Navy and working on all the big ships. I was in Greece once and heard 'You'll Never Walk Alone' being played on a little tape recorder. This guy in an American uniform came up to me and said: "Phil Thompson, I worked with your dad. What a guy!" I was thrilled when he said that. My dad's not in brilliant health, but he remains a fighter. He's a fantastic granddad to the kids and a great friend.

My mum was a Trojan. How she brought us all up in that three-bedroomed house is anyone's guess, but we always got by. My nan would come round every Friday with two bags of shopping to help out. Mum made sure I had everything I needed to develop my football career. It was so sad the day she died because she had been such a wonderful person and a great mum.

Of course, I also dedicate this book to my own close family. Everyone says their own kids are brilliant. It's all about how youngsters are brought up. Marg and myself learned from our parents. The boys are great.

Philip is into his own little property business. Dan is trying to work his way into the music industry. I can see him being a top producer with a record company one day. Max is so intelligent and focused and says he would like to be a doctor. He can be whatever he wants. He's good at sports as well and excellent at his swimming and tennis. Josh is multi-talented in sport. He's also clever. I don't know where Max and Josh get their academic ability from. Marg and myself look at each other and shrug. Josh can also play any sport, but he loves his tennis.

All the children have all attended St Edward's College in Liverpool's Sandfield Park. It has been a wonderful school. We wanted to give them all a great chance in life.

I would not have stopped any of them if they had wanted to go into football, but nor would I have pushed them. You will have realised that we are proud of every one of them and shed a tear when each was born. The four are good kids and it's nice when other people speak highly of them. I've tried to ensure that they also have humility, learning from my own parents.

Certainly, none of them are big headed about who their dad is. People can be cruel in school, particularly when your dad gets sacked in a high profile way. They can be difficult times. I remember when I was Liverpool's assistant manager and results began to go the wrong way. They handled it superbly. They were Thompsons and took it all in their stride.

Of course, my biggest tribute goes to Marg. She has been so strong in everything we have done. She is a typical Kirkby girl, strong-willed and strong-minded, but very loving. She has been a fantastic mum to the kids and has helped in every way. She reminds me of her own mum in that respect. Marg is one of four girls. Her sisters are Pauline, Ann and Elaine. They are a lovely family.

Like all couples, we have been through difficult times. Before we were married we would split up and then get back together. Our love beat everything. I've said that the other players might say that I was henpecked or under the thumb. If I had to be under anyone's thumb then I'm happy for it to be Marg's. She helped to save my career. Our wedding took place in June 1981, a few weeks after my proudest football moment, winning the European Cup. We were wed in St Joseph's in Kirkby by Father Jimmy Collins, who later christened all of our children in the same church. Our marriage has got stronger and stronger.

Obviously we had hard times dealing with her parents' deaths and the loss of my mum, but we always come out closer. I know she will always be there for me and I will always be there for her.

It was through Marg that I finally decided to do this book. I had left it too long and she said I should do it for the children. She wanted me to put my story down in black and white. It will be great when the kids can sit down and read it. Hopefully they will be proud and understand what we have been through. I hope to be a granddad one day and hopefully this book will be something for my grandchildren to treasure. It's all because of Marg.

I would like to finish by mentioning my third 'family' – the great friends I played with in those legendary Liverpool teams down the years and the fans with whom I built up such a close relationship with. I am a Liverpudlian and always will be. I often get together with my former teammates and as soon as we meet all of that camaraderie that we built up down the years comes straight back. Obviously we get together a lot, but not so much at the scene of our greatest triumphs – the mighty Anfield.

That is why a game that took place on Sunday, March 27, 2005, was so special. Unfortunately, it came about because of a disaster that rocked the world – the Asian Tsunami that on December 26, 2004 devastated huge stretches of coastline from Sumatra to Thailand.

Early in the following New Year my great pal David Johnson phoned me and said he was contacting all the ex-players to see if we could get a fund-raiser going. He had come up with the idea of playing a star-studded game at Anfield between ex-Liverpool legends and showbiz stars. I felt he would get a massive response for all the right reasons.

David said the game would take a couple of months to organise, but that it would be a fantastic opportunity to get all the lads together again on our own field of dreams. Another former Liverpool player, Jason McAteer was thinking down the same lines and in the end four people came together to get things moving, including local actor Steven Fletcher and football agent David Lockwood. I should say that Johnno was the man who first highlighted the potential to me. He is a good guy with a big heart and I knew he believed totally in the exercise.

The end product was a marvellous day at Anfield. It raised hundreds of thousands for the Tsunami fund, which was crucial. At the same time it made a lot of older footballers extremely happy. I know the showbiz celebrities enjoyed the experience, not least our great friend Sue Johnston of Royle Family fame. Sue is a wonderful person and a great actress. She has also been a true friend down the years, through good times and bad. Sue is almost as big a Liverpudlian as I am and I'm sure she would have preferred to be out there on the pitch rather than watching the match from her seat in the SKY hospitality box at Anfield.

The former players were ecstatic as we turned out again in front of 40,000 spectators who were able to marvel again at legends like Ian Rush, John Barnes, Alan Hansen, Robbie Fowler, John Aldridge and many more household names. The attendance was astounding. I have played in big testimonial games that were nowhere near as exciting as this.

There were celebrities and heroes all over the pitch and we took it seriously. We had to because the showbiz side had some good players and they were out to beat us. Our pride was at stake and when that is the case with any group of Liverpool players something very special happens. When Kenny Dalglish made an appearance with 20 minutes to go that capped it all. The result was irrelevant, but I should point out for the record that we won!

The part I enjoyed most was before the game in the Hope Street Hotel where we met. I was sitting with the lads having a pre-match meal. The Mickey-taking started as soon as we sat down. We could have stayed all day, but we had a match to play. We have our Christmas parties, but this was something else. It was an hour-and-a-half of laughter as the others joined in. It was like being in a time warp. I could hear Shanks, Bob, Joe and Ronnie in my mind's eye saying: "Boys, there is no such thing as a friendly!"

Because of my dodgy knees and a calf strain I knew I couldn't play for long, but I was like a kid again, really excited by the prospect. In the end I only managed 15 minutes. Then big Jan Molby, one of the playing stars of the day, operated at the back with Alan Hansen. What a partnership.

It was just like getting on a bike again. Everything came back. After 20 years we were still going into positions we knew were instinctively right. Okay, maybe it was more pass than pass and move, but we knew we had to do the business with my dear old friend Ronnie Moran on the bench. I knew that if we did something wrong he would still be giving us a bollocking. We will probably never experience that again as a group and this meant we revelled in every second.

After the match we went back to the Newz Bar on Water Street in Liverpool's city centre. The day raised more than half-a-million pounds and that is a credit to everyone who turned up.

For the players, it had been an amazing trip in a football time capsule. I closed my eyes and heard Shanks speaking to me again: "You are going to play for this club for years. You will captain this club one day. You will go on and play for England."

Thanks boss. I hope I did you proud.

An Agreement made the 29th

day of **August** 19 **69** between **P.B. Robinson**

of **Anfield Road Liverpool 4.**

in the COUNTY OF **Lancaster**

the Secretary of and acting pursuant to Resolution and Authority for and on

behalf of the **Liverpool** FOOTBALL CLUB

of **Liverpool** (hereinafter referred to as the Club)

of the one part and **Philip Bernard Thompson**

of **64 Stoneley Road Kirkby Nr Liverpool**

in the COUNTY OF **Lancaster** Apprentice Football Player

(hereinafter referred to as the Player) of the other part **Whereby** it is agreed

as follows :—

1. The Player hereby agrees to play in an efficient manner and to the best of his ability for the Club.

2. The Player shall attend the Club's ground or any other place decided upon by the Club for the purposes of or in connection with his training as a Player pursuant to the instructions of the Secretary, Manager, or Trainer of the Club, or of such other person, or persons as the Club may appoint.

3. The Player shall do everything necessary to get and keep himself in the best possible condition so as to render the most efficient service to the Club, and will carry out all the training and other instructions of the Club through its representative officials.

4. The Player shall observe and be subject to all the Rules, Regulations and Bye-Laws of The Football Association, and any other Association, League, or Combination of which the Club shall be a member. And this Agreement shall be subject to any action which shall be taken by The Football Association under their Rules for the suspension or termination of the Football Season, and if any such suspension or termination shall be decided upon the payment of wages shall likewise be suspended or terminated, as the case may be.

5. The Player shall not engage in any business or live in any place which the Directors (or Committee) of the Club may deem unsuitable, provided that the Club shall, at the request of the Player or his Parent or Guardian, allow the Player to continue his further education or take up suitable vocational training.

6. If the Player shall be guilty of serious misconduct or breach of the disciplinary Rules of the Club, the Club may, on giving 14 days' notice to the said Player, or the Club may, on giving 28 days' notice to the said Player, on any reasonable grounds, terminate this Agreement and dispense with the services of the Player in pursuance of the Rules of all such Associations.

10. In consideration of the observance by the said player of the terms, provisions and conditions of this Agreement, the said P.B. Robinson on behalf of the Club hereby agrees that the said Club shall pay to the said Player the sum of £7/-/- per week from 29th Aug. 1969 to 21st Jan. 1970 and £ 8/-/- per week from 22nd Jan 1970 to 21st Jan 1972 and £ per week from to and £ per week from to and £ per week from to

11. This Agreement (subject to the Rules of The Football Association) shall cease and determine on 21st Jan 1972 unless the same shall have been previously determined in accordance with the provisions hereinbefore set forth.

Fill in any
other pro-
visions
required

As Witness the hands of the said parties the day and year first aforesaid

Signed by the said P.B. Robinson and Philip Bernard Thompson

In the presence of the Parent or Guardian of the Player

(Signature)

(Occupation) Coach

(Address) Anfield Road Liverpool 4.

Philip Thompson *(Player)*

P B Robinson *(Secretary)*

Other titles produced by Sport Media:

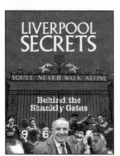

Sport Media
A Trinity Mirror Business

All of these titles are available to order by calling 0845 143 0001.